Applied
Sport
Psychology

Applied
Sport
Psychology

PERSONAL GROWTH TO PEAK PERFORMANCE

Jean M. Williams, editor
University of Arizona

Mayfield Publishing Company

Library of Congress Catalog Card Number: 85-063737
International Standard Book Number: 0-87484-729-X

Manufactured in the United States of America
10 9 8 7 6

Mayfield Publishing Company
1240 Villa Street
Mountain View, CA 94041

Sponsoring editor: James Bull
Manuscript editors: Marie Enders and
Claire Hunt Comiskey
Managing editor: Pat Herbst
Production editor: Jan deProsse
Art director: Cynthia Bassett
Cover Photograph: David Madison
Technical illustrator: Elaine Wang
Production manager: Cathy Willkie
Compositor: Progressive Typographers, Inc.
Printer and binder: George Banta Company

Contents

Part Two

Part Three

Psychological Considerations: Burnout, Injury, and Termination from Athletics   325

Preface

An increasing number of coaches and athletes are turning to applied sport psychology to gain a competitive edge — to learn, among other things, ways to manage competitive stress, control concentration, improve confidence, increase communication skills, and promote team harmony. Only recently has the level of scientific and experiential knowledge about psychological interventions for enhancing performance become sufficient to warrant books that attempt to translate this knowledge into practical suggestions and exercises.

Applied Sport Psychology: Personal Growth to Peak Performance is one of the first books written specifically to introduce coaches and sport psychologists to psychological theories and techniques that can be used to enhance the performance and personal growth of athletes from youth sport to elite levels. This book focuses primarily on two dimensions: (1) techniques for developing and refining psychological skills to enhance performance and (2) suggestions for establishing a learning and social environment that will maximize the skill and personal growth of athletes.

Applied Sport Psychology is particularly well-suited as a text for classes in psychology of coaching and applied sport psychology. The book will also be a valuable reference for practicing coaches and sport psychologists who did not have the opportunity for such training in their own formal education. Here are the reasons that we think this book is exceptionally well-suited for these classes:

WRITTEN SPECIFICALLY FOR SPORT PSYCHOLOGISTS AND COACHES

The growing body of knowledge and interest in applied sport psychology is perhaps best indicated by the half dozen or so books published in the last few years on mental skills for peak performance. Most of these books were written primarily for the athlete. Their coverage is thus not comprehensive enough for the coach or sport psychologist who must apply psychological constructs across a wide variety of situations and deal with many different athletes. Books previously written for coaches and sport psychologists are typically general textbooks that attempt to cover the entire field of sport psychology. Thus their coverage of applied issues — and particularly psychological interventions for enhancing performance and personal growth — is superficial compared to the in-depth coverage provided in this text.

xiii

BASED ON THE LATEST RESEARCH AND PRACTICE

This book reflects the latest research and practice in applied sport psychology. Each chapter is an original contribution written or revised during 1985. Although the primary focus was on application, theoretical and research foundations have been provided in each chapter, whenever appropriate. When using the book as a textbook for a graduate course, the instructor may want to supplement the book with readings from the research studies cited by the contributors.

COMPREHENSIVE COVERAGE OF TOPICS

No previous text in applied sport psychology encompasses the comprehensive approach taken here. The first chapter discusses the past, present, and future of sport psychology. The remainder of the book is divided into three parts: Part One covers learning, motivation, group dynamics, desirable leadership behaviors, and social interactions in sport. For clarity and simplicity, some of these chapters have been written in the vernacular of the coach. The reader is cautioned, however, not to conclude that these chapters are only useful for coaches. Sport psychologists frequently find it necessary to work with coaches in areas such as improving communications skills, building team rapport, and fostering more effective leadership behaviors. Also, the same principles of learning, motivation, and social interaction that help to increase a coach's effectiveness apply to the sport psychologist teaching mental skills and interacting with athletes. Thus the knowledge and insight gained from reading the chapters in Part One may be equally as appropriate for current and prospective sport psychologists. Therefore, in those instances where we have addressed only the coach, it should be assumed that we are also addressing the sport psychologist.

Part Two of the book addresses mental training for peak performance. This section begins with a chapter on the psychological characteristics of peak performance; other chapters discuss identifying ideal performance states, managing stress and energy levels, training in imagery, identifying optimal attentional styles, controlling concentration, building confidence, setting and achieving goals, and using self-hypnosis. The section concludes with a chapter on the integration and implementation of a psychological skills training program.

Part Three treats athletic staleness and burnout, psychological considerations in injury and rehabilitation, and termination from athletics. This section is unique because coaches and sport psychologists have only recently begun to address and explore these facets of the athlete's career. No sport psychology book has dealt with all of these issues, even though they are crucial to athletes' performance and personal development.

The appropriateness of these chapters for certain courses will depend on the students' backgrounds and interests. The book was planned to provide a complete coverage of psychological theories, techniques, and issues relevant to the enhancement of athletes' performance and personal growth. We intend for the reader, or course instructor, to select those chapters that are appropriate for their course. For example, Chapters 2 and 3 concern motor skills learning and principles of reinforcement and feedback; this material might be redundant if the reader already has a thorough background in motor learning. Chapter 4 on coach-parent relationships may interest only those individuals who are working, or plan to work, in a setting where athletes are still living with their parents; whereas Chapter 22 on termination from athletics may interest only individuals who work with athletes who are nearing retirement or dropping out of athletics.

WRITTEN BY LEADING EXPERTS IN SPORT PSYCHOLOGY

The contributors to this volume are aptly qualified: They are all leading scholars and practitioners in sport psychology. They work with athletes from youth sport to Olympic and professional levels, and most have illustrious backgrounds as elite athletes and/or coaches.

INTEGRATED ORGANIZATION AND WRITING STYLE

The book has the major advantage of drawing upon the diverse expertise and perspectives of 25 sport psychologists, but it avoids the common disadvantage of disparate coverage and diverse writing styles frequently found in edited textbooks. The content and sequencing of chapters has been carefully coordinated to assure comprehensive coverage and progressive development of concepts yet eliminating undesirable overlap and inconsistency in terminology. Writing focus, styles, and organization have been standardized as much as possible. Each chapter cites appropriate research and theory, makes application to the world of sport, and provides examples and training exercises whenever appropriate. Each chapter also begins with an introduction that highlights the content of the chapter and ends with a conclusion or summary of the major psychological constructs and skills.

APPLICATION EXAMPLES

The numerous examples given throughout the book greatly facilitate the translation of psychological theory and constructs into everyday practice. Many of these examples involve well-known professional and amateur sportspeople. The examples cut across more than 40 sports and provide important anecdotal evidence that can be used to motivate athletes to develop psychological skills for their sport. These real-life examples are frequently supplemented with hypothetical examples created by the authors to clarify appropriate applications.

APPLIED SPORT PSYCHOLOGY PROVIDES MANY BENEFITS

The rewards are many for those who choose to dedicate themselves to the pursuit of athletic excellence through use of the theories and techniques of applied sport psychology. Coaches and athletes acknowledge the importance of mental factors in athletic development and performance, yet the time athletes actually spend practicing mental skills belies this view. In publishing this book, we have made a serious effort to help abolish that inconsistency by supplying the knowledge necessary for providing a salutory and beneficial psychological climate. The benefits that can be derived from this text will arise not just in athletic performance, but in overall performance outside of athletics and, perhaps most importantly, in general personal growth and increased sense of self-worth.

ACKNOWLEDGMENTS

I wish to thank all the contributors who participated in this project and thus shared their vast expertise with the readers. Whatever contribution this book makes to applied sport psychology and to the field of athletics will be in large measure a consequence of their efforts.

I am also indebted to the fine editorial staff at Mayfield Publishing Company, most particularly Jim Bull and Jan deProsse, for their support and skill. Additionally, my sincere appreciation goes to Donna Mae Miller, Marie Enders, and Claire Comiskey for their outstanding work in copyediting; the clarity and consistency of the writing and organization was greatly enhanced by their efforts.

Finally, my thanks to the following colleagues for their insightful reviews of the manuscript: Elizabeth Brown, University of Maryland; James Ellwanger, Briar Cliff College; Deborah L. Feltz, Michigan State University; Richard Montgomery, San Jose State University; E. Dean Ryan, University of California, Davis; Robert N. Singer, Florida State University; and Maureen R. Weiss, University of Oregon.

Jean M. Williams

Contributors

JEAN M. WILLIAMS is an associate professor in the Department of Exercise and Sport Science at the University of Arizona. She teaches courses in sport psychology, stress management, and psychological training for peak performance. Dr. Williams has been a consultant for numerous intercollegiate athletes and teams. She has over ten years of collegiate coaching experience in men's and women's fencing, and her women's teams have been nationally ranked. Dr. Williams has edited two books in sport psychology and published numerous research articles in refereed journals. She is past chair of the AAHPERD Sport Psychology Academy and current secretary–treasurer of the Association for the Advancement of Applied Sport Psychology.

STEPHEN H. BOUTCHER is in the fourth year of his doctoral studies in Exercise Science at Arizona State University. He has worked with Dan Landers on a variety of research projects exploring the psychological effects of exercise, the arousal–attention relationship, and the effects of stressors on different psychophysiological variables. His special interests also include enhancing the performance of closed-skill athletes through highly specific mental training programs. He has been a varsity athlete in soccer, rugby, and golf and has coached rugby at the collegiate level.

LINDA BUNKER is associate dean for Academic and Student Affairs and director of the Motor Learning Laboratory at the University of Virginia. She has authored or coauthored six books, including *Mind Mastery for Winning Golf; Mind, Set and Match; Sport Psychology: Maximizing Sport Performance;* and *Motivating Kids Through Play.* Her research interests include aspects of cognitive and emotional influences in the acquisition and performance of motor skills. In college Dr. Bunker was a varsity athlete in tennis, field hockey, and basketball. She is currently serving as a consultant for the National Golf Foundation. Her professional leadership experience includes serving on the National Youth Sport Coalition and as chair of the AAHPERD Sport Psychology Academy.

ALBERT V. CARRON is a professor of sport psychology in the Faculty of Physical Education and the Department of Psychology at the University of Western Ontario. Dr. Carron coached football for four years at the university level and also coached a variety of minor sport teams. His general research focus has been in the area of group dynamics, with a specific interest in social interaction, leadership, and group cohesiveness. Dr. Carron has conducted research supported by the Canadian Amateur Diving Association, the Federation of Canadian Archers, and Sport Canada. He is the author of *Social Psychology of Sport* and *Motivation: Implications for Coaching and Teaching.*

P. (CHELLA) CHELLADURAI is an associate professor of sport management in the Faculty of Physical Education at the University of Western Ontario. He obtained his doctorate in Management Sciences from the University of Waterloo. His research interests have mainly centered around leadership in sports. Dr. Chelladurai is the author of *Sport Management: Macro Perspectives.* As a youth in India, he was a national basketball player, coach, and referee.

DANIEL GOULD is an associate professor in the Department of Physical Education at the University of Illinois. His research interests include the study of athlete motivation, competitive stress, and the psychological effects of athletic competition on children. Dr. Gould is extensively involved in disseminating the results of sport psychological research to athletes and coaches through clinics, publications, and consultations. He has consulted with novice and elite international-caliber athletes in a wide variety of sports ranging from figure skating and dressage to wrestling and baseball. He is a former wrestler, football and baseball player. Dr. Gould also serves as director of the U.S. Wrestling Science and Medicine Program.

DOROTHY V. HARRIS is a professor and coordinator of the Graduate Program in Sport Psychology at Pennsylvania State University. She is a world-renowned educational sport psychologist, past president of NASPSPA, a former member of the Managing Council of the International Society of Sport Psychology, ISSP treasurer, and editor of the ISSP Newsletter. Dr. Harris is a prolific author who has written two books, edited five, and contributed to numerous others. She is also an accomplished speaker. She spent a sabbatical at the Olympic Training Center in 1980 and has continued to work with numerous Olympic and national teams and athletes.

KEITH P. HENSCHEN is an associate professor in the Department of Physical Education at The University of Utah. He is Director of the Sport Psychology Graduate Program and has published numerous research articles and spoken extensively concerning the practical applications of sport psychology. His research interests include intervention strategies, athlete performance assessment, and performance psychology for the handicapped. Dr. Henschen is a recognized consultant for numerous college and professional sport teams. He is currently the Chairman of the Sport Psychology Committee for the U.S. Gymnastics Federation.

STEVEN R. HEYMAN is a licensed clinical psychologist and currently an associate professor and director of clinical training in the Clinical Psychology Doctoral Program at the University of Wyoming. Dr. Heyman's interests in sport psychology developed from his personal involvement with high-risk sports, including scuba diving, hang gliding, and skydiving. His research interests within sport psychology include personality and performance, high-risk sports, and hypnosis. He has worked primarily with individual athletes, including swimmers, boxers, football players, and powerlifters.

THELMA STERNBERG HORN received her doctorate in sport psychology from Michigan State University and is currently an assistant professor with the Department of Human Kinetics at the University of Wisconsin—Milwaukee. Her major research interests center around children's perceptions concerning their physical competence and the influence of adult behavior on children's psychosocial growth. Prior to her graduate work in sport psychology, Dr. Horn taught physical education and English at the high school level in Michigan and Colorado. She has had extensive coaching experience at both interscholastic and intercollegiate levels and continues to work as a consultant and clinician with coaches and teachers in youth sport programs.

MAYNARD HOWE holds a doctorate in psychology with specializations in clinical and industrial psychology. He is now an executive consultant and a vice president of Behavioral Management Institute, a Minnesota-based consulting firm that brings products and services from the behavioral sciences to corporations throughout the world. Dr. Howe's areas of interest include motivation, self-esteem, stress management, and sport psychology. He has also made major contributions to professional and Olympic athletes, teams, and organizations in the areas of motivation, assessment, and performance enhancement.

DANIEL M. LANDERS is professor of Physical Education and chair of the interdisciplinary doctoral program in Exercise Science at Arizona State University. He has been editor of the *Journal of Sport Psychology* since its inception in 1978. Dr. Landers serves on a National Academy of Science committee and is a member of the Sport Psychology Task Force of the U.S. Olympic Committee. His research has focused on the arousal–performance relationship, including attention/concentration and stress-reducing coping strategies. He has served as a sport psychologist for collegiate teams, professional teams, and national Olympic teams in the U.S., Canada, and Korea.

MIMI C. MURRAY received her doctorate from the University of Connecticut and is currently professor at Springfield College. Dr. Murray has been a very successful gymnastics coach: Her teams at Springfield College won three Division I National Championships; she was selected to coach the U.S. team of the World University Games and was named "Coach of the Year." She has authored *Gymnastics for Women: The Spectator, Gymnast, Coach and Teacher* and has been a commentator on ABC's "Wide World of Sports." As a sport psychologist, Dr. Murray has published many articles and lectured throughout the United States. Before the 1984 Olympics, she served as a sport psychologist with the U.S. Equestrian Team.

ROBERT M. NIDEFFER has been a professor on the faculties of the University of Rochester, The California School of Professional Psychology, and San Diego State University. He has been involved in sport psychology since 1969 and is currently self-employed as the President of Enhanced Performance Associates. Dr. Nideffer has published extensively in the sport psychology and stress management areas, with nine books and over one hundred articles to his credit. He has worked with Olympic-level and professional athletes in a wide variety of sports and has been a member of policy-setting committees in the United States, Canada, and Australia.

BRUCE C. OGILVIE is professor emeritus in the Department of Psychology at San Jose State University. Dr. Ogilvie is a world-renowned pioneer in applied sport psychology; he has researched, consulted, and published in the area of performance and the high-performance person since 1955. He has contributed over 140 publications on issues ranging from children in sport, identification of psychological factors that contribute to performance success, and the development of performance-enhancing strategies. Dr. Ogilvie has served as team psychological consultant for numerous U.S. Olympic teams as well as professional football, basketball, baseball, hockey, and soccer teams. He has also been a private-practice consultant for elite athletes from various sports.

JOSEPH B. OXENDINE is a professor in the Department of Physical Education at Temple University. After competing in three sports at the college level, he played professional baseball for three years in the Pittsburg Pirate minor-league system. Dr. Oxendine taught and coached at the high school level before completing the doctoral program at Boston University. At Temple University he has conducted research on practice conditions, information feedback, and the role of arousal on motor performance. He has taught graduate and undergraduate courses in skill learning and sport psychology and is the author of *Psychology of Motor Learning*.

ERIK PEPER teaches at the Center for Interdisciplinary Science at San Francisco State University, and is director of the Biofeedback and Family Therapy Institute. He is past president of the Biofeedback Society of America and has published books and articles on biofeedback, including *Mind/Body Integration, From the Inside Out: A Self-Teaching and Laboratory Manual for Biofeedback.* Dr. Peper has been a consultant to musicians, artists, athletes, and the U.S. rhythmic gymnastics team. His research focuses on biofeedback and psychophysiology to enhance optimal performance.

KENNETH RAVIZZA is an associate professor in the Department of Health, Physical Education and Recreation at California State University at Fullerton. His research has examined the nature of peak performance in human movement activities. Dr. Ravizza has functioned as mental training specialist with the Fullerton gymnastics, softball, and baseball teams for the past six years. He worked for two years with the 1984 U.S. Women's Olympic field hockey team, and he is presently implementing a program with the California Angels baseball team. He has also developed and presented stress management programs for health care and school staffs, cancer patients, battered women, private business groups, and prison inmates.

ROBERT J. ROTELLA is director of Sport Psychology at the University of Virginia. Dr. Rotella was named twice to "Outstanding College Athletes of America" and was awarded All-American honors in lacrosse. He has also coached high school basketball and college lacrosse teams. His research interests have focused on stress, anxiety, self-confidence and sport performance. Dr. Rotella has written numerous books and articles on applied sport psychology; his books include *Mind Mastery for Winning Golf; Mind, Set and Match;* and *Scientific Foundations of Coaching.* He has also served as consultant for the University of Virginia athletic teams, the University of Notre Dame, and professional athletes from football, basketball, baseball, and golf.

ANDREA SCHMID is professor of Physical Education at San Francisco State University. As a two-time Olympian, she received gold, silver, and bronze medals in gymnastics. She coached the 1975 U.S. world championship team and judged five world championships in rhythmic gymnastics. She is a member of F.I.G. and the U.S.G.F. Sport Psychology Committee. Dr. Schmid has been a sport psychology consultant to college athletes and the U.S. rhythmic gymnastics team. She has published books and articles and lectured on sport psychology at national and international conferences. Her research interest focuses on optimal performance.

RONALD E. SMITH received his doctorate in psychology from Southern Illinois University and was a Fellow at UCLA's Neuropsychiatric Institute. He is currently professor of psychology and director of clinical psychology training at the University of Washington. Dr. Smith has long been involved in baseball and softball as player and coach; he has coached championship youth and adult teams. His major research interests are the study of coaching behaviors and the development of training programs designed to increase psychological coping skills. Dr. Smith serves as a consultant to youth, collegiate, and professional sports organizations. He is president-elect of the Association for the Advancement of Applied Sport Psychology.

FRANK L. SMOLL is an associate professor of sport psychology and motor development in the Psychology Department at the University of Washington. His research has focused on developing and testing intervention programs designed to improve the quality of youth sports. While attending Ripon College, he played on championship basketball and baseball teams. In the area of applied sport psychology, Dr. Smoll has extensive experience in conducting psychologically oriented coaching clinics (Coach Effectiveness Training) and workshops for parents of young athletes. He is actively involved as a consultant to numerous youth sport organizations.

WILLIAM F. STRAUB is a professor in the Department of Physical Education at Ithaca College. Before becoming involved in sport psychology, Dr. Straub was an accomplished athlete and high school coach; his teams won league championships in baseball, basketball, football, and wrestling. He has published extensively in scholarly journals and has edited two books. Dr. Straub has also chaired the AAHPERD Sport Psychology Academy and is current publications director of the Association for the Advancement of Applied Sport Psychology. As a consultant, he has worked for Cornell University, the Washington Redskins, and the Philadelphia Eagles.

LARS-ERIC UNESTÅHL received his doctorate at Uppsala University and is currently a professor in Psychology at Örebro University in Sweden. His main areas of research interest are clinical and experimental hypnosis and physical and creative performance. He has written and edited seven books and over seventy research articles. Dr. Uneståhl serves on the Council of the International Society of Hynopsis and the International Society of Sport Psychology. He organized the Sixth World Congress in Hypnosis and Psychosomatic Medicine and the Sixth World Congress in Sport Psychology. He was a national athlete in track and field, and during the last fifteen years he has served as a consultant for Swedish and Olympic teams and elite athletes from many countries.

ROBIN S. VEALEY is an assistant professor in the Department of Health, Physical Education and Recreation at Miami University. Dr. Vealey completed a doctorate in sport psychology at the University of Illinois and now focuses her research on the areas of self-confidence and achievement behavior in sport, competitive anxiety, and coaching behavior. She also serves as sport psychologist for the U.S. nordic ski team and regularly consults with various athletes and teams. Before beginning her career in sport psychology, Dr. Vealey taught and coached at Linfield College in Oregon; her basketball and volleyball teams achieved national recognition, and she was named as a finalist for National Coach of the Year.

1

Sport Psychology: Past, Present, Future

JEAN M. WILLIAMS

University of Arizona

WILLIAM F. STRAUB

Ithaca College

Within the past 20 years, a new field of sport science has been recognized. It is called sport psychology, and it is concerned with both the psychological factors that influence participation in sport and exercise and the psychological effects derived from that participation. Sport psychologists study motivation, personality, aggression and violence, leadership, group dynamics, exercise and psychological well-being, thoughts and feelings of athletes, and many other dimensions of participation in sport and physical activity. Among other functions, modern-day sport psychologists teach sport psychology classes, conduct research, and work with athletes and coaches to help improve performance and enhance the quality of the athletic experience.

Coaches were interested in the psychological aspects of athletic competition even before there was a science called sport psychology. For example, in the 1920s Knute Rockne, the coach of the fighting Irish of Notre Dame, popularized the pep talk by making it an important part of his coaching philosophy. We should note, however, that Rockne did not attempt to psych up his team for every contest. He only used the pep talk for special occasions. In contrast, coaching interest in contemporary sport psychology involves more than a mere concern for psyching up athletes for competition.

Applied Sport Psychology focuses on only one facet of sport psychology, that of identifying and understanding psychological theories and techniques that can be applied to sport to enhance the performance and personal growth of athletes. This area of applied sport psychology has grown tremendously in recent years as evidenced by the numbers of coaches and athletes now looking to sport psychology for a competitive edge. These individuals are turning to various psychological training programs to learn, among other things, ways to manage competitive stress, control concentra-

1

tion, improve confidence, and increase communication skills and team harmony. The goal of psychological training is to learn to consistently create the ideal mental climate that unleashes those physical skills which allow athletes to perform at their best. The authors of subsequent chapters will discuss the preceding factors and also present other psychological principles and techniques that can be used to enhance performance and personal growth. But, first, in this chapter we will provide a brief overview of the past, present, and future of sport psychology. Primary emphasis will be given to sport psychology practices in North America and the iron curtain countries of Eastern Europe. The coverage is not all-inclusive but selective to the focus of the book. For a more comprehensive overview, see Wiggins (1984), Salmela (1984), Shneidman (1979), and Alderman (1984).

HISTORY OF SPORT PSYCHOLOGY IN NORTH AMERICA

Coleman Griffith, a psychologist who is considered by many to be the father of sport psychology in North America, was the first person to research sport psychology over an extended period of time. Griffith was hired by the University of Illinois in 1925 to help coaches improve the performance of their players. He wrote two books, *Psychology of Coaching* (1926) and *Psychology of Athletics* (1928), that are considered to be classics. He also established the first sport psychology laboratory in North America and taught the first course in sport psychology. By modern definition, Griffith was as much interested in motor learning as he was in sport psychology. Following Griffith's contributions in the 1920s and 1930s, very little extensive study occurred in sport psychology (except for research on personality and the influence of stress on performance) until the late 1960s.

Another book entitled *Psychology of Coaching* was published in 1951. Written by psychologist John Lawther, it resulted in coaches' becoming increasingly interested in learning more about such important topics as motivation, team cohesion, and interpersonal relations. What made Lawther's message particularly appealing was the fact that he also coached the Pennsylvania State University varsity men's basketball team.

During the 1960s, two San Jose State University psychologists, Bruce Ogilvie and Thomas Tutko, created considerable interest in sport psychology with their book *Problem Athletes and How to Handle Them* (1966). According to Ogilvie, this book "moved the coaching world off dead center." After extensively researching the personality of athletes, Ogilvie and Tutko developed the controversial Athletic Motivation Inventory, a paper-and-pencil test that purported to measure the motives of athletes. Despite some criticism of their work, Ogilvie and Tutko were the leading applied sport psychologists during the 1960s. They did a great deal of consulting with college and professional teams and did much to foster public interest in sport psychology. Because of Dr. Ogilvie's many contributions, he has been called the father of applied sport psychology in North America.

The 1960s also witnessed the first attempts to bring together groups of individuals interested in sport psychology. In the early part of the decade, sport psychology began to organize on an international level with the formation of the International Society of Sport Psychology (ISSP) in Rome. Dr. Ferruccio Antonelli, an Italian psychiatrist, was elected the first president and provided leadership during the early years. Miroslav Vanek, a Czech, has been president since 1973. The ISSP publishes the *International Journal of Sport Psychology* and hosts worldwide meetings. These gatherings are particularly important because they provide a forum for sharing research and fostering the exchange of ideas by sport psychologists from different countries.

The second international meeting of ISSP was hosted in 1968 in Washington, D.C., by the newly formed North American Society for Psychology of Sport and Physical Activity (NASPSPA). The first annual meeting of NASPSPA was held in 1967, prior to the American Alliance for Health, Physical Education, and Recreation Conference in Las Vegas, Nevada. Dr. Arthur Slatter-Hammel was the first NASPSPA president. According to Salmela (1981), NASPSPA has developed into the single most influential academic professional sport psychology society in the world. Its annual meetings are well attended by scholars in motor learning, motor development, and sport psychology. The 1960s also saw the formation of the Canadian Society for Psychomotor Learning and Sport Psychology (CSPLSP), which was founded by Robert Wilberg of the University of Alberta in 1969 under the auspices of the Canadian Association for Health, Physical Education, and Recreation. The organization became independent in 1977. Both NASPSPA and CSPLSP have been extremely influential in fostering increased interest and research in sport psychology.

The decade of the 1970s marks the period in which sport psychology in North America really began to flourish and to be recognized more widely as a separate discipline within the sport sciences. Systematic research by ever-increasing numbers of sport psychologists played a major role in this coming of age. In fact, the primary goal of sport psychologists in the 1970s was advancing sport psychology's knowledge base through experimental research. We should note, however, that there was no clear focus or agreement as to what the knowledge base should be. Consequently, research topics were very diverse and were directed toward many target populations. Topics typically came from mainstream psychology.

The earlier interest in personality research declined in the 1970s because of heated debates about the validity of personality traits and the paper-and-pencil tests used to assess the personality traits of athletes. Many sport psychologists continued to believe that internal mechanisms (i.e., traits) govern behavior, but these psychologists also became aware of the effect of environmental variables. The interactionism paradigm, which considers person and environmental variables and their potential interaction, began to surface and gain more and more credibility as a viable approach to the understanding of athlete behavior.

According to data gathered by Salmela (1984) from a questionnaire study completed by 1980, North American sport psychology researchers spent a majority of their time (52.6%) testing nonathletes. An athletic history was presumably not important because the aim of the research was to create and test new basic theory and conceptual models. The researchers did spend 38.5% of their time testing elite athletes. Unlike researchers in North America, those in Eastern Europe primarily had an applied research focus: improving the sport performance of elite athletes. Consequently, Eastern Europeans spent 54.6% of their research time on elite athletes and only 27.5% on nonathletic populations (Salmela, 1984).

The experimental quality of North American research improved throughout the 1970s. Earlier research, which was methodologically and theoretically weak, was replaced by better research design and more sophisticated statistics. The increased quality and volume of sport psychology research is perhaps best reflected in the establishment in 1979 of a separate research journal, the *Journal of Sport Psychology*.

In the late 1970s and early 1980s, sport psychology began to reflect a more cognitive focus by devoting increasing attention to athletes' thoughts and images. How athletes think influences how they perform. Negative thinking, the "I can't" attitude, seems to be associated with performance failure. The 1983 New York City marathon provides an excellent example of how inner dialogue can influence the performance of runners. Geoff Smith, an Englishman, led for most of the race. Within approximately 300 meters of the finish line, Rod Dixon, a New Zealander, passed Smith and won the race. The difference between first and second place was 9 seconds, or about 50 yards. William P. Morgan (1984), a well-known sport psychology authority, indicated that Dixon's success may have been aided by his cognitive strategy. According to newspaper reports, Dixon stated, "With a mile to go I was thinking, 'A miler's kick does the trick,' and 'I've got to go, I've got to go.'" By contrast, with 600 yards to go, Smith is reported to have said, "My legs have gone." Later Smith noted, "I was just running from memory. I thought I was going to stumble and collapse." In fact, Smith did collapse at the finish line. Today, many sport psychologists who work in the area of applied sport psychology have developed techniques to train athletes to think positively by focusing on what they want to happen as opposed to what they do *not* want to happen. Perhaps the results of the 1983 New York marathon would have been different if Smith had employed these techniques.

The growth of cognitive sport psychology has also led to renewed interest in visualization. Athletes who naturally image themselves performing well or who are trained to image successful performances appear to both learn and perform better. Consequently, imagery and cognitive interventions have become an integral part of most mental training programs. See Chapters 13 and 14 for a detailed description of how these procedures work and how they can be trained.

The interest in cognitive sport psychology paralleled an increase in field research in sport psychology. This greater emphasis on field research played a major role in advancing knowledge in applied sport psychology. Research has been conducted on topics such as identifying coaching behaviors most effective in promoting learning and personal growth; discovering ways to enhance team harmony and coach – athlete communications; learning how to set and use goals; determining psychological characteristics of successful performers; developing psychological training techniques; and identifying psychological factors considered important in dealing with burned-out, injured, and retiring athletes. Although much still needs to be learned and tested in regard to these topics in applied sport psychology, important advances have been made. These advances, which are integral to enhancing performance and personal growth, will be addressed specifically in the following chapters.

The growing interest and knowledge base in applied sport psychology is also reflected in the recent formation of the Association for the Advancement of Applied Sport Psychology (AAASP). John Silva, University of North Carolina sport psychologist, played the primary role in forming AAASP, whose first organizational meeting was held at Nags Head, North Carolina, in the fall of 1985. The purpose of AAASP is to extend the existing services of organizations such as ISSP, NASPSPA, and the American Psychological Association (APA) by providing a forum that specifically addresses applied aspects of sport psychology, aspects such as the promotion of applied research, the advancement of knowledge regarding interventions, and the examination of professional issues such as ethical standards, qualifications for becoming a sport psychologist, and potential certification of sport psychologists.

HISTORY OF SPORT PSYCHOLOGY IN EASTERN EUROPE

Sport psychology in the iron curtain countries of Eastern Europe is of particular importance to people interested in peak performance. These nations have a long history of giving a great deal of attention to the applied aspects of sport psychology — more specifically, the enhancing of elite athletes' performance through applied research and direct intervention. As a consequence of this emphasis, sport psychologists in Eastern Europe play an active role at all levels in the selection, training, and competitive preparation of athletes.

Sport psychology in Eastern Europe is a highly esteemed field of academic and professional concern as evidenced by State support and the acceptance of sport psychologists in national psychological associations. In some nations, sport psychologists have even been awarded the title of academician, a title that elevates the recipient to the level of a national hero. All of this is because in these countries sport excellence is considered to be an important propaganda tool in advancing their political system and sport psychologists are viewed as central figures in facilitating the athlete's quest for excellence.

Although Salmela (1981) characterized the Eastern European approach to sport psychology as "made in the Soviet Union," he also indicated that there were individual differences in kind and degree of the basic Soviet model. Despite the attempts of many North American scholars to determine what Eastern European sport psychologists are doing, an aura of mystery surrounds the practice of sport psychology in these countries. This is partly because their scholars have been reluctant to share openly their research and techniques for enhancing performance.

Vanek and Cratty (1970) reported that the first interest in sport psychology in Eastern Europe can be traced to a physician, Dr. P. F. Lesgaft, who described in 1901 the possible psychological benefits of physical activity. The first research articles were published by Puni and Rudik in the early 1920s. The Institutes for Physical Culture in Moscow and Leningrad were also established in the early 1920s, and the beginning of sport psychology can be traced to them.

Garfield (Garfield & Bennett, 1984), who visited with a group of Soviet sport psychologists and physiologists while lecturing in Milan in 1979, reported that "the extensive investment in athletic research in the communist countries began early in the 1950s as part of the Soviet space program" (p. 13). Russian scientists successfully explored the possibility of using ancient yogic techniques to teach cosmonauts to control psychophysiological processes while in space. These techniques were called self-regulation training or psychic self-regulation and were used to voluntarily control such bodily functions as heart rate, temperature, and muscle tension, as well as emotional reactions to stressful situations such as zero gravity. Nearly 20 years passed before these methods were systematically applied to the Soviet and East German sport programs. According to Kurt Tittel, director of the Leipzig Institute of Sports (a 14-acre sport laboratory employing 900 people, over half of whom are scientists) in East Germany, new training methods similar to psychic self-regulation were responsible for the impressive victories by East German and Soviet athletes during the 1976 Olympics (Garfield & Bennett, 1984).

Salmela (1984) reported that sport psychology research in Eastern European countries has been more limited in scope than in North America because of greater governmental control. Rather narrowly focused five-year research plans are determined by the State with the advice of its sport psychologists. All sport psychology researchers within the country are required to coordinate and streamline their research efforts to accomplish the stated research objective. Salmela (1981) also indicated that this research focus has tended to be of a field variety and applied primarily toward top-level achievement in sport. This is not surprising considering each State's heavy emphasis on sport excellence and the easy access by sport psychologists to elite athletes. Most of the Eastern European sport institutes where athletes are trained have teams of sport psychologists. Salmela (1984), on a visit to a major sport institute in Bucharest, Romania, reported meeting with a team of eight sport psychologists. A sport psychology faculty of that size is considered normal for that type of sport institute. In contrast, in North America it is uncommon for an institution to have more than one person specifically trained in sport psychology.

Although most North American sport psychologists would find government-dictated research endeavors abhorrent, a large-scale, unified approach to a particular research topic does have advantages. Salmela (1984) cited one positive example that was a consequence of knowledge gained from a constrained focus of attention. All Eastern European countries have successfully inaugurated as many as 30 hours of theory and practice of training in self-control for all elite athletes. Equivalent types of programs have been implemented on only a limited basis in North America.

The exact training techniques employed by Eastern European sport psychologists are not known, but it is believed that autogenic training, visualization, and self-hypnosis are key components (see Chapters 13, 14, and 18 for a description of these techniques). Because of government-funded research and widespread integration of sophisticated mental training programs with rigorous physical training, some authorities believe Eastern Europe is ahead of North America in the development and application of applied sport psychology.

FUTURE DIRECTIONS IN NORTH AMERICAN SPORT PSYCHOLOGY

What will be the future of sport psychology in North America? Will sport psychologists become more applied in focus, taking a more active role in educating coaches and athletes regarding psychological training techniques for enhancing performance and personal growth? Will college and professional teams hire sport psychologists? If so, what kinds of services will future psychologists be qualified to provide? How should sport psychologists be trained and by whom? Should minimal standards be established and used to certify future sport psychologists? What should be the future directions in sport psychology research? Will laboratory- and theory-oriented research continue to be the principal method of investigation? Will interest in conducting research on the psychology of performance and techniques for training psychological skills continue to expand? If the trend toward conducting field studies continues, will sport psychology lose academic respectability? These and other questions abound as we consider the future of sport psychology. The field of sport psychology is undergoing considerable change. You might even say it is having an identity crisis. Who sport psychologists are, what the nature of their work is, and related issues have not been completely determined.

The future of sport psychology hinges upon the answers to the preceding questions. At this time, however, it is impossible to provide definitive answers. Nevertheless, there are sources from which answers to these questions can at least be realistically conjectured. Among these sources are the writings of other sport psychologists, the opinions of individuals currently holding leadership roles in sport psychology, and the results of a recent research study that surveyed a panel of sport psychology experts in order to determine their predictions for the future of sport psychology.

First, how are future sport psychologists likely to be trained, what will be their role in working with athletes, and will they be certified? Many of the comments that follow are taken from an article by Robert Nideffer (1984), a prominent San Diego clinical sport psychologist. The advancement of sport psychology in North America has been primarily a consequence of sport psychologists' being trained in physical education or related departments. Most of these individuals had minimal formal training in psychology or, at best, a minor emphasis. With only a few exceptions, psychologists in the American Psychological Association did not initially show much interest in sport psychology. This may be changing, however, because of better education of APA members regarding the field of sport psychology, increased consumer demand for the services of sport psychologists, and the demands of economic necessity created by not having enough traditional psychology jobs to go around.

Some individuals actually fear that in the future psychologists may take control of the field of applied sport psychology. If this occurs, these individuals are concerned that psychologists who are primarily trained in a clinical model will emphasize psychopathology rather than the performance-enhancement educational model currently used by most people receiving their degrees through physical education or related departments. Also, individuals trained only in psychology would not have an adequate knowledge of the sport sciences and the demands of the athletic arena. Concerns regarding a therapy model are legitimate because some data suggest that over 90% of all athletes are very stable psychologically.

At the other extreme, people who are trained as clinicians have seen serious clinical problems in sport, and they are convinced that taking only an educational model approach to sport psychology is inadequate. Individuals lacking training in clinical psychology might not be sensitive to underlying psychopathology and might, therefore, use psychological training techniques that could precipitate a problem they are incapable of handling.

According to Nideffer, NASPSPA and CSPLSP might start taking a more active interest in addressing the issues of training and certification as more psychologists move into sport psychology because of the growing interest in application. Previously, the more academically oriented members of NASPSPA and CSPLSP were not sure there was even a sufficient knowledge base on which sport psychology services could be provided. Such members also did not want applied issues to dominate the organizations they had founded. Although NASPSPA and CSPLSP previously did not choose to define what a sport psychologist is, how he or she should be trained, and whether there should be certification, these organizations were sufficiently concerned with applied issues to formulate an ethical code of standards to guide the behavior of their members (see Nideffer, 1984, for a description of these standards).

Even if NASPSPA and CSPLSP continue to choose not to be involved in the professional issues noted above, we believe the relatively new Association for the Advancement of Sport Psychology, and perhaps the APA, most assuredly will address them. At some future time guidelines will be established for the training and certification of sport psychologists. The training guidelines will surely merge the disciplines of psychology and sport science, but exactly how that will be done and who will house relevant programs remains to be seen. There may even be separate training guidelines and role descriptions for clinical sport psychologists, educational sport psychologists, and research sport psychologists. In fact, the United States Olympic Committee's Sports Medicine Committee is currently using such guidelines. The USOC's role descriptions and minimal educational and experiential requirements for these roles can be found in the 1983 *Journal of Sport Psychology* (vol. 5, pp. 4–8).

Meanwhile, the prospective future sport psychologist and his or her adviser must take responsibility for getting the right balance in course work between the disciplines of psychology and sport science. Until the various issues are satisfactorily resolved, Nideffer recommends that an individual choose a graduate program that will prepare him or her for licensure — not because training in sport science is less important but because the right to call oneself a psychologist is restricted by law to those with formal training in psychology. We should note that this recommendation was made for people who are interested in independent practice in sport psychology. When private practice is the objective, we would add to Nideffer's recommendation that people try to select a university where the psychology department has recognized expertise in sport psychology or where a minor in sport psychology is available from the physical education or a related department.

The issue of training and qualifications for providing certain types of psychological training programs is also relevant for coaches and athletic departments that are in a position of selecting a sport psychologist to work with their athletes and/or coaching staff. It is essential that the sport psychologist's credentials and experience be carefully scrutinized to determine whether his or her qualifications parallel the goals of the services being sought.

Some insights on future directions in sport psychology also come from an address given by Robert N. Singer, president of ISSP, at the VI International Society of Sport Psychology meeting in Copenhagen, Denmark, in June 1985 (Singer, 1985). Because of the applied nature of sport psychology and its diversified and broad framework, Singer (1985) is not optimistic about scholarly recognition of the field, but he does think sport psychology will become a more accepted, active, and integral part of sports medicine. He also thinks it likely that until the early 1990s sport psychologists will primarily focus on practical questions and issues such as helping elite athletes try to become more elite. At this time Singer sees the following research questions to be of particular interest and importance to applied sport psychologists: Which type of anxiety-reduction program is most effective and for what kind of problem and what type of person? What is the best way to train processes related to selective attention and attentional focus? What is the content of the best psychological training programs?

Singer (1985) further identified 11 major research areas that he thinks will receive attention in the late 1980s and early 1990s: (1) kids and sport learning, (2) sport-specific psychological tests, (3) predicting athletic success, (4) analyzing cognitive processes, (5) self-management, coping techniques, (6) the development and training of pertinent psychological processes, (7) motivation, (8) comprehensive psychological programs for athletes, (9) longitudinal data on athletes, (10) psychological outcomes derived from programs of vigorous physical activity, and (11) cross-country psychological comparative data on athletes.

Perhaps the most definitive data on the future of sport psychology come from Thueson and Jarman's (1985) research predicting future trends in sport psychology by using the Delphi technique with a panel of 37 sport psychology experts who completed a series of three questionnaires, the return rate of which was 92%. Of those who responded, 76% were from physical education or related departments, 15% were from psychology departments, and 9% were in private practice or other positions.

The experts predicted 26 future trends in sport psychology, including the following: (1) more emphasis will be placed upon the psychological factors affecting elite performers, (2) there will be an increase in the use of sport psychologists in the United States Olympic program, (3) more emphasis will be placed upon the practical application of knowledge gained through research, (4) there will be increased interest in sport psychology courses by both coaches and athletes, (5) there will be more research with nonathletes on psychology of exercise and/or health psychology dealing with things such as well-being, stress reduction, etc., (6) there will be increased emphasis on applied research, (7) there will be an increase in the number of unqualified people in sport psychology, and (8) a journal of applied sport psychology will be published.

The experts also predicted that many of these trends will not become a reality until 1990. Even if this is the case, the future appears bright for applied sport psychology. Much-needed research on practical and theoretical questions appears likely to continue. Because of the current interests and demands of coaches and athletes, more sport psychologists than ever before will be providing psychological training programs for enhancing performance and long-term personal growth and development. As the discipline of sport psychology continues to mature and become more specialized, its ultimate future will depend upon the ability of sport psychologists to support and advance one another's interests and needs.

SUMMARY

Sport psychology, the youngest of the sport sciences, is concerned with the psychological factors that influence participation in sport and exercise and with the psychological effects derived from participation. Today many athletes and coaches look to sport psychology for a competitive edge by seeking psychological training programs in order to learn, among other things, ways to manage competitive stress, control concentration, improve confidence, and increase communication skills and team harmony.

The roots of sport psychology in North America go back to Coleman Griffith, a psychologist who was hired in 1925 by the University of Illinois to help improve the performance of its athletes. Griffith taught the first course in sport psychology, established the first sport psychology laboratory in North America, and wrote the first psychology of coaching book. Following Griffith's contributions in the 1920s and 1930s, very little happened in sport psychology until the 1960s. The 1960s witnessed the first attempts to bring together groups of individuals interested in sport psychology, which resulted in the formation of three sport psychology associations. During the 1970s, sport psychology in North America really began to flourish. Systematic research by increasing numbers of sport psychologists played a major role in this coming of age. Research topics were very diverse and were channeled toward many populations. During the late 1970s and early 1980s, it became very popular to apply psychological theories and techniques to sport to enhance the performance and personal growth of athletes.

In contrast, sport psychology in the countries of Eastern Europe has a long history of devoting a great deal of attention to enhancing the performance of elite athletes through applied research and direct intervention. Sport psychologists in these countries are viewed as central figures in facilitating an athlete's quest for excellence. Thus, they are held in great esteem because sport excellence is considered an important propaganda tool in advancing the political system of Eastern Europe. Because of government-funded research and widespread integration of sophisticated mental training programs with rigorous physical training, some authorities believe Eastern Europe is ahead of North America in the development and application of sport psychology.

The future of sport psychology in North America hinges upon the answers to many questions: Who will seek the services of sport psychologists? What services will sport psychologists be qualified to supply? How should sport psychologists be trained? What should be future research directions in sport psychology? Answers to these questions are now being proposed by sport psychology experts.

REFERENCES

Alderman, R. B. (1984). The future of sport psychology. In J. M. Silva, III, & R. S. Weinberg (Eds.), *Psychological foundations of sport* (pp. 45–54). Champaign, Ill.: Human Kinetics.

Garfield, C. A., & Bennett, H. Z. (1984). *Peak performance.* Los Angeles: Tarcher.

Griffith, C. R. (1926). *Psychology of coaching.* New York: Scribner's.

Griffith, C. R. (1928). *Psychology of athletics.* New York: Scribner's.

Lawther, J. D. (1951). *Psychology of coaching.* Englewood Cliffs, N.J.: Prentice-Hall.

Morgan, W. P. (1984). Mind over matter. In W. F. Straub & J. M. Williams (Eds.), *Cognitive sport psychology* (pp. 311–316). Lansing, N.Y.: Sport Science International.

Nideffer, R. M. (1984). Current concerns in sport psychology. In J. M. Silva, III, &

R. S. Weinberg (Eds.), *Psychological foundations of sport* (pp. 35–44). Champaign, Ill.: Human Kinetics.

Ogilvie, B., & Tutko, T. (1966). *Problem athletes and how to handle them.* London: Pelham.

Salmela, J. H. (1981). *The world sport psychology sourcebook.* Ithaca, N.Y.: Mouvement Publications.

Salmela, J. H. (1984). Comparative sport psychology. In J. M. Silva, III, & R. A. Weinberg (Eds.), *Psychological foundations of sport* (pp. 23–24). Champaign, Ill.: Human Kinetics.

Shneidman, N. N. (1979). *The Soviet road to Olympus: Theory and practice of Soviet physical culture and sport.* Toronto: The Ontario Institute for Studies in Education.

Singer, R. N. (1985). *Current perspectives on motor learning and sport psychology.* Paper presented at the VI International Meeting of the International Society of Sport Psychology, Copenhagen, Denmark.

Thueson, N. C., & Jarman, B. Q. (1985). *Predicting future trends in sport psychology.* Paper presented at the annual meeting of the North American Society for Psychology of Sport and Physical Activity, Gulfport, Miss.

U.S. Olympic Committee (1983). U.S. Olympic Committee establishes guidelines for sport psychology services. *Journal of Sport Psychology, 5,* 4–7.

Vanek, M., & Cratty, B. J. (1970). *Psychology and the superior athlete.* New York: Macmillan.

Wiggins, D. K. (1984). The history of sport psychology in North America. In J. M. Silva, III, & R. S. Weinberg (Eds.), *Psychological foundations of sport* (pp. 9–22). Champaign, Ill.: Human Kinetics.

Part One

Learning, Motivation, and Social Interaction in Sport

2   Motor Skill Learning for Effective Sport Performance

JOSEPH B. OXENDINE

Temple University

All athletic coaches recognize that sport performance depends upon many factors. Some factors are essentially determined by heredity (size and physique, speed potential, muscular power, agility, etc.); other factors are the result of effort on the part of the individual and are more temporary. The latter factors include skill level, motivation, and mental control. This chapter will focus on the development of motor skills, particularly emphasizing the processes involved in the learning, teaching, and coaching of sport skills.

The teacher or coach must understand that the overall learning climate is crucial for effective development of motor skills. The coach who establishes a good climate will find that skills are acquired more rapidly and will ultimately reach a higher level. Well-learned skills become routine habits that can be performed flawlessly under the most intense, intimidating competition. Further, learning that has been efficient and has taken place under favorable conditions is more likely to result in a positive attitude about the activity, thus assuring enjoyment and continued participation. Unfortunately, sport skills are too often taught under stressful, monotonous, or generally confusing conditions, all of which lead to negative attitudes and avoidance tendencies. Effective teaching saves time in the learning process so that students can achieve a more advanced level or acquire additional skills within the same time frame.

To be an effective athletic coach, one must be an excellent teacher. This requires expertise in the sport itself, familiarity with the learning process, and effectiveness in communication. The teacher-coach must have the ability to detect performance errors, to give the learner clear feedback about those errors, and to provide reinforcement when even the slightest improvement is noted.

Merely being a good performer of a sport skill does not ensure that one can teach that skill. Years ago at my university a former National Football League running back was hired as an assistant (backfield) coach. The young man, who was in his early 30s and still in near playing condition, depended upon the technique of demonstration to teach the running backs. Whenever a university runner had difficulty in executing a particular play, the assistant coach promptly grabbed the ball and demonstrated the proper technique. Subsequent errors resulted in additional demonstration from the coach. The behavior of neither the players nor the coach seemed to be altered by these demonstrations. The players often failed to understand what they were doing wrong, and the coach was unable to isolate the specific error and clearly communicate that information to the players. The coach could demonstrate, but he could not analyze and instruct. In short, he had not learned to teach.

Like a physician, automobile mechanic, or troubleshooter assigned to resolve an electrical breakdown, a coach as a teacher must be able to analyze a performance, spot the flaws, and provide clear remedial suggestions. Drill sergeants in the army can demonstrate the proper technique in a bayonet drill, a rifle firing position, or a marching maneuver, but they may not be able to help an individual who is having a special problem with one of these techniques. Good teachers and coaches must be able to do more than "teach it the way it was taught to me." Rather, they must understand how learning takes place and be skillful in providing timely cues, rewards, and encouragement.

THE LEARNING PROCESS

Motor skill learning is a physical *and* mental process. Therefore, effective skill learning can take place only when the learner is both physically and mentally committed to the task. We are inclined to forget mental demands when we observe highly skilled players perform, or when we ourselves perform well-established skills. Even highly complex motor skills can become habit, requiring no conscious thought. However, such was not the case in the early stages of learning those skills, even the more basic skills. For example, one who observes a 12-month-old in the process of taking her or his first steps cannot help but realize that the child is devoting every bit of physical and mental energy to this endeavor.

From the most basic skills, such as walking, to those considered to be more complex, such as riding a bicycle, driving a car, doing a back somersault on the balance beam, or throwing a screwball, the early stages of learning require a high involvement of both mental and physical capacities. A casual approach to skill learning results in casual results. This is evident in situations where a high school student is giving a halfhearted effort toward a chemistry lesson, or a disinterested fifth grader is being taught a folk dance. Therefore, Mary Lou Retton can perform a complex gymnastics routine "effortlessly" and Michael Jordan can forcefully drive around an opponent and shoot a "soft" fall-away jump shot, but such was not always the case. The early development of their skills required these athletes' full mental concentration.

The learning of motor skills and verbal skills is very similar in their requirement of mental attention and concentration. However, motor skills not only require a person to think but to make coordinated movements in response to verbal instruction, demonstration, or imagined performance.

The thoughtful, active process of skill learning can be sensed in the very early stages. For example, the 10-year-old girl who is a novice springboard diver goes through this process in learning the one-and-one-half forward somersault. First she observes the coach or another diver demonstrate the dive, or she may simply listen to the coach's description of the body movements or mechanics required for the performance. She then attempts to perform the dive, that is, to put her own body through the sequence of movement as observed or visualized. During and following her first attempt, she has some sense of the correctness of the response, even without being told. This (internal) feedback may be in the form of a painful belly flop or the clear realization that she entered the water feet first rather than head first. Now she attempts to understand the relationship between her self-initiated movement responses and the results. After this initial try, the young girl not only reflects on her own ideas about the performance but usually receives information from the coach and advice on how to improve on the next trial. She may also receive comments from classmates or other divers. Taking this internal (kinesthetic) and external (coaching) feedback into account, she now plans the second dive. She mentally rehearses the dive, making use of her own ideas as well as those corrective suggestions of others. After the second, third, and subsequent trials, she attempts to make use of all of the information to improve future trials. She makes constant adjustments based on mentally rehearsing the dives in light of the information she receives. The novice diver who approaches the task more casually, or who practices while resorting to simple trial-and-error efforts, does not learn nearly as fast. Such effort is not only frustrating but largely ineffective.

PHASES OF MOTOR SKILL LEARNING

The process of skill learning may be better understood by reviewing the phases or steps that one goes through in progressing from the novice stage to an advanced level. The clearest model of this process was developed by Fitts (1964) who described three phases in skill learning: the cognitive, the associative, and the autonomous phases. Robb (1972) has discussed similar stages in skill learning as plan-formation, practice, and automatic-execution phases. On the other hand, Adams (1971) discussed only two phases, using the term *verbal-motor* to parallel Fitts' first two phases and the term *motor* to approximate the autonomous phase.

Although Fitts' phases are not clearly distinct, or separate, they do provide some insight into the evolutionary process in skill learning. He referred to the *cognitive phase* as the beginning period during which the learner focuses on gaining an understanding of how the skill is to be performed. The coach or teacher explains or describes the task. In addition, he or she may provide demonstrations, films, charts, or other visual cues. During this period the learner uses "cognition" or mental processes to gain an understanding of how the task is to be performed. The learner also makes several initial attempts to perform the task. Kinesthetic feedback and other types of information that may be self-evident are coupled with verbal feedback from coaches or peers. This is all designed to provide an understanding of the requirements for performing the task. The cognitive phase is a relatively short period in the overall learning process.

The *associative phase,* also referred to as the practice or fixation phase, is a much longer period. During this phase the learner practices the skill to the point of mastery. Improvement is made, rapidly at first, and then less and less change is necessary as performance approaches the optimal level. Toward the end of the associative phase, the performance places less and less mental demand upon the learner. Feedback from the coach continues to be important, while the learner develops an increasing ability to detect errors—that is, to self-monitor the performance. During the associative phase the learner progresses from a rank beginner to an advanced-level performer.

The *autonomous phase* emerges when the learner is able to perform the skill with perfection (or at a maximal level of proficiency) without conscious thought. At this time the skill has been practiced to the point of becoming a habit. It can be performed with full efficiency while the learner is thinking about other matters. In addition, an "executive plan" is established that automatically sets into motion the motor responses, in proper sequence, once the decision is made to perform the task. A cybernetic (self-monitoring or automatic control) process takes over and relieves the individual of having to think about the skill that he or she is performing at the time.

All adults have developed certain motor skills to the autonomous level. Some are fairly basic skills such as walking, riding a bicycle, eating soup with a spoon, and writing. Others are more advanced but can still be performed by many people without their thinking about the motor response itself. These skills can include activities such as juggling three tennis balls while holding a conversation, driving an automobile in traffic, swimming the crawl stroke with coordinated flutter kick and breathing, and playing a game of catch.

Highly sophisticated skills can also be developed to the point of automation by talented people who have engaged in years of practice. For example, some skilled typists can type 100 words per minute from a manuscript while holding a conversation with officemates. The Olympic gymnast or figure skater can perform a complex routine while devoting little thought to the actual skills involved. The NBA guard can dribble the basketball downcourt at full speed on a fast break and change course by dribbling behind his back. He does this without looking at the ball and while thinking about the best strategy for getting the ball to the basket. During such a play he considers the position and movement of his opponents, as well as his teammates. He considers delivering a bounce pass to the right or to the left or perhaps faking in one direction and driving for the basket himself, or pulling it short and shooting a 15-foot jump shot, or slowing down and taking the ball outside to set up a play. He does all of this while dribbling the ball at full speed, *giving no thought to the mechanics of dribbling;* and there is rarely an error in the dribble itself. He is "programmed" to perform the fundamental skills of basketball, which include dribbling.

Each of these tasks, the high-speed typing, the gymnastics, the figure skating, and the dribbling are complex motor tasks that require some native ability as well as a great deal of practice before one reaches the autonomous phase. Yet each of these experts began as a novice, comparable to the child beginning the walk, or the American adult in a Chinese restaurant attempting to use chopsticks for the first time. Progressing from the cognitive, through the associative, and arriving at the autonomous phase requires an amount of practice and a period of time that are dependent upon the abilities of the individual, the efficiency of the learning environment, and the complexity of the task itself. Certainly high-speed dribbling, complex figure skating maneuvers, and a circus juggling act require more time and practice to master than does a sit-up or a simple dance routine.

Some speculate that it requires approximately eight years for a person to reach his or her full potential in a major sport such as gymnastics or ice skating. This appears to be substantiated by reports that today's female Olympic performers in these sports, competing at the ages of 16 to 18, actually began serious training at around 8 to 10 years of age. Three decades ago it was more customary for performers to begin training during their early teens and reach a peak in their early 20s.

FEEDBACK

The single most important factor in the control of learning is the provision of effective feedback (information about the quality of the performance) to the learner. Without feedback, learning is practically nonexistent. After all, if people do not know how they are doing, there is no reason for them to change their behavior. Furthermore, if they arbitrarily make a change, there is no assurance that it will be in the right direction. Since the time of Thorndike's classic experiment with line drawing in 1931, other researchers (Bennett, Vincent, & Johnson, 1979; Salmoni, 1980; Trowbridge & Cason, 1932) have repeatedly shown the essential nature of information feedback.

Kinds of Feedback

With some sport skills, information about the correctness of a response is readily apparent to performers; that is, they can *see* how they did. This is *intrinsic feedback.* For example, the basketball player can see whether the free-throw shot went into the basket. It is easy to see where the arrow lands in the archery target, whether one clears the bar in the high jump, how many pins are knocked down in bowling, or whether the tennis ball lands in the service area. In such activities it is not necessary for anyone to provide information as to the results of the performances. Such information is clearly evident to the performer. However, even in these situations it is often helpful to have a coach who can tell the performer *why* a particular response failed or to point out what particular response caused a performance to succeed.

On the other hand, in many sports the performer has no clear idea of how well he or she is doing. In such situations *extrinsic feedback* becomes necessary. This may be provided by a coach or other means such as a videotape, clock, bell, or similar signal. In track, the runner does not know his or her time in a 400-meter trial run until informed by another person or a clock. Neither does the long jumper know the distance of the jump until a measure is taken and reported by an official. Novices in gymnastics, dance, ice skating, and diving have minimal information about the quality of their performance until they are informed by the coach or other observers.

The role of the coach in providing feedback is important even when some performance information is already available to learners. For example, a bowler sees that the ball is repeatedly veering off into the left gutter but has no idea of what is causing it. A coach may be able to point out that during follow-through the arm is pulling across the left shoulder, therefore pulling the ball off to the left. Consequently, focusing attention on a follow-through that is straight past the visual line may correct the problem. A golfer may have no idea why he has developed a sudden tendency to slice the ball until the coach points out a newly developed flaw in his swing. Similarly, a tennis player may be consistently serving too long, or a springboard diver may be going over too far during her entry into the water.

A teacher or coach who can provide accurate and understandable feedback is important to performers at all levels of the performance scale, from novice to elite. Clearly, the beginner in any sport needs early and consistent instruction as well as regular feedback. What is not as often understood is that performers at average and even advanced levels also need feedback. Major league pitchers at the peak of their careers sometimes run into slumps that are not attributable to any physical or emotional problem they can detect. At this point the pitching coach must set aside a period to work with such pitchers and attempt to determine what they are doing differently, and how the problem can be corrected. At this high level of performance, problems are usually very subtle; errors in movement response are so slight that only a highly skilled coach can detect them.

The baseball coach who trots out to the mound to confer with a pitcher who has developed a wildness may have noticed that the pitcher's stride is uncharacteristically long, or that the pitcher is leaning too far backward to get more speed on the ball, or that he is releasing too early. Only a very knowledgeable coach, and one who is thoroughly familiar with the particular player, is able to provide this type of helpful information.

Athletes who are the very best in the world, Wayne Gretzky, Martina Navratalova, John McEnroe, Joan Benoit, and Carl Lewis, all need coaches. They all have periods when they are not performing at their maximum and are usually mystified as to why this is so. It is easy to understand why this is true with young people such as pitcher Dwight Gooden, gymnast Mary Lou Retton, or runner Zola Budd, but it is not so easily understood with old pros such as Jack Nicklaus or Jimmy Conners. Still, these people cannot see themselves as a coach does and thus cannot always self-correct, so they wisely return to their coaches when serious problems develop.

Some Techniques to Augment Feedback

Providing timely and effective feedback to learners is not a simple matter. Even when the movement faults are obvious to the coach and the appropriate corrective responses are clear, transmitting this information to learners so that they can comprehend and use it is not always easy. Frequently the learner is unable to translate the verbiage into meaningful movement behavior. At other times the learner simply does not believe what he or she is being told. Consequently, the ability to effectively communicate feedback to learners is often as troublesome as actually detecting the movement errors.

All experienced teachers and coaches can recall occasions when they have observed movement errors in learners and have informed those individuals about the problems, only to have the problems persist. Such difficulties do not arise because the learners are unintelligent, though it may seem so. They are not uninterested in improving; neither are they deliberately trying to be cantankerous. They simply are unable to put into effect what they are being told. Given this situation the coach must become innovative in communicating.

In teaching a beginning bowling class, I had difficulty in getting learners to follow through properly, to use a full arm swing in a plane that was in a line parallel to the target. Many in the class had a tendency to follow through across the left shoulder so that the ball veered to the left of the target. Despite my admonitions about the improper follow-through, such behavior persisted. Most often the players argued that they had indeed followed through properly. To correct this, on a subsequent occasion I moved up behind a bowler and sharply yelled, "See?" just at the point of the errant follow-through (while the arm was still to the left). On several occasions I actually grabbed the arm and held it at the erroneous position so that the bowler could not doubt the accuracy of my comment. Having finally convinced the bowler of the problem, it was then necessary to provide a mechanism for correcting the behavior. I instructed the bowlers to concentrate on making a "V" with the thumb and forefinger and, during the follow-through, sighting the 1 – 3 pocket within the "V." By devoting their attention to synchronizing the hand position with the target many learners quickly established the habit of a straight-ahead follow-through.

Movement errors in sport are many and varied. Recognizing these and effectively communicating them to the performer, along with providing hints for correcting the problems, are the mark of a good coach. I used one such technique when I found that young baseball players, when sliding into a base, had a tendency to put down the palms of their hands to cushion the fall. Their habit of dragging their hands along the ground often led to bruised hands and also slowed down the slide. To correct this I had the players practice sliding with pebbles in both hands and concentrating on holding those pebbles throughout the slide. Having all pebbles in their hands at the conclusion of the slide provided feedback that they had not opened their hands during the slide.

Young baseball batters, and sometimes older ones, have a tendency to overstride during the swing. Placing an object (such as a block of wood) a few inches in front of the striding foot is an effective technique in that if the foot strikes the block, the batter receives immediate feedback that he or she has overstrode. Another technique for the same problem is to tie the player's ankles together with a rope, allowing only enough slack for a proper stride. Batters who have a tendency to exaggerate a hitch (the dropping of the hands prior to the forward swing) can be given feedback if the coach holds a flat board or stick under the hands during the swing. The hands making contact with the board provide evidence of the hitch.

Novelty ideas are often effective in dramatizing feedback in a variety of sport and other motor activities. A dance teacher, who after failing to break the tendency of one dancer to slump over during performance, actually taped a 12-inch ruler to the dancer's body (from the navel area to approximately one inch under the chin). Thereafter any tendency to drop the chin resulted in immediate and annoying feedback. Branch Rickey, the general manager of several major league baseball teams, used to stress for pitchers the importance of a full follow-through during delivery. Evidence of what Rickey considered an adequate follow-through was that the throwing hand actually swept across the grass at the end of the delivery. When the hand did not touch the grass, this was feedback that the follow-through was inadequate. Some track coaches, trying to get their sprinters to maintain relaxed forearms and hands, have had runners carry an egg in each hand during practice runs. Some runners may not consciously be aware of tension in their hands, but cracked eggs can provide dramatic evidence of such tension.

The use of imaginative ideas for providing feedback is limited only by the ingenuity of the coach or teacher. Many unusual techniques are available in all sports. They can be very helpful in providing information that is not easily communicated with traditional verbal instructions. However, in using these unusual or gimmicky ideas, one must guard against having the learner begin to lean too heavily on these techniques as props. Long-term use of props can result in unanticipated problems. A learner may begin to concentrate on a prop rather than the proper movement response.

ARRANGING PRACTICE SCHEDULES

Great care must be devoted to the scheduling of practice sessions for maximum learning and performance efficiency. The length of practice periods and the spacing between those periods are strategic. After a period of time in a given activity, performance efficiency and learning drop off. Numerous studies (Cook & Hilgard, 1949; Harmon & Oxendine, 1961; Hovland, 1940; Pyle, 1915; Travers, 1977) have shown that continued practice frequently becomes a waste of time. In order to avoid a serious drop in efficiency, coaches should devote more attention to the length of practice sessions and organization within those sessions.

The term *burnout* has been popularized recently in reference to a reduction in efficiency and enthusiasm by people in high-pressure positions, including business executives, professional people, athletic coaches, and others in positions of leadership. It is now being recognized that one cannot indefinitely sustain a high level of energy and concentration in the same activity without periodic breaks from that activity. On a short-term basis, athletes and whole teams have been described as being "flat," "stale," or having "left their game on the practice field." The problem, therefore, is not limited to high-level executives; neither is it limited to those who have served in the same role for years on end.

Effects of Inhibition

Psychologists have used the term *inhibition* to refer to the phenomenon of work reduction resulting from continued performance in the same activity (Hull, 1943). Inhibition acts as a type of negative drive on performance. The condition is not restricted to years or months of activity but may occur within a single work period. Neither is it restricted to people in high-pressure jobs. Inhibition can occur with those in any work setting. The debilitating effects of inhibition increase the longer one performs, the more often the task is repeated, and the greater the energy and vigor devoted to the task. Whereas the term *burnout* is more often used in regard to someone who has been engaged in an activity on a sustained basis for many months or years and whose decreased performance is clear to all, it is important to realize that the results of inhibition may be much more subtle and may occur within one work or practice session. In addition, the effects of inhibition are not limited to adults in work situations; they also occur with school-age children, and the effects occur during enjoyable activities, including sports.

Practice sessions in sports should be scheduled so as to promote maximum learning and performance. This can be done only if careful attention is paid to avoiding the development of inhibition. Relatively *short practices* lead to efficient performances whereas long, repetitive practices lead to decreases in performance. In addition, those sessions that are *spaced* (that include rest periods between work sessions) are more productive.

Scheduling Daily Practice Sessions

Coaches need to understand that the factor which depresses performance during prolonged practices is not necessarily fatigue. Obviously, when fatigue occurs both learning and performance are diminished. However, even when the performer is not tired in any detectable manner, performance may still lessen. The reason for this decline in performance is inhibition, which begins to emerge a short time after the beginning of a work or practice session.

Maximum gains or improvement take place soon after the beginning of practice on a particular task. For example, people do not generally improve as much during the second 10 minutes of a drill as they do during the first 10 minutes. In practical terms, people do not benefit as much from the second 10 swings in batting practice as from the first 10 swings, from the second 10 tennis serves as the first 10. This is true even though the performers are not "tired."

Coaches can make use of these principles (short, spaced practices) without actually sacrificing practice time or drill on particular skills. For example, if the baseball coach decides that a total of 30 batting practice swings are necessary on a particular day, he or she should schedule players to take those swings in three interrupted "rounds" of 10 swings each. During the "rest" periods between those rounds, the coach can effectively engage the players in infield practice, base running, strategy sessions, or any other activity. Then players can return to the batting cage for practice better able to benefit from batting practice.

The buildup of inhibition for a given activity will subside even while the players are fully involved in a different activity. A *change in activity* essentially results in "rest" from the original skill being practiced. A period of as little as 10 minutes between the "rounds" of batting practice will prove advantageous. Thus inhibition differs from fatigue in that fatigue requires a period of idleness for recuperation.

Coaches should organize practices so as to avoid sustained, repetitive drills. For example, the high school basketball coach who wishes to devote 60 minutes to fundamental drills in dribbling, shooting the 12-foot jump shot, and passing should not schedule 20 minutes of sustained drill on each activity. Two rounds of 10 minutes practice on each is preferable. Obviously, this same sort of scheduling can be applied to field hockey, volleyball, gymnastics, football, or any other sport. Not only do such breaks increase performance levels, they also prevent athletes from getting lulled into boredom; the breaks are likely to keep athletes more alert.

The concept of practice scheduling should also be considered in terms of seasonal arrangements. For example, after the basketball team has been practicing or playing games on a fairly sustained basis for three months, the coach should, by mid-February, be taking precautions to prevent the long-term buildup of inhibition or genuine burnout. Without attention to this, a drop-off in performance late in the season often occurs even though players are not fatigued and are highly motivated by upcoming tournaments. Coaches will find that by shortening overall practices and even having players take periodic days off late in the season they can enhance performance and generate greater "hunger" for the game. The same phenomenon occurs with higher-level, even professional, athletes. Slumping major league baseball players often find that intensifying their practices does not work as well as getting away from the activity for a period of time. Consequently, the regular player who is benched for a few games often returns with a new alertness and enthusiasm, as well as improved performance.

WHOLE AND PART PRACTICE

New sports or games may be presented to the learner in terms of the total activity or a part thereof. The manner in which material is organized for presentation makes a difference in immediate learning and in performance over the long run. Organizing learning material into "wholes" or "parts" is an important issue in all types of learning. *Whole learning* refers to the practice or study of the total activity, or a major part thereof, from the beginning. *Part learning* occurs when the activity is broken down into its component parts and each part is practiced and learned prior to commencing the next part. In a practical situation, work sessions may not be totally whole or part, but may follow a whole-part-whole or a progressive part pattern. An AAHPERD publication (1981) presents a synthesis of the literature on whole and part learning.

There are distinct advantages to both the whole and part methods, and there are circumstances under which one or the other is preferable. The essential advantage of the whole method is that ultimately the separate parts of the activity, once learned, are more likely to be performed in a smooth, continuous fashion. Undue adherence to the part method is likely to develop a series of well-learned skills that are disconnected and are performed in a disjointed and segmented fashion when combined into a whole. Learning a sport requires both learning the individual skills and *connecting* them into a cohesive unit.

The part method is often advantageous in learning a complex activity because it usually provides the learner with a sense of having accomplished something. Using the whole method for such complex and difficult tasks sometimes gives the learner the impression that nothing has been learned, thus leading to confusion and discouragement.

Years ago Gestalt psychologists emphasized the concept that the whole is greater than the sum of its parts. We have come to realize the truth of this idea in many areas of human endeavor, including sports. For example, the game of basketball involves more than the isolated skills of dribbling, passing, shooting, rebounding, or other skills we could identify. Certainly the game has all of those skills, but it also includes the blending of those parts into game play. To become an excellent basketball player one must not only develop good skills but also develop the ability to make a quick transition from recovering a rebound to an outlet pass, from a dribble to a pass, or from the reception of a pass to a full-speed lay-up shot. Recently it has become popular to refer to "transition games" — games characterized by a team's ability to switch rapidly from defensive play to attacking offensive play after intercepting a pass or gaining a rebound.

Extensive practice of the separate skills (parts) of basketball does not automatically result in speed and skill in putting the skills together. Consequently, it is important to practice the connective or transitional skills of the game. Such skills are developed when the whole game, or at least a major portion of it, is practiced at once. You have probably observed half-court basketball practices where all action stops as soon as the defensive team intercepts a pass or gains a rebound. There will certainly be times when this is desirable (when all emphasis is on the offensive play of one team), but it fails to take advantage of the opportunity for the team to practice the rapid transition from offense to defense or from defense to offense.

Individual skills, whether in team activities or individual sports, should be analyzed to determine their relation to other skills within a particular sport. Skills that are performed together in continuous fashion in actual play should be joined together in practice. This does not mean that the whole game must be performed continuously. For example, when there is a break in the action, then there is no point in continuing the activity, at least from the point of view of combining skills into a whole. After a successful basket or free throw or when a whistle stops play, there is nothing to be connected with the prior or subsequent activity.

The need to unite isolated skills into "wholes" is evident in all sports. Coaches must analyze each sport to determine the individual skills that need to be united. For example, in baseball it is essential that shortstops be able to field ground balls that require them to range far to the right or to the left. It is also important that they be able to throw accurately and forcefully to first and second base. However, it is also important that shortstops be more than good fielders of ground balls and good throwers. They must be able to field a ball that is hit to either side *while making the necessary preparatory movements* for delivering a strong throw to the base. Practicing the two skills separately (the part method) will not prepare them for making the total play (fielding and throwing) in one quick and fluid movement. In like manner, as middle persons in a double play, shortstops must run to second base as soon as the ball is hit to the right side, then receive the ball while positioning themselves and making a strong throw to first base. Only through such "whole" practice will shortstops be able to receive the ball and get it away in one quick motion.

There are clearly times when parts of an activity should be practiced separately. For example, when one particulr skill or phase of the overall activity is causing difficulty, concentration and practice of this particular component is appropriate, for a time. This allows additional practice where it is most needed. However, one must guard against working on an isolated skill too long lest it become disconnected from the surrounding skills. In fact, after such part practice, the combined routine should be practiced so as to avoid this problem.

MENTAL PRACTICE

As pointed out earlier, skill learning is a mental as well as a physical process. However, coaches and teachers of motor skills often devote nearly all their attention to athletes' physical involvement with a skill. Athletes are put through physical conditioning. Then they are instructed to go through the movement responses, sometimes at full speed and other times at half speed. After initial trials they are given feedback and instructed to take another trial. Often they have had bodily parts passively manipulated through the response. Until recently the emphasis on physical response has largely neglected the cognitive aspects of motor skill learning. Rarely have learners been told how to *think* about the skills during the learning process.

Convincing research (Corbin, 1966; Oxendine, 1969; Richardson, 1967; Start, 1960, 1962) is available to show that skill learning can take place by merely thinking about performing a skill. There is also evidence that better learning takes place when both physical and mental practice are formally involved than when only one of the processes is used. When the intellectual process is prominently involved, learners understand a skill better and remember it better than when they simply go through the motions physically.

The relative lack of formal instruction for mental practice does not mean that the process has not been used in sport learning and performance. In fact, cognition has no doubt been used in sport performance since the beginning of time. One can often notice performers, both novice and elite, hesitate just prior to beginning so as to (seemingly) better plan the performance in their minds. The novice diver about to attempt a springboard dive for the first time, the Olympic gymnast ready to begin an uneven parallel bar routine, and the professional bowler at the ready position all seem to devote some thought to the upcoming performance. Whether they are rehearsing it in the most effective manner is not certain. Most often this mental activity is self-initiated, is without helpful instruction from the coach, and is no doubt often haphazard. Whether or not to engage in mental rehearsal is usually left to the discretion of the learner, as is the matter of how to do it. Wise teachers and coaches will take advantage of such occasions to promote effective mental practice.

Many young people daydream about duplicating the athletic feats of their heroes. They proceed to score a perfect 10 in a gymnastics routine, hit a towering home run in the bottom of the ninth inning to win the championship, or calmly sink two free throws with one second remaining on the clock to win the game. Such fantasizing may actually be helpful in preparing the individual for the ultimate performance. However, whether to engage in such practice and, if so, how to do it should not be left entirely to chance. Part II of this book will provide specific instruction in mental practice techniques.

TRANSFER IN MOTOR SKILLS

One of the most practical things a teacher or coach can do is to take advantage of the many and diverse transfer possibilities in sports. Promoting transfer tends to maximize learning that has already taken place by expanding its application to other activities. Transfer may take place between different skills (intertask) or from one motor response to another within the same skill (intratask). Not only do movement responses transfer among sports but so do principles of play and strategy. Wherever such transfer takes place, it saves the time and energy that would be required for developing these skills or strategies in a new sport.

Transfer of skill refers to the effect that any established skill has on the learning or performance of a second skill. The effect can be either helpful (positive) or harmful (negative). In either case it is essential that the teacher-coach be aware of the possibilities in order to enhance positive transfer where possible and avoid the development of negative transfer.

Deciding what skills actually transfer, and are therefore helpful, is a complex matter. Although we can assume motor responses which are identical, or nearly so, result in positive transfer, we cannot assume that taking part in a slightly similar task is helpful. In fact, learning a second task of vague similarity is often a hindrance, making it more difficult than if the first task had not been learned.

Except for a few studies in the past several decades (Lindeburg & Hewitt, 1965; Nelson, 1957a, 1957b), the possibilities for transfer in sport have not been extensively explored. However, some opportunities for positive transfer seem clear:

1. From the soccer kick to the field goal kick in football.
2. From rebound tumbling to springboard diving, in terms of rotary and curvilinear body control.
3. Follow-through techniques in throwing (baseball, softball, football, bowling) and swinging (baseball, tennis, golf, handball, squash).
4. Use of the concept of overloading (two on one, three on two, etc.) in offensive play in basketball, soccer, field hockey, lacrosse, and other team sports.
5. Strategies from tennis to racquetball, including footwork, body positioning, and knowledge of rebounds.
6. From the sprinter's start in track to running back's start in football.
7. From soccer to field hockey, lacrosse, and basketball in terms of (a) footwork and body position and (b) field position in relation to teammates, opponents, and the goal or basket.

Totally dissimilar motor responses and very general sports situations neither help nor hinder a second activity. However, as noted earlier, *slightly* similar responses frequently cause problems. For example, baseball and golf swings have some similarity in that they both involve striking a ball with a club. They both require a full, two-handed swing with a follow-through. However, the baseball player brings to the golf game established movement patterns that can hinder the golf swing, patterns that have not been developed by the person who does not play baseball. The bent arms, the baseball grip, and the swing across the body all tend to play havoc with an individual when he or she attempts to develop a proper golf swing. The more "habitual" the baseball patterns are, the greater is the tendency to carry them over into the golf swing.

Other incidents of negative transfer can be noted in almost all sports where there is seeming similarity among movement responses. For example, the individual who has correctly learned to hold the wrist firm when stroking a tennis ball will find this habit inappropriate when hitting the shuttlecock in badminton. Therefore, in terms of the badminton stroke, the tennis player will be at a disadvantage when compared with the person who has never played tennis. The more firmly established the tennis stroke has become, the more difficult it will be to break the habit. A handball player accustomed to playing the four-wall game will be at a distinct disadvantage when beginning to play the game without a back wall. The experienced kick boxer who switches to the more "legitimate" prize fighting will be embarrassed, and perhaps disqualified, if in the heat of battle, he reacts to an opening by landing a clean reverse kick on his surprised opponent.

It is probable that after entering high school most people rarely learn any motor skills that are entirely new to them. Rather, new skills are really combinations of old skills or variations of previously learned responses. People learn to combine, to adapt, and to refine or extend skills. They also learn how to learn. People learn to solve new problems with motor skills just as they do with verbal skills.

Teachers and coaches can maximize the transfer of skills and reduce negative transfer effects by adhering to the following teaching principles:

1. Where movement patterns between two skills are similar, teachers should point out those similarities to learners. Transfer is not automatic because learners do not always recognize the similarities and consequently do not apply them. As an example, for transfer purposes it is helpful for the coach to emphasize the generality of the follow-through concept, whether in the soccer kick, baseball throw, bowling delivery, tennis stroke, or volleyball spike.

2. Where transfer possibilities exist, it is helpful if the first skill is well learned. The more thoroughly the movement pattern is learned in the first situation, the more easily it can be transferred to other skills.

3. To maximize skill transfer, basic concepts, principles, and generalizations relating to movement and sport should be taught. Information that is broadly applicable should be clearly communicated to the learner. Such information is then more likely to be applied. Principles of friction, momentum, rebound, and inertia have wide applicability in sports. A thorough understanding of these concepts can aid the athlete in making use of them in a wide variety of appropriate activities.

4. As in all teaching, the use of a variety of illustrations or techniques will enhance the chance that a learner will understand a concept and thus use it in a new setting. Simply verbalizing a concept regarding transfer will not ensure that the learner fully appreciates its importance and general applicability.

SUMMARY

First and foremost, effective coaches must be good teachers. Although coaches may have other important assets, such as being innovative strategists, skilled motivators, and effective personal counselors, if they are not also good teachers they are working at a distinct disadvantage and are probably doomed to failure.

The athletic coach must be able to instruct in a range of situations: from helping the hurdler correct a troublesome leg position to establishing the teamwork needed in a baton handoff with the relay team. The instructional role of the coach is most crucial with players in the early stages of their learning and competition.

The successful coach must provide effective feedback, carefully schedule practices, use whole and part practices wisely, emphasize the use of mental rehearsal, and attend to transfer possibilities among skills. In short, the successful coach must thoroughly understand the learning process.

REFERENCES

Adams, J. A. (1971). A closed-loop theory of motor learning. *Journal of Motor Behavior, 3,* 111–150.

American Alliance for Health, Physical Education, Recreation and Dance (1981). *Motor Learning* (Basic Stiff Series I, A. Rothstein, scholar).

Bennett, I. C., Vincent, W. J., & Johnson, C. J. (1979). Effects of precision of grading systems on learning a fine motor skill. *Research Quarterly, 50,* 715–722.

Cook, B. S., & Hilgard, E. R. (1949). Distributed practice in motor learning: Progressively increasing and decreasing rests. *Journal of Experimental Psychology, 39,* 169–172.

Corbin, C. (1966). The effects of mental practice on the development of a unique motor skill. *NCPEAM Proceedings.*

Fitts, R. M. (1964). Perceptual-motor skills learning. In A. W. Melton (Ed.), *Categories of human learning.* New York: Academic Press.

Harmon, J. M., & Oxendine, J. B. (1961). Effects of different lengths of practice periods on the learning of a motor skill. *Research Quarterly, 32,* 34–41.

Hovland, G. C. (1940). Experimental studies in rote-learning theory: Vol. VII. Distribution of practice with varying lengths of lists. *Journal of Experimental Psychology, 27,* 271–284.

Hull, C. L. (1943). *Principles of behavior.* New York: Appleton-Century-Crofts.

Lindeburg, F. A., & Hewitt, J. E. (1965). Effect of an oversized basketball on shooting ability and ball handling. *Research Quarterly, 36,* 164–167.

Nelson, D. O. (1957a). Effect of swimming on the learning of selected gross motor skills. *Research Quarterly, 28,* 374–378.

Nelson, D. O. (1957b). Studies of transfer of learning in gross motor skills. *Research Quarterly, 28,* 364–373.

Oxendine, J. B. (1969). Effect of mental and physical practice on the learning of three motor skills. *Research Quarterly, 40,* 755–763.

Pyle, W. H. (1915). Concentrated versus distributed practices. *Journal of Educational Psychology, 5,* 247–258.

Richardson, A. (1967). Mental practice: A review and a discussion, part I. *Research Quarterly, 38,* 95–107.

Robb, M. D. (1972). *The dynamics of motor-skill acquisition.* Englewood Cliffs, N.J.: Prentice-Hall.

Salmoni, A. W. (1980). The effects of precision of knowledge of results on the performance of a simple line drawing task for children and adults. *Research Quarterly for Exercise and Sport, 51,* 572–575.

Start, K. B. (1960). The relationship between intelligence and the effect of mental practice on the performance of a motor skill. *Research Quarterly, 31,* 644–649.

Start, K. B. (1962). The influence of subjectively assessed games ability on gain in motor performance after mental practice. *Journal of Genetic Psychology, 67,* 169–173.

Thorndike, E. L. (1931). *Human learning.* New York: Appleton-Century-Crofts.

Travers, R. M. W. (1977). *Esssentials of learning* (4th ed.). New York: Macmillan.

Trowbridge, M. H., & Cason, H. (1932). An experimental study of Thorndike's theory of learning. *Journal of General Psychology, 7,* 245–260.

3   Principles of Positive Reinforcement and Performance Feedback

RONALD E. SMITH

University of Washington

Much of human interaction consists of attempts to influence the behavior of other people. As a coach, you try to influence your players in many important ways. One of your most important goals is to create a good learning situation in which athletes can acquire the technical skills needed to succeed as individuals and as a team. Another priority for most coaches is to create a social environment in which the participants can experience positive interactions with one another. This is certainly a key factor in building team cohesion, in making athletes more receptive to your coaching, and in fostering a supportive environment in which athletes can develop dedication, mental toughness, and other valued traits. Indeed, virtually everything you do as a coach can be viewed as an attempt to increase certain desired behaviors and to decrease undesirable behaviors.

The psychology of coaching (including the many principles discussed in this book) is essentially a set of strategies designed to increase your ability to influence the behavior of others more effectively. It is often said that stripped of its jargon and complexities, psychology is basically the application of common sense. The principles to be discussed in this chapter — positive as opposed to aversive control, reinforcement, and performance feedback — make good sense. But more importantly, they have been shown in research to be among the most effective ways to increase motivation, morale, enjoyment of the athletic situation, and performance.

POSITIVE AND AVERSIVE APPROACHES TO INFLUENCING BEHAVIOR

There are two basic approaches to influencing the behavior of others. Psychologists refer to these as *positive control* and *aversive control*. Both forms of control are based on the fact that behavior is strongly influenced by the consequences it produces. Responses that lead to positive or desired consequences are strengthened, and their likelihood of occurring in the future is increased. Conversely, behaviors that result in undesirable or unpleasant consequences are less likely to recur. Positive and aversive control underlie what has been termed the *positive approach* and the *negative approach* to coaching (Smoll & Smith, 1979).

The positive approach is designed to strengthen desired behaviors by motivating players to perform them and by rewarding them when they occur. The second approach, the negative approach, involves attempts to eliminate unwanted behaviors through punishment and criticism. The motivating factor in this approach is fear. Observational studies of coaches indicate that most coaches use a combination of positive and aversive control (Smith, Zane, Smoll, & Coppel, 1983).

In our society, aversive control through punishment is perhaps the most widespread means of controlling behavior. Our entire system of laws is backed up by threats of punishment. Similarly, fear of failure is one means of promoting school achievement, social development, and other desired behaviors. The reason that punishment is the glue that holds so much of our society's fabric together is that, for the most part, it seems to work. It is the fastest way to bring behavior under control. In sports, it finds one mode of expression in the negative approach to coaching.

Frequently in sport, we hear the statement, "The team that makes the fewest mistakes will win." And, indeed, this is usually the case. Many coaches therefore develop coaching tactics that are oriented toward eliminating mistakes. The most natural approach is to use aversive control. To get rid of mistakes, we simply punish athletes who make them. The assumption is that if we make players frightened enough of making mistakes, they are more likely to perform well. We do not have to look far to find examples of highly successful coaches who are "screamers" and whose teams seem to perform like well-oiled machines. Other less experienced coaches may therefore conclude that this is the most effective way to train athletes. They, too, adopt this aspect of the successful coaches' behavior, perhaps to the exclusion of other teaching techniques that are probably the true keys to the success of the "screamers."

There is clear evidence that punishment and criticism can decrease unwanted behaviors. Unfortunately, the evidence is equally compelling that punishment has certain undesirable side effects that can actually interfere with what a coach is trying to accomplish. First and foremost is the fact that punishment works by arousing fear. If used excessively, punishment promotes the development of fear of failure, and this is undoubtedly the least desirable form of athletic motivation. If it becomes the predominant motive for athletic performance, it not only decreases enjoyment of the activity but also increases the likelihood of failure. The athlete who has a strong fear of failure is motivated not by a positive desire to achieve and enjoy the thrill of victory but by a fear of the agony of defeat. Athletic competition is transformed from a challenge into a threat. Because high anxiety disrupts motor performance and interferes with thinking, the athlete with a high fear of failure is prone to "choke" under pressure because he or she is concentrating more on the feared consequences of mistakes or failure than on what needs to be done in a positive sense. Research has shown that athletes having high fear of failure not only perform more poorly in competition but are also at greater risk for injury, enjoy the sport experience less, and are more likely to drop out (Orlick & Botterill, 1975; Smith & Smoll, 1983). The research literature also shows that the quickest and most effective way to develop fear of failure is by punishing people when they fail (Smith, Smith, & Smoll, 1983).

Punishment has other potential side effects that most coaches wish to avoid. A predominance of aversive control makes for an unpleasant teaching situation. It arouses resentment and hostility that may be masked by the power difference that exists between coach and athlete. It may produce a kind of cohesion among players based on their mutual hatred of the coach, but most coaches would prefer other bases for team cohesion. It is even possible that players may consciously or subconsciously act in ways that sabotage what the coach is trying to accomplish. Moreover, coaches occupy a role that is admired by athletes, and they should not overlook their importance as models for young people who are developing socially. The abusive screamer is certainly not exhibiting the kinds of behaviors that will contribute to the personal growth of athletes who emulate the coach.

Does this mean that coaches should avoid all criticism and punishment of their athletes? Not at all. Sometimes these behaviors are necessary for instructional or disciplinary purposes. But they should be used sparingly and with a full appreciation for the potential negative side effects that have been discussed. The negative approach should *never* be the primary approach with athletes. This is particularly the case where child athletes are concerned, but it also applies at higher competitive levels. Our observation has been that abusive coaches may enjoy success and may even be admired by some of their players, but they run the risk of losing other players who could contribute to the team's success and who could profit personally from an athletic experience. Those who succeed through the use of aversive control usually do so because (a) they are also able to communicate caring for their players as people, so that the abuse is not taken personally; (b) they have very talented athletes; and/or (c) they are such skilled teachers and strategists that these abilities overshadow their negative approach. In other words, such coaches win *in spite of,* not because of, the negative approach they espouse.

Fortunately, there is an alternative to the negative approach that accomplishes everything aversive control does, and much more, without the harmful side effects. The positive approach is aimed at strengthening desired behaviors through the use of encouragement, reward (psychologists prefer the term *positive reinforcement*), and technical instruction. From this point of view, the best way to eliminate mistakes is not to try to stamp them out with punishment but rather to strengthen the *correct* behaviors. The motivational force at work here is a positive desire to achieve rather than a negative fear of failure. Mistakes are seen not as totally negative occurrences but as, in the words of John Wooden, "stepping stones to achievement" that provide the information needed to improve performance. The positive approach, through its emphasis on improving rather than on "not screwing up," fosters a more positive learning environment and tends to promote more positive relationships among coaches and athletes. Research has clearly shown that athletes like positive coaches better, enjoy their athletic experience more and report higher team cohesion when playing for them, and perform at a higher level when positive control techniques are used (Martin & Hyrcaiko, 1983; Smith, Smoll, & Curtis, 1979).

The cornerstone of the positive approach is the skillful use of positive reinforcement to increase motivation and to strengthen desired behaviors. Another highly effective technique is the use of performance feedback. These specific techniques are now discussed.

POSITIVE REINFORCEMENT: GETTING GOOD THINGS TO HAPPEN

A positive reinforcement is any consequence that increases the likelihood of a behavior that it follows. For our present purposes, positive reinforcement is similar to the concept of reward. The use of reinforcement to strengthen behavior requires that a coach (a) find a reinforcer that works for a particular athlete and (b) make the occurrence of reinforcement dependent upon performance of the desired behavior.

Choosing Effective Reinforcers

Choosing a reinforcer is not usually difficult, but in some instances, the coach's ingenuity and sensitivity to the needs of individual players may be tested. Potential reinforcers include social behaviors such as verbal praise, smiles, nonverbal signs such as applause, and physical contact such as a pat on the back. They also include the opportunity to engage in certain activities (such as extra batting practice) or to play with a particular piece of equipment. Social reinforcers are those most frequently employed in athletics, but even here you must decide what is most likely to be effective with each player. One player might find praise given in the presence of others highly reinforcing, whereas another might find it embarrassing. The best way to find an effective reinforcer is to get to know each player's likes and dislikes. In some instances, you may elect to praise an entire unit or group of players; at other times, you may direct reinforcement at one player. If at all possible, it is a good idea to use a variety of reinforcers and vary what you say and do so that you do not begin to sound like a broken record. In the final analysis, the acid test of your choice of reinforcer is whether it affects behavior in the desired manner.

The effectiveness of verbal reinforcement can be increased by combining it with a specific description of the desirable behavior that the player just performed. For example, you might say, "Way to go, Bob! Your head stayed right down on the ball on that swing." In this way, you combine the power of the reinforcement with an instructional reminder of what the player should do. This also cues the athlete to what you want him or her to concentrate on.

Selecting and Reinforcing Target Behaviors

Systematic use of reinforcement forces you to be specific in your own mind about exactly which behaviors you want to reinforce in a given athlete at a particular time. Obviously, you will not want to reinforce everything an athlete does correctly. The most effective use of your reward power is to strengthen skills that a player is just beginning to master. In many instances, complex skills can be broken down into their component subskills, and you can concentrate on one of these subskills at a time until the player has mastered it. For example, you might choose to concentrate entirely on the pattern run by a pass receiver with no concern about whether the pass is completed. This is where your knowledge of the sport and of the mastery levels of your individual players is crucial. Athletes can enjoy lots of support and reinforcement long before they have completely mastered the entire skill if you are attentive to their instructional needs and progress. Such reinforcement will help to keep motivation and interest at their maximum.

We have all marveled at the complex behaviors performed by animals in circuses, at amusement parks, and in the movies. These behavioral feats are brought about by the use of a positive reinforcement procedure known as *shaping*. At the beginning of training, the animal was incapable of anything even approximating the desired behavior. The trainer thus began with some behavior the animal was already performing and began reinforcing that behavior. Then, over time, the requirements for reinforcement were gradually altered so that the animal had to perform acts that more and more closely resembled the final desired behavior until that behavior had been shaped by the systematic application of reinforcement. This same procedure can be used to shape athletic skills. Start with what the athlete is currently capable of doing, and then gradually require more and more of the athlete before giving reinforcement. It is important that the shift in demands be realistic and that the steps be small enough so that the athlete can master them and be reinforced. Used correctly, shaping is one of the most powerful of all the positive control techniques.

An Example of a Successful Reinforcement Program

The systematic use of positive reinforcement to improve the performance of a youth football team's offensive backfield was described by Komaki and Barnett (1977). Three different plays run out of the wishbone offense were selected by the coach. Each of the plays was broken down into five stages judged to be crucial to the execution of the play and was presented to the players accordingly. For example, one of the plays included the following stages: (1) quarterback-center exchange, (2) quarterback spin and pitch, (3) right halfback and fullback lead blocking, (4) left halfback route, and (5) quarterback block. Breaking down the plays in this manner allowed the coach to respond to the elements that were run correctly and to give specific feedback to the players about their execution of each of the five stages.

During the first phase of the experiment, data were carefully collected on how often the stages of each play were executed correctly. Then the coach began to systematically apply reinforcement procedures to Play A. Each time the play was run in practice, the coach checked off the elements that had been successfully executed and praised the players for the stages that were run successfully. Reinforcement was not applied when Plays B and C were run. After a period of time, the reinforcement procedure was shifted to Play B only, and later to Play C only. Applying the technique to only one play at a time permitted a determination of the specific effects of reinforcement on the performance of each of them.

A comparison of the percentage of stages executed correctly before and after introduction of the reinforcement procedure indicated that performance increased for all three plays, but only after reinforcement was introduced. The level of performance for Play A improved from 61.7% to 81.5% when reinforcement was applied, but execution of B and C did not improve until reinforcement was also applied to them. When this occurred, execution of Play B improved from 54.4% to 82%, and execution of Play C improved from 65.5% to 79.8%. Clearly, the systematic use of reinforcement led to a substantial improvement in performance. Other studies have shown similar performance improvement in gymnastics, swimming, baseball, golf, and tennis (see Martin & Hyrcaiko, 1983).

Schedules and Timing of Reinforcement

One of the most frequently asked questions about reinforcement is how consistently it should be given. Fortunately, a great deal of research has been done concerning the effects of *schedules of reinforcement,* the pattern and frequency with which reinforcement is administered. The most important distinction is between *continuous* and *partial* schedules. On a continuous schedule, every correct response is reinforced. On a partial schedule, some correct responses are reinforced and some are not.

A coach has two related challenges. First, he or she must instruct athletes in specific skills until they master them. Then the coach must figure out ways to maintain the skills so that players will continue to perform them. A knowledge of the effects of reinforcement schedules can assist in meeting both challenges.

During the initial stages of training, reinforcement should be given on a continuous schedule. The frequent reinforcement not only strengthens the desired response but also provides athletes with frequent feedback about how they are doing. Once the behavior is learned, however, reinforcement should be shifted to a partial schedule. Research has shown that behaviors reinforced on partial schedules persist much longer in the absence of reinforcement than do those that have been reinforced only on a continuous schedule. People will put a great many coins into slot machines, which operate on partial schedules; people are unlikely to persist long in putting coins into soft drink machines that do not deliver. Thus, the key principle in using schedules is to start with continuous reinforcement until the behavior is mastered, then to shift gradually to partial reinforcement to maintain a high level of motivation and performance.

The timing of reinforcement is another important consideration. Other things being equal, the sooner after a response that reinforcement occurs, the stronger are its effects on behavior. Thus, whenever possible, try to reinforce a desired behavior as soon as it occurs. If this is not possible, however, try to find an opportunity to praise the athlete later.

Reinforcing Effort and Other Desirable Behaviors

To this point, the use of reinforcement to strengthen skills has been described. It is important to realize, however, that reinforcement can be used to strengthen other desirable behaviors. For example, you can use the positive approach to reduce the likelihood of disciplinary problems by reinforcing compliance with team rules. There is no reason why a coach should not recognize and reinforce exemplary conduct on the part of particular players or the team as a whole. One of the most effective ways of avoiding disciplinary problems is by strengthening the opposite behaviors through reinforcement. Similarly, instances of teamwork and of players' support and encouragement of one another should be reinforced whenever possible. This strengthens these desirable behaviors and also creates an atmosphere in which the coach is serving as a positive model by supporting them. Research has shown that the best predictor of liking for the coach and desire to play for him or her in the future is not the won-lost record of the team but how consistently the coach applies the positive approach and avoids the use of punishment (Smith, Smoll, & Curtis, 1979).

One of the most important points of all has been saved until last. What you choose to reinforce is of critical importance. It is easy to praise a player who has just made a great play. It is less natural to reinforce a player who tried but failed. Reinforce *effort* as much as you do results. After all, the only thing players have complete control over is the amount of effort they make; they have only limited control over the outcome of their efforts. As a coach, you have a right to demand total effort, and this is perhaps the most important thing of all for you to reinforce. If players have had good technical instruction, are free from self-defeating fear of failure, and are giving maximum effort, then performance and winning will take care of themselves within the limits of the players' ability. John Wooden, the legendary "Wizard of Westwood," placed great emphasis on this concept:

> You cannot find a player who ever played for me at UCLA that can tell you he ever heard me mention "winning" a basketball game. He might say I inferred a little here and there, but I never mentioned winning. Yet the last thing that I told my players, just prior to tipoff, before we would go on the floor was, "When the game is over, I want your head up—and I know of only one way for your head to be up—and that's for you to know that you did your best. . . . This means to do the best *you* can do. That's the best; no one can do more. . . . You made that effort.

PERFORMANCE FEEDBACK

Positive reinforcement not only serves as a reward for desirable behavior but also as a form of performance feedback. In other words, it communicates the message that performance has met or exceeded the coach's standards. When it is possible to measure desired and undesired behaviors objectively, the coach can utilize the highly effective tool of performance feedback to increase motivation and performance.

In recent years, there has been a surge of interest in objective feedback as a technology for improving job performance in business and industry. The evidence indicates that performance feedback is a highly effective tool. A recent review of 18 studies carried out in a variety of job settings found increases in objective performance indicators averaging 53% after systematic performance feedback procedures were instituted (Kopelman, 1982–83). Specific work behaviors improved an average of 78%, and overall productivity an average of 16%. These increases were recorded over intervals ranging from eight weeks to four years.

Performance feedback is a prominent feature of what many successful coaches do. For example, psychologists Roland Tharp and Ronald Gallimore (1976) charted all of John Wooden's behaviors during 15 practice sessions. They found that 75% of Wooden's comments to his players contained instructional feedback. Most of his comments were specific statements of what to do and how the players were or were not doing it. Indeed, Wooden was five times more likely to inform than to merely praise or reprimand.

How Feedback Motivates and Instructs

There are a variety of reasons why objective feedback is so consistently effective in motivating increased performance. For one thing, feedback can correct misconceptions. Athletes, like other people, often have distorted perceptions of their own behavior. Objective evidence in the form of statistics or numbers can help correct such misconceptions and may motivate corrective action. For example, it can be a sobering experience for a basketball player who fancies himself a great ball handler to learn that he has more turnovers than assists.

Feedback also creates internal consequences by stimulating athletes to experience positive (or negative) feelings about themselves. An athlete who is dissatisfied with his or her level of performance not only may be motivated to improve but will experience feelings of self-satisfaction that function as positive reinforcement when subsequent feedback indicates improvement. Such self-administered reinforcement can be even more important than external reinforcement from the coach in bringing about improved performance. Promoting self-motivation in athletes also reduces the need for coaches to reinforce or punish. When feedback is public, as in the posting of statistics, the actual or anticipated reactions of others can serve as an additional motivator of increased effort and performance. Improvement is also likely to result in reinforcement from teammates.

A final motivational function of objective feedback is in relation to formal goal-setting programs. Because goal setting is discussed in detail elsewhere in this volume (see Chapter 10), it is sufficient to point out that successful goal-setting programs usually involve the identification of specific desired consequences and the behaviors required to achieve them. Feedback on the behaviors needed to achieve the desired goal can be helpful, if not essential, in monitoring progress.

Feedback has instructional as well as motivational effects. It helps direct behavior. Objective performance feedback provides information about (a) the specific behaviors that should be performed, (b) the levels of proficiency that should be achieved in each of the skills, and (c) the athlete's current level of proficiency in those activities. This instructional function of feedback can be especially valuable when execution of a given skill is broken down into its stages or components, as was done in the football study described earlier. When the skill is a highly complex one, such as hitting a baseball, objective feedback on how frequently a hitter executes each of the essentials (e.g., keeping the bat in the correct position, shifting one's weight correctly, striding with the hips closed, keeping one's head down during the swing, etc.) can be very valuable in pinpointing areas of strength and weakness so that attention can be directed toward correcting mistakes. The information provided by subsequent objective feedback allows both coach and athlete to monitor progress in a more useful fashion than by depending on a more global measure of proficiency, such as batting average.

Implementing a Performance Measurement and Feedback System

As in the application of positive reinforcement programs, a successful feedback program requires that you identify specific and measurable behaviors or consequences. What you decide upon must be something that can be counted. The performance measures can be fairly global (e.g., number of rebounds per minute) or more specific and dealing with subskills (e.g., percentage of rebound plays in which the opponent is boxed out). Because successful execution does not always result in a successful outcome, it is sometimes preferable to use a measure of successful execution. For example, some baseball coaches keep statistics on the percentage of times the batter hits either a line drive or a hard ground ball in preference to batting average. In other words, select the specific behaviors you want to track, and then develop a system for measuring them. At this stage, it is important to communicate with players so that they agree that the behaviors are important ones. Try to elicit suggestions from the players so that they feel a sense of involvement in the program.

In many instances, you can choose between measuring a desired behavior or its undesirable counterpart. In line with the positive approach to coaching, choosing the correct behavior for feedback rather than the mistake (or, at the very least, presenting both) is strongly recommended. This puts you in the position of reinforcing improvement rather than punishing or criticizing mistakes. It also focuses players' attention on what they should do rather than on what they should not do.

The measurement and feedback system you choose is limited only by your own ingenuity and awareness of the specific behaviors that you want to promote. Some coaches have developed "total performance indexes," which include a variety of behaviors. For example, basketball coach Lute Olson has devised an index in which negative behaviors such as turnovers, missed free throws, and defensive mistakes are subtracted from positive behaviors such as points scored, rebounds, and assists. Coach Don James has a highly detailed performance feedback system that involves the percentage of plays in which each football player successfully carried out his specific assignment. The measures are derived from game films and are posted after every game and scrimmage. They also provide an objective basis for selecting starters and allocating playing time.

Finally, it is important to note that performance feedback measures can be derived not only for individual players but also for subgroups or even for the team as a whole. Such measures can help to promote team cohesion by emphasizing the importance of teamwork and by providing a specific measure of group performance.

Reinforcement and performance feedback techniques can be applied to sports in many ways. Given the success they have enjoyed in a wide variety of performance settings, these strategies have the potential to increase coaching effectiveness at all competitive levels, from children's programs to the demanding and exacting realm of the professionals.

SUMMARY

This chapter has focused on some of the advantages of a positive approach to coaching, an approach that involves the use of reinforcement to strengthen desired behaviors and to promote the development of a positive motivation for success rather than fear of failure. Objective performance feedback on specific aspects of performance is a highly successful motivational and instructional technique. Both systematic reinforcement and objective feedback require that the coach identify specific behaviors that are important to individual and team success. This is in itself a highly desirable practice, for it focuses both coach and player attention on exactly what needs to be mastered and executed. It also promotes goal setting based on specific behaviors rather than on more general goals that are difficult to measure. Systematic use of positive reinforcement and objective feedback has yielded impressive results in many performance settings, including sports, and their utilization is appropriate at all competitive levels of athletics.

REFERENCES

Komaki, J., & Barnett, F. T. (1977). A behavioral approach to coaching football: Improving the play execution of an offensive backfield on a youth football team. *Journal of Applied Behavior Analysis, 10,* 657–664.

Kopelman, R. E. (1982–83). Improving productivity through objective feedback: A review of the evidence. *National Productivity Review, 24,* 43–55.

Martin, G. L., & Hyrcaiko, D. (1983). *Behavior modification and coaching: Principles, procedures, and research.* Springfield, Ill.: Charles C. Thomas.

Orlick, T., & Botterill, C. (1975). *Every kid can win.* Chicago: Nelson-Hall.

Smith, N. J., Smith, R. E., & Smoll, F. L. (1983). *Kidsports: A survival guide for parents.* Reading, Mass.: Addison-Wesley.

Smith, R. E., & Smoll, F. L. (1983). Psychological stress in youth sports: Sources, effects, and intervention strategies. In N. J. Smith (Ed.), *Sports medicine: Health care for young athletes.* Evanston, Ill.: American Academy of Pediatrics.

Smith, R. E., Smoll, F. L., & Curtis, B. (1979). Coach effectiveness training: A cognitive-behavioral approach to enhancing relationship skills in youth sport coaches. *Journal of Sport Psychology, 1,* 59–75.

Smith, R. E., Zane, N. S., Smoll, F. L., & Coppel, D. B. (1983). Behavioral assessment in youth sports: Coaching behaviors and children's attitudes. *Medicine and Science in Sports and Exercise, 15,* 208–214.

Smoll, F. L., & Smith, R. E. (1979). *Improving relationship skills in youth sport coaches.* East Lansing: Michigan Institute for the Study of Youth Sports.

Tharp, R. G., & Gallimore, R. (1976). What a coach can teach a teacher. *Psychology Today, 9,* 74–78.

4

Coach – Parent Relationships: Enhancing the Quality of the Athlete's Sport Experience

FRANK L. SMOLL

University of Washington

The rapid growth in the scope and popularity of youth sports for females as well as males extends to both interscholastic athletics and to programs conducted under the auspices of agency or community-based organizations (e.g., YMCA, CYO, Little League Baseball). Although debate rages concerning certain aspects of athletic competition for children, it is generally agreed that coaches occupy a central and critical role in determining the outcomes of participation. They teach physical skills and mastery of the sport, and they promote higher levels of physical fitness. Coaches also become significant adults in the lives of many young athletes and can thus have a profound positive influence on personal and social development. In addition, the involvement of parents in the athletic enterprise can serve to bring families closer together and heighten the value of the sport experience (Martens, 1978; Smith, Smith, & Smoll, 1983).

The "athletic triangle," consisting of coach, athlete, and parent, is a natural aspect of youth sports, and a coach's success in dealing with parents can be very important to the success of a program. Through their cooperative efforts, many parents productively contribute to youth sport programs. Unfortunately, however, the negative impact that some parents have is all too obvious. Some parents, out of ignorance, can undermine the basic goals of youth sport programs and rob youngsters of benefits they could derive from participation. Hopefully, as a coach, you will be able to channel parents' genuine concerns and good intentions in a way that supports what you are trying to accomplish.

This chapter provides information to assist you in communicating effectively with parents, thereby increasing the chances of a desirable sport outcome for all concerned. After completing this chapter, you should have a better understanding of (a) the objectives of youth sports, including a "healthy" philosophy of winning, (b) parent roles and responsibilities, (c)

47

how to achieve effective two-way communication with parents, and (d) how to organize and conduct sport meetings with parents.

OBJECTIVES OF YOUTH SPORTS

There are many possible benefits of participating in youth sports. Some of them are physical, such as attaining sport skills and increasing health and fitness. Others are psychological, such as developing leadership skills, respect for authority, competitiveness, cooperativeness, sportsmanship, self-reliance, and self-confidence. These are many of the positive traits that fall under the heading of "building character." Athletics are also an important social activity in which young people can make new friends and acquaintances. Furthermore, sports can strengthen family unity. And, of course, they are (or should be) just plain *fun*!

What about *winning*? The common notion in sports equates success with victory. However, with a "winning is everything" philosophy, young athletes may lose opportunities to develop their skills, to enjoy participation, and to grow as people. Well-informed coaches realize that success is not synonymous with winning games, and failure is not the same as losing. Rather, the most important kind of success comes from striving to win and giving maximum *effort*. The only thing players can control is the amount of effort they give. They have incomplete control over the outcome that is achieved. Athletes should be taught that they are never "losers" if they give maximum effort in striving for excellence (Smoll & Smith, 1981).

This philosophy of success is relevant to parents as well as coaches. In fact, it may be more important for parents to understand its meaning. They can apply it to many areas of their child's life in addition to athletics.

What about the objectives that young athletes seek to achieve? Gould (1980) summarized the results of two studies which indicated that young athletes most often participate in organized sports for the following reasons: (a) to have fun, (b) to improve their skills and learn new skills, (c) to be with their friends or make new friends, (d) for thrills and excitement, (e) to succeed or win, and (f) to become physically fit. You may wish to give these consideration when establishing your goals for the season. Furthermore, you should be aware that none of these objectives is achieved automatically through participation in sports. Coaches, parents, and sport officials should be part of a team trying to achieve common goals. By working together to reduce chances of misunderstanding and problems, the objectives can be achieved. Parents should be encouraged to view their involvement in youth sports as an integral part of their child-rearing responsibilities.

Another issue requiring clarification is the difference between youth and professional models of sport. Youth sports are best viewed as an educational medium for the development of desirable physical and psychosocial characteristics — as miniature life situations in which youth can learn to cope with realities they will face in later life. Thus, athletics provide a setting within which an *educational process* can occur. On the other hand, professional sports are a huge commercial enterprise. Financial success is of primary importance and depends heavily on a product orientation, namely, winning. Because of this, these two models reflect very different philosophies about the primary goals and functions of sport.

PARENTS' ROLES AND RESPONSIBILITIES

To begin, parents must realize that children have a right to participate in sports. This includes the right to choose *not* to participate (Martens & Seefeldt, 1979). Parents should encourage participation, but children should not be pressured, intimidated, or bribed into playing. In fulfilling their responsibility, parents should counsel their children, giving consideration to the sport selected and the level of competition at which the children want to play. Of course, parents should also respect their children's decisions.

Parents can enjoy their children's participation more if they acquire an understanding and appreciation of the sport. This includes knowledge of basic rules, skills, and strategies. Coaches can serve as valuable resources by answering parents' questions and by referring parents to a community/school library or to a bookstore for educational materials. In addition, coaches should devote part of an early season practice to a lecture-demonstration of the fundamentals of the sport, and parents having little background in the sport should be encouraged to attend this session.

Some parents unknowingly become a source of stress to young athletes. All parents identify with their children to some extent and thus want them to do well. Unfortunately, in some cases, the degree of identification becomes excessive. The child becomes an extension of the parents. When this happens, parents begin to define their own self-worth in terms of how successful their son or daughter is. The father who is a "frustrated jock" may seek to experience through his child the success he never knew as an athlete. Or the parent who was a star may be resentful and rejecting if the child does not attain similar achievements. Some parents thus become "winners" or "losers" through their children, and the pressure placed on the children to excel can be extreme. A child *must* succeed or the parent's self-image is threatened. Much more is at stake than a mere game, and the child of such a parent carries a heavy burden. When parental love and support are dependent on adequacy of performance, sports are bound to be stressful (see Passer, 1982; Smith & Smoll, 1982).

As a coach, you may be able to counteract this tendency by explaining the identification process to parents. Tell them that if they place excessive pressure on children, they can decrease the potential that sports can have for enjoyment and personal growth. A key to reducing parent-produced stress is to impress on parents that youth sport programs are for young athletes and that children and youth are *not* miniature adults. Parents must acknowledge the right of each young person to develop athletic potential in an atmosphere that emphasizes participation, personal growth, and fun.

To contribute to the success of your sport program, parents must be willing and able to commit themselves in many different ways. Al Rosen (1967), a former major league baseball player, developed some questions that can serve as important reminders of the scope of parent responsibilities:

1. *Can the parents give their child up?* This requires putting the child completely in your charge and trusting you as coach to guide his or her sport experience. It involves accepting your authority and the fact that you may gain some of the child's admiration that once was directed solely at the parent.

2. *Can the parents admit their shortcomings?* Parents must be convinced that the proper response to a mistake or not knowing something is an honest disclosure. They must not hesitate to openly discuss it with their child.

3. *Can the parents accept their child's triumphs?* This sounds easy, but it is not always so. Some parents do not realize it, but fathers in particular may be competitive with their sons. If a boy does well in a contest, his father may point out minor mistakes, describe how others did even better, or bring up something more impressive from memories of his own sport achievements.

4. *Can the parents accept their child's disappointments?* Accepting a child's disappointments may mean watching him or her lose a contest while others triumph, or not being embarrassed, ashamed, or angry when their 10-year-old cries after losing. When an apparent disappointment occurs, parents should be able to help their children to see the positive side of the situation.

5. *Can the parents show their child self-control?* Parents should be reminded that they are important role models for their children's behavior. Your coaching task becomes much more difficult if parents lose control of themselves at contests. You can hardly be expected to teach sportsmanship and self-control to youngsters whose parents obviously lack these qualities.

6. *Can the parents give their child some time?* Some parents are very busy, which becomes a problem because they are interested and want to encourage their children. The best advice you can give them is never to promise more time than they can actually deliver. You should recommend that parents ask their children about their sport experiences and make every effort to watch at least some of their contests.

7. *Can the parents let their child make his or her own decisions?* This is an essential part of growing up and a real challenge to parents. You should encourage them to offer suggestions and guidance relative to sports, but ultimately, within reasonable limits, they should let the child go his or her own way. All parents have ambitions for their child, but they must accept the fact that they cannot mold the child's life. Sports can offer an introduction to the major process of letting go.

The most noticeable parent problem is misbehavior at contests. As part of their responsibilities, parents should watch their children compete in sports. But their behavior should meet acceptable standards. In this regard, Martens & Seefeldt (1979) recommend the following rules:

1. Parents should remain seated in the spectator area during the contest.
2. Parents should not yell instructions or criticisms to the children.
3. Parents should make no derogatory comments to players or other parents of the opposing team, to officials, or to league administrators.
4. Parents should not interfere with their children's coach. They must be willing to relinquish the responsibility for their children to the coach for the period of the contest.

TWO-WAY COMMUNICATION

Parents have a right to know what is happening to their children. For this reason, coaches should be willing to answer questions and remain open to parent input. Remember that *communication is a two-way street.* If you keep the lines of communication open, you will be more likely to have constructive and enjoyable relations with parents.

Fostering two-way communication does not mean that parents are free to be disrespectful toward you in word or action. Rather, it is an open invitation for parents to express their concerns with the assurance that they will be heard by you. There is, however, a proper time and place for interaction with you. That time is not during practice or during a contest. It is best not to discuss areas of disagreement in the presence of the children.

The most common cause of coach–parent conflicts is the difference in a coach's and parent's opinion about the young athlete's abilities. In this regard, implementation of a performance measurement system (described in Chapter 3) not only provides valuable feedback to athletes but can be an objective source of performance evaluation for parents. Nevertheless, sometimes parents will disagree with what you are doing as a coach. The main thing is not to get defensive. Listen to what they have to say. You might find some of their suggestions helpful. However, even if you do not agree, you can at least *listen*. Realize that *you* are the coach and have the final say. Remember that no coach can please everyone. No one can ask any more of you than to be the best coach you can be.

In establishing good communication with parents, you should be aware that most parents are really enthusiastic and have a true concern for their children. Sometimes, however, parents simply do not realize the trouble they are causing. Instead of being angry with them, recognize that they have a problem—one that you can help solve. Your task is to point out to these people, tactfully and diplomatically, the negative influences of their actions and get them to become more constructive and helpful. Some common types of problem parents are identified below. In addition to describing their traits, recommendations are included for dealing with them.

Disinterested Parents

Distinguishing characteristic   The noticeable characteristic of disinterested parents is their absence from team activities.

What you should do   Find out why certain parents do not participate and contribute. Make sure that you avoid the mistake of misjudging parents who are actually interested but have good reasons (work, sickness, etc.) for missing activities. Explaining the value of sports and the importance of parents' enthusiasm to their children may provide parents with a new interest in the activities of their children. In this situation, the athletes need help, too. Encourage them; show that you are really interested in them as people.

Overcritical Parents

Distinguishing characteristics   Overcritical parents often scold and berate their child. Such parents are never quite satisfied with their child's performance. They give the impression that it is more "their" game than it is the athlete's.

What you should do   As discussed earlier, some parents unconsciously relate the success or failure of their child with their own success or failure. As a result, they are often hard on their children. You should attempt to make overcritical parents aware of this problem as tactfully as possible. Explain how constant criticism can cause stress and emotional turmoil for their youngsters, turmoil that actually hinders performance. Tell them why you prefer to use praise and encouragement to motivate and instruct young people, and how parents can do the same.

What you can say "Mr. Jones, I know you're only trying to help Billy, but when you criticize him as much as you do, he gets so nervous that his playing becomes worse, and that certainly takes any fun out of it for him." *Or* "Mr. Jones, if you were to encourage your son instead of criticizing him so much, the game would be a lot more enjoyable for both of you. After all, it's the kids' game. They play for fun, and too much criticism spoils it for them."

Screaming Parents from Behind the Bench

Distinguishing characteristics Some parents seem to have leather lungs and large vocal cords. They often sit directly behind the bench, which makes them a distinct danger to the well-being of your eardrums. They frequently rant and rave and virtually drown out anyone else speaking in the area, including you. Everyone is a target for their verbal abuse — team members, opponents, coaches, officials.

What you should do Do not get into an argument with a screaming parent. It will not do any good and will probably make things worse. During a break in the game (halftime, between periods), calmly, tactfully, and privately point out to the person that such yelling is a poor example for the young athletes. Ask other parents to help out by working with this person during games. Also, you can give him or her a job that will help the team (scouting opponents, keeping stats, looking after equipment, etc.). This may provide a greater sense of responsibility and help the screamer to keep quiet. If the screaming persists, seek assistance from league officials.

What you can say "I know it's easy to get excited, but these kids are out here to have a good time. Try not to take the game so seriously, O.K.?" *Or* "Listen, why don't we get together after the game and you can give me some of your ideas on coaching. I'd rather have them afterward because during the game, they're very confusing."

Sideline Coaches

Distinguishing characteristics Parents who assume the role of sideline coaches are often found leaning over the bench making suggestions to players. They may contradict your instructions and disrupt the team.

What you should do Again, do not confront such a parent right away. Advise your players that during practices and games, you are the coach and that you want their full attention. Listening to instructions from others may become confusing. Tell the parent privately how confusing it is for the athletes when two or more people are telling them what to do. You might ask the parent to be either a full-time assistant coach or a full-time spectator.

What you can say   "Mrs. Jones, I appreciate your concern and enthusiasm for the team, but when you are coaching Kay from the sidelines, it becomes confusing and distracting to her. I know you've got some good ideas, and I want to hear them. But please, after the game."

Overprotective Parents

Distinguishing characteristics   Most often, overprotective parents are mothers of the athletes. Such parents are characterized by their worried looks and comments whenever their son or daughter is playing. Overprotective parents frequently threaten to remove their child because of the dangers involved in the sport.

What you should do   You must try to eliminate the fear of injury by reassuring the parent that the game is fairly safe. Explain the rules and equipment that protect the player. Point out how good coaching, program administration, and officiating add to the safety of the sport.

What you can say   "Mrs. Jones, we try to make the game as safe as possible for the athletes. You've got to remember that I wouldn't be coaching kids if I didn't care about them or if I thought the sport was dangerous for them." *Or* "Mrs. Jones, I care about each one of these kids, and I would never let any of them do anything that I thought would endanger them."

THE COACH–PARENT MEETING

Successful coaches are aware of the importance of securing the aid and support of well-informed parents. Rather than facing the task of dealing with problem parents, a preseason meeting is the *key* to reducing the chances of having unpleasant experiences. In other words, having a coach–parent meeting is well worth the additional time and effort!

This section is a *guide* for planning and conducting effective coach–parent meetings. Because each coach is unique, we urge you to evaluate the information and suggestions and make modifications to suit your personal situation.

Purpose of the Meeting

The overall objective of a coach–parent meeting is to improve parents' understanding of youth sports. Their input can then increase the value of sport participation for their children's physical, psychological, and social development.

Planning and Preparation

It will take approximately 1¼ hours to cover the necessary topics. The meeting does not have to be elaborate to be successful. However, the importance of your being well prepared and organized cannot be overemphasized. To improve organizational quality, develop and follow a written program outline.

Schedule the meeting as early in the season as possible. Be sure that the facility you select is easily accessible and has a meeting room of adequate size, with appropriate features (seating, lighting, etc.). Use a letter of invitation to notify parents. Include brief statements about the objective of the meeting, its importance, and information about the date, time, location, and directions. Send a team roster, with addresses and telephone numbers, along with the letter. Follow-up telephone calls are recommended to remind parents about the meeting.

Content and Conduct of the Meeting

As stated earlier, effective communication is based on two-way sharing. Therefore, in conducting the meeting, draw parents into discussion instead of lecturing to them. You can do this by (a) encouraging parents to ask questions and (b) directing questions to them from time to time. Also, in creating an open atmosphere for exchange, it is very important to show respect for the parents. Make them feel that they are a contributing part of the meeting rather than a mere audience.

Opening (5 minutes) Begin the meeting by introducing yourself and your assistant coach(es). In welcoming the parents, it is important to let them know that you appreciate their interest and concern. Praise them for attending. Next, establish your credibility by giving background information. Tell them about your experience in the sport, your experience as a coach, and special training that you have had (e.g., workshops, clinics). Finally, point out the purpose of the meeting, and tell them how you will provide information about fundamentals of the sport (invite them to attend a practice session).

Objectives of youth sports (10 minutes) After the opening remarks, there should be a discussion of the objectives of children's athletics. Focus on those goals that are a major part of your coaching. Also, find out which objectives the parents would like to have emphasized. As pointed out earlier, if coaches and parents work together to reduce misunderstandings, the objectives can be achieved.

Details of your sport program (10 minutes)   Present details about the operation of your sport program. In addition to other items that you might think of, consider giving attention to the following: (a) equipment needed and where it can be purchased, (b) sites and schedules for practices and contests, (c) length of practices and contests, (d) team travel plans, (e) major team rules and guidelines, (f) medical examinations, (g) insurance, (h) fund-raising projects, and (i) midseason and postseason events.

You should also provide information about what is expected of the athletes and parents relative to the program details. Some coaches find it useful to organize a parent committee, giving the committee the task of coordinating parent involvement in many activities of the season.

Coaching roles and relationships (10 minutes)   Parents will benefit from knowing about your coaching style. In addition to describing the *positive approach* that you will be using, encourage parents to reinforce this approach in interactions with their children.

Parents' roles and responsibilities (20 minutes)   Informing parents about their roles in youth sports and the responsibilities you expect them to fulfill is the most important part of the meeting. Discuss the following topics, which were covered earlier in this chapter:

1. Counseling children about sport selection and the level of competition at which they want to play—conferring with and *listening* to them.
2. Dangers of overidentification by parents with their children—the negative impact of this process.
3. Parents' commitments—the seven important questions (see pages 50–51) to which parents must be able to honestly answer yes.
4. Rules for parent behavior at contests—as the coach, you are responsible for the team, and as parents, they are responsible for their own behavior.

Coach–parent relations (5 minutes)   Tell parents of your willingness to discuss any problems that might arise—two-way communication. You should let them know what times and places are best suited for discussions with you.

Closing (20–30 minutes)   The coach–parent meeting should be concluded with a question–answer session. There is an effective technique for starting a question–answer period. You can take the lead in raising questions. Stimulate parent involvement by asking the first few questions, and then guide the discussion. If you do not know the answer to a question, do not be ashamed to admit it. The parents will appreciate your honesty. Rather than giving a weak or incorrect response, indicate that it is a question you can both seek an answer to. Finally, at the end of the meeting, remember to thank the parents again for attending.

The coach–parent meeting is a vitally important tool for developing parent involvement and support. A successful meeting will help promote solidification of the "athletic triangle" (coach-athlete-parent) and lead to a positive youth sport experience.

SUMMARY

This chapter has dealt with a frequently neglected aspect of youth sports, namely, interactions between coaches and parents. Consideration was given to promoting effective coach–parent relationships in order to improve the quality of the athlete's sport experience. In so doing, the following major points were emphasized:

1. Coaches and parents play important roles in young athletes' sport experiences.
2. Participation in youth sports can improve physical skills and fitness, build "character," promote social competence, bring families closer together, and provide enjoyable recreational experiences for young people.
3. Young athletes should be taught that they are never "losers" if they give maximum effort in striving for excellence.
4. Most youth participate in sports to have fun, to learn new skills, and to make new friends. Research has shown that winning is relatively unimportant to them as compared with these other goals.
5. Parents should not pressure, intimidate, or bribe their children into playing a sport.
6. Parents should learn basic sport rules, skills, and strategies.
7. Coaches should serve as valuable resources and answer parents' questions as best as possible.
8. A key to reducing parent-produced stress is to impress on them that youth sports are for the young athletes.
9. Parents must be able to endorse their child's participation in youth sports and support your program.
10. Parents must conform to acceptable standards of behavior at contests.

11. In working with parents, it is essential to develop and maintain open, healthy communication with them.
12. Effective communication is a two-way street requiring both speaking and listening skills.
13. Holding a preseason coach–parent meeting is the key to avoiding unpleasant experiences.
14. The main objective of a coach–parent meeting is to improve parents' understanding of youth sports.

REFERENCES

Gould, D. (1980). *Motivating young athletes.* East Lansing: Michigan Institute for the Study of Youth Sports.

Martens, R. (1978). *Joy and sadness in children's sports.* Champaign, Ill.: Human Kinetics.

Martens, R., & Seefeldt, V. (1979). *Guidelines for children's sports.* Washington, D.C.: American Alliance for Health, Physical Education, Recreation, and Dance.

Passer, M. W. (1982). Psychological stress in youth sports. In R. A. Magill, M. J. Ash, & F. L. Smoll (Eds.), *Children in sport* (2nd ed.) (pp. 153–177). Champaign, Ill.: Human Kinetics.

Rosen, A. (1967). *Baseball and your boy.* New York: Funk & Wagnalls.

Smith, N. J., Smith, R. E., & Smoll, F. L. (1983). *Kidsports: A survival guide for parents.* Reading, Mass.: Addison-Wesley.

Smith, R. E., & Smoll, F. L. (1982). Psychological stress: A conceptual model and some intervention strategies in youth sports. In R. A. Magill, M. J. Ash, & F. L. Smoll (Eds.), *Children in sport* (2nd ed.) (pp. 178–195). Champaign, Ill.: Human Kinetics.

Smoll, F. L., & Smith, R. E. (1981). Developing a healthy philosophy of winning in youth sports. In V. Seefeldt, F. L. Smoll, R. E. Smith, & D. Gould, *A winning philosophy for youth sports programs* (pp. 17–24). East Lansing: Michigan Institute for the Study of Youth Sports.

5

The Self-fulfilling Prophecy Theory: When Coaches' Expectations Become Reality

THELMA STERNBERG HORN

University of Wisconsin—Milwaukee

In 1968 Rosenthal and Jacobson published the results of an experiment they had conducted with teachers and students in 18 elementary school classrooms. This research study, which was appropriately titled "Pygmalion in the Classroom," had been designed to find out whether the academic progress of students could actually be affected by their teachers' expectations or beliefs concerning their intellectual abilities. To investigate the issue, Rosenthal and Jacobson informed the sample of teachers that certain children in each of their classes had been identified, via scores on a standardized test of academic ability, as latent achievers or "late bloomers" who could be expected to show big gains in academic achievement over the coming school year. In actuality, the identified children had been selected at random from the total group, and there was no reason to expect that they would show any greater academic progress than their classmates. At the end of the school year, however, many of the targeted children, especially those in the lower elementary grades, had made greater gains intellectually than had children who were not so identified. Rosenthal and Jacobson concluded that the false information given to the teachers had led them to hold higher expectations for the targeted children and then to act in ways that would stimulate better performance from those students. Thus, the authors were suggesting that the teachers' expectations served as self-fulfilling prophecies by initiating a series of events that ultimately caused the expectations to be fulfilled.

The publication of this study elicited considerable interest among other researchers, some of whom responded with criticism of the Pygmalion study for a variety of methodological and statistical flaws (e.g., Elashoff & Snow, 1971; Thorndike, 1968). The ensuing controversy concerning the legitimacy of the self-fulfilling prophecy phenomenon stimulated an impressive amount of research throughout the 1970s. Although most of these investigations were oriented toward the study of expectancy effects in the academic classroom, some of them were conducted in physical education classrooms (e.g., Crowe, 1977; Martinek & Johnson, 1979) and more recently in competitive sport contexts (Horn, 1984; Rejeski, Darracott, & Hutslar, 1979). Within the last decade, several excellent reviews of this literature have been compiled (e.g., Brophy, 1983; Brophy & Good, 1974; Martinek, 1981). Based on a thorough examination of the expectancy research, the authors of these reviews have generally concluded that teachers' expectations certainly do have the potential to affect the academic progress of individual students. This poses a major problem when the expectancy is below the students' capabilities. However, the reviewers are also careful to point out that the self-fulfilling prophecy phenomenon does *not* occur in all instructional situations. Many teachers and coaches are not "Pygmalion-prone" and thus do not allow their expectations to affect the performance or the achievement of their students and athletes.

Such variation among teachers and coaches implies that those who are aware of and understand the self-fulfilling prophecy phenomenon can avoid becoming Pygmalion-type coaches or teachers. Therefore, it is the purpose of this chapter to present coaches and prospective coaches with information concerning the expectation-performance process. In the following pages, we will examine *how* coaches' expectations or judgments of their athletes can influence the athletes' performance and behavior. Specifically, we will identify (a) the processes by which coaches form expectations concerning individual athletes, (b) how such expectations influence coaching behavior, (c) how the coaches' behavior can affect the athletes' performance and psychological growth, and finally (d) how the athletes' performance and behavior can ultimately conform to the coaches' original expectations. The chapter will conclude with a discussion of the ways in which coaches can individualize their interactions with athletes to facilitate the performance of all athletes.

THE EXPECTATION-PERFORMANCE PROCESS

According to the self-fulfilling prophecy theory, the expectations that coaches form about the ability of individual athletes can serve as prophecies that dictate or determine the level of achievement each athlete will reach. Several researchers who have studied the self-fulfilling prophecy phenomenon in educational contexts (e.g., Brophy & Good, 1974; Martinek, 1981) have proposed a sequence of steps to explain how the expectation-performance connection is accomplished. This model or sequence of events can also be used to describe how the self-fulfilling prophecy phenomenon can occur in athletic settings.

Step 1. The coach develops an expectation for each athlete, an expectation that predicts the level of performance and type of behavior which that athlete will exhibit over the year.

Step 2. The coach's expectations influence his or her treatment of individual athletes. That is, the coach's behavior toward each athlete differs according to the coach's belief concerning the athlete's competence.

Step 3. The way in which the coach treats each athlete affects the athlete's performance and rate of learning. In addition, differential communication tells each athlete how competent the coach thinks he or she is. This information affects the athlete's self-concept, achievement motivation, and level of aspiration.

Step 4. The athlete's behavior and performance conform to the coach's expectations. This behavioral conformity reinforces the coach's original expectation, and the process continues.

We will now examine each of these steps in detail.

Step 1: Coaches Form Expectations

At the beginning of an athletic season, most coaches form expectations for each athlete on their teams. These expectations are really initial judgments or assessments regarding the physical competence or sport potential of each athlete and are based on certain pieces of information that are available to the coach. In particular, the research indicates that teachers, and by implication coaches, most often use two types of categories of information.

The first category contains what we can label as *person cues* and includes such informational items as the individual's socioeconomic status, racial group, gender, physical attractiveness, body size, and style of dress. The exclusive use of any or all of these person cues to form judgments about an athlete's physical competence would certainly lead to inaccurate and very stereotypic expectations. Fortunately, according to the research on expectancy effects, it appears that most coaches do not form their expectations solely on demographic or physical appearance cues but also use behaviorally based information. Thus, coaches additionally use *performance information* such as the athlete's scores on certain physical skills tests, the athlete's past performance achievements (e.g., previous season statistics or related sport accomplishments), as well as other teachers' or coaches' comments concerning the athlete's performance and behavior. Coaches also base initial impressions of athletes on observation of their behavior in practice or tryout situations (e.g., observation of the player's motivation, enthusiasm, pleasantness, response to criticism, interaction with teammates, etc.).

Although the initial expectations formed by most coaches are based on information from a variety of sources, individual coaches probably differ in regard to the weight they assign to each source. That is, some coaches may particularly value the comments of other coaches in evaluating an athlete during recruitment or at the beginning of the season, whereas other coaches may place greatest emphasis on the player's physical attributes (e.g., speed, size, strength, body build, etc.). Therefore, two coaches could form two different sets of expectations for the same athlete on the basis of what sources of information each valued most.

It obviously follows, then, that a coach's initial judgment of an athlete may be either accurate or inaccurate depending on the source(s) of information used. Accurate assessments of a player's competence generally pose no problem as they usually do not affect the player's subsequent performance. However, inaccurate expectations (i.e., expectations that are either too high or too low) that are *also* inflexible can be very disruptive for the athlete and can interfere with his or her optimal athletic progress. Consider, for example, the coach who misjudges a particular athlete at the beginning of the season and falsely believes that individual to be less competent than he or she really is. If the coach's expectation or judgment is flexible (i.e., changes when the athlete demonstrates better performance than expected), then the initial false expectation does not cause a problem. In contrast, a coach who is very inflexible and resistant to modifying initial beliefs may well "see" only what she or he expects to see from that player. That is, all evidence of skill errors by the athlete will reinforce the coach's belief that the athlete is incompetent, and all skill success will either be ignored or simply considered by the coach to be "lucky" events and not indicative of the athlete's sport skill. This coach's initial expectation, then, is not only inaccurate and inflexible, but it also affects the way in which the coach reacts or responds to that player. This type of situation leads to the second step in the sequence of events comprising the self-fulfilling prophecy phenomenon.

Step 2: Coaches' Expectations Affect Their Behavior

The expectations that coaches typically form for each athlete at the beginning of an athletic season do not necessarily or automatically act as self-fulfilling prophecies. Expectations do, however, have the potential for doing so if they affect the coaches' treatment of their athletes.

Much of the research on the self-fulfilling prophecy phenomenon has focused on this issue by asking the crucial question, "Do teachers and coaches treat students or athletes they believe have high ability (i.e., high-expectancy individuals) differently from students or athletes they believe have low ability (i.e., low-expectancy individuals)?" Generally, this question has been studied by observing and recording the type, frequency, and quality of instructional behavior that teachers and coaches exhibit toward

---

Example 1

Kim and Sue, who are teammates on their school's varsity basketball team, stay after practice to play a game of one-on-one. Their coach comes over to watch. When Kim (a high-expectancy athlete) executes a successful fake and drive, the coach responds with approval but also stops the game to provide Kim with further instruction (i.e., what she should do in a similar situation if the weak side defender had moved across the key). Later when Sue (a low-expectancy player) executes the same successful fake and drive, the coach responds with approval only ("Good move, Sue") but then goes on to show *Kim* how she should have prevented or defended against such an offensive move.

---

individual students and athletes. Again, the overall conclusion from this research (see reviews by Brophy, 1983; Brophy & Good, 1974; Martinek, 1981) indicates that *some* teachers and coaches do indeed show differential instructional behaviors to these two groups of students and athletes. Applying the results of this research to the athletic setting, we could expect the Pygmalion-type coach to show differential behavior to high- and low-expectancy athletes in regard to (a) the frequency and quality of interactions the coach has with individual athletes, (b) the quantity and quality of instruction given to each athlete, and (c) the frequency and type of performance feedback given to each athlete.

In the first behavioral category, *frequency and quality of coach-athlete interactions,* a Pygmalion-prone coach typically shows less tendency to initiate interpersonal contact (either of a social or a skill-related nature) with athletes he or she believes to be less skilled. As a result, the coach spends significantly more time with athletes who are highly skilled (see Example 1 of expectancy-biased communication). In addition, the quality of coach-athlete interactions may also differ, with high-expectancy players being shown more warmth and positive affect (e.g., smiling, head nodding, and personal contact) than their low-expectancy teammates.

Perhaps of greater consequence is the differential treatment that high- and low-expectancy players may receive in regard to the *quantity and quality of instruction.* If a coach firmly believes that certain players on her or his team do not have the requisite athletic competencies to be successful (i.e., the low-expectancy players), that coach may, first of all, reduce the amount of material and/or skills those players are expected to learn, thus establishing a lower standard of performance for them. Second, the coach may allow the low-expectancy players less time in practice drills. Thus, these athletes may spend relatively more practice time in nonskill-related activities such as shagging balls, waiting in line, and keeping score. Finally, the coach may be less persistent in helping low-expectancy athletes to learn a difficult skill.

Example 2
During a practice scrimmage, Kim (the high-expectancy player in Example 1) is having problems running a particularly difficult offensive pattern. The coach stops the team drill and spends three or four minutes helping Kim learn the pattern. When Sue (the low-expectancy athlete) later evidences the same difficulty, the coach removes her from the scrimmage team by saying to another player, "Sally, come here and take Sue's place. Let's see if *you* can run this play."

The Pygmalion-prone coach tends to give up on a low-expectancy player who fails after two or three attempts to learn a new skill but will persist in working with a high-expectancy player who is having the same difficulty (see Example 2).

   In addition to differences in the quality of instruction, researchers have also found differences in the *type and frequency of feedback* that coaches give to high- and low-expectancy players. One of the primary ways in which coaches respond differently to individual athletes is in their use of praise and criticism. Some researchers investigating expectancy issues in the classroom (e.g., Brophy & Good, 1970; Cooper & Baron, 1977) and in the motor skill instructional setting (e.g., Martinek & Johnson, 1979; Rejeski, Darracott, & Hutslar, 1979) have found that teachers and coaches give high-expectancy students and athletes more reinforcement and praise after a successful performance than they do low-expectancy individuals. In contrast, other researchers have found that low-expectancy students and athletes are the ones who receive proportionately more reinforcement (e.g., Horn, 1984; Kleinfeld, 1975; Weinstein, 1976). However, the latter researchers have additionally noted that the higher frequency of reinforcement or praise given by coaches and teachers to these low-expectancy individuals may actually be qualitatively suspect because the reinforcement is often given inappropriately (i.e., given for a mediocre performance or for success at a very easy task). See Example 3. Therefore, it appears that

---

Example 3
During the course of a varsity volleyball match, a hitter approaches the net for a spike. Seeing her opponents put up a single block, she reaches out to "tip" the ball around the block. No point is scored, but the ball is kept in play. The athlete, who is a high-expectancy player, is told by her coach, "O.K., Pat, at least you kept the ball in play. But next time you go up against a single block, *hit* the ball. Your spike is good enough to get it through that block." If, however, a low-expectancy player executes that same play, the Pygmalion-type coach might respond with approval only: "Great work, Linda, you kept the ball *away* from the block. That was smart."

Pygmalion-prone coaches may (a) provide low-expectancy athletes with less frequent reinforcement and/or (b) give them less appropriate and less beneficial feedback after successful performances.

Observation of teachers' and coaches' feedback has also revealed differences in the amount of corrective or technical instruction given. In the sport setting, such differential treatment may be especially evident in the feedback coaches provide their athletes following a performance. As illustrated in Example 4, high-expectancy performers receive informational and corrective feedback that tells them how to improve their performance. In contrast, low-expectancy performers receive a positive communication from the coach but no accompanying technical information to tell them what they can do to improve their performance. These differences in feedback responses may well be due to the different expectations the coach holds for the various athletes. For example, because the coach fully expects Dan's performance to improve, he is more apt to provide Dan with technical information to help him achieve skill success. However, the low expectations the coach holds for Pete lead the coach to believe that corrective instruction may be fruitless and certainly not useful for Pete.

Finally, coaches may also differ in the type of attribution they use to explain the cause of the high- and low-expectancy athletes' successful or unsuccessful performances. Although this aspect of performance feedback has received very little research attention, we certainly might speculate that a coach's beliefs concerning the competence or incompetence of selected players on his or her team would induce that coach to verbalize different attributions for the athletes' performance outcome. For instance, the coach in Example 5 holds different perceptions or expectations concerning the physical competence of Scott (a high-expectancy player) and Steve (a low-expectancy player). These expectations lead the coach to attribute players' performance to different causes. When Steve reaches first base safely, the

---

Example 4
Dan and Pete have both joined an age-group swimming team. Although both swimmers begin the season at the same level of performance, their coach has very high expectations for Dan's improvement and ultimate success because of his "natural" physical attributes. The coach does not have the same high expectations for Pete. At the first meet of the season, both swimmers take fifth place in their respective events. The coach responds to Dan's performance by telling him that he can considerably reduce his time if he improves his technique on the turns. The coach concludes with the comment, "We'll work on those turns all next week so you'll be ready for the next meet." In contrast, the coach responds to Pete's fifth-place performance by saying, "Good job, Pete. Hang in there."

Example 5
During a baseball game, Steve (a low-expectancy athlete) hits a pitched
ball sharply toward the left side of the infield. The shortstop makes a
nice backhanded move for the ball and fields it. Although he then
slightly mishandles it, he does throw it hard to first for a close play, with
the runner (Steve) being called safe. The coach comments, "What a
break, Steve! We were lucky he [the shortstop] bobbled it, or you would
have been out." However, in a similar situation with Scott (a high-
expectancy player) as the batter/runner, the coach responds to the same
performance by exclaiming, "Way to hit the hole, Scott, and great speed!
You beat the throw again!"

coach immediately, and in this case verbally, attributes that success to the
opposing team's error (i.e., a lucky break for Steve). In comparison, the
coach verbally attributes the same performance by Scott to Scott's ability
(i.e., his batting prowess and speed). Similarly, the coach's response to these
athletes' performance errors may also be affected by the coach's judgment
of each player's ability. In Example 6, the coach attributes Scott's lack of
success in stealing a base to poor positioning and thus suggests that the
performance can be corrected. The coach attributes a similar failure by
Steve to Steve's lack of ability (i.e., his lack of speed).

These examples illustrate how the expectations that coaches form for
individual athletes on their teams can affect coaches' perceptions of actual
events. Such different perceptions, in turn, can lead to differences in
coaches' responses to athletes' performances.

Although the research clearly suggests that some teachers and coaches
do treat high- and low-expectancy athletes and students differently, we
need to exercise caution in regard to those findings and not jump to the
conclusion that it is essential for coaches to treat all athletes on their teams
in exactly the same way. Because athletes differ in their skills as well as in
their personalities, coaches are well advised to individualize their instruc-

Example 6
Later in the game described in Example 5, Scott (the high-expectancy
player) attempts to steal second without the coach's giving a steal sign.
Scott is easily thrown out. As he reaches the dugout, the coach tells him,
"Good try, Scott. That would have been a good pitch to steal on, but you
didn't have a big enough lead to go. Next time . . ." When Steve (the
low-expectancy player) attempts the same performance, the coach
angrily responds, "What are you doing out there? I didn't tell you to
go . . . you're too slow to steal second, especially on that catcher."

tional behavior to accommodate the uniquenesses of each athlete. There-fore, it is important, at this point, to emphasize that observable differences in a coach's behavior toward individual athletes on his or her team do *not* automatically imply that the coach is acting in a biased manner and that the progress of her or his athletes will be impeded. If the differences in the coach's behavior are designed to and actually do facilitate the performance and achievement of *each* athlete, then such differential coaching behavior is appropriate. However, if the differential treatment an athlete or a group of athletes *consistently* receive from their coach in practices and games limits the athletes' ability or opportunity to learn, then such differential coaching behavior is dysfunctional, and the coach's expectations may be serving as self-fulfilling prophecies.

Step 3: Coaches' Behavior Affects Athletes' Performance and Behavior

The third step in the sequence of events comprising the self-fulfilling proph-ecy phenomenon occurs when a coach's expectancy-biased treatment of an individual athlete affects that athlete's performance and psychological growth. It is easy to understand how the biased behavior described in the preceding section is likely to maximize the athletic progress of high-expect-ancy athletes while limiting the achievements of their low-expectancy teammates. Players who are *consistently* given less effective and less inten-sive instruction or who are allowed less active time in practice drills will not show the same degree of skill improvement as their teammates who are given optimal learning opportunities. In Examples 1 and 2, Kim and Sue are obviously not being given the same quality of instruction. If this instruc-tional behavior is typical of the treatment that these athletes receive from their coach over the season, we might well anticipate that after a certain period of time, Kim's basketball skills will be considerably better than Sue's. Their coach will attribute these skill differences to what she believes to be the innate differences in Kim and Sue's basic athletic talent. Given the observed variation in the coach's instructional behavior toward these two athletes, it is equally likely that the coach's original expectation or judg-ment concerning each athlete's sport potential actually determined, rather than just predicted, the level of achievement that Kim and Sue reached. The coach's expectations, then, served as self-fulfilling prophecies by setting in motion a series of events (i.e., consistent differences in the quality of in-struction) that ultimately caused the original expectations to be fulfilled.

In addition to the negative effects that a coach's biased instructional behavior has on an athlete's rate of learning and level of achievement, such behavior can also affect the athlete's psychological growth. Recent research in sport psychology has demonstrated that the type of instructional behav-iors a coach exhibits in games and in practices is associated with changes in athletes' self-concept and perceived competence over the course of a season (Horn, 1985; Smith, Smoll, & Curtis, 1979). This association between coaches' behavior and athletes' self-perceptions is quite consistent with several psychological theories (e.g., Harter, 1981; Weiner, 1979) which suggest that the evaluation or feedback that adults provide is an important source of information that children and adolescents use to determine how competent or incompetent they are.

In the athletic setting, then, the type of feedback that coaches give to individual athletes may affect the athletes' self-perceptions (e.g., their self-confidence, self-efficacy, and anxiety) by communicating to the athletes how competent or skilled the coach thinks they are. Occasionally, of course, the coach communicates this evaluative information directly to the athletes. More commonly, however, coaches communicate their judgments or beliefs concerning the athletes' abilities in more subtle or indirect ways. Specifically, the coach's reinforcement patterns (i.e., the level of performance or type of behavior the coach rewards) provide the athletes with information that tells them how skilled the coach thinks they are. In Example 3, Linda and Pat have demonstrated the same level of performance, but each receives a different response from the coach. This differential feedback may communicate to these athletes what standard of performance each is expected to achieve. Linda, who is clearly reinforced for that level of performance, may also be receiving information telling her that she is at the maximum level she is capable of achieving. However, Pat is led to believe that her performance, while acceptable, can and should be improved because she has the requisite skills to perform at a higher level.

Similarly, the amount and frequency of corrective instruction a coach provides after a skill error may also tell each athlete how competent or skillful the coach thinks he or she is. In Example 4, for instance, the coach responds to Dan's fifth-place performance with corrective feedback, thus overtly telling him that his performance can be improved with effort and covertly supplying him with the perception that he is capable of a higher level of skill. In contrast, although the coach gives Pete a positive and encouraging response for a similar level of performance, the coach does not give Pete the additional information to tell him that he can improve his performance and thus is capable of achieving at a higher level. Thus, the coach has indirectly communicated his expectations or judgments concerning each athlete's level of ability.

In a recent study investigating coaches' feedback in the interscholastic athletic context (Horn, 1984), it was found that junior high softball coaches gave their low-expectancy female athletes proportionately more reinforcement or praise in response to skill successes during games than they gave their high-expectancy athletes. In response to skill errors, however, these coaches provided their high-expectancy athletes with more criticism and

corrective instruction but tended to ignore more frequently (give no response to) the mistakes of their low-expectancy athletes.

Research reported in the educational psychology literature (Meyer,
1982) has demonstrated that differential feedback responses do indeed
provide performers with information concerning their abilities. Individuals
who received more reinforcement than other performers for the same level
of performance were perceived by themselves and others to have lower
ability. In situations where performers exhibited the same performance
errors, the individuals who received criticism were perceived by themselves
and others to be more competent than those who received a neutral response following failure. It appears, then, that the evaluative feedback
given by coaches to individual athletes is indeed providing the athletes with
information concerning their competence. Certainly the differential feedback that low- and high-expectancy athletes receive from Pygmalion-prone
coaches may affect the athletes' perceptions or beliefs concerning their own
skill competence.

Finally, as noted in the previous section, coaches may also communicate their beliefs concerning an athlete's skill ability by the attribution they
make for the athlete's performance. Such attribution provides the athlete
with information concerning his or her competence. When a coach attributes an athlete's successful performance to the athlete's innate ability
(e.g., Example 5) the athlete develops a high expectancy for future success
and a positive attitude toward the sport activity. In contrast, when a coach
attributes successful performance to luck, the attribution does not encourage an athlete to believe that he or she can attain the same performance in
the future and provides the athlete with no information concerning personal competence. Similarly, a coach's attributing a skill error to lack of
effort, lack of practice, or some other athlete-controlled factor will do more
to facilitate future motivation, decrease feelings of helplessness, and encourage a positive attitude than attributing the athlete's failure to lack of
ability. In Example 6, Scott's performance failure is attributed by his coach
to incorrect skill execution (a controllable and correctable error), whereas
Steve's failure is attributed to his lack of speed (a less controllable and less
correctable cause). The differential messages carried via these coaching
communications may affect each athlete's future performance and motivation.

Step 4: The Athlete's Performance Conforms to the Coach's Expectations

The final step in the chain of events comprising the self-fulfilling prophecy
phenomenon occurs when the athlete's performance and behavior conform to the coach's original expectation. This behavioral conformity is, in

itself, a very important component in the chain of events because it reinforces for the coach that his or her initial judgment of the athlete was on the
mark. This confirms for the Pygmalion-prone coach that he or she is a very
accurate judge of sport potential and can recognize true athletic talent at the
beginning of the season. Such "success" may reinforce or intensify the
coach's Pygmalion tendencies.

As a final point in regard to the self-fulfilling prophecy process, it is
important to recognize that all athletes do *not* allow their coach's behavior
or expectations to affect their performance or psychological responses. Just
as all coaches are *not* Pygmalion-prone, so too all athletes are not susceptible
to the self-fulfilling prophecy. Earlier research in the coaching effectiveness
area (Smith, Smoll, & Curtis, 1979) has suggested that the self-perceptions
of some athletes are more easily affected by their coach's evaluative feedback than are the self-perceptions of their teammates. It is likely that individuals who tend to be very dependent on their coach's feedback to provide
them with information concerning their competence would be most easily
"molded" by their coach's expectations. In contrast, athletes who are resistant to the Pygmalion process may not use the coach's feedback as a sole
source of information to tell them how competent they are. If such athletes
do receive biased feedback from a coach, they may respond by discounting
that information and using other informational sources (e.g., feedback
from peers, parents, or other adults) to form their perceptions of how
competent or skilled they are. Thus, even if a coach shows biased treatment
of an individual athlete, the self-fulfilling prophecy process will short-cir-
cuit if the athlete is resistant to his or her coach's bias. It is important to
note, then, that all four steps in the sequence are essential if the self-fulfilling prophecy phenomenon is to occur in the athletic setting.

BEHAVIORAL RECOMMENDATIONS FOR COACHES

The research and theory detailed in the preceding pages illustrate how
coaches' expectations and behavior can affect the performance and psychological growth of individual athletes on their teams. This information can
and should be used to promote positive coach–athlete interactions. Therefore, the following recommendations are offered to coaches and prospective coaches for their use in evaluating and perhaps modifying their own
behavior in the athletic setting.

   1. *Coaches should determine what sources of information they use to form
preseason or early season expectations for each athlete.* Performance-based information sources are generally more reliable and accurate predictors or indicators of an individual's physical competence than are such person cues as

the athlete's gender, racial or ethnic heritage, socioeconomic status, and physical appearance.

2. *Coaches should realize that their initial assessments of an athlete's competence may be inaccurate and thus need to be revised continually as the season progresses.*

3. *During practices, coaches need to keep a running count of the amount of time each athlete spends in nonskill-related activities* (i.e., shagging balls, waiting in line, etc.). Certainly it is advisable for coaches to ask a friend or another coach to observe their practices and record the amount of time a starter (usually a high-expectancy athlete) and a nonstarter (usually a low-expectancy athlete) spend in practice drills.

4. *Coaches should design instructional activities or drills that provide all athletes with an opportunity to improve their skills.* In planning practice activities, the Pygmalion-type coach typically uses skill drills that are most appropriate for the highly skilled players. When the less skilled athletes cannot keep up, the coach then gives up on these athletes because he or she believes that their failure is inevitable because of low skill abilities. The more effective coach, upon finding that his or her less skilled players cannot master the skill, will implement instructional activities designed to help them ultimately achieve success (e.g., break the skill down into component parts, employ performance aids, and/or ask the athlete to stay a few minutes extra after practice for more intensive work).

5. *As a general rule, coaches should respond to skill errors with corrective instruction that tells each athlete what she or he can do to improve the skill performance.*

6. *Coaches should emphasize skill improvement as a means of evaluating and reinforcing individual athletes* rather than using absolute performance scores or levels of skill achievement. To the degree that a coach conveys the attitude that *all* athletes can *improve* their skill performance, no matter what their present level, then positive expectations can be communicated to each athlete.

SUMMARY

Coaches' preseason judgments of individual athletes can serve as self-fulfilling prophecies by initiating a series of events that cause the coaches' initial expectations to become reality. This self-fulfilling prophecy phenomenon can be most detrimental when a coach forms an initial expectation that is inaccurate and underestimates an athlete's true ability. The coach's biased judgment of the athlete's sport potential, in turn, causes the coach to provide that player with less frequent and less effective instruction. Not only does such biased coaching behavior ultimately interfere with the athlete's opportunity to learn, but it also has a negative effect on his or her motivation and self-confidence. When the athlete subsequently exhibits an inability to perform well and a lack of motivation in practice situations, the coach's original but false judgment of incompetence is fulfilled.

Fortunately, the research that has been conducted in academic classrooms as well as in physical activity settings shows that all coaches are not Pygmalion-prone. That is, some coaches do not allow their preseason judgments of individual athletes to affect the quality of their interaction with those players. It seems likely that coaches who are made aware of the effects that their expectations may have on athletes and who are trained to monitor their own instructional behavior may become more effective in working with individual athletes. The results of this research demonstrate that it is important that researchers and coaches more closely examine coaching behavior as one of the major factors that affect the performance and psychological growth of young athletes.

REFERENCES

Brophy, J. (1983). Research on the self-fulfilling prophecy and teacher expectations. *Journal of Educational Psychology, 75,* 631–661.

Brophy, J., & Good, T. (1970). Teachers' communication of differential expectations for children's classroom performance: Some behavioral data. *Journal of Educational Psychology, 61,* 365–374.

Brophy, J., & Good, T. (1974). *Teacher–student relationships: Causes and consequences.* New York: Holt, Rinehart & Winston.

Cooper, H., & Baron, R. (1977). Academic expectations and attributed responsibility as predictors of professional teachers' reinforcement behavior. *Journal of Educational Psychology, 69,* 409–418.

Crowe, P. (1977). *An observational study of expectancy effects and their mediating mechanisms on students of physical education activity classes.* Unpublished doctoral dissertation, University of North Carolina at Greensboro.

Elashoff, J., & Snow, R. (1971). *Pygmalion reconsidered.* Worthington, Ohio: Chas. Jones.

Harter, S. (1981). The development of competence motivation in the mastery of cognitive and physical skills: Is there still a place for joy? In G. C. Roberts & D. M. Landers (Eds.), *Psychology of motor behavior and sport—1980* (pp. 3–29). Champaign, Ill.: Human Kinetics.

Horn, T. S. (1984). Expectancy effects in the interscholastic athletic setting: Methodological considerations. *Journal of Sport Psychology, 6,* 60–76.

Horn, T. S. (1985). Coaches' feedback and changes in children's perceptions of their physical competence. *Journal of Educational Psychology, 77,* 174–186.

Kleinfeld, J. (1975). Effective teachers of Eskimo and Indian students. *School Review, 83,* 301 – 344.

Martinek, T. (1981). Pygmalion in the gym: A model for the communication of teacher expectations in physical education. *Research Quarterly, 52,* 58 – 67.

Martinek, T., & Johnson, S. (1979). Teacher expectations: Effects on dyadic interactions and self-concept in elementary age children. *Research Quarterly, 50,* 60 – 70.

Meyer, W. (1982). Indirect communications about perceived ability estimates. *Journal of Educational Psychology, 74,* 888 – 897.

Rejeski, W., Darracott, C., & Hutslar, S. (1979). Pygmalion in youth sports: A field study. *Journal of Sport Psychology, 1,* 311 – 319.

Rosenthal, R., & Jacobson, L. (1968). *Pygmalion in the classroom: Teacher expectations and pupils' intellectual development.* New York: Holt, Rinehart & Winston.

Smith, R. E., Smoll, F. L., & Curtis, B. (1979). Coach effectiveness training: A cognitive-behavioral approach to enhancing relationship skills in youth sport coaches. *Journal of Sport Psychology, 1,* 59 – 75.

Thorndike, R. (1968). Review of Pygmalion in the classroom. *American Educational Research Journal, 5,* 708 – 711.

Weiner, B. (1979). A theory of motivation for some classroom experiences. *Journal of Educational Psychology, 71,* 3 – 25.

Weinstein, R. (1976). Reading group membership in first grade: Teacher behaviors and pupil experience over time. *Journal of Educational Psychology, 68,* 103 – 116.

6   The Sport Team as an Effective Group

ALBERT V. CARRON

University of Western Ontario

Membership and involvement in groups is a fundamental characteristic of our society. We band together in a large number and variety of groups for social reasons or to carry out more effectively some job or task. Thus, each of us interacts daily with numerous other people in group settings — in the family, at work, in social situations, on sport teams. The result is a reciprocal exchange of influence; we exert an influence on other people in groups, and in turn, those groups and their members have an influence on us. Two examples serve to illustrate just how powerful this influence can be:

In January 1980, Tony Conigliaro, a former Boston Red Sox baseball player, was driving with his brother when he suffered a massive heart attack — he experienced "sudden death." At least six minutes passed before CPR was administered and his heart was stimulated into activity. However, he remained in a coma for four days, and the prognosis for any significant recovery was bleak. A lack of oxygen to the brain for as few as four minutes can produce permanent brain damage. Also, people who are comatose for the length of time Conigliaro was are almost never able to walk, talk, or look after themselves totally again.

Conigliaro's family refused to believe the prognosis. They were at his side constantly, talking, encouraging, providing love and affection. Slowly, Conigliaro fought back, began to talk, and showed improvements that astounded his doctors. In fact, as Maximillian Kaulback, one of his doctors, stated, "This case is beyond science. . . . I wouldn't be surprised if someday it was proven that the input of the family in cases like this is significant" (quoted in McCallum, 1982, p. 72). The incident is powerful and moving; it also illustrates the importance of the family's influence — its love, concern, and physical and emotional support. The second illustration, however, shows another side of group influence.

On August 9 and 10, 1969, Charles Manson and four accomplices, three women and a man, brutally and senselessly killed seven people. Actress Sharon Tate, who was pregnant, and four others were killed the first night and Leno and Rosemary La Bianca the second. The two sets of victims were

75

not related in any meaningful way, and there was no apparent motive for the murders. After the longest trial in American history, Manson and his accomplices were found guilty. The question of how such an atrocity could come about was more difficult to puzzle out. Psychiatrist Joel Hochman, commenting on the role of one of Manson's female accomplices, reported that "we might suggest the possibility that she may be suffering from a condition of *folie a famille,* a kind of shared madness within a group situation" (quoted in Bugliosi & Gentry, 1974, p. 461). Vincent Bugliosi, the prosecutor for the case, also felt that the influence of the group was significant. He described the Manson group as follows:

> There was also love, a great deal of love. To overlook this would be to miss one of the strongest bonds that existed among them. The love grew out of their sharing, their communal problems and pleasures, their relationship with Charlie. They were a real family in almost every sense of that word, a sociological unit complete to brothers, sisters, substitute mothers, linked by the domination of an all-knowing, all-powerful patriarch. (Bugliosi & Gentry, 1974, p. 484)

These anecdotes serve to illustrate the dramatic influence that groups can have on their members. In the Conigliaro case, the influence was a positive one, whereas in the Manson case, the influence was negative and destructive. The fundamental question is how groups can come to exert such influence. From a coaching perspective, insight into this issue could produce possible prescriptions for the development of a positive, productive sport group—an effective, cohesive team. In this chapter, we discuss the nature of groups and offer some suggestions for the development of effective groups in sport settings.

THE GROUP DEFINED

Just what is a group? Of what does it consist? A number of definitions have been suggested and each serves to highlight some special feature or characteristic of a group. Some of the more important features of a group are that it has a collective identity, a sense of shared purpose, structured patterns of interaction, structured methods of communication, personal and task interdependence, and interpersonal attraction (Carron, 1980).

A football team* can be used to illustrate each of these definitional components. For example, a collective identity exists when individual team members, fellow teammates, and nonteam members all view the group as a

---

* This example is taken from Carron, 1981, pp. 246–247, and is used with the permission of Human Kinetics, Champaign, Illinois.

unit distinguishable from other units: "We are teammates on the University of Xebec Scullers." The sense of shared purpose or objectives readily develops from the strong task-oriented nature of sport. With a football team, this can vary from an awareness and agreement on short-term objectives (attend weight-training sessions in the off-season) or long-term ones (win the championship).

Numerous examples are available for the structured patterns of interaction that exist within a team. The interrelated blocking assignments for various offensive plays and the defensive responsibilities under different alignments are unique task interactions within any specific team. Any newcomer to a football team requires some time to become completely familiar with the specific system. Similarly, the differentiation made explicitly or implicitly between rookies and veterans early in training camp (locker-room assignments, uniform distinctions, hazing practices) is an example of the patterned social interactions existing within any sport team.

The argot of football in general — blitz, drive block, fly, curl, trap — and the specific manner in which it is selectively used on particular teams provides one example of an existing structured mode of communication. The specific terminology used to convey particular offensive and defensive assignments (R-221, Man, Z-Curl) is another. Although members of a team can readily transpose these apparently meaningless symbols into something meaningful, the nonteam member or uninitiated observer cannot.

Personal and task interdependence are inherent within the nature of sport itself; the rules of sport dictate the size, general structure, and organization of the sport team. Thus, an individual cannot play football alone; a specific number of players is permitted on the field at any given time; there are general rules on how they must be aligned; interaction with the opposition must conform to designated behavioral standards and so on. In essence, then, each team member is inextricably bound to teammates if competition is desired.

Finally, although there are documented exceptions, interpersonal attraction generally evolves from sport team participation. Therefore, attraction is usually present in some degree on most teams although it is neither a necessary nor sufficient property in terms of the definition of a sport team.

Distinguishing Between a Group and a Collection of Individuals

Individuals who study groups often make an important distinction between a group and a collection of individuals. Alvin Zander, the former director of the Research Center for Group Dynamics at the University of Michigan, discussed this issue when he pointed out the following:

A group is a collection or set of individuals who interact with and depend on each other. A number of persons jointly engaged in an activity—traveling on a sightseeing tour, picking apples in an orchard, working in a personnel department, attending a seminar—are not necessarily a group, but it may become one. We know that people have formed a group when they talk freely, are interested in the achievement of their set as a whole, feel that associates are helpful, try to assist colleagues, refer to their collectivity as "we" and to other social bodies as "they," and faithfully participate when members gather. A body of people is not a group if the members are primarily interested in individual accomplishments, are not concerned with the activities of other members or see others as rivals, and are often absent. (Zander, 1982, pp. 1–2)

On the sport team, the general rule is that the coach or leader must develop the sense of "we" and reduce the importance of "I." A number of general techniques can assist in this process. Depending upon the type of sport and the age of the participants, some are more effective than others.

Developing the Team Concept

Research has shown that some of the most important factors for developing a group out of a collection of individuals are proximity, distinctiveness, similarity, and the establishment of group goals and rewards (Shaw, 1981; Zander, 1982).

Individuals who are in close *proximity*, who are physically close to each other, have a greater tendency to bond together. Physical proximity by itself is not always sufficient; but being in close contact and having the opportunity for interaction in combination with distinctiveness, similarity, and the establishment of group goals and rewards does hasten group development.

Some situations in sport that ensure physical proximity among group members include having a specific team locker room, residence, or training table. In youth sport situations, scheduling games that require the team to travel together in a bus or car is also beneficial. The important point is that group members should be placed in situations where interaction is inevitable.

A second factor is *distinctiveness*. As a set of individuals becomes more separate, more distinctive from others, its feelings of oneness and unity also increase. Traditionally, distinctiveness is achieved through team uniforms and mottos, by having special initiation rites, by providing special privileges or demanding special sacrifices. Many of the factors that make athletes distinct from the general population are taken for granted. These include year-round intensive training programs, reduced time for social activities or part-time employment. The coach should highlight such factors to develop a feeling of commonality. Finally, emphasizing the sense of tradition and the history of the organization or team can contribute to the feeling of distinctiveness.

A third factor is *similarity* — similarity in attitudes, aspirations, commitments, ability. As Zander (1982) noted:

> Birds of a feather flock together, and create a more distinct entity when they do. People too form a better unit if they are alike, and an effective leader develops oneness within a set by encouraging likeness among members. To do this, she recruits persons who will interact well because of similar purpose, background, training, experience, or temperament. . . . Persons whose beliefs do not fit together well have a hard time forming a strong group. (p. 3)

On sport teams, members' differences in personality, ethnicity, racial background, economic background, ability, and numerous other factors are inevitable. What the coach must do is work to develop a similarity in attitude about factors such as the group's performance goals, expectations for individual behavior, and the code of conduct for practices, games, and situations away from the sport environment.

A fourth factor that influences the development of a team concept is the establishment of *group goals and rewards.* In most group activities, including track and field, swimming, baseball, and even basketball, hockey, and soccer, there is an opportunity for the gifted individual competitor to obtain special recognition and rewards. This is inevitable. However, to ensure that a concept of unity develops, the coach must emphasize the group's goals and objectives and the rewards that will accrue to the group if these are achieved. Individual goals and rewards should be downplayed.

A final technique for promoting a team concept is to have more satisfied or prestigious team members make personal sacrifices for the group (Zander, 1982). This not only produces a sense of commitment and involvement in the individual, but it shows other team members how the welfare of the team is perceived by important group members.

THE STRUCTURE OF THE GROUP

When a set of individuals is brought together for the first time (e.g., at training camp, at the first practice session, or at organizational meetings in the off-season), a number of structural aspects characteristic of all groups begin to emerge. These result from the interactions among individual members, their perceptions of one another, and their expectations for themselves, other individuals, and the group. The emergence of these structural characteristics is inevitable and essential if the set of individuals is to become a group that functions effectively. The structural characteristics discussed in this chapter are group roles and norms. Although the two are similar in some respects, a significant distinction between them is that a *role* is a property of individual group members whereas a *norm* is a property of the group itself.

Group Roles

A role is a set of behaviors that are expected from the occupants of specific positions within the group. Thus, when we think of the "role of a coach," a number of expectations for behavior come to mind; instruct athletes; set up the team's offensive and defensive alignments; liaise with parents, the media, and the general public; organize practices, and so on.

Within every group, there are two general categories of roles, formal and informal (Mabry & Barnes, 1980). As the term suggests, *formal* roles are explicitly set out by the group or organization. Coach, team captain, manager are examples of explicit leadership roles within a team; spiker and setter in volleyball; forward, guard, and center in basketball; and scrum half and prop in rugby are examples of explicit performance roles. The sport team, as an organization, requires specific individuals to carry out each of these roles. Thus, individuals are trained or recruited for these roles, and specific expectations are held for their behavior.

On the other hand, *informal* roles evolve as a result of the interactions that take place among group members. Some examples of the informal roles that often emerge on a sport team are leader (which may or may not be the team captain), enforcer, police officer, social director, and team clown.

Not surprisingly, research has consistently shown that when individual group members understand their roles (which is referred to as *role clarity*), accept their roles (which is referred to as *role acceptance*), and attempt to carry out their roles to the best of their ability (which is referred to as *role performance*), the group's effectiveness is improved (Schriesheim, 1980). Furthermore, role clarity, role acceptance, and perceived role performance are also associated with a number of other important group processes such as communication, cohesiveness, conformity, and goal-directed behavior.

In an attempt to help coaches assess the degree to which each of these three important variables is present within a sport team, Carron and Grand developed the Team Climate Questionnaire (Carron & Grand, 1982; Grand & Carron, 1982). A copy is provided on pp. 89–91.

Group Norms

A norm is a standard for behavior that is expected of members of the group. It may be task irrelevant or task relevant; in either case, a norm reflects the group's consensus about behaviors that are considered acceptable. The treatment of team managers or trainers by the athletes is one example of a task irrelevant norm. On one team, the manager might be regarded and treated as little more than an unpaid servant; on another team, he or she might be considered a member of the coaching team. In both cases, new team members quickly become aware of the standard of behavior considered acceptable and begin to act accordingly.

One of the best known, most heavily researched issues relating to task relevant norms is the *norm for productivity*. One example of this occurs in industrial settings when a level or rate of performance is established by the group as acceptable. Then productivity that is above that standard ("rate busting") or below it ("malingering") is not sanctioned by the group.

In sport, similar situations can arise. In the movie, *Chariots of Fire*, for example, the British sprinter Harry Abrahams was chided by his Cambridge dons for hiring a professional trainer — for becoming too serious. Similarly, when Pete Rose broke into major league baseball he was nicknamed "Charlie Hustle" for the intensity he brought to all aspects of his behavior on the field. The implicit suggestion is that he was too intense.

Another important aspect of group norms is their stability. It has been demonstrated experimentally that an arbitrary norm can persist for four or five generations after the original members have been removed (Jacobs & Campbell, 1961). Thus, if a sport team develops negative norms, such as abusive behavior toward officials or other team members, a laissez-faire attitude toward training, a reliance on individual versus team goals, the norms can persist over a number of seasons unless steps are taken to eliminate them.

Enhancing Group Structure

A National Hockey League coach once observed that the worst thing that could happen to a team was to have its enforcer score a few goals in successive games. The enforcer would then begin to see himself as and prefer the role of goal scorer to the detriment of the team as a whole.

The roles that individuals are expected to perform should be clearly spelled out. In other words, the behavioral requirements of a role should be made as explicit as possible. Merton (1957) pointed out that the occupants of a role generally have a different perspective of the role's requirements than do other members of the group. Thus, if the sixth best player on a basketball team is to be used as a defensive specialist only, the coach should point this out. Otherwise that person may see his or her role in an entirely different way.

In terms of role acceptance, it is also beneficial to set out any contingencies associated with role performance. "We plan to use you as a defensive specialist only. If you cannot or do not want to play this role, you will probably get very little playing time this year."

Both role clarity and role acceptance can be improved through an effective goal-setting program. Goal setting serves four important functions: it directs the individual's attention and actions toward appropriate behaviors, it motivates the individual to develop strategies to achieve the goal; it contributes to increased interest in the activity; and it leads to prolonged effort (Carron, 1984a). All of these contribute to role clarity and acceptance. (See Chapter 10, "Goal Setting for Peak Performance," for specific guidelines on how to set effective goals.)

Role acceptance is also enhanced when the coach minimizes the status differences among roles. Thus, the success of the total team and the importance of all roles for team success should be continually emphasized. When all group members perceive that their responsibilities are important and make a contribution to the common good, they more willingly accept and carry them out.

Establishing positive group norms (standards) is extremely important in sport teams — particularly if an inappropriate norm is in operation. One technique that has been used successfully is to enlist the formal and informal leaders of the group as active agents. If group leaders (in addition to the coach) accept and adhere to specific standards, other group members soon follow.

In some instances, the group leaders may be resistant to change. This poses a problem because on sport teams, the formal and informal leaders are usually the most highly skilled. If this is the case, the coach must decide how important the new standard is to the long-term success of the organization. In the event that the new standard is considered to be very important, the coach may have to release the resistant team members.

Zander (1982) has discussed a number of other methods for establishing and enforcing group standards. Some of the proposals advanced by Zander for the group leader (or coach in this case) include the following:

- Show individual team members how the group's standards can contribute to the achievement of desirable qualities in the team, more effective team performance, and a greater sense of team unity.
- Point out to all team members how their contributions toward developing and maintaining the standards can contribute to the team's success.
- Develop a method of assessing whether there is adherence to the group's standards, and then reward those team members who do adhere and sanction those who do not.

The coach as a leader obviously has significant input into any standards adopted by the team. However, whenever possible, he or she should give the team an opportunity to participate in decision making. Group members adhere best to those decisions in which they have had input.

THE DYNAMICS OF THE GROUP

Groups are dynamic, not static, in nature. They exhibit life and vitality, interaction, and activity. The vitality may be reflected in many ways — some positive, others negative. For example, at different times, the group and its members may be in harmony; at other times, conflict and tension may predominate. Or, in some instances, communication may be excellent between leaders and members, but in others, it may be nonexistent. As a final example, commitment to the group's goals and purposes may vary sharply. In this section, we discuss cohesiveness, one of the dynamic aspects of group life, and outline techniques for enhancing it in sport teams.

Cohesiveness has been defined as the "dynamic process which is reflected in the tendency for a group to stick together and remain united in the pursuit of its goals and objectives" (Carron, 1982, p. 124). The reference to *dynamic* in this definition is an acknowledgment that the way individual group members feel about one another and about the group and its goals changes with time and experience. Generally, the longer groups stay together, the stronger their bonding becomes. But cohesiveness is not static; it develops and then declines slightly, develops again, and then declines throughout the course of a group's existence.

Properties Associated with Cohesiveness

A number of important group properties are associated with group cohesiveness. One of these is *communication.* Quite simply, the level of communication relating to task and social issues increases as the group becomes more cohesive. Group members are more open with one another, they volunteer more, they talk more, and they listen better. In short, the exchange of task information and social pleasantries increases with cohesiveness.

There is also greater *conformity* to group standards for behavior and performance in cohesive groups. Recently formed groups have minimal influence over their members. But as the group develops and becomes more cohesive, adherence to explicit norms for behavior ("Practice starts at 4:30") as well as implicit norms ("Everyone will arrive on the field by 4:15") increases. Failure to conform can lead to different sanctions or types of punishment. For example, the group can control the amount of interaction it permits members, their degree of involvement in decision making, and their accessibility to task and social rewards. Controlling the opportu-

nity to interact and to influence the group is probably the most powerful
sanction the group possesses. As a group increases in cohesiveness, its
members place increasing value on social approval and the opportunities to
interact with other group members. Therefore, they show an increasing
tendency to adhere to the group norms and to give way to the group
influence — even if that influence is directed toward the performance of
deviant behavior (such as was the case in the Manson killings) or the
maintenance of an inappropriately low work quota (i.e., a low norm for
productivity).

The *perception* the group has about itself and about other groups and/or
nongroup members also becomes distorted with increased group cohesiveness. On the one hand, the group tends to be very favorable in its perception
of its own members and to overvalue its own contributions, importance,
and performance. On the other hand, the group undervalues the contributions, importance, and performance of other groups or nongroup members.
Jewell and Reitz (1981) have pointed out that this turning inward can lead
to some difficulties for a new formally appointed leader. The new leader will
not be readily accepted, and any proposed changes to existing practices will
be met with resistance.

This situation is often encountered in sport when a new coach replaces
a highly popular, highly successful predecessor. The group makes constant
comparisons between the two leaders' personalities, methods, and so on.
And because a cohesive group tends to overvalue its own membership and
undervalue outsiders, the new coach will encounter initial difficulties in
being accepted.

Another property associated with cohesiveness is *productivity*. Traditionally it has been assumed that there is a direct, positive relationship
between the two; as cohesiveness increases, productivity increases. Research in management science, psychology, and sport, however, has shown
that the picture is not quite that simple. For example, when R. M. Stogdill
(1972) reviewed studies that had been carried out with a variety of different
groups, he found that cohesiveness was positively related to performance in
12, negatively related in 11, and unrelated to performance in 11. According
to Stogdill, the key factor that influences the relationship between cohesion
and performance is the group's norm for productivity (see Table 6.1). If
group cohesiveness is high and the norm for productivity is high, performance will be positively affected (number 1). Conversely, if cohesion is high
and the norm for productivity is low (number 4), performance will be low or
negatively affected. When cohesiveness is low, groups with a high norm
(number 2) will outperform groups with a low norm (number 3).

Carron and Chelladurai (1981) have suggested that the nature of the
sport task is also an important factor. In sports where individuals perform
alone and a team score is obtained by using the individual scores in some

TABLE 6.1
The Interactive Effects of Group Cohesiveness and the Group Norm for Productivity on Individual and Group Performance

		GROUP COHESION	
		HIGH	LOW
GROUP NORM FOR PRODUCTIVITY	HIGH	Best performance (1)	Intermediate performance (2)
	LOW	Worst performance (4)	Intermediate performance (3)

additive fashion (e.g., swimming, track and field, golf), cohesiveness is less important for performance than is the case in interactive sports (e.g., basketball, hockey). The rationale, of course, is that cohesiveness is a group property and, therefore, will have its most significant impact on performance when the group's task requires active cooperation among team members.

Enhancing Group Dynamics

Previously we pointed out that groups are dynamic, not static, that they exhibit life and vitality, interaction and activity. One important implication of this is that they are, therefore, subject to change, to growth, to modification, and to improvement. And the coach is probably in the best position to influence change in a positive direction.

Yukelson (1984), in a discussion of group motivation, has presented nine effective ways to enhance coach–athlete communication systems and team harmony:

- Open communication channels by providing opportunities for athlete input. Communication is a group process, and mutual trust and respect are essential in order to keep the channels open.
- Develop pride and a sense of collective identity within the group by setting out realistic team, individual, and subunit goals. Feelings of pride and satisfaction develop when individuals and groups attain challenging but realistic goals.
- Strive for common expectations on what types of behavior are appropriate. "An organizational philosophy should specify not only the desired objectives the group is striving to achieve but also the strat-

egy, operating procedures, or means to reach these goals as well" (pp. 236–237).

- Value unique personal contributions by emphasizing the importance of each of the roles that are necessary for group performance.
- Recognize excellence by rewarding exceptional individual performance. If realistic objectives are set out and each individual clearly understands his or her role, the outstanding execution of that role should be recognized to enhance feelings of pride and commitment in the group and its members.
- Strive for consensus and commitment by involving the total team in goal-setting activities.
- Use periodic team meetings to resolve conflicts. Many explosive situations can be resolved by encouraging open communication within the team.
- Stay in touch with the formal and informal leaders in the team. The team members with high prestige and status are not only a barometer for assessing the group's attitudes and feelings, they are also effective agents for implementing necessary changes.
- Focus on success before discussing any failures. A positive group climate is developed if the positive nature of group and individual performance is highlighted before errors and omissions are discussed.

Carron (1984b) has suggested some other practical methods to enhance group cohesiveness:

- Avoid an excessively difficult schedule early in a season if at all possible. Failure has been shown to reduce group cohesiveness, the pride individual members have in their group, and their commitment to the group's goals and activities.
- Encourage the development of a group identity through team jackets, social functions, and initiation practices.
- Avoid excessive personnel turnover to the extent that this is compatible with eligibility requirements and group needs. There is a strong correlation between team stability and group cohesiveness.
- Rotate roommate assignments and dining table placements to avoid the development of cliques. Whenever possible, provide for opportunities in which interaction among diverse cliques becomes inevitable.

Athletic teams are a special type of group. Coaches can help their teams become more effective groups by drawing upon the wealth of research information that has been developed over a number of years in management science, social psychology, sociology, and physical education. Given the influence that groups have on their members, a knowledge of group structure and group dynamics is essential for coaches. Gaining an understanding of the nature of group structures and group dynamics will provide an excellent base from which to weld athletes into a more effective team.

SUMMARY

This chapter has focused on the factors that contribute to the development of the sport team into an effective group. The important features of a group are that its members have a collective identity, a sense of shared purpose, structured patterns of interaction, structured methods of communication, personal and task interdependence, and interpersonal attraction. These features can be improved. Some techniques used to develop a stronger team concept are to place members in closer physical proximity, to highlight the distinctiveness of the group, and to emphasize group rather than individual goals.

Groups develop specific structural characteristics, including roles and norms. Group roles can be formal or informal, but the important considerations from a coach's perspective are to ensure that team members understand their specific roles (role clarity), are satisfied with them (role acceptance), and strive to carry them out (role performance). There are two types of norms: task relevant and task irrelevant. Coaches can use a number of techniques to enhance these two important structural properties.

Cohesiveness is a dynamic process that contributes to group development, group maintenance, and a number of other important group properties, including communication, conformity, intragroup perceptions, and productivity. Coaches can use a number of techniques to enhance cohesiveness and group dynamics in general.

REFERENCES

Bugliosi, V., & Gentry, C. (1974). *Helter skelter: The true story of the Manson murders.* New York: W. W. Norton.

Carron, A. V. (1980). *Social psychology of sport.* Ithaca, N.Y.: Mouvement Publications.

Carron, A. V. (1981). Processes of group interaction in sport teams. *Quest, 33,* 245–270.

Carron, A. V. (1982). Cohesiveness in sport groups. Interpretations and considerations. *Journal of Sport Psychology, 4,* 123–138.

Carron, A. V. (1984a). *Motivation: Implications for coaching and teaching.* London, Ontario: Sports Dynamics.

Carron, A. V. (1984b). Cohesion in sport teams. In J. M. Silva and R. S. Weinberg (Eds.), *Psychological foundations of sport.* Champaign, Ill.: Human Kinetics.

Carron, A. V., & Chelladurai, P. (1981). Cohesion as a factor in sport performance. *International Review of Sport Sociology, 16,* 21–41.

Carron, A. V., & Grand, R. R. (1982). *Team climate questionnaire: Form B.* London, Ontario: Faculty of Physical Education, University of Western Ontario.

Grand, R. R., & Carron, A. V. (1982). Development of a team climate questionnaire. In L. M. Wankel and R. B. Wilbert (Eds.), *Psychology of sport and motor behavior: Research and practice.* Edmonton, Alberta: Department of Recreation and Leisure Studies, University of Alberta.

Jacobs, R. C., & Campbell, D. T. (1961). The perpetuation of an arbitrary tradition through several generations of a laboratory microculture. *Journal of Abnormal and Social Psychology, 62,* 649–658.

Jewell, L. N., & Reitz, H. J. (1981). *Group effectiveness in organizations.* Glenview, Ill.: Scott, Foresman and Company.

Mabry, E. A., & Barnes, R. E. (1980). *The dynamics of small group communication.* Englewood Cliffs, N.J.: Prentice-Hall.

Merton, R. K. (1957). *Social theory and social structure* (rev. ed.). New York: The Free Press.

McCallum, J. (1982). Faith, hope and Tony C. *Sports Illustrated, 57,* 58–72.

Schriesheim, J. F. (1980). The social context of leader–subordinate relations: An investigation of the effects of group cohesiveness. *Journal of Applied Psychology, 65,* 183–194.

Shaw, M. E. (1981). *Group dynamics: The psychology of small group behavior* (3rd. ed.). New York: McGraw-Hill.

Stogdill, R. M. (1972). Group productivity, drive, and cohesiveness. *Organizational Behavior and Human Performance, 8,* 26–43.

Yukelson, D. P. (1984). Group motivation in sport teams. In J. M. Silva and R. S. Weinberg (Eds.), *Psychological foundations of sport.* Champaign, Ill.: Human Kinetics.

Zander, A. (1982). *Making groups effective.* San Francisco: Jossey-Bass.

APPENDIX

TEAM CLIMATE QUESTIONNAIRE: FORM B*

The Team Climate Questionnaire is designed to measure some important group constructs within athletic teams. Specifically these constructs are role clarity, role acceptance, and perceived role performance.

Role clarity, the cognitive component of role involvement, reflects the degree to which there is a knowledge and understanding among team members insofar as performance expectations, responsibilities, and assignments are concerned. Thus, for example, the responsibilities associated with carrying out the team's offense and defense are clearly understood by team members generally.

The second construct, role acceptance, reflects the affective component of role involvement—the approval and satisfaction associated with the assigned role. Thus, for example, there could be general understanding within the team concerning assigned roles but a general dissatisfaction with the assignments. Satisfaction, of course, represents role acceptance.

Perceived role performance taps the behavioral domain of role involvement—the degree to which the team in general holds the perception that assigned responsibilities are being carried out.

Questionnaire

The questionnaire is made up of 30 items—10 in each of the 3 scales. The subjects are required to respond to the 30 statements about the team on a 7-point scale which is anchored at the two extremes by "strongly disagree" and "strongly agree." The score on any specific scale is computed by obtaining the mean response for a subject from the 10 pertinent items. A representative score for the total team is then derived by determining the mean response for all subjects tested from the group.

Scoring Key

For *role clarity*, items 1, 7, 10, 13, 19, 22, 25, 28 are scored from strongly agree = 7 to strongly disagree = 1. Items 4 and 16 are scored from strongly agree = 1 to strongly disagree = 7.

For *role acceptance*, items 3, 6, 9, 12, 15, 18, 24, 30 are scored from strongly agree = 7 to strongly disagree = 1. Items 21 and 27 are scored from strongly disagree = 7 to strongly agree = 1.

* Carron & Grand, 1982. Used with permission.

For *perceived role performance,* items 2, 5, 11, 14, 17, 23, 26, 29 are scored from strongly agree = 7 to strongly disagree = 1. Items 8 and 20 are scores from strongly disagree = 7 to strongly agree = 1.

All teams differ in the degree to which different team members understand their assignments and responsibilities, carry them out, mesh as a unit, and so on. The following questions are designed to assess your perceptions of the team you are on. There are no right or wrong answers. Some of the questions may seem repetitive but please answer all questions.

Circle a number from 1 to 7 to indicate your level of agreement with each of the statements. The scale used is

Strongly disagree					Strongly agree	
1	2	3	4	5	6	7

1. As a team, we understand our offensive assignments.		1	2	3	4	5	6	7
2. As a team, we try to change the way we play to satisfy the coach.		1	2	3	4	5	6	7
3. The talent is put to good use on this team.		1	2	3	4	5	6	7
4. The team is uncertain about what is expected of it during a game.		1	2	3	4	5	6	7
5. As a team, we carry out our game assignments.		1	2	3	4	5	6	7
6. As a team, we are satisfied with our coach's expectations of us.		1	2	3	4	5	6	7
7. As a team, we understand our defensive assignments.		1	2	3	4	5	6	7
8. As a team, we don't change the way we play to satisfy the coach.		1	2	3	4	5	6	7
9. As a team, we are satisfied with the input we have in team decisions.		1	2	3	4	5	6	7
10. As a team, we can get answers from our coach if we are not sure what to do.		1	2	3	4	5	6	7
11. As a team, we try to conform to rules relating to behavior away from the field.		1	2	3	4	5	6	7
12. Team members are satisfied with their role on this team.		1	2	3	4	5	6	7

13. As a team, we all understand how our
    role fits into the overall team plan.   1   2   3   4   5   6   7

14. As a team, we all try to play according
    to the team's system or style.   1   2   3   4   5   6   7

15. As a team, we are all satisfied with the
    opportunities to exert leadership.   1   2   3   4   5   6   7

16. As a team, we receive conflicting advice
    or instructions from our coach.   1   2   3   4   5   6   7

17. As a team, we all carry out our game
    assignments.   1   2   3   4   5   6   7

18. As a team, we are all satisfied with our
    offensive responsibilities.   1   2   3   4   5   6   7

19. As a team, we know what is expected of
    us away from practice and game situa-
    tions.   1   2   3   4   5   6   7

20. The team does what it wants rather
    than what the coach expects.   1   2   3   4   5   6   7

21. On the team, there is dissatisfaction
    with many of the game assignments.   1   2   3   4   5   6   7

22. As a team, we are told regularly how we
    are doing our job.   1   2   3   4   5   6   7

23. Team members try to carry out the roles
    they are assigned.   1   2   3   4   5   6   7

24. Team members are satisfied with their
    defensive responsibilities.   1   2   3   4   5   6   7

25. Team members understand their re-
    sponsibilities during the game.   1   2   3   4   5   6   7

26. As a team, we try to go along with team
    decisions.   1   2   3   4   5   6   7

27. As a team, we are dissatisfied with our
    assignments.   1   2   3   4   5   6   7

28. As a team, we know if our performance
    is acceptable to the coach.   1   2   3   4   5   6   7

29. The team sticks to our system during a
    game.   1   2   3   4   5   6   7

30. Team members are satisfied with the
    team's offensive and defensive systems.   1   2   3   4   5   6   7

7 Leadership Effectiveness

MIMI C. MURRAY

Springfield College

The study of leadership has been a dominant concern of social scientists and behavioral psychologists for many decades. Stogdill (1974) provides more than 3000 references to the topic of leadership. Nevertheless, there still appears to be no generally accepted definition of leadership. Burns (1978), author of *Leadership*, a Pulitzer Prize-winning book, observed that leadership is one of the least understood phenomena on earth. Yet the search for qualities that lead to successful leadership is a search that occupies the attention of numerous investigators. Unfortunately, there is a paucity of research and conceptual literature about leadership in sport situations even though coaching requires one to be a leader.

When people are asked, "Who is a leader?" many respond by naming politicians such as presidents, senators, governors, or mayors. Others name military leaders such as Patton, Napoleon, and Alexander the Great or business leaders of whom the most prominent of late seems to be Iacocca. Successful coaches such as Lombardi, Bryant, Shula, Landry, Stengel, Durocher, Lasorda, Auerback, and Wooden are frequently included in the lists. Because coaches are leaders, coaching effectiveness can be maximized through understanding the concepts of leadership.

Sport psychologists also serve in a leadership capacity, although from a different perspective than that of coaches. Thus, although this chapter is often written in the lexicon of the coach, and may initially appear to be aimed exclusively at the coach, such is far from the case. Knowledge of the basic principles of leadership presented in this chapter will help sport psychologists deal more effectively with athletes; it will also help them to more fully understand effective coach–athlete communications and help coaches to become more effective leaders.

This chapter describes several approaches to leadership and attempts to relate these theoretical frameworks to dimensions of leader behavior in sports.

WHAT IS LEADERSHIP?

Some authorities (Stogdill, 1974; Barrow, 1977) define leadership as the behavioral process of influencing the activities of an organized group toward specific goals and the achievement of those goals. Others simply define leadership as the process whereby an individual influences others to do what he or she wants them to do. This is a seemingly simplistic concept, however, since leadership is often far more complex. Attempts to understand leadership should also be concerned with why people comply rather than just how one person influences another.

Schein (1970) suggested that people comply because of a psychological contract. This theory implies that individuals will do many things because they believe they should, and for what they do, they expect reciprocation in the form of remuneration, perks, and privileges. Coaches and sport psychologists need to be aware of the rewards or reinforcements their athletes expect. The athlete who complies with the wishes or demands of the leader might expect to win, to be positively reinforced, to get to play, and/or to receive a higher status. In essence, the cost-benefit ratio needs to balance. Consequently, both the leader and the athlete strike a bargain or a psychological contract with each other and with the team. Whether or not an athlete complies may be somewhat dependent on how she or he views authority. Individuals have learned to respond to authority through their experiences with parents, teachers, coaches, and other authority figures. Indirectly, individuals also learn how to respond to authority through the modeling portrayed in books, magazines, TV, and the movies. Legitimate power is often granted to coaches and sport psychologists when athletes feel it is right for these people to tell them what to do. In a later section of this chapter, we will discuss ways in which leaders can increase their potential influence or power.

LEADERSHIP THEORIES AND IMPLICATIONS

Can theories be developed to help characterize the qualities and/or behaviors of effective leaders? Research on leadership theories has attempted to identify personal qualities and behaviors that are most likely to result in leader effectiveness and to determine what influence, if any, specific situational factors have on these variables. It was hoped that such knowledge could be used in both the selection and training of individuals who are likely to become effective leaders. Such research has resulted in testing trait, behavioral, and situational approaches to leadership theory.

Trait Approach

Assessing personality characteristics and traits to determine whether effective leaders have similar qualities is the same approach as one that was initially directed at trying to understand why certain people are successful athletes. The results of trait or factor theory studies as applied to athletes and coaches has left us without any conclusive results or information. No readily identifiable personality traits are related to leadership status or leadership effectiveness in *all* situations. A more viable explanation for effective leadership is that leadership qualities are situationally specific. Further, characteristics related to leadership do not operate separately but in combination. If we could begin to address these qualities or traits as dispositional, we might gain more valuable insights. *Dispositional* means that behavior associated with a given training can vary from situation to situation but individuals keep the same relative position regardless of the situation; that is, the most assertive individual will always respond with the highest level of assertiveness.

Research on dispositions associated with successful business executives indicates that these individuals are dominant, self-confident, assertive, high in levels of aspiration, and generally successful throughout life (Dunette, 1965). In 1971, Ghiselli found the following dispositions related to leader success as determined by upward mobility and rated job success: self-perceived intelligence, initiative, supervisory ability, and self-assurance. For more information on traits associated with successful leaders, refer to Stogdill (1974) for an excellent review.

The work of Hendry (1974) and Ogilvie and Tutko (1966) established the stereotype of the typical coach/physical educator as someone who needs to be in control and is inflexible, domineering, and emotionally inhibited. Sage (1975) did not concur with these findings, which seemingly indicate that coaches are highly authoritarian, dogmatic, and manipulative. Sage's reservations were based upon the small number of samples and the sampling techniques employed. Even if this questionable stereotype is correct, these dispositions may be necessary for successful leadership under many situations found in sport, such as stressful game situations. For example, during a 30-second time-out, the coach should be informing the athletes of the strategies to be used when the game resumes. This is obviously not the time for participatory or democratic decision making. Further, qualities such as authoritarianism, when present in coaches, may be only part of their sport personalities and are not necessarily present or apparent in other situations in their lives.

The authoritarian personality profile does merit further elaboration and understanding since it is a typical description of sport leadership — whether a false one or not. Authoritarians generally avoid unstructured situations because such situations are perceived as being threatening. The inability to cope with ambiguous situations may result from the authoritarian's continuing to utilize old responses for new stimulus conditions, even when these responses provide less than satisfactory results. Such inability could help to explain the "this is the way I was coached; it was good enough for me, and it is good enough for them" syndrome often found in coaching. Unfortunately, the practices of many coaches are often at odds with the most current sport knowledge in motor learning, sport psychology, exercise physiology, and biomechanics. Is it because many coaches cannot cope with change? This may also provide insight into why so many coaches can be threatened by insignificant social change such as longer hair styles for men a few years ago and, more currently, male athletes wearing an earring. Those male authoritarians who are most threatened by such social changes probably define their masculinity in and through sport. Thus, anything perceived as deviating from their masculine image, based upon their older, unchanged social values, would be abhorred by them.

Interestingly, research has shown authoritarian males to have lower moral reasoning, a higher need for social approval, impulsiveness in decision making, and greater frequency in making errors (Podd, 1972). Perhaps this is why some typically authoritarian coaches have been known to harass referees, humiliate players, and throw clipboards and chairs during a game. Can these behaviors be ethically justified and do they provide an appropriate leadership role model?

According to Triandis (1971), authoritarians typically avoid introspection, approve of severe punishment, and tend to hold strong prejudices. Could this help to explain why sport in some situations is still sexist and racist and sometimes filled with physical and psychological abuses for athletes? A more recent study of authoritarianism and associated attitudes sheds some light on the behavior of some male coaches and athletic directors in regard to females in sport. Males who were more concerned with winning at the expense of sportsmanship and who were also the highest in authoritarianism had negative attitudes about women, admired the traditional male roles, and were opposed to equality (Maier & Laurakis, 1981). You may be aware of a recent example of the foregoing type of behavior as portrayed in the remarks of Bobby Knight, Indiana basketball coach and U.S. coach for the 1984 Olympics. "I don't like people very well because most of them lack intestinal fortitude or they lack integrity. Women in particular bother me. I don't like women at all. I can't bear all the small talk and social amenities that women put you through."

In summary, the factor/trait approach to examining leadership has attempted to determine whether there is a universal personality for leadership success. This approach is also called the great person (man) theory of leadership. There are some common trends, but the overall results of this research have been quite equivocal. It appears that both situational and individual factors, and the interaction of these factors, are needed to determine who will emerge as a successful leader.

Situational Theories

Situational factors have a great effect on leadership success and leadership style in using certain approaches. Some situational factors that are important to leadership success are the characteristics of subordinates, the organizational situation, and the demands of the specific situation. Of particular interest to those of us in sport are the interactions of coaches and sport psychologists (leaders) with athletes (subordinates) in a specific situation.

Fiedler (1967), in his contingency model, argues that leadership style, the group, and the situation interact to affect group performance and satisfaction. Fiedler believes that a leader's style is a result of the leader's own needs and personality. He also suggests that leadership style is considered a stable personality characteristic that is well-established. According to him, the two classifications of leadership style are being people-centered or being task-centered. Fiedler proposed that if leadership style is not flexible and the organization is not productive, the organizational structure should be changed or the leader replaced. If one accepts Fiedler's theory, then leadership style is generalizable regardless of the situation.

The studies in sport using Fiedler's contingency approach have proved interesting. Danielson (1976) found that the most effective coaching in ice hockey was person-oriented (personal relations emphasized) rather than task-oriented. In a study involving volleyball, Bird (1977) found that winning women's volleyball coaches in the more skillful Division I programs were person-oriented. The results were the opposite in less skillful Division II programs.

There appear to be no direct and simple answers to such questions as, Is group effectiveness caused by how a leader behaves, or does the leader behave in a certain way because of the group's performance? It would be extremely difficult and unwise to assume any cause-effect relationships on the basis of the limited and somewhat contradictory research evidence available. Flexibility, which can be very disturbing for many authoritarians, would appear to be an ideal approach to coaching because of the variability of the situational nature of the sport milieu. Chelladurai reaches a similar conclusion in the following chapter when he discusses leadership style and decision making.

In *The Next American Frontier*, author Robert Reich's major emphasis is that traditional management in the United States is the greatest threat to American prosperity. Presently, management is bureaucratic, top-heavy, and authoritarian. Reich suggests we look at the management style in countries such as Japan, Germany, and France, which have the fastest-growing industries. The new *flexible* management systems in these countries focus on smaller work teams and employee problem solving. Can this information be applied to coaching? According to Maslow, the greatest leaders are those who are humble and flexible while also having the strength of character to make decisions that may not be popular (as cited in Sage, 1973).

Behavioral Theories

More recent research on leadership theory has focused upon actual leadership behaviors, or how a leader leads rather than what a leader is (trait). This approach examines the behavior of leaders as related to group effectiveness or the productivity and satisfaction of group members.

Research on behavioral theories has expended much effort on the influence the leader allows subordinates in decision making. From such research a classification system developed by which leaders were described as autocratic or dictatorial, participative or democratic, laissez-faire or free rein. Little attention will be given here to leadership styles because they are covered in Chapter 8.

The impetus for and concern with leadership behaviors was first initiated in business management areas, as was the factor/trait approach to studying leadership. The majority of earlier studies (1940s and 1950s) were conducted by researchers at Ohio State University. From these studies, two leader behavior characteristics related to group effectiveness emerged. The first was consideration, and the second was initiating structure. Consideration reflects job relationships in which there is mutual trust, respect for others' ideas, and attention to others' feelings. Leaders who scored high in consideration had good rapport and communication with others. Initiating structure refers to how leaders define and structure their roles for goal attainment. Leaders who scored high in initiating structure were active in directing group activities, communicating, scheduling, and experimenting with new ideas. According to the Ohio State studies, successful leaders score high on both consideration and initiating structure.

After World War II, some interesting studies on organizational effectiveness were conducted at the University of Michigan. The Michigan studies described a leader as being either production-centered or employee-centered (Stogdill, 1974) but not both. These classifications are self-evident. Later studies have revealed that leaders can be *both* employee-centered and production-centered, and the most effective leaders tend to score high on both behaviors.

When these various behavioral theories were applied to sport, it was found that the behaviors of coaches most desired by athletes were competitive training, providing social support, and being rewarding (Chelladurai & Saleh, 1978). Massimo (1973), in asking a large number of gymnasts what were the behaviors they desired most in a coach, found desired behaviors were ordered in importance from use minimal verbiage, have a sense of humor, use individual psychology, and have technical competency, to appreciate the sociology of the team. I have used Massimo's statements and expanded upon them in the ways noted below. Although the desirable leadership behaviors were initially identified for coaches and have been expanded using the terminology of coaches, most of the behaviors are probably equally true for sport psychologists and their interactions with athletes.

1. *Use minimal verbiage.* Too many people overcoach. This may be due to an insecurity, to trying too hard, or simply to not knowing any better. An example of how to correct this is to select only one or two corrections for a group or an athlete to work on in each skill or effort. Once these corrections are selected, *briefly* verbalize the key analysis points for each correction and perhaps physically demonstrate the incorrect and correct movements. Then put the athletes in an appropriate drill.

2. *Have a sense of humor.* Although this behavior is desirable, one must be careful to not overuse humor. Sarcasm is not a desirable form of humor. Humor involves laughing at oneself and with others, not at another.

3. *Use individual psychology.* This implies dealing with each team member as an individual. Some athletes need considerable coaching and attention, and others can almost coach themselves. Fairness as a concept is something that athletes seem to get hung up on. There is no way in which a coach can appear to be completely fair. Some athletes will always get more of the coach's attention on a given day than will others. Perhaps if the team understands why the coach is giving more time to a certain athlete, other members will be more understanding. This involves good communication skills. All athletes have different needs, and the coach should attempt to determine those needs and, within her or his own philosophy, provide for them.

4. *Have technical competency.* Anyone who is willing to learn and cares enough to take the time to understand correct movement mechanics and strategies and fundamental principles of exercise physiology, motor learning, and psychology can effectively coach most sports. A person can acquire knowledge of a particular sport and factors influencing the learning process. This knowledge should not be equated with personal skill in performing. One can be a very effective coach and not be able personally to perform well, just as one can be an outstanding athlete and still not have the technical competencies and personal skills to be an effective coach.

5. *Appreciate the sociology of the team.* The coach not only must deal with the individuals on the team but also with how those individuals interact. This means that the coach should know what the team's "personality" is. The coach should not blow out of perspective minor animosities between

team members. If animosities go too far, then the coach should end them, diplomatically and emphatically.

HOW LEADERS CAN INCREASE THEIR INFLUENCE OR POWER

Power is the basis of followers complying with a leader's wishes. When a leader/coach is successful at influencing another person, the leader/coach has demonstrated power. In the influence process, this power is initiated and is the force that causes things to happen. Thus the utilization of power is leadership. Power comes partly from being in a position of authority. The coach by virtue of her or his position has control and is perceived as more valid than other members of the team. Consequently, the coach can exert a great deal of influence of either a positive or negative nature upon the behaviors of the team members. Although to a lesser extent, the same can be said of a sport psychologist assigned to work with a team.

What specific measures can leaders take to ensure greater influence or power other than that granted by virtue of position? Paying attention to appearance, demonstrating self-confidence and expertise, appropriately allocating rewards and sanctions, and being an example to admire and emulate are all ways in which coaches and sport psychologists can increase their potential influence.

Appearance: First Impression

Visualize Tom Landry, the perennially successful coach of the Dallas Cowboys. What were your first impressions of this great coach? He is always well-groomed, dressed in a tie and jacket at games; he appears to be fit; he seems to be in complete control of himself and his team regardless of the circumstances or intensity of the situation. At the other extreme, what are your impressions of the coach who never changes from a practice warm-up jacket and shirt, is overweight and out of shape, smokes on the sidelines, shouts obscenities at athletes and officials, and appears to be gearing up for a volcanic explosion in tense and close situations?

You may want to resist the initially "superficial" notion that appearance is or should be important in effective leadership, and yet it is. Often our first impressions of people are inadequate and distorted, yet these approximations are critical starting points for predicting influence and the quality of social interaction to follow. Certainly, there are and have been successful coaches whose appearance and behavior have been less than exemplary, but they are the exceptions.

Pat Head Summitt, women's basketball coach at the University of Tennessee and 1984 U.S. Olympic coach, is another example to be admired. Athletes' immediate impressions of her are that she is extremely well-groomed, dynamic, enthusiastic, intense, fit, and in total control. Because of these first impressions and the influence that emanates from them, she must be a formidable force against whom to recruit. The Rosenthal effect, or a self-fulfilling prophecy, can be initiated by the coach who looks and acts like a winner. That is, the coach who behaves like a winner is more likely to become a winner.

Referent Power

Referent power (French & Raven, 1959) is based upon the attraction exerted by an individual on another person or on a group. The stronger the attraction, the greater the power will be. The influence occurs because people identify with one another. Referent power is task specific and is more likely to occur when an individual demonstrates skill or competence at certain tasks or has expert power granted because of education, experience, and appearance. Shouldn't most coaches and sport psychologists have referent power?

Identification with a leader occurs when the leader possesses personal characteristics and qualities valued by the group or team such as appearance, demonstrated knowledge, and the ability to express the values and concerns of her or his followers.

Charisma

Some leaders receive loyalty and commitment because they possess the illusive quality called charisma. This kind of influence is unique to the leader and group and thus cannot be transferred to another person. Political history is punctuated by charismatic leaders: John F. Kennedy, Martin Luther King, Jr., Adolf Hitler, George Patton, Geraldine Ferraro, and Gloria Steinem are a few examples.

Who would be on your list of charismatic coaches? If these coaches retired or resigned, would those who follow in their positions exhibit the same charisma? Obviously not. Unfortunately, in many instances, the charismatic leader is the most difficult of all to replace. The most inappropriate and ineffective behavior for the new coach is to attempt to emulate or behave as the previous charismatic coach. Coaches need to develop and establish their own styles. How very different from one another are outstanding coaches from the past such as Lombardi, Bryant, Hayes, Auerbach, and Wooden. Each was a uniquely distinct individual as a coach. No one else could exactly duplicate their leadership style and charisma. We are all individuals, and our personalities differ greatly; therefore, we should not attempt to imitate someone else's behavior. Charisma cannot be copied; it is individually created.

Allocation of Rewards and Sanctions

If a leader can influence others, it is frequently because others depend upon her or him. As previously discussed, this influence can arise from psychological identification because the leader has the power to allocate rewards or sanctions. The rewards can be objective or subjective. For example, some professional and college coaches have the authority to provide objective rewards such as salaries, tuition, room and board, books, etc., as well as subjective rewards such as approval or disapproval. The majority of coaches deal with subjective rewards on a regular basis. They are not very tangible.

Some athletes are able to motivate themselves completely (internal motivation) whereas others need help from their peers, family, coach, and additional significant others (external motivation). The leader's role is much easier when he or she is involved with an athlete who is internally motivated. The leader's influence will be lessened if he or she does not appropriately motivate the athlete who needs external motivation. For example, when Jerry Kramer was asked how his coach, Vince Lombardi, motivated individual players, Kramer responded by saying that Lombardi knew who needed pats on the back, who needed to be kicked, and who needed various shades between the extremes. Lombardi had the ability to differentiate among the athletes and knew how to motivate each athlete properly and at the proper time (Kaplan, 1983). (See Chapters 2 and 3 for specific suggestions regarding effective motivation.)

Role Model: An Example to Follow

A coach must not expect any more from an athlete than what the coach is willing to give or be. Athletes will emulate the coach's behavior. This means that the coach should be committed to exemplifying as well as enforcing the rules for the players. For example, if there is a punctuality rule, then the coach should abide by it too.

Control of emotions is another expectation most coaches have for their athletes. This is a worthy expectation, for people cannot function maximally in terms of physical performance or interpersonal relations if they lose emotional control. Decision making, information processing, speed and coordination, objectivity, reasonableness, and the acuity of the senses are just a few of the factors that are adversely affected by loss of emotional control. If such negative consequences occur for the player who loses control, can similar negative consequences be assumed for the coach who loses control? Coaches who lose emotional control are not performing at their optimal level, and they are also presenting a negative role model. If coaches can misbehave on the sidelines, why can't athletes misbehave on the sidelines or lose their tempers while performing?

Planning and commitment are also behaviors coaches expect from their athletes. In his autobiography, Lee Iacocca, "Chrysler's savior," stresses over and over again that much of his managerial success is due to his own personal commitment to planning and his insistence that his employees also plan. Iacocca believes that the discipline of writing down one's goals is the first step toward making them happen.

Not only is goal setting appropriate and important for athletes, it is critical for coaches and sport psychologists. Setting goals is only the beginning. Goals also need to be evaluated, and progress in meeting goals needs to be appropriately reinforced. For example, Iacocca reviews and establishes goals on a quarterly basis. He feels it makes people accountable to themselves, while forcing leaders to reconsider their goals and not to lose sight of their dreams. Iacocca's quarterly review is a contract between a leader and follower and is signed by each. (For more detailed information on how to set effective goals and what strategies help to achieve these goals, see Chapter 10.)

Goals can be used to plan athletic practices down to the smallest detail. Such practices are extremely positive ways in which a coach or sport psychologist can facilitate teaching and learning. During games, Bear Bryant carried reminders on a piece of paper. Among the things that he had written down were "Don't forget — use time-outs intelligently — double time-out — run clock down last play — ORDERLY BENCH."

In summary, having an appropriate appearance, exhibiting conduct that exemplifies the behavior expected from athletes, balancing the cost-benefit reinforcement ratio for complying with the leader's wishes, and complete planning and goal setting are specific behaviors all leaders can use to improve their credibility and influence. Improvement in any of these areas can potentially increase one's effectiveness as a leader.

DEVELOPING LEADERSHIP WITHIN THE TEAM

In terms of identifying leaders within a team, a coach should be attuned to functional leadership that arises spontaneously in a climate of trust. Such a climate is present when coaches accept the uniqueness of each team member, including what might appear as deviant behavior, provided this behavior does not have a negative impact on the effectiveness of the team or the satisfaction of its members. Leadership within a team should go to the most competent. Natural leaders will usually surface if there is a climate of acceptance and if athletes are encouraged to provide input and leadership. A coach can help certain athletes in demonstrating or developing their leadership abilities by giving those individuals responsibilities, small at first, and then reinforcing positively their successful attempts at leadership.

Human relations within a team can be improved if everyone is aware of expectations, if the rules and regulations are clearly stated, if team procedures are well written and available, and if responsibilities that do not overlap are clearly defined. Following are some suggestions for building effective team leaders:

1. Identify potential leaders and provide opportunities for leadership within the team.
2. Use these athlete leaders, as well as leaders such as athletic trainers, managers, and assistant coaches, wisely by delegating authority and responsibility to them.
3. Deal with all athletes and assistant leaders as individuals.
4. Keep communication open and direct rather than having team leaders serve as a "buffer" between the coach and other athletes.

CONCLUSION

Coaches play a very significant role in the skill and personal development of their athletes. Consequently their influence, power, and effect cannot be negated! Being a good leader involves an appreciation of leadership theory and knowledge of how a coach can maximize influence and followership through positive role modeling, planning, preparation, and being true to oneself. Coaches must accept their athletes' as well as their own individuality. Coaches who fail miserably are often those who attempt to imitate or emulate other coaches. With insight, knowledge, and sensitivity toward individual differences, all coaches can be successful.

In leadership theory as well as coaching experience, it is evident that there are specific implications of what the coach as a leader should do:

1. Master and apply current knowledge in regard to sport physiology, psychology, and biomechanics.
2. Develop interpersonal skills including the communication skills of speaking, writing, observing, understanding defensive mechanisms, motivating, and listening. Of all the communication skills, coaches are generally the weakest at listening. Interpersonal interactions are critical to sport success, and communication is the key (Mancini & Agnew, 1978).
3. Eliminate all sexist, racist, and dehumanizing language.

4. Eliminate any attitude that involves the humiliation of losers and the glorification of winners.
5. Encourage the athletes, and oneself, to view the opponent as a challenge and not an enemy.
6. Understand the effects of social reinforcement on individual performance.
7. Control one's own arousal level and be an example of the ideal emotionality perceived for successful performance.
8. Help the athletes set their *own* goals. Emphasize the process (participation and playing as well as possible) and not the outcome goal (winning). This is an important concept because goals should be something that an individual can accomplish or control. An athlete can control her or his own performance but not an opponent's.
9. Live in the present. Do not constantly remind athletes of former winners or of the potential for team success two years hence.
10. Provide opportunities for success through the provision for good practices, good game conditions, sensible scheduling, and a pleasant atmosphere. The administrative aspects of a coach's job cannot be overlooked. Planning, preparation, and budgeting are important functions that affect leadership performance. A coach must be a teacher, a leader, and an administrator.
11. Be rational and humanistic.

There seems to be a new concern for the human aspects in sport. Fortunately, athletes are increasingly portrayed as people and are losing, somewhat, their superhero status. John Naisbitt (1984), in his bestseller *Megatrends*, reminds us of the massive social changes we are constantly being bombarded with and that, with increases in technology, we must not forget the importance of personal touches—hitech/hitouch. Bear Bryant was indeed a rare coach for he was able to change with the times. He was "the only one of his generation to coach as successfully in an era when football players use hair dryers in the locker room as he did when they wore crew cuts" (Phillips, 1980, p. 70). As coaches and sport psychologists, we should commit to leadership in sport that is dedicated to the ethics and morality of positive growth for all athletes.

REFERENCES

Barrow, J. C. (1977). The variables of leadership: A review and conceptual framework. *Academy of Management Review, 2,* 231–251.

Bird, A. (1977). Team structure and success as related to cohesiveness and leadership. *Journal of Social Psychology, 103,* 217–233.

Burns, J. M. (1978). *Leadership.* New York: Harper & Row.

Chelladurai, P., & Saleh, S. (1978). Preferred leadership in sport. *Canadian Journal of Applied Sport Sciences, 3,* 85–97.

Danielson, R. (1976). Contingency model of leadership effectiveness: For empirical investigation of its application in sport. Motor learning, sport psychology, pedagogy and didactics of physical activity, *Monograph 5.* Quebec City, Canada.

Dunette, M. (1965). *Personnel selection and placement.* Belmont, Calif.: Wadsworth.

Fiedler, F. (1967). *A theory of leadership effectiveness.* New York: McGraw-Hill.

French, J., & Raven, B. (1959). The bases of social power. In D. Cartwright (Ed.), *Studies in social power.* Ann Arbor: Research Center for Group Dynamics, University of Michigan.

Ghiselli, E. (1971). *Explorations in managerial talent.* Santa Monica, Calif.: Goodyear.

Hendry, L. (1968). Assessment of personality traits in the coach–athlete relationship. *Research Quarterly, 39,* 543–551.

Hendry, L. (1974). Human factors in sport systems. *Human Factors, 16,* 528–544.

Iacocca, L., with Novak, W. (1984). *Iacocca.* New York: Bantam.

Kaplan, E. (1983, January 30). The legend of Vince Lombardi. *Family Weekly.*

Maier, R., & Laurakis, D. (1981). Some personality correlates of attitudes about sports. *International Journal of Sport Psychology, 12,* 19–22.

Mancini, V., & Agnew, M. (1978). An analysis of teaching and coaching behaviors. In W. Straub (Ed.), *Sport psychology: An analysis of athlete behavior.* Ithaca, N.Y.: Mouvement Publications.

Massimo, J. (1973). A psychologist's approach to sport. Presentation to New England Gymnastic Clinic, Newton, Mass.

Naisbitt, J. (1984). *Megatrends.* New York: Warner Books.

Ogilvie, B., & Tutko, T. (1966). *Problem athletes and how to handle them.* New York: Pelham Books.

Phillips, B. (1980, September 29). Football's supercoach. *Time.*

Podd, M. (1972). Ego identity status and morality: The relationship between two developmental contracts. *Developmental Psychology, 6,* 497–507.

Reich, R. (1983). *The next American frontier.* New York: Times Books.

Sage, G. H. (1973). The coach as management: Organizational leadership in American sport. *Quest, 19,* 35–40.

Sage, G. (1975). An occupational analysis of the college coach. In D. Ball & L. Loy (Eds.), *Sport and social order.* Reading, Mass.: Addison-Wesley.

Schein, E. (1970). *Organization psychology.* New York: Prentice-Hall.

Stogdill, R. (1974). *Handbook of leadership: A survey of theory and research.* New York: The Free Press.

Triandis, H. C. (1971). *Attitude and attitude change.* New York: John Wiley & Sons.

8 Styles of Decision Making in Coaching

P. CHELLADURAI

University of Western Ontario

All of the various activities carried out by a coach involve decision making, which is defined as the process of selecting an alternative from among many choices to achieve a desired end. For example, the coach has to decide what performance goals to pursue, what activities or programs will lead to the attainment of those goals, who of the available athletes should be selected, what should be the assignments for the selected athletes, and what are ways of motivating the athletes. In addition to these fundamental concerns, the coach needs to make decisions about practice and tournament schedules, travel arrangements and uniform selection, and other routine matters. Every one of the coach's decisions has a strong impact on the team and its performance. Thus, as has been said of management, coaching is, in essence, the art and science of decision making.

Apart from the concern with making good decisions, the coach is also faced with the question of how much participation in decision making he or she should allow the members of the team. This is an important concern since member participation may ensure that good decisions will be made and, at the same time, enhance the motivation of the athletes. Insofar as the coach has sole authority over the degree and manner of members' participation, he or she must have a clear grasp of the advantages and disadvantages of such participation and the conditions under which the participation will be most fruitful. This chapter focuses on this specific issue and discusses theory and research on the topic. But, first, the process of decision making must be isolated from factors that confound the issue. Three confounding factors in the coaching context are leader's personality, leader's mannerisms, and the substance of a decision.

DECISION MAKING AND PERSONALITY

The issue of decision styles in coaching has been clouded by the exclusive focus on the personality of the coach. For instance, a number of authors have suggested that coaches, influenced by their personality, tend to be either autocratic or democratic in all instances without reference to the nature of the problems facing them. In contrast, recent theorists suggest that instead of labeling coaches as autocratic or democratic, we should be analyzing the problem situation and designating it as calling for an autocratic or democratic decision-making style.

DECISION MAKING AND LEADERS' MANNERISMS

One also must guard against confusing the coach's mannerisms and affectations with his or her decision style. For instance, consider a football coach who presents his playbook for the season to the quarterback with the apparently menacing command: "This is your bible. You better master it." In contrast, another coach may present his playbook with a smile and the comment: "Here is the playbook I drew up during the summer. You may get a kick out of reading it." The obvious difference in their mannerisms should not be allowed to mask the fact that both coaches autocratically decided on the plays.

STYLE AND SUBSTANCE OF DECISIONS

An important issue regarding leadership style is that the "style" of decision making has been confounded with the "substance" of the decision. For instance, in Fiedler's (1967) contingency model of leadership effectiveness, a leader is deemed to be either task oriented or relations oriented. In addition, the task-oriented leader is regarded as being relatively more autocratic and the relations-oriented leader as relatively more democratic.

Recently, however, there has been an attempt to separate the decision style of the leader from other leadership behaviors. To illustrate, five dimensions of leader behavior in coaching are identified and described in Table 8.1. Of these, training and instruction and positive feedback relate more directly to the task and its performance whereas social support relates to the personal needs of the athletes. The remaining two dimensions refer to the social process of decision making. It has been found that experienced male athletes prefer more autocratic behavior and at the same time more social support than less experienced athletes (Chelladurai & Carron, 1982). The point is that in earlier leadership theories an autocratic style of decision making and socially supportive behavior were deemed to be negatively related, but recent theories and research indicate that these dimensions of leader behavior are independent of each other.

TABLE 8.1
Leader Behavior Dimensions in Sports

Dimension	Description
Training and instruction behavior	Behavior of the coach aimed at improving the performance of the athletes by emphasizing and facilitating hard and strenuous training; by instructing them in the skills, techniques, and tactics of the sport; by clarifying the relationship among the members; and by structuring and coordinating the activities of the members.
Democratic behavior	Behavior of the coach which allows greater participation by the athletes in decisions pertaining to group goals, practice methods, and game tactics and strategies.
Autocratic behavior	Behavior of the coach which involves independence in decision making and which stresses personal authority.
Social support behavior	Behavior of the coach characterized by a concern for individual athletes, for their welfare, for positive group atmosphere, and for warm interpersonal relations with members.
Rewarding (positive feedback) behavior	Behavior of the coach which includes providing reinforcements for an athlete by recognizing and rewarding good performance.

Source: Chelladurai & Saleh (1980).

DECISION-MAKING PROCESSES

Decision making as a significant component of leadership has been viewed from two perspectives: as a cognitive process and as a social process.

Decision Making as a Cognitive Process

The emphasis in decision making as a cognitive process is on the rationality of the decision. That is, the concern is with evaluating the available alternatives and selecting the best one to achieve a desired end. Decision makers can arrive at rational decisions only after defining the problem clearly, identifying relevant constraints, generating possible and plausible alternatives, evaluating and ranking the alternatives according to some selected criterion, and then selecting the best alternative in terms of some prespecified criterion. In this view, generating alternatives and evaluating them become crucial to decision making. Thus, the focus here is on the objective and optimal use of available information.

Decision Making as a Social Process

In the context of coaching, the social process refers to the degree to which members of the team are allowed to participate in decision making and the varying degrees of influence the members have on the decisions. Thus, the social process of decision making may vary from strictly autocratic decision making by the coach to varying degrees of participation by members (e.g., consultation with one or a few members, consultation with all members, group decision making, and delegation). These variations have been called the *decision styles* of the coach (Chelladurai & Haggerty, 1978).

PARTICIPATIVE DECISION MAKING

Before discussing the theory and research concerning decision styles in coaching, we will first consider the advantages and disadvantages of team members' participation in decision making.

Advantages

Participation by athletes in decision making beneficially affects the team and its performance in three specific ways. First, such participation enhances the rationality of the decision insofar as there is more information available in a group to generate and evaluate alternate pathways to a goal. Thus, the "quality" of the decision is ensured. Second, once a participative decision is made, the members feel that it is their own decision, and such feelings of ownership result in proper and efficient execution of the decision. Member participation increases the "acceptance" of the decision. Finally, participation in decision making is said to contribute to the personal growth of the members by facilitating their feelings of self-worth and self-confidence. This humanistic point of view has led several theorists to emphasize increased participation by members. In the athletic context, Sage (1973) advised that coaches should become more aware of the needs of their athletes and should allow greater participation in deciding on team membership, practice methods, team strategy, and so forth.

Disadvantages

Three notable disadvantages are associated with participative decision making. First, participative decisions are time consuming. Anyone who has ever served on a committee has experienced tangential discussions and arguments over trivial issues.

A second disadvantage is that groups are relatively less effective in solving complex problems that require the decision maker(s) to keep a number of factors in perspective and to think through a series of steps and procedures that link all the relevant factors. Under such circumstances, the group is less likely to make an optimal decision than the best member in the group.

Kelley and Thibaut (1969) provided a good example of the contrast between a simple and complex problem: the solution of a crossword puzzle versus the construction of a crossword puzzle. The solution of a crossword puzzle is a relatively simple problem in which the group will be more proficient than individual members. This is so because the group can generate a greater number of alternatives, each of which can easily be judged as correct or incorrect according to the criteria provided. Furthermore, one need not be concerned with all of the words in the puzzle at the same time. On the other hand, the construction of a crossword puzzle is more complex because the whole set of words and associated criteria must be kept in perspective and linked in a coherent and logical manner. According to Kelley and Thibaut (1969), the best individual in the group is likely to be more efficient than the group as a whole in this type of task.

A sport specific example of the same concept would be to involve the defensive football squad in identifying why they are having trouble defending against a specific offensive pattern and then to have them follow up by planning what kind of practice is needed to correct the weakness. This relatively simple problem could easily be resolved by means of participative decision making. The decision would probably result in much more effective action by the players in resolving the problem than if the coach had merely told them what to do. Although there is merit in involving athletes in simple problems such as the preceding, it would probably be inefficient and ineffective to expect the defensive squad to deal with the more complex problem of drawing up the entire defensive game plan for an upcoming competition.

The third disadvantage of participative decision making is that its efficacy is heavily dependent upon the degree of integration within the group. If the group is marked by internal conflict and rivalry, participation in decision making may result in one of two negative outcomes. First, the internal conflict may be further accentuated; one subgroup may feel that it has won the argument, but the other may not accept the decision. This conflict is not conducive to effective implementation of the decision. The other possibility is that the subgroups may "smooth over" the issue and arrive at a compromise solution that is not optimal.

In addition to the disadvantages described above, which may be inherent in participation per se, a number of attributes of a problem situation may preclude or restrict member participation in decision making. Thus, it is necessary to analyze the mix of relevant characteristics of the situation before selecting the appropriate decision style. The following sections deal with a framework purported to facilitate such analyses and the research results thereof.

A NORMATIVE MODEL OF DECISION STYLES IN COACHING

In 1978 Chelladurai and Haggerty proposed a normative model of decision styles in coaching, based largely on the works of Vroom and his associates (Vroom & Jago, 1974; Vroom & Yetton, 1973) and on heuristics. Briefly, their model identifies the following seven problem attributes deemed relevant to the athletic context:

1. *Time pressure.* Many of the decisions in the sport context, as in the case of military units in action, have to be made under great time pressure. The lack of time may preclude participative decisions.

2. *Decision quality required.* Some problems require optimal solutions, but in other cases, the coach may be satisfied with any one of several minimally acceptable alternatives. Chelladurai and Haggerty illustrated this distinction in the selection of a captain versus a quarterback in football.

> The functions of a captain can be carried out by any one of several members of a team (in fact, some teams elect a different captain for each game) and hence are not crucial; but the quarterback's function is more instrumental to the team's success and his abilities cannot be supplemented by other members. (1978, p. 7)

Therefore, the coach should be more concerned about the quality of the decision in selecting a quarterback than in selecting a captain.

3. *Information location.* Information is the basis of high-quality decisions in any context. Such information in athletics relates to the strategies and tactics of the sport; its rules and their interpretations; and to the athletes, their capabilities, attitudes, needs, and preferences. The decision style adopted by the coach should allow for the participation of all of those who possess the information so that a high-quality decision can be made. At the same time, the coach should guard against the "pooling of ignorance," which results when members without the necessary expertise and knowledge participate in decisions.

4. *Problem complexity.* On the basis of Kelley and Thibaut's (1969) work discussed earlier, Chelladurai and Haggerty suggested the following:

> Accordingly, the coach or one player (i.e., a player who possesses the necessary information) is more likely to make the optimal

decision than a group in the selection of plays to be used in specific competitive situations, where the relative abilities of the players, the appropriateness of the sequence of events, and the various options and their consequences all must be held in perspective. (1978, p. 7)

5. *Group acceptance.* It was noted previously that the acceptance of a decision by the group is essential for effective implementation of the decision. However, acceptance of some decisions may not be critical.

For instance, a basketball coach may decide to use a full-court press, but it is the players who have to implement the decision. Only if they accept the press as appropriate and as within their capabilities will it be effective. On the other hand, acceptance of a decision to practice foul shots every day is not critical, as it is quite specific and its execution can easily be monitored. (Chelladurai & Haggerty, 1978, p. 7)

6. *Coach's power.* The coach's power base may consist of one or more of the following: (a) control over rewards, (b) control over punishments, (c) the authority residing in the position of a coach, (d) the interpersonal liking and admiration the athletes have for the coach, and (e) the expertise, superior knowledge, and past performance of the coach. It should be pointed out that group acceptance emanating from the coach's referent and expert power is of real essence. The other three bases of power (reward, coercion, and legitimacy) only elicit compliance, not acceptance.

7. *Group integration.* Group integration is "a concept encompassing the quality of interpersonal relations on the team and the relative homogeneity of the team in terms of ability and tenure" (Chelladurai & Haggerty, 1978, p. 8). If the team is not integrated, the participative process will not yield optimal decisions and may weaken the already fragile team consensus and team spirit.

The next component of the normative model is the specification of variations in the decision process. Chelladurai and Haggerty have proposed three decision styles:

1. *Autocratic style.* In the autocratic style, the coach makes the final decision. Although consultation with one or more players is included within the autocratic style in this model, other authors (e.g., Vroom & Yetton, 1973) prefer to treat this consultation process as a separate style of decision making.

2. *Participative style.* In participative decision making, the group, which includes the coach as just another member, makes the decision.

3. *Delegative style.* In the delegative style, the coach delegates the decision making to one or more members. The coach's involvement is restricted to announcing the decision and/or implementing it.

Having specified the attributes of a problem situation and the three decision styles, Chelladurai and Haggerty presented the model in the form of a flowchart as shown in Figure 8.1. The attributes are listed as questions at the top of the chart. The decision maker is required to follow the branches of the flowchart as indicated by the yes or no responses to the questions. At the terminal nodes, the appropriate decision styles are indicated.

Although Chelladurai and Haggerty acknowledged that their model was fashioned after the framework provided by Vroom and Yetton (1973), there are considerable differences between the two approaches. Therefore the results of empirical research carried out with the Vroom and Yetton model cannot be used to substantiate the Chelladurai and Haggerty model. Thus, the latter remains a heuristic model without any empirical base. Furthermore, the two studies conducted in this regard are not entirely supportive of the model. The next section further elucidates these research efforts.

RESEARCH ON DECISION STYLES IN COACHING

A study by Gordon (1983) was the first attempt to test the Chelladurai and Haggerty model in its entirety. Gordon's study was concerned with soccer coaches' self-reports on what decision styles they would use in any given situation and on what other coaches would use in the same situation, as well as with soccer players' preferences for a specific decision style in a given situation and their perceptions of what decision style their coaches would use in the same situation.

Chelladurai and Arnott's study (1985) was concerned only with the preferences of university-level basketball players of both sexes. Furthermore, their study included only four of the seven problem attributes (quality requirement, coach's information, problem complexity, and group integration). They argued that these four attributes were more critical in the determination of players' preferences.

In both studies, the categories of decision styles were autocratic, consultive, participative, and delegative. It must be noted that these authors, in contrast to Chelladurai and Haggerty, separated the consultive style from the autocratic style. The consultive style was defined as the coach's making the final decision after consulting with one or more members of the team.

The results of the two studies are summarized in Table 8.2. The notable finding of both studies was that the delegative style was totally rejected by the respondents. Obviously this finding is contrary to the normative model (see Figure 8.1) wherein the delegative style was prescribed in 7 of the 15 situations. The normative model prescribed the delegative style only under the simultaneous occurrence of the conditions that (1) the coach does not

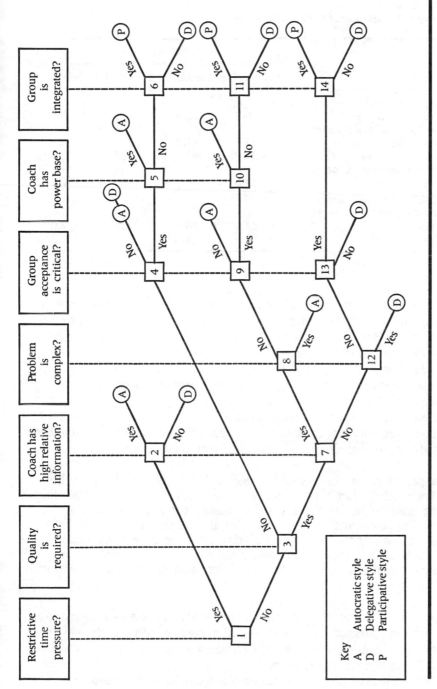

FIGURE 8.1

A Normative Model of Decision Styles in Coaching

Source: Reprinted from "A Normative Model of Decision-Making Styles in Coaching," by P. Chelladurai and T. R. Haggerty, 1978, *Athletic Administration, 13*(1), p. B. Used with permission.

TABLE 8.2
Percentage Distribution of Decision Style Choices

	Decision styles			
	Autocratic	Consultive	Participative	Delegative
Soccer (Gordon, 1983)				
Coaches' own choices	46.3	33.3	18.5	1.9
Coaches' perceptions of other coaches' choices	45.5	41.2	12.5	0.8
Players' preferences	31.2	41.9	24.9	2.0
Players' perceptions of coaches' choices	43.0	39.6	15.4	2.0
Basketball (Chelladurai & Arnott, 1984) Players' preferences				
Females	33.0	18.1	46.9	2.0
Males	38.9	25.8	34.1	1.2

have the necessary information, which prohibits him or her from making the decision, and (2) the group is not integrated, which precludes the participative style. However, this line of reasoning overlooks the relative influences of team members in the three decision styles. For instance, Chelladurai and Arnott (1985) argued that the four decision styles could be placed on a continuum on the basis of the degree of the coach's influence in the decisions. That is, the coach's influence ranges from 100 percent in the autocratic style to 0 percent in the delegative style, as shown in Figure 8.2. However, from the players' perspective, both the autocratic style and the delegative style exclude them from participation (see Figure 8.2).

> Apparently, members would forego their influence in favor of the coach rather than in favor of another teammate(s). . . . One possible explanation for this result could be that sharing of the decision-making power with one or more (but limited) members from the group is antithetical to the egalitarian notion inherent in a team. That is, such delegation to a few athletes may be construed as preferential treatment by the rest of the team. (Chelladurai & Arnott, 1985, pp. 21–22)

It appears that when the coach does not possess the necessary information, it needs to be collected through consultation with the athletes. However, it is not clear whether consulting with a limited number of members will be acceptable to the rest of the team.

Two additional pieces of information from Table 8.2 need to be ex-

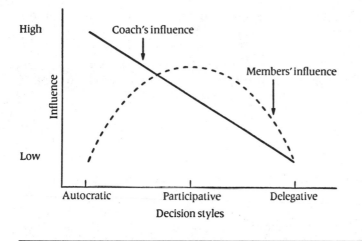

FIGURE 8.2
Coach's and Members' Relative Influence in Three Decision Styles

plored further. First, it must be noted that the preceding studies were concerned with team sports. It could be that individual sports present a vastly different picture. Vroom and Yetton (1973) have indicated that the social process of decision making in dyadic settings is different from that in group settings. Second, in Chelladurai and Arnott's study, the females preferred more participation than the males. This is consistent with past research (Chelladurai & Saleh, 1978), but it is not known whether these sex differences in preferences do actually translate into differences in the decision styles of those who coach men's teams and women's teams. Additional research is needed before any definitive statements can be made on these issues.

The findings by Chelladurai and Arnott — which showed that when the coach was deemed to have the necessary information, the subjects preferred a more autocratic style and when the group was deemed to be integrated, the subjects preferred more participation — are consistent with theory and previous research. However, less participation was preferred when the quality requirement was high and the problem was complex, as well as when quality was not required and the problem was simple. More participation was preferred when one of these attributes was present in the absence of the other.

These results suggest that the democratic selection of a captain and/or the starting five in basketball, for instance, may not have the desired effects. Such decisions may be considered trivial since the captain acts merely as a figurehead without any vested authority. With regard to the election of the starting five, there is no substance to the decision as long as the coach reserves the right to substitute players at the first whistle.

SUMMARY

Theories relating to the social process of decision making and the related research indicate that it is more useful to assume that situations call for autocratic or participative decision making rather than merely to categorize coaches as autocratic or democratic. This is not to deny the influence of the coach's personality but to point out that the coach's personality is only part of the total situation, which includes the team members' personalities and preferences and the type of problem involved.

There is a common tendency to view the autocratic style as something evil, indulged in only by despots and dictators as a device for furthering their own interests. Contrastingly, the participative style is viewed as a humanistic approach aimed at the welfare of the members. Coaches and athletes need to understand that these contrasting decision styles are not value laden and that the autocratic style can be associated with humanism and benevolence.

Finally, research in the area of decision styles, although rather limited, clearly shows that the autocratic style is quite acceptable to the athletes in certain circumstances. It appears that coaches need to select a decision style appropriate to the particular situation rather than being guided by a belief that participative decisions are always superior and/or always preferred.

REFERENCES

Chelladurai, P., & Arnott, M. (1985). Decision styles in coaching: Preferences of basketball players. *Research Quarterly for Exercise and Sport, 56* (1), 15–24.

Chelladurai, P., & Carron, A. V. (1982, May). *Task characteristics and individual differences, and their relationship to preferred leadership in sports.* Paper presented at the annual meeting of the North American Society for the Psychology of Sport and Physical Activity, College Park, Maryland.

Chelladurai, P., & Haggerty, T. R. (1978). A normative model of decision styles in coaching. *Athletic Administrator, 13,* 6–9.

Chelladurai, P., & Saleh, S. D. (1978). Preferred leadership in sports. *Canadian Journal of Applied Sport Sciences, 3,* 85–92.

Chelladurai, P., & Saleh, S. D. (1980). Dimensions of leader behavior in sports. Development of a leadership scale. *Journal of Sport Psychology, 2* (1), 34–45.

Fiedler, F. E. (1967). *A theory of leadership effectiveness.* New York: McGraw-Hill.

Gordon, S. (1983, July). *Decision-making styles in university soccer coaching.* Paper presented at the FISU conference, World University Games, Edmonton, Canada.

Kelley, H. H., & Thibaut, J. W. (1969). Group problem solving. In G. Lindzey & E. Arconson (Eds.), *The handbook of social psychology* (2nd ed., Vol. 4, pp. 1–101). Reading, Mass.: Addison-Wesley.

Sage, G. H. (1973). The coach as management: Organizational leadership in American sport. *Quest, 19,* 35–40.

Vroom, V. H., & Jago, A. G. (1974). On the validity of the Vroom–Yetton model. *Journal of Applied Psychology, 63,* 151–162.

Vroom, V. H., & Yetton, R. N. (1973). *Leadership and decision making.* Pittsburgh: University of Pittsburgh Press.

Part Two

Mental Training for Peak Performance

9 Psychological Characteristics of Peak Performance

Peak performances are those magic moments when an athlete puts it all together — both physically and mentally. The performance is exceptional, seemingly transcending ordinary levels of play. Competitively, these performances often result in a personal best. They are the ultimate high, the thrilling moment that athletes and coaches work for in their pursuit of excellence. Unfortunately, they also are relatively rare and, according to many athletes, nonvoluntary. But are they truly nonvoluntary? Can athletes be trained so that peak performances occur more frequently? If not to produce a peak performance, can they be trained so they consistently play closer to their optimal level?

To answer these questions, it is first necessary to know if there are any common characteristics that identify peak performances. For example, is there an ideal body/mind state associated with peak performance? If so, is this ideal state similar from one athlete to another or one sport to another? More importantly, if common qualities are identified, can they be trained?

First, it is safe to assume that peak performance is a consequence of both physical and mental factors. Mind and body cannot be separated. A precondition to peak performance is a certain level of physical conditioning and mastery of the physical skills involved in performance. For many decades, athletic and sport science communities have been devoted to improving physical training programs. Obviously, the higher the level of physical skill and conditioning, the more potential control the athlete has over his or her performance. Within this minimal physical skill framework, one must realize that peak performance is relative — contingent upon each athlete's present level of ability. Thus, concern for enhancing peak performance may be as relevant to the coaches and sport psychologists who work with less skilled youth sport athletes as it is to coaches and sport psychologists who work with professional or elite amateur athletes.

OVERVIEW OF PEAK PERFORMANCE

This chapter is not concerned per se with physical skill characteristics and physical training programs that enhance the likelihood of peak performance. Instead, its focus is on the mental side of peak performance and how the mind interacts with the body in ultimately producing performance. Most athletes and coaches will acknowledge that at least 40 to 90 percent of success in sports is due to mental factors. The higher the skill level, the more important the mental aspect becomes. In fact, on the elite competitive level, it is not uncommon to hear that the winner invariably comes down to who is the strongest athlete — mentally — on a given day! For example, after winning seven gold medals at the Montreal Olympics, Mark Spitz was quoted as saying, "At this level of physical skill, the difference between winning and losing is 99 percent psychological." In *Golf My Way*, Jack Nicklaus states that mental preparation is the single most critical element in peak performance. This is not a particularly surprising statement considering that Nicklaus believes golf is 90 percent mental.

If the mental side of performance is so important to success, then perhaps an ideal internal psychological climate exists during peak performance. Over the last decade, there has been a tremendous surge of research on psychological aspects of peak performance. The remainder of this chapter will reflect what has been learned from this research and from the insights of people who have worked with athletes in psychological training.

Before identifying some of these research findings and insights, I must offer a caution. Do not think that the field of sport psychology has found all the answers. It certainly has not, and the evidence to support some of its answers is still quite tenuous. In addition to not having all of the answers, sport psychologists have probably not even identified all of the questions yet! There is, however, a growing foundation for understanding the mental side of performance and possibilities for improving performance through psychological skills training. This chapter, and the following chapters in this section, will attempt to reflect the latest state of knowledge and the current thinking and practices of those involved in mental training for peak performance.

THE PEAK PERFORMANCE PSYCHOLOGICAL PROFILE

Before we can think in terms of psychological skills training, it is necessary to know if there is an optimal psychological state for peak performance. If such a state can be identified for programs or for a given individual, then there is a foundation for developing a mental skills training program, provided these skills can be trained. There are at least three excellent sources for helping to identify the psychological characteristics underlying successful athletic performance. One is the data that have been generated from researchers who have asked athletes to recall their subjective perceptions during the greatest moment they ever had while participating in sport. The second source is the data generated from studies that have compared the psychological characteristics of successful and less successful athletes—for example, athletes who were Olympic qualifiers compared to nonqualifiers or collegiate athletes who were successful compared to less successful collegiate athletes. The third source of information comes from people who have asked top athletes, coaches, and scouts what they think it takes to be successful in their given sport.

Psychological Characteristics During Peak Experiences in Sport

Ken Ravizza (1977), the author of Chapter 11, "Increasing Awareness for Sport Performance," was one of the first sport psychologists to publish a study on the subjective experiences of athletes during their "greatest moment" in sport. He interviewed 20 male and female athletes from a variety of competitive levels who related experiences in 12 different sports. Over 80 percent of the athletes reported having the following perceptions:

Loss of fear—no fear of failure

No thinking of performance

Total immersion in the activity

Narrow focus of attention

Effortless performance—not forcing it

Feeling of being in complete control

Time–space disorientation (usually slowed down)

Perceive universe to be integrated and unified

Unique, temporary, involuntary experience

In trying to determine where "mental toughness" comes from and to answer other questions about the mental aspects of sports training, Jim Loehr, Head of the Center for Athletic Excellence in Denver, Colorado, interviewed hundreds of athletes. He asked them to describe how they felt when they were playing at their best. What were their psychological experiences prior to and during a peak athletic experience? The athletes gave surprisingly similar accounts. According to Loehr, "It was, they said, like playing possessed, yet in complete control. Time itself seemed to slow down, so they never felt rushed. They played with profound intensity, total concentration and an enthusiasm that bordered on joy" (1984, p. 67). Loehr further clarified the relationship between optimal sport performance and confidence and arousal by compiling the following composite of athletes' interview statements:

"I felt like I could do almost anything, as if I were in complete control. I really felt confident and positive." Regarding arousal,

"I felt physically very relaxed, but really energized and pumped up. I experienced virtually no anxiety or fear, and the whole experience was enjoyable. I experienced a very real sense of calmness and quiet inside, and everything just seemed to flow automatically. . . . Even though I was really hustling, it was all very effortless." (cited in Garfield & Bennett, 1984, p. 37, 95)

Loehr concluded that the probability of good performance could be substantially increased if the following combination of feelings could be triggered and maintained: high energy (challenge, inspiration, determination, intensity), fun and enjoyment, no pressure (low anxiety), optimism and positiveness, mental calmness, confidence, being very focused, and being in control.

Loehr's research has been corroborated by Charles Garfield (Garfield & Bennett, 1984), President of the Peak Performance Center in Berkeley, California. In interviews with hundreds of elite athletes, Garfield identified eight mental and physical conditions that athletes described as being characteristic of the feelings they have at those moments when they are doing something extraordinarily well:

1. *Mentally relaxed.* This was described most frequently as a sense of inner calm. Some athletes also reported a sense of time being slowed down and having a high degree of concentration. By contrast, loss of concentration was associated with a sense of everything happening too fast and being out of control.
2. *Physically relaxed.* Feeling of muscles being loose with movements fluid and sure.
3. *Confident/optimistic.* A positive attitude, feelings of self-confidence and optimism. Being able to keep poise and feelings of strength and control even during potentially threatening challenges.
4. *Focused on the present.* A sense of harmony that comes from the body and mind working as one unit. No thoughts of the past or future. The body performs automatically, without conscious or deliberate mental effort.
5. *Highly energized.* A high-energy state frequently described as feelings of joy, ecstasy, intensity, and being "charged" or "hot."
6. *Extraordinary awareness.* A state of mind in which the athletes are acutely aware of their own bodies and of the surrounding athletes. They report an uncanny ability to know what the other athletes are going to do, and they respond accordingly. Also a sensation of being completely in harmony with the environment.
7. *In control.* The body and mind seem to do automatically exactly what is right — yet there is no sense of exerting or imposing control.
8. *In the cocoon.* The feeling of being in an envelope, being completely

detached from the external environment and any potential distractions. Also a sense of complete access to all of one's powers and skills. Athletes "in the cocoon" are able to avoid loss of concentration and accelerated, tight-muscled, out-of-control feelings.

Psychological Differences Between Successful and Unsuccessful Athletes

Some researchers question the scientific rigor of research based on interviews. They are cautious about drawing conclusions from interviews out of fear that an interviewer can influence the outcome of an interview. Instead, they prefer to rely on objective, standardized tests. One has to agree that there is always the "experimenter variable" in interview research, but this is greatly lessened when the interviewers have been trained to exhibit as little bias as possible and also to ask questions designed to test a subject's earlier answers.

For those who may be skeptical of interview data, another source of psychological peak performance information concerns research on why some individuals might outperform others. This data comes from researchers who have used objective paper and pencil inventories to compare the psychological characteristics of successful and less successful athletes.

In the mid-1970s, Mahoney and Avener designed an objective questionnaire to assess various psychological factors such as confidence, concentration, anxiety, self-talk, imagery, and dreams. Most of the questionnaire items employed an 11-point Likert-type scale. This basic tool (or variations of it) has been used by researchers to study athletes in the sports of gymnastics, wrestling, tennis, racquetball, and diving. When Mahoney and Avener (1977) compared 1976 U.S. Olympic qualifiers and nonqualifiers in men's gymnastics, they found that the finalists coped more easily with competitive mistakes, were better able to control and utilize anxiety, had higher self-confidence and more positive self-talk, had more gymnastics-related dreams, and had more frequent imagery of an internal versus external nature. External imagery occurs when a person views himself or herself from the perspective of an external observer, such as seeing oneself on television or videotape. Internal imagery requires an approximation much more like the actual perspective when the skill is performed physically, that is, imagining being inside the body and experiencing the same sensations as one might expect in actual physical execution.

Following are the results from a sampling of other studies that employed a design similar to Mahoney and Avener's. Better performers on the Memphis State University racquetball team had higher self-confidence in training and competition, reported fewer doubts, had more racquetball thoughts in everyday situations, and had dreams and imagery that were more likely to portray successful performance (Meyers, Cooke, Cullen, & Liles, 1979). Canadian National Wrestling Team qualifiers compared with nonqualifiers were higher in self-confidence, closer to reaching their maximum athletic potential, more able to block anxiety one hour prior to and during competition, and experienced fewer negative self-thoughts one hour prior to competition (Highlen & Bennett, 1979). In a wrestling study comparing placers and nonplacers in a Big Ten wrestling tournament, the placers were more self-confident, closer to their athletic potential, more frequent users of attentional focusing to prepare for the meet, and more positively affected by seeing themselves as the underdog (Gould, Weiss, & Weinberg, 1981). The divers who competed successfully enough in Canada's National Championship to subsequently qualify for Canada's Pan American Diving Team had more self-confidence, higher concentration, lower anxiety during competition, and more self-talk and imagery. They also reported more vividness and better control of their imagery (Highlen & Bennett, 1983).

On the basis of the results of these studies, and similarly designed studies that have not been summarized here, there appear to be some commonalities in the psychological characteristics of more successful athletes. The most consistent finding is higher levels of self-confidence for the more successful competitors. Without exception, the researchers reported that the better athletes believed in themselves more than the less successful athletes. Most of the researchers also reported better concentration. Successful athletes were less likely to get distracted and kept a more task-oriented focus of concentration versus a preoccupation with outcome thoughts or thoughts of messing up. Generally, the successful athletes also were more preoccupied with their sport and in a more positive way. This was reflected by more thoughts, imagery, daydreams, and dreams relative to their sport, with the content tending to be more positive. In a number of the studies, successful athletes were found to have less anxiety immediately before and during competition. Sometimes higher anxiety was found one day to one week before competition, but as the competition drew closer, the successful competitors brought their anxiety to lower levels than the less successful competitors. Most of the better athletes also had a higher ability to rebound from mistakes. One might conjecture that this could be a consequence of higher self-confidence, more optimal control of anxiety, and better concentration skills.

Can one assume that the psychological differences between the successful and less successful athletes were critical to performance differences? This may well be the case, but the design of the preceding studies does not permit that conclusion. Those studies were only correlational; they did not test a cause and effect relationship. Other untested history and selection variables might have caused the differences. For example, perhaps these psychological differences did not contribute to performance outcome so much as reflect previous experience and success levels (Heyman, 1982).

What Top Sport People Think It Takes to "Make It"

Another way to identify potential peak performance characteristics is to ask the best athletes, coaches, and scouts what it takes to "make it" at the highest level in their sport. A study by Orlick (sport psychologist) and Reed (exercise physiologist) did just that (Orlick, 1980). They found disagreement from sport to sport regarding the physical attributes necessary for excellence but almost total agreement across sports on the necessary psychological attributes for success. Commitment and self-control were identified as the two key psychological ingredients for excellence.

For example, regarding commitment, when Orlick and Ross interviewed many of the top coaches and scouts in the National Hockey League, words like *desire, determination, attitude, heart,* and *self-motivation* were most often mentioned as the crucial factors that determine who does and does not make it at the professional level. Few athletes can reach high levels of excellence without high levels of personal commitment. One way for coaches and sport psychologists to assess levels of commitment and also to build commitment is to use the principles of goal setting (see Chapter 10). What level of commitment coaches can reasonably expect from athletes obviously depends upon the level and type of competition, e.g., youth sport participant, professional athlete, Olympic team member, nonscholarship compared to full-scholarship collegiate athlete). Regardless of the level or type of competition, those athletes who have the goal of being the best they are capable of or being one of the best in their sport need higher levels of commitment than athletes with less challenging goals. Achieving the highest standard possible requires that an athlete must want it more than others, be willing to train harder and longer (expending more hours and more effort and concentration during practices), and be willing to make sacrifices.

According to these top athletes, coaches, and scouts, high commitment alone is not sufficient to achieve real athletic success. Maturity and self-control are also needed. This means being *able to do things in big games and tight situations* as well as in normal games and situations. This requires *staying cool* and *confident* and *maintaining composure.* One way top coaches and scouts assessed composure was to look at how athletes reacted to bad officiating calls. Athletes who remained cool and who tried to calm their teammates under such circumstances were considered more desirable prospects. Being *mature* and *positive, reacting well to mistakes,* being *able to accept criticism* (even when undeserved), and *not being afraid to fail* (not holding back, having the courage to go for it in challenging situations) were other qualities used to describe self-control.

Conclusions

This chapter began with the questions, "Is there an ideal body/mind state associated with peak performance?" and "If so, is this ideal state similar from one athlete to another or one sport to another?" Regardless of the source of data or the nature of the sport, a certain psychological profile appears to be linked with successful performance. Although there are numerous individual variations, in most cases this general profile is depicted by the following characteristics:

Self-regulation of arousal (energized yet relaxed, no fear)

Higher self-confidence

Better concentration (being appropriately focused)

In control, but not forcing it

Positive preoccupation with sport (imagery and thoughts)

Determination and commitment

These commonalities in psychological qualities have led many researchers and practitioners to conclude that the presence of the right emotional climate helps mobilize physiological reactions that are essential to performing at one's best. A negative psychological climate, such as feelings of frustration, fear, anger, and worry, typically does the opposite. It may trigger reactions such as tight muscles and poor concentration. Thus, even though adequate cause and effect data are lacking, current thinking and practice in applied sport psychology tends to assume that level of performance is a direct reflection of the way one is thinking and feeling rather than that the emotional state is a consequence of performance outcome. In actuality, both views could be correct: a circular relationship would be quite logical—that is, optimal mental states lead to better performance, and being successful enhances desirable mental states.

According to Loehr (1984) and others, this ideal performance state (IPS) does not just happen. Top-level athletes have identified their own IPS and have learned, intentionally or subconsciously, to create and maintain this state voluntarily so that their talents and physical skills thrive. Achieving one's own ideal internal psychological climate is not a simple task. The mental skills needed to trigger and sustain this IPS are learned through knowledge and practice just as the physical skills and strategies of the game are learned. It appears that some gifted athletes seem to be able to perfect these mental techniques on their own, but most athletes need to be taught specific training techniques. Fortunately, knowledge in applied sport psychology has advanced to the point that such techniques are now available. Although much still needs to be learned and tested, there is a sufficient base of knowledge to implement systematic mental skills training. Many athletes who have been exposed to such systematic training believe that they have both improved their performance level and learned to perform more consistently at their best.

The remaining chapters in this section of the book specifically address the psychological states associated with peak performance and, when appropriate, provide techniques for learning to create and maintain desirable mental and physiological states. Chapter 11 is unique in that its purpose is to help coaches and sport psychologists learn how to assist each athlete in identifying his or her own internal psychological climate for peak performance and to identify those factors that tend to enhance or detract from this ideal internal climate. Such an awareness is the first step in mental skills training. In the chapters that follow, it becomes obvious that peak performance need not be a unique, temporary, involuntary experience. It is a product of the body and mind, and it can be trained. Just as improving physical skills, strategies, and conditioning increases the likelihood of peak performance, learning to control psychological readiness and the ideal mental climate for peak performance also enhances performance.

REFERENCES

Garfield, C. A., & Bennett, H. Z. (1984). *Peak performance: Mental training techniques of the world's greatest athletes.* Los Angeles: Tarcher.

Gould, D., Weiss, M., & Weinberg, R. (1981). Psychological characteristics of successful and nonsuccessful Big Ten wrestlers. *Journal of Sport Psychology, 3,* 69–81.

Heyman, S. R. (1982). Comparisons of successful and unsuccessful competitors: A reconsideration of methodological questions and data. *Journal of Sport Psychology, 4,* 295–300.

Highlen, P. S., & Bennett, B. B. (1979). Psychological characteristics of successful and nonsuccessful elite wrestlers: An exploratory study. *Journal of Sport Psychology, 1,* 123–137.

Highlen, P. S., & Bennett, B. B. (1983). Elite divers and wrestlers: A comparison between open- and closed-skill athletes. *Journal of Sport Psychology, 5,* 390–409.

Loehr, J. E. (1984, March). How to overcome stress and play at your peak all the time. *Tennis,* pp. 66–76.

Mahoney, M. J., & Avener, M. (1977). Psychology of the elite athlete: An exploratory study. *Cognitive Therapy and Research, 1,* 135–142.

Meyers, A. W., Cooke, C. J., Cullen, J., & Liles, L. (1979). Psychological aspects of athletic competitors: A replication across sports. *Cognitive Therapy and Research, 3,* 361–366.

Orlick, T. (1980). *In pursuit of excellence.* Champaign, Ill.: Human Kinetics.

Ravizza, K. (1977). Peak experiences in sport. *Journal of Humanistic Psychology, 17*(4), 35–40.

10 Goal Setting for Peak Performance*

DANIEL GOULD

University of Illinois

In recent years a number of training strategies have been identified as ways of assisting athletes in achieving personal growth and peak performance. Goal setting is one such technique. In fact, goal setting has not only been shown to influence the performance of athletes of varied age and ability levels but has also been linked to positive changes in important psychological states such as anxiety, confidence, and motivation. It is clearly a technique that coaches and sport psychologists should regularly employ.

Unfortunately, goal setting is not always effectively employed by the coach/sport psychologist practitioner. It is falsely assumed, for example, that because athletes set goals on their own, these goals will automatically facilitate performance. This is seldom the case, however, as many athletes set inappropriate goals or do not set goals in a systematic fashion. Similarly, practitioners often forget to initiate the follow-up and evaluation procedures that are necessary if goal setting is to be effective. To effectively use goal setting, then, practitioners must understand the goal-setting process and the many factors that can affect it.

This chapter has a fourfold purpose. First, psychological and sport psychological research and theory on goal setting will be briefly examined. Second, a number of fundamental goal-setting guidelines will be discussed. Third, a system for effectively initiating goal-setting procedures with athletes will be presented. And, fourth, common problems that arise when setting goals will be identified and solutions forwarded. The principles and recommendations derived in this chapter are based both on research and on what sport psychologists have learned while using goal-setting interventions with athletes in a variety of settings.

* The author would like to thank Linda Bump, Linda Petlichkoff, and Jeff Simons for their helpful comments on early drafts of this chapter.

GOAL-SETTING RESEARCH AND THEORY

Before examining the research on goal setting and theoretical explanations for the relationship between goal setting and performance, we must first define goals and distinguish between various types of goals.

Defining Goals

Although any number of definitions could be offered for the term *goal*, Locke, Shaw, Saari, and Lathram (1981) have generated the most widely accepted definition. For these investigators, a goal is defined as "attaining a specific standard of proficiency on a task, usually within a specified time limit" (Locke et al., 1981, p. 145). From a practical perspective, then, goals focus on achieving some standard, whether it be increasing one's batting average by 10 percentage points, lowering one's time in the 800 meters or losing five pounds. This definition also implies that such performance standards will be achieved within some specified unit of time such as by the end of the season, within two weeks, or by the end of practice.

Even though the definition by Locke and his associates provides a good general description of a goal, sport psychologists have at times found it useful to make specific distinctions between types of goals. McClements (1982), for instance, has differentiated between *subjective goals* (e.g., having fun, getting fit, or trying one's best), *general objective goals* (e.g., winning a championship or making a team), and *specific objective goals* (e.g., increasing the number of assists in basketball or decreasing a pitcher's earned run average in softball). Similarly, Martens, Christina, Harvey, and Sharkey (1981) and Burton (1983, 1984) have made distinctions between *outcome goals,* which represent standards of performance that focus on the results of a contest between opponents or teams (e.g., beating someone), and *performance goals,* which focus on improvements relative to one's own past performance (e.g., improving one's time in the mile). These distinctions are important because evidence suggests that specific objective goals, as well as performance goals, are most useful when attempting to change behavior.

Goal-Effectiveness Research

Extensive psychological research has been conducted on the topic of goal setting. Typically, this research has involved a comparison of the performance of subjects who set goals or certain types of goals (e.g., specific-explicit goals) with the performance of subjects who are simply told to do their best or are given no goals. Studies sometimes manipulate other factors such as subject characteristics (e.g., race, educational level, personality) or situational variables (e.g., the presence or absence of feedback).

Psychological research on goal setting is impressive in that it has been conducted in a variety of laboratory and field settings and used in a wide variety of tasks ranging from truckloading to brainstorming sessions; it has also employed diverse samples of subjects, including elementary school children, uneducated laborers, managers, and scientists. In addition, a clear pattern of results has emerged with ready implications for sport psychology specialists and coaches alike.

The most important result generated from this line of research is that goal setting clearly and consistently facilitates performance. In their excellent and comprehensive review of well over one hundred studies on goal setting, for example, Locke et al. (1981) concluded that "the beneficial effect of goal setting on task performance is one of the most robust and replicable findings in the psychological literature. Ninety percent of the studies showed positive or partially positive effects. Furthermore, these effects are found just as reliable in the field setting as in the laboratory" (p. 145). Thus, a review of the psychological research clearly shows that goal setting is a powerful technique for enhancing performance.

Given the abundance of research on goal setting and the consistent pattern of results found in the psychological literature in general, it is surprising that the topic has been almost virtually ignored in the sport psychological literature. In fact, to date, only a few studies (Botterill, 1977; Burton, 1983, 1984) have been conducted on the topic.

Nevertheless, the results of these initial investigations show much promise. Botterill (1977), for instance, had youth ice hockey players perform an exercise endurance task under various combinations of goal difficulty, goal explicitness-specificity, and goal-type (group, subject, or experimenter set) conditions. Consistent with the psychological literature, the results revealed that goal setting facilitated performance. Similarly, difficult goals were more effective in enhancing performance than easy goals, and explicit goals were more effective than general "do your best" goals. Finally, it was concluded that explicit, difficult, and group set goals were most effective in enhancing endurance task performance.

In a more recent field investigation, Burton (1983) examined the effects of a goal-setting training program on the performance and cognitions (e.g., levels of self-confidence, motivation, and state anxiety) of male and female intercollegiate swimmers. In a five-month goal-setting program, performance as opposed to outcome goals were employed and an attempt was made to explain why goal setting influences performance by relating goals to other psychological constructs such as confidence and state anxiety. The results revealed that swimmers who participated in the goal-setting training program learned to focus highest priority on performance goals and those swimmers high in goal-setting ability demonstrated better performance and more positive cognitions. Furthermore, a related study conducted with

National Sports Festival swimmers supported these findings, demonstrating that goals were positively related to performance and positive psychological attributes (Burton, 1984).

In summary, the results of the psychological and sport psychological research literature provide strong support for using goal-setting procedures to facilitate athletic performance. Moreover, these findings are further strengthened by the fact that they have been demonstrated in studies using varied tasks and largely different subject populations in both laboratory and field settings.

Theoretical Explanations for the Relationship Between Goal Setting and Performance

The old adage that there is nothing more practical than a good theory is an appropriate way to view the goal-setting process. It is important to know that goal setting influences performance, but it is equally important for coaches and sport psychologists to understand how and why goal setting is effective, especially when problems occur in goal setting and the practitioner must assess the situation and make adjustments to solve the problems.

Two explanations have been proposed to describe how goals influence performance. Locke and his associates (1981) suggested a mechanistic theory to explain the goal–performance relationship in general. Burton (1983) proposed a second theory specifically to explain how goal setting influences performance in the athletic domain; this theory is more cognitive in orientation.

In their mechanistic theory, Locke et al. (1981) contend that goals influence performance in four ways. First, goals direct the performer's attention and action to important aspects of the task. Thus, by setting goals, a basketball player's attention and subsequent action will be focused on improving specific skills such as blocking out under the boards or decreasing turnovers as opposed to becoming a better ball player in general. Second, goals help the performer mobilize effort. For example, by setting a series of practice goals, a swimmer will exhibit greater practice effort in attempting to achieve these objectives. Third, goals not only increase immediate effort but help prolong effort or increase persistence. As a case in point, the boredom of a long season is offset and persistence is increased when a wrestler sets a number of short-term goals throughout the year. Finally, research has shown that performers often develop and employ new learning strategies through the process of setting goals. Golfers, for instance, may learn new methods of putting in an effort to achieve putting goals that the golfers have set in conjunction with their coach.

In contrast to the Locke et al. theory (1981), Burton's cognitive theory

(1983) focuses solely on how goal setting influences performance in athletic environments. Athletes' goals are linked to their levels of anxiety, motivation, and confidence. That is, when athletes focus solely on outcome or winning goals, unrealistic future expectations often result; such expectations can lead to lower levels of confidence, increased cognitive anxiety, decreased effort, and poor performance. Unlike outcome goals, performance goals are both in the athlete's control and flexible. Moreover, when properly employed, performance goals assist the athlete in forming realistic expectations. This, in turn, results in optimal levels of confidence, cognitive anxiety, and motivation and, ultimately, in enhanced performance.

When setting goals, then, coaches and sport psychologists should make every effort to become aware of the mechanisms causing performance changes to occur. Simply stated, theorists indicate that performance changes occur because of the influence of goals on such psychological attributes as anxiety, confidence, and motivation; the directing of attention to important aspects of the skill being performed; the mobilization of effort; increases in persistence; and the fostering of the development of new learning strategies.

GOAL-SETTING GUIDELINES

The previously reviewed research clearly shows that goal setting facilitates performance. It is misleading to think, however, that all types of goals are equally effective in enhancing athletic performance. The research conducted by Botterill (1977) and Burton (1983) indicates that this is not the case. Their work has produced specific guidelines concerning the most effective types of goals to use. Similarly, sport psychologists (Bell, 1983; Botterill, 1983; Carron, 1984; Gould, 1983; Harris & Harris, 1984; McClements & Botterill, 1979; O'Block & Evans, 1984; Orlick, 1980) who have had extensive experience in employing goal-setting techniques with athletes have been able to derive a number of useful guidelines for those interested in utilizing such techniques, the most important of which are summarized below.

Set Specific Goals in Measurable and Behavioral Terms

Explicit, specific, and numerical goals are more effective in facilitating behavior change than general "do your best" goals or no goals at all. Therefore, it is of the utmost importance that in the athletic environment goals be expressed in terms of specific measurable behaviors. Goals such as doing one's best, becoming better, and increasing one's strength are least effective. More effective goals include being able to high jump 6 feet 5 inches by the end of the season or increasing one's maximum lift on the bench press to 240 pounds. If athletes are to show performance improvements, specific measurable goals must be set!

Set Difficult but Realistic Goals

Locke and his associates (1981) have found a direct relationship between goal difficulty and task performance. That is, the more difficult the goal, the better the performance. It must be remembered, however, that this relationship is true only when the difficulty of the goal does not exceed the performer's ability. Unrealistic goals that exceed the ability of an athlete only lead to failure and frustration. Thus, it is recommended that goals be set so that they are difficult enough to challenge athletes but realistic enough to achieve (McClements, 1982).

Set Short-Range as Well as Long-Range Goals

When asked to describe their goals, most athletes identify long-range objectives such as winning a particular championship, breaking a record, or making a particular team. However, a number of sport psychologists (Bell, 1983; Carron, 1984; Gould, 1983; Harris & Harris, 1984; O'Block & Evans, 1984) have emphasized the need to set more immediate short-range goals. Short-range goals are important because they allow athletes to see immediate improvements in performance and in so doing enhance motivation. Additionally, without short-range goals, athletes often lose sight of their long-range goals and the progression of skills needed to obtain them.

An effective way to understand the relationship between short- and long-range goals is to visualize a staircase. The top stair represents an athlete's long-range goal or objective and the lowest stair his or her present ability. The remaining steps represent a progression of short-term goals of increasing difficulty that lead from the bottom to the top of the stairs. In essence, the performer climbs the staircase of athletic achievement by taking a step at a time, accomplishing a series of interrelated short-range goals.

Set Performance Goals as Opposed to Outcome Goals

North American society places tremendous emphasis on the outcome of athletic events. Because of this, most athletes are socialized to set only outcome goals (e.g., winning, beating a particular opponent). Unfortunately, outcome goals have been shown to be less effective than performance goals (Burton, 1983, 1984).

It has been theorized that outcome goals have several inherent weaknesses (Burton, 1983, 1984; Martens et al., 1981). First, athletes have, at best, only partial control over outcome goals. For example, a cross-country competitor can set a personal best but fail to achieve the outcome goal of winning because he or she came in second. Despite his or her superior effort, this runner could not control the behavior of the other competitors.

A second important weakness of outcome goals is that when they are employed by athletes, the athletes usually become less flexible in their goal adjustment practices. For example, an athlete who sets an outcome goal of winning every game and loses the initial contest will often reject goal setting altogether. However, an athlete who sets an individual performance goal such as decreasing his or her 100-meter breaststroke time by five tenths of a second and fails to achieve this goal is more likely to reset the goal to one tenth of a second.

In summary, by emphasizing personal performance goals, coaches create greater opportunities for meeting the success needs of all athletes. Those highly gifted competitors who easily exceed the performances of their opponents learn to compete against themselves and, in turn, reach new performance heights. Similarly, the less skilled athletes on the team are no longer doomed to failure; they learn to judge success and failure in terms of their own performance, not solely on the basis of peer comparisons.

Set Goals for Practice and Competition

Setting goals that only relate to competition is a frequently made mistake when implementing a goal-setting program. This does not imply that setting competitive performance goals is inappropriate; rather, it suggests that practice goals should not be forgotten (Bell, 1983).

Common practice goals may include starting practice on time, making five sincere positive statements to teammates during practice, running to and from all drills, and achieving various performance standards. These are typically not the most frequently cited goals of athletes, but they take on special significance when one considers the amount of time athletes spend in practice as opposed to competition. Moreover, most athletes report that it is easier to get up and motivated for a game or match whereas additional motivation is often needed for daily practices.

Set Positive Goals as Opposed to Negative Goals

Goals can be stated in either positive (e.g., increase the percentage of good first serves in tennis) or negative terms (e.g., decrease the percentage of bad first serves in tennis). Although it is sometimes necessary for athletes to set goals in negative terms, it has been suggested that, whenever possible, goals should be stated positively (Bell, 1983). That is, identify behaviors to be exhibited as opposed to behaviors that should not be exhibited. Instead of having goal tenders in ice hockey strive to decrease the number of unblocked shots, have them set goals of increasing the number of saves they can make. This positive goal-setting procedure helps athletes focus on success instead of failure.

Identify Target Dates for Attaining Goals

Not only should goals describe the behavior of focus in specific measurable terms, but they should identify target dates for goal accomplishment. Target dates help motivate athletes by reminding them of the urgency of accomplishing their objectives in realistic lengths of time.

Identify Goal Achievement Strategies

All too often goals are properly set but never accomplished because athletes fail to identify goal achievement strategies. An important ingredient for any effective goal-setting program, then, is the identification of ways of achieving goals. For example, a basketball player who has set a goal of increasing her foul shot percentage by 5 percentage points may want to identify a goal achievement strategy of shooting 25 extra foul shots after every practice. Similarly, a wrestler needing to lose 10 pounds prior to the start of the season should identify an achievement strategy of cutting out a midafternoon snack and running two additional miles a day.

Record Goals Once They Have Been Identified

It is easy for athletes to focus attention on their goals soon after those goals have been set. Over the course of a long season, however, goals are sometimes forgotten. Therefore, it is useful for athletes to record their goals in written form and place them where they will be seen (e.g., in their lockers). Additionally, Harris and Harris (1984) recommend that athletes keep notebooks, recording goals, goal achievement strategies, and goal progress on a daily or weekly basis. Finally, Botterill (1983) suggests that the coach develop a contract stating all goals and goal achievement strategies for each athlete. Each athlete then signs his or her contract, and the coach keeps the contracts on file. Later the coach can use the contracts to remind the athletes of their goals.

Provide for Goal Evaluation

Based on their review of the research, Locke and his associates (1981) concluded that evaluative feedback is absolutely necessary if goals are to enhance performance. Therefore, athletes must receive feedback about how present performance is related to both short- and long-range goals. In many cases, feedback in the form of performance statistics like batting average, assists, goals scored, or steals made is readily available. Other goals, however, require that the coach or sport psychologist make special efforts to provide evaluative feedback. For instance, a coach helping an athlete control his or her temper on the field may have a manager record the number of times the player loses his or her temper in practice. Similarly, a softball coach helping outfielders attain their goal of efficiently backing up one another may have an observer record the number of times players move into correct positions after the ball is hit. In Chapter 15 Bunker and Williams suggest that the sport psychologist trying to help an athlete become more aware of his or her negative thoughts might have the athlete put a box of paper clips in a pocket; then during practice the athlete transfers one paper clip at a time to another pocket for each negative thought.

Provide Support for Goals

A goal-setting program will not succeed unless it is supported by those individuals who are paramount in the athlete's life. This typically includes the coach, the athlete's family, and teammates. Therefore, efforts must be made to educate these individuals as to the types of goals the athlete sets and the importance of their support in encouraging progress toward the goals. For instance, if an athlete sets performance goals as opposed to outcome goals but significant others in the athlete's life only stress the outcome of the game or match, it is unlikely that performance goals will change behavior. Simply stated, significant others must understand the goal-setting process and support it!

A GOAL-SETTING SYSTEM FOR COACHES

Goal-setting research and guidelines provide coaches with the information necessary for implementing goal-setting techniques with athletes. To be successful in implementing goal-setting procedures, however, coaches must develop and employ a goal-setting system. Botterill (1983) has outlined the essentials of such a system in detail. Of the many elements Botterill discusses, three seem paramount and can be incorporated into a three-phase goal-setting system: (1) the planning phase, (2) the meeting phase, and (3) the follow-up/evaluation phase.

The Planning Phase

Coaches will be ineffective if they attempt to set goals without first spending considerable time in planning them. Before discussing goals with athletes, for instance, coaches must identify individual and team needs. These needs may focus on any number of areas such as player fitness, individual skills, team skills, playing time, sportsmanship, and enjoyment.

Following this needs analysis, coaches must identify potential team and individual goals. Most coaches can identify a large number of potential goals for their athletes so it is important for them to consider how likely it is that their athletes will agree to and accomplish the goals. In doing so, coaches should consider the athletes' long-range goals, individual potential, commitment, and opportunity for practice.

Finally, coaches must begin to consider possible strategies that they can use to help their athletes achieve their goals. For example, a segment of each practice could be devoted to the accomplishment of identified goals or extra practices could be held for this purpose.

In essence, goal setting involves commitment and effort on the part of coaches as well as athletes. Therefore, coaches must be ready to initiate the goal-setting process with well-planned assessments of their athletes' abilities and established priorities.

The Meeting Phase

Once coaches have considered individual athlete and team needs, they should schedule goal-setting meetings. The first of these meetings should include the entire team. At the first meeting coaches should convey basic goal-setting information (e.g., the value of setting goals, areas in which to set goals, types of goals to set, the importance of performance goals) and ask the athletes to think about their general objectives for participation, as well as specific team and individual goals. Coaches must then give the athletes time to reflect upon their reasons for participation and to formulate potential goals.

A few days after the initial meeting, a second meeting should be held for the purpose of discussing some of the athletes' goals. It is especially important to examine goals in respect to their importance, specificity, and realistic nature. It is also desirable to examine possible strategies for achieving these goals.

In most cases, it will be impossible to set specific goals for each athlete during these initial group meetings. Therefore, coaches must also hold a number of meetings with individual athletes and small subgroups (e.g., forwards, centers, and guards in basketball). In these meetings, individual goals should be recorded, specific strategies for achieving these goals identified, and goal evaluation procedures determined. Before and after practice are often the most effective times for holding such meetings.

The Follow-Up/Evaluation Phase

As previously stated, goal setting will not be effective unless evaluative feedback is provided to athletes. Unfortunately, because of the hectic nature of the season, this is often forgotten. It is, therefore, a good idea to schedule goal evaluation meetings throughout the season. At these meetings, subgroups of athletes should discuss their goals and progress made toward achieving them and also reevaluate unrealistic goals or goals that cannot be achieved because of injury or sickness.

Finally, to facilitate goal follow-up and evaluation, coaches should develop systematic ways of providing feedback. Figure 10-1 contains such a system for the sport of basketball. Prior to the season, the coach prints up goal achievement cards that are completed by the athlete during the preseason or seasonal meetings. These cards contain places for the athletes to rate their present skills, identify specific goals, describe goal achievement strategies, and develop goal evaluation schedules. In addition, performance evaluation cards are printed (see Figure 10.1) and used to evaluate performance on a percentage scale (0% = poor, 100% = excellent). The evaluation cards are completed after various competitions and when combined with other available statistics serve as feedback for weekly goal follow-up meetings.

COMMON PROBLEMS IN SETTING GOALS

Goal setting is not a difficult psychological skill to use. However, it would be a misconception to think that problems do not arise when setting goals. Some of the more frequently encountered problems include attempting to set too many goals too soon, failing to recognize individual differences in athletes, setting goals that are too general, failing to modify unrealistic goals, failing to set performance goals as opposed to outcome goals, and failing to create a supportive goal-setting atmosphere. Each of these problems is addressed below.

Setting Too Many Goals Too Soon

A natural mistake that occurs when one first implements a goal-setting system is to set too many goals too soon. For example, it is not uncommon for coaches and athletes to set five or ten specific goals. This usually has negative results. The athletes have so many individual goals that they cannot properly monitor performance, or if they do monitor performance, they find the record keeping to be overwhelming and lose interest. A more effective approach is to prioritize goals and focus on accomplishing the one

Goal Achievement Card—Basketball

| Name | B. Jones | | | Date | 9-27-85 | | |
| Position | Forward | | | Years Experience | 2 | | |

Skill–Activity	Strong	Average	Needs improvement	Specific goal	Strategy	Target Date

Shooting
    lay-ups
    jump shots
    free throws
	✓	✓	✓	To correctly execute 8 out of 10 jump shots from the 8' to 10' range	Shoot 4 sets of 10 jump shots before practice every day	Oct. 27

Ball handling		✓				
Rebounding	✓					

Performance Evaluation Card—Basketball

| Name | B. Jones | Date | 12-4-85 |
| Position | Forward | Game | 3 |

Skill–Activity	Available statistics/Coach performance rating (0–100%)	Comments
Overall offensive play	80%	
Overall defensive play	94%	

Shooting
    lay-ups
    jump shots
    free throws
	70%
	2 for 2
	2 for 6
	3 for 4
		Jump shot—release ball at peak of jump

Ball handling turnovers	90% 1	
Rebounding	90%	

FIGURE 10.1

Sample Goal Achievement and Performance Evaluation Cards for the Sport of Basketball

or two most important ones. When these goals are achieved, the athletes then focus on the next most important prioritized goals. As the athletes become more experienced in goal setting, they also learn to handle greater numbers of goals more efficiently. In essence, coaches and sport psychologists must first teach their athletes how to set and accomplish goals so that later on the athletes can set goals independently.

Failing to Recognize Individual Differences

Not all athletes will be excited about setting goals, and some may even have negative attitudes about doing so. Coaches and sport psychologists must expect this and not overreact. Forcing athletes to set goals is ineffective, for individual commitment is needed. Rather, expose all of the athletes to goal setting and then work with those who show interest. Over time, their success will convince other less committed athletes to begin setting goals.

Setting Goals That Are Too General

Throughout this chapter we have emphasized the need for setting specific, measurable goals. Unfortunately, this does not always occur. Coaches, sport psychologists and athletes who are inexperienced goal setters will often set goals that are too general. Improving one's first serve in tennis, executing a better Yamashita vault in gymnastics, and lessening the frequency of negative thoughts are too vague. These goals are more effectively stated as increasing the number of good first serves from 50% to 55% in tennis, improving the Yamashita vault by sticking the landing eight out of ten times, and reducing negative thoughts to five, or less, during each practice session. When stating goals, coaches, sport psychologists and athletes must always ask, "How can we make this goal measurable and specific?"

Failing to Modify Unrealistic Goals

In his extensive five-month study of goal setting, Burton (1983) found that competitive collegiate swimmers had problems readjusting goals once they were set. Although the swimmers had little difficulty raising their goals once they were achieved, a number of athletes failed to lower goals that became unrealistic because of illness or injury. Coaches must recognize this problem and continually emphasize the appropriateness of lowering goals when necessary.

Failing to Set Performance Goals

The work of Martens et al. (1981) and Burton (1983, 1984) has demonstrated the value of setting performance goals as opposed to outcome goals.

To many athletes, however, winning or outcome goals are the only worthy goals. This is psychologically destructive and illogical, but it occurs because of the tremendous emphasis Americans place on winning. Coaches must be aware of this problem and continually emphasize the attainment of performance goals. For instance, coaches must continually remind athletes that great performances will typically lead to the best possible outcomes. Finally, coaches must realize that changing their athletes' perception of the importance of outcome versus performance goals may take a long-term effort.

Failing to Create a Supportive Goal-Setting Atmosphere

To reiterate, coaches and sport psychologists cannot set goals for their athletes or force them to participate in the goal-setting process. The athletes must be self-motivated and committed to the program. For this reason, leaders need to create a supportive goal-setting atmosphere, and in creating such an atmosphere, communication style is critical. Leaders must act as facilitators of goal-setting discussions, not as dictators (Botterill, 1983). They must share limitations with athletes and identify unrealistic goals, while simultaneously avoiding pessimistic remarks and put-downs. In essence, coaches and sport psychologists must adopt a positive communication style that includes good listening skills, a sincere orientation, and a positive approach.

SUMMARY

This chapter has provided strong empirical and experiential support for the utility of using goal setting in helping athletes attain personal growth and peak performance. Goals are effective because they influence psychological states such as self-confidence, direct attention to important aspects of the task, mobilize effort, increase persistence and foster the development of new learning strategies. A number of recognized guidelines should be followed when goal setting with athletes. These include setting behaviorally measurable goals, difficult yet realistic goals, short range as well as long range goals, performance as opposed to outcome goals, practice and competition goals, and positive as opposed to negative goals. Equally important guidelines are identifying target dates for attaining goals, identifying goal achievement strategies, recording goals once they have been identified, providing goal evaluation procedures and providing for goal support. Lastly, common problems must be recognized which arise when goal setting. These include setting too many goals too soon, failing to recognize individual differences, setting goals that are too general, failing to modify unrealistic goals, failing to set performance goals, and failing to create a supportive goal setting atmosphere. These problems can be easily avoided or controlled if they are recognized at the onset of the goal setting process.

Like other psychological skills, goal setting is not a magic formula that guarantees success. Goal setting is a tool, a very effective tool, that when combined with hard work and discipline can help coaches, sport psychologists and athletes reap the fruits of personal athletic growth and peak performance. It is highly recommended, then, that coaches and sport psychologists at all levels of competition engage in goal setting with their athletes.

REFERENCES

Bell, K. F. (1983). *Championship thinking: The athlete's guide to winning performance in all sports.* Englewood Cliffs, N.J.: Prentice-Hall.

Botterill, C. (1977, September). *Goal setting and performance on an endurance task.* Paper presented at the Canadian Psychomotor Learning and Sport Psychology Conference, Banff, Alberta, Canada.

Botterill, C. (1983). Goal setting for athletes with examples from hockey. In G. L. Martin and D. Hrycaiko (Eds.), *Behavior modification and coaching: Principles, procedures, and research.* Springfield, Ill.: Charles C. Thomas.

Burton, D. (1983). *Evaluation of goal setting training on selected cognitions and performance of collegiate swimmers.* Unpublished doctoral dissertation, University of Illinois, Urbana, Ill.

Burton, D. (1984, February). Goal setting: A secret to success. *Swimming World,* pp. 25–29.

Carron, A. V. (1984). *Motivation: Implications for coaching and teaching.* London, Ontario, Canada: Sports Dynamics.

Gould, D. (1983). Developing psychological skills in young athletes. In N. L. Wood (Ed.), *Coaching Science Update.* Ottawa, Ontario, Canada: Coaching Association of Canada.

Harris, D. V., & Harris, B. L. (1984). *The athlete's guide to sports psychology: Mental skills for physical people.* Ner York: Leisure Press.

Locke, E. A., Shaw, K. N., Saari, L. M., & Lathram, G. P. (1981). Goal setting and task performance. *Psychological Bulletin, 90,* 125–152.

Martens, R., Christina, R. W., Harvey, J. S., Jr., & Sharkey, B. J. (1981). *Coaching young athletes.* Champaign, Ill.: Human Kinetics.

McClements, J. (1982). Goal setting and planning for mental preparations. In L. Wankel & R. B. Wilberg (Eds.), Psychology of sport and motor behavior: Research and practice. *Proceedings of the Annual Conference of the Canadian Society for Psychomotor Learning and Sport Psychology.* Edmonton, Alberta, Canada: University of Alberta.

McClements, J. D., & Botterill, C. B. (1979). Goal setting in shaping of future per-
    formance of athletes. In P. Klavora and J. Daniel (Eds.), *Coach, athlete, and the
    sport psychologist.* Champaign, Ill.: Human Kinetics.

O'Block, F. R., & Evans, F. H. (1984). Goal setting as a motivational technique. In J.
    M. Silva & R. S. Weinberg (Eds.), *Psychological foundations of sport.* Champaign,
    Ill.: Human Kinetics.

Orlick, T. (1980). *In pursuit of excellence.* Champaign, Ill.: Human Kinetics.

11

Increasing Awareness for Sport Performance

KENNETH RAVIZZA

California State University at Fullerton

Bases loaded, 3 – 2 count, two outs, game tied. This type of pressure situation frequently confronts athletes during performance, and all too often the coach's instructions are, "just relax" or "concentrate." This type of generalized advice tells the athlete that the coach has recognized a lack of concentration, and frequently this results in even more pressure.

The underlying basis for the emerging field of peak performance sport psychology involves teaching the athlete the importance of the recognition, or awareness, of the need to do something to gain control. Athletes will not be aware of the need to gain control unless they first identify their own ideal performance state (see Chapter 9) and can contrast that state with the present one. Thus, awareness is the first step to gaining control of any pressure situation. For example, the athlete must be aware of his or her emotional state, or arousal level, and adjust it as needed to reach the optimal arousal level for performance. Then the athlete must attend to the appropriate focal points that will fine-tune or lock in his or her concentration. For example, a softball player will only get two or three great pitches to hit in a game. The player must be fully focused on each pitch so that when the great pitch comes, he or she is ready to make solid contact. The lack of awareness demonstrated by many athletes is often a by-product of the sport socialization process, whereby the athlete is encouraged to follow orders and not to question the coach's authority. More and more, coaches are beginning to take a less dogmatic approach because they realize that dependency often results from a strictly authoritarian coaching style.

Furthermore, lack of awareness in athletes is almost always the result of excessive concern with achieving the end result. For example, the baseball player in the pressure situation focuses on the end result of getting a hit. Awareness and control are part of the process of skill execution, specifically, execution in the present moment. The anxiety lies in the end result. Thus, the baseball player must focus on key components of hitting, such as taking the signal, stepping into the box, taking the practice swings to get the rhythm, then focusing on the pitcher, then fine-tuning the concentration to

149

the release area. At this point the athlete is totally focused on the task at hand and is ready to react spontaneously to the situation with controlled intensity. This type of appropriate focus of attention is essential in order to maximize performance.

The athlete's challenge is to focus on basic skills even when the athlete's pulse rate may increase significantly. The situation can be perceived as speeded up or out of the usual perspective because of the perceived threat of the situation. This chapter does not suggest a multitude of performance changes; instead, it suggests that the athlete be encouraged to become aware of his or her own ideal performance state and *routine* behaviors that he or she is already using to achieve this state. Many of the techniques we talk about in sport psychology are performed instinctively by the athlete. Awareness of these instinctive routines provides the athlete with something to focus on to regain control. Sport psychologists have contributed to enhancing performance by providing a structure or consistent framework for the various mental skills the athlete has often developed and practiced haphazardly.

This structure clarifies for the athlete the fact that there is a relationship between the various things that the athlete does to maximize performance. When the athlete can begin to understand that the imagery skills that are used for pregame preparation can also be used for concentration and relaxation training (as well as for academic studies), he or she has a better sense of control. Control is the key issue because the athlete's anxiety level tends to decrease with a feeling of control.

The purpose of this chapter is to discuss the importance of awareness in reaching peak performance in sport. Awareness will be presented as the first essential step in goal setting and self-regulation as it relates to skill development and the management of performance stress. The final section will discuss specific methods that the athlete can use to develop heightened awareness.

THE IMPORTANCE OF AWARENESS IN ATHLETICS

Every sport requires athletes to execute basic skills. The athletes must stand alone and accept the responsibility for their performance. During the off-season, individual responsibility is an even more crucial aspect since it is then that athletes must put in hours of isolated, rigorous training and self-coaching to develop and refine essential skills. Athletes must perform the skills, reflect on the feedback gained from the performance, make corrections and refinements, and then make the skills feel natural through a multitude of repetitions and refinements.

Athletes must recognize their strengths and weaknesses so that they can maximize their strengths and correct their weaknesses. Goal setting can be used to facilitate performance enhancement. At first, athletes want to be told what their goals should be, but it is essential that the athletes make the major contribution to establishing individual goals. This requires the athletes to reflect upon and evaluate their past performance. The coach gains a great deal of insight about the athletes' awareness on the basis of this evaluation of perceived strengths and weaknesses. The goals should be *performance* goals, such as, "I will be more consistent at the foul line by shooting 50 shots a day with the goal of hitting 60% by the end of two weeks and 65% after one month." This is different from an *outcome* goal, such as, "I want to improve my foul shooting." The goals should be as specific as possible and of various duration: short-term, intermediate, and long-range.

Goal setting requires awareness because the athlete first sets the goals, then strives to reach them, then proceeds to evaluate the performance feedback, and finally, adjusts the goals appropriately (Harris & Harris, 1984; McClements & Botterill, 1979).

AWARENESS AS IT RELATES TO SKILL DEVELOPMENT

Athletes must learn the difference between merely performing skills and experiencing skills. For example, try this exercise. Raise your right arm over your head five times—one . . . two . . . three . . . four . . . five— and halt. Now deeply inhale as you slowly raise your right arm over your head. Breathe slow and steady as you feel the movement, experience the muscles involved, feel the gentle stretch through the different muscles, feel that extension all through the arm, and now slowly let the arm down.

The difference between just going through the motions and really experiencing the skills hinges on the awareness involved. Feldenkrais (1972), a movement specialist, offers the following analogy:

> A man without awareness is like a carriage whose passengers are the desires, with the muscles for horses, while the carriage itself is the skeleton. Awareness is the sleeping coachman. As long as the coachman remains asleep the carriage will be dragged aimlessly here and there. Each passenger seeks a different destination and the horses pull different ways. But when the coachman is wide awake and holds the reins the horses will pull and bring every passenger to his proper destination. (p. 54)

Like the coachman, athletes must gain control of muscles, emotions, and thoughts and integrate them into a smooth performance. When athletes are aware and focused upon the sport experience, they exert more control over the situation. They recognize sooner when their balance is off, when too much tension is present in certain muscle groups, or when thoughts have become self-defeating. Aware athletes are more attuned to subtle fluctuations in the flow of the contest and can adjust that much sooner. Aware athletes can conserve vital energy by exerting no more than the needed effort.

Learning the Basics

Awareness requires that athletes totally focus their attention on the task. This ability must be developed in practice. Coaches want their athletes to be intense and totally involved in practice because this aids in creating quality practice time. Many coaches also realize the importance of mental training for performance, but the challenge is to find time for it. For this reason, it is important to incorporate awareness training with the physical skills that are already being performed in practice. For example, coaches and sport psychologists should encourage athletes to develop concentration as they stretch before practice by feeling the stretch and breathing into it. This type of stretching develops concentration in that the athletes are tuned in to their body as they stretch.

With the 1984 U.S. Olympic Women's Field Hockey Team, we established a set warm-up procedure for practice to aid the athletes in mentally and physically preparing for practice. The players began by stretching, then hit the ball back and forth to work out any kinks, and finally executed focused hitting. *Focused hitting* involves hitting the ball to exact locations, for example, to the receiver's right, middle, and left. This sequence is followed for five minutes. These are basic field hockey skills, but there is a difference when they are done with awareness. If the player's attention is on other aspects of the day, such as a party coming up or an argument with a friend, consistency in the focused hitting drill will be impossible.

This type of drill has two major advantages for the coach. First, visible objective performance demonstrates whether or not the athlete is concentrating. More importantly, awareness training is incorporated into the practice of basic skills. As a result, additional practice time is not required for mental training. This sophisticated approach to basic skills allows coaches to make the most of practice time by integrating mental or awareness skills training with basic fundamentals.

During one practice the Cal State Fullerton baseball team engaged in the focused bat and catch drill for 90 minutes because they had not been hitting exact locations consistently. This emphasis on basics was crucial because the players realized the coach was serious about executing the basics. The difference between performing the basics and focusing on the basics lies in the players' awareness. Athletes must learn to concentrate when the pressure is on, and the focal points for concentration become the basic skills. Augie Garrido, Cal State Fullerton's baseball coach, gives the following example:

> We are really working on having the players clear their minds. Yesterday one player was given a bunt signal and he proceeded to pop out. His next time at the plate he was in a bunting situation and tried to bunt but missed. So I called him over and said, "You've tried two times and failed, and you are about to fail again because you still have the other two times on your mind. Give yourself the best chance to be successful by seeing the ball and bunting the ball. You can do that. Stay right with the ingredients of bunting. You've done it a hundred times, but you have got to get the other times off your mind." The player proceeded to lay down a perfect bunt. (1982)

When athletes practice physical skills and mental skills together, their confidence increases because they are ready and experienced in the subtle skill of concentration.

The All-or-None Syndrome

Awareness develops in the sport process. This is where the athlete experiences self-control. Gymnasts learning new moves cannot expect to master them immediately. A series of progressions must be worked through. Often, in the midst of this process, gymnasts feel they have *either* hit the move *or* missed. If they hit it, they are delighted, but if they miss, frustration begins to set in. The challenge is to maintain motivation throughout the hours of practice.

At Cal State Fullerton we have established gradations of execution for the athletes to evaluate their skill development. For example, even if a move is "missed," certain aspects of the movement were probably successful, and it is important that they be identified. Similarly, in baseball a pitcher is told that he needs to raise his arm on a fastball release. The number 5 is given for the ideal release distance and a 1 is given for a side-arm release. After each pitch the player is asked to assign a numerical value from 1 to 5 to his arm location. It is essential that the athlete reflect on the position of his arm because this requires awareness. The coach can then give an evaluation from 1 to 5. This aids the athlete in beginning to adjust his awareness to what the proper position feels like (based on a principle from Gallwey, 1974). If a video recorder is available, the performance feedback is even more specific.

When athletes gain more awareness, they can make more accurate adjustments in their performance. This ability to refine the subtle intricacies of performance is a critical skill as athletes reach for maximum performance. In addition to improving self-control, the athletes experience a feeling of growing success. Even though the outcome is not perfect, players develop a more positive attitude about the skill and will keep their motivation level where it needs to be.

Playing the Edge of Peak Performance

To reach their full sport potential, athletes must learn to play the performance edge. For example, they must learn to control that delicate balance between power and grace. Every sport has components that must be balanced appropriately to maximize performance. This type of control necessitates that athletes be aware. They must monitor their performance in order to recognize when it is at its peak. In athletic training and conditioning, there are many times when athletes push too hard or do not push hard enough. At such times, the athletes need to relate to their movement experience with the precision of a surgeon so that they can make needed adjustments. For example, a runner constantly monitors her body for subtle messages so that she can make adjustments to reach that edge of peak performance.

One awareness technique I use with runners is the blindfold run. A blindfolded runner and a partner run a specified distance together, with the partner providing physical support and removing any dangers. The blindfold alters the runner's perspective as the runner is now totally focused on the present moment. Usual thoughts and distractions are suspended by the new perspective. After about five minutes into the run, the athlete experiences running in a more aware fashion.

Coaches and sport psychologists are encouraged to discuss with their athletes this idea of playing the edge so that each athlete can begin to understand and identify where that edge is for him or her. Figure 11.1 and the Appendix suggest ways of keeping records of the mental aspects of performance.

Awareness in Managing Performance Stress

To move consistently toward peak performance, each athlete must know and be aware of his or her own experience of optimal performance. The athlete has to learn to control the excitement of the sport situation so that his or her energy can be channeled into the performance, or to reorganize when the arousal level is too low and activate it as needed. To gain this control the athlete must learn how competitive stress affects individual performance. (See Chapter 12 for more information on this topic.) The first step is to be aware of one's arousal level and then to adjust it as needed. The athlete must recognize which situations or stressors tend to negatively affect his or her performance. Knowledge of the stressful areas allows for the development of a strategy to prepare and cope effectively with them.

PERFORMANCE FEEDBACK SHEET

Name _____

Opponent _____

1. What were your stressors for today's game?

2. How did you experience the stress (thoughts, actions, body)?

3. How was your level of arousal for today's game? What were your feelings at
   these various points?   0 ————— 5 ————— 10
                          Too Low   Perfect   Too High

   a. Bus ride to game: _____
   b. Warm-up on field, court, etc.: _____
   c. Just before the game: _____
   d. During the game: _____

4. What techniques did you use to manage the stress and how effective were you in
   controlling it?

5. How was your self-talk?   (Describe.)

6. What did you learn from today's game that will help you in your next game?

7. What mental training techniques were most effective for you?

8. Briefly describe one play or segment of the game that you enjoyed.

9. How would you rate your play? _____   1 ————— 5 ————— 10
                                            Terrible   OK   Great

10. Briefly describe how you felt about today's game.

11. Anything you want to say:

FIGURE 11.1
Sample Performance Feedback Sheet

For example, playing in front of a crowd or in the presence of scouts is stressful; thus, the athlete can mentally prepare to deal with the situation to avoid surprise. The athlete has time to get support from teammates and the coaching staff and also to develop his or her own strategy.

Once the athlete understands the stressors, the next step is to be aware of the way that stress is experienced, because the manifestations of stress vary greatly among individuals. For example: "As the pressure mounts, my shoulders and neck tighten, my thoughts jump around, and I tend to get jittery." Changes in breathing are another bodily cue that often signals too much stress. Train your athletes to become sensitive to how their breathing responds to stress. For example, do they start to breathe more rapidly and shallowly? Do they hold their breath? Do they have difficulty breathing? These manifestations of stress may be perceived as problems, but they can be used as signals to provide feedback to the athlete as to whether the arousal level is appropriate. The athlete gains this personal knowledge by reflecting on previous performances and essentially using sport experiences like a biofeedback machine.

The athlete's consistent focus on his or her thoughts and feelings and use of appropriate interventions allow the athlete to maintain an optimal performance state. Interventions may include relaxation and activation techniques, concentration methods, thought control, and basic breathing techniques. (See Chapters 13 – 18 for specific techniques.) There are also times when the athlete must recognize that it is time just to flow with the experience and let it happen (Ravizza, 1984). Once again, the sport journal described in the Appendix helps the athlete develop this awareness because it provides a mechanism for recording and evaluating sport performance.

TECHNIQUES FOR DEVELOPING AWARENESS

There are many techniques to increase awareness. Three specific methods are journal keeping, performance feedback sheets and group discussions. The sport journal provides a structured method to reflect on sport performances and to capitalize on the wealth of experiential knowledge gained from the performance. The journal guidelines in the Appendix ask questions about stressors, manifestations of stress, and feelings associated with performance, concentration, and skill execution. After your teams play a game, discuss what the members have learned so that you and they can establish new goals or modify earlier ones.

Following selected performances, give your players feedback sheets similar to the one shown in Figure 11.1 so that they can process the subjective information gained from each contest. This procedure helps the players systematically learn from the experience and bring closure to their performance so that they can begin to focus on the next performance. This is particularly helpful in tournament play where the athletes have to perform many times during a short period.

With the athletes' permission, coaches and sport psychologists can read these journals and provide additional feedback. Writing feelings in a journal or on a feedback sheet is often perceived by athletes as less threatening than actual verbal discussions. On the other hand, such writing often forges an understanding that promotes discussion. (In some cases, coaches have also worked with English teachers to capitalize on the athletes' interest in writing about the experiential aspects of sport performance to develop English writing skills.)

Group discussion is another method that coaches and sport psychologists can use to increase athlete awareness. Coaches should provide their athletes with an opportunity to discuss a performance by delicately encouraging but not requiring them to do so. Sport psychologists should do the same thing after practice of certain mental training techniques. Sometimes coaches and sport psychologists can foster this form of communication through one-on-one discussions. Coach/sport psychology practitioners should share their perspective or expertise but also encourage the athletes to talk about the experience. Ask questions about arousal and confidence levels, stressors, and manifestations. Every team is capable of this type of interaction but such dialogue is frequently difficult to facilitate at first. As the athletes become much more aware of the needs of their teammates, team cohesion will be more likely to result. In turn, new insights into the athletes' own sport performance are gained. For example, one athlete responds to stress by withdrawing. An understanding of this by teammates relieves stress because other people now know that this is one method used to mentally prepare for performance. There is nothing "wrong" with an athlete who is quiet.

A good time to begin group discussions is after a positive experience because the feelings are nonthreatening. For example, after a great practice, coaches can ask the athletes to discuss what made the practice so good. How was it different from a nonproductive practice session?

In regard to specific methods of increasing awareness, it is important that the practitioner do what they are comfortable with. However, it is strongly suggested that coaches and sport psychologists slowly integrate the various methods discussed in this chapter.

SUMMARY

Developing awareness is a critical element of peak performance because it provides athletes with the experiential knowledge to gain control of the performance. Awareness is the first step in raising self-control in sport participation. Initially, athletes need to become aware of their ideal performance state. Next athletes need to recognize when they are no longer at that ideal state. As athletes develop the awareness skills, they will recognize earlier when they are not focused or aroused appropriately. This early recognition aids athletes in gaining control before it is lost. The sooner a deviation is recognized the easier it is to get back on course. Athletes with a range of interventions can use them to get their mental–emotional and physical states to more nearly approximate what they have found leads to peak performance. Among the various techniques for developing awareness, journal keeping and group discussion are particularly helpful.

REFERENCES

Feldenkrais, M. (1972). *Awareness through movement.* New York: Harper & Row.

Gallwey, T. (1974). *The inner game of tennis.* New York: Random House.

Garrido, A. Interview with author. Fullerton, California, 7 December 1982.

Harris, D., & Harris, B. (1984). *The athlete's guide to sport psychology: Mental skills for physical people.* New York: Leisure Press.

McClements, J., & Botterill, C. (1979). Goal setting in shaping of future performance of athletes. In P. Klavora & J. Daniel (Eds.), *Coach, athlete and the sport psychologist.* Champaign, Ill.: Human Kinetics.

Ravizza, K. (1984). Qualities of the peak experience in sport. In J. Silva and R. Weinberg (Eds.), *Psychological foundations for sport.* Champaign, Ill.: Human Kinetics.

APPENDIX

GUIDELINES FOR KEEPING
A SPORT JOURNAL

The sport journal is a tool to help you further develop your mental skills for sport performance. The first step to gain self-control is to develop an awareness of your sport performance so that you can recognize when you are pulled out of the most appropriate mental state for you. The journal provides you with an opportunity to record the different intervention strategies that you experiment with to regain control. The long-range goal is to develop various techniques that you can implement in stressful situations to perform to your utmost ability.

If you choose to, the journal also can be a place where you can record your feelings and the personal knowledge that you are gaining about yourself, the game, your teammates, and any other factors. This is one of the few times in your life that you will ever direct so much energy toward one specific goal. There is a lot to learn from your pursuit of excellence. This journal will give you something to reflect back on after your high-level participation is completed.

The journal also can serve as a place where you can express your feelings in writing and drawings. It is beneficial to get these feelings out in some manner so that they don't build up and contribute to unproductive tension. The use of colored pens is often helpful to express yourself. You do not have to make an entry every day, but date the entries you do make. The journal is an informal record of your thoughts and experiences as you train for high-level performance.

If you choose to have someone read your journal, please feel comfortable to delete any parts that you think are too personal to share. The intention of someone who is reviewing you should be to guide you and make *suggestions* that may facilitate your self-exploration in reaching your goals.

I would suggest that you try this technique, but it is not for everyone. If you choose not to, that is your choice.

1. *Peak Performance.* What does it feel like when you play and/or practice at your best? Describe some of your most enjoyable experiences playing your sport. What have you learned from these moments when you are fully functioning?
2. *Stressors.* Outside the sport — write down your thoughts about var-

ious events outside your sport that are distracting to you. Parents, boy/girlfriends, peers, job hassles, financial issues, community (hometown expectations), etc. On the field — importance of contest, location, spectators, etc.

3. *Coaching Staff.* What do you need from your coaches? What can you give them in order to reach your goals? What can you do to make your relationship with your coaches more productive?

4. *Teammates.* What do you want from your teammates? What can you give them? How do you relate and work with your teammates? Write about your relationship with other teammates. Any unfinished business?

5. *Confidence.* At this time how confident are you in regard to achieving your goals? What can you do differently to feel more confident? What can you ask of yourself, coach, and/or teammates?

6. *Manifestations of Your Stress.* How do you experience high levels of anxiety in performance? Physiologically, thoughts and behavioral reactions. What did you do to intervene and keep in balance?

7. *Awareness and Concentration.* What changes do you observe in your performance when you are aware? What concentration methods are you experimenting with? What are your focal points for various skills?

8. *Relaxation Training.* How are your relaxation skills developing? Are there any parts of your body that are more difficult than others to relax? What method is best for you? In what manner are you able to relate this to your play? How quickly can you relax?

9. *Thought Control.* How is your self-talk affecting your performance? Write out some of your negative self-talk and make it positive.

10. *Centering/Concentration Skills.* What are you doing to concentrate appropriately before the contest and during the contest? What has been successful? Unsuccessful? Describe your preperformance routine.

11. *Imagery.* How are your imagery skills developing for you? Do you see a TV screen-type image or is it more of a feeling image? At what point do you notice lapses in concentration? How clear are your images? Can you control the speed and tempo of the image?

12. *Controlling Your Arousal Level.* What are you doing to control your arousal level? What are you doing to increase arousal and intensity? What are you experimenting with to reduce arousal levels? What is working for you and what is not working?

13. *Pressure Situations.* How are you handling pressure situations? What are you doing differently? What are you doing to learn to cope more effectively?

14. *Quality Practice Time.* What do you do to mentally prepare for practice? How do you keep your personal difficulties from affecting your play? What are you doing to take charge? What works for you and what hasn't worked?
15. *Anything You Want to Address.*

12   Arousal – Performance Relationships

DANIEL M. LANDERS and
STEPHEN H. BOUTCHER

Arizona State University

Most athletes at some time or another have suffered from inappropriate levels of arousal. Consider, for a moment, the following illustrative examples. A U.S. Olympic weight lifter in international competition surprisingly deviates from his customary preparatory routine before a lift and totally forgets to chalk his hands. As might be expected, the lift is missed. A gymnast preparing for a high flyaway dismount from the still rings suddenly focuses on self-doubts concerning his ability to perform the stunt without the presence of a spotter. These doubts, coupled with an increased fatigue level brought about by a long routine, cause him to freeze and release the rings prematurely. Finally, a sprinter who appears lackadaisical and lethargic during precompetition workouts records one of her worst times during competition.

These are just a few examples of what athletes and coaches usually refer to as lack of concentration, choking under pressure, or failure to get the athlete "up" for competition. Sport competition can generate much anxiety and worry, which in turn can affect physiological and thought processes so dramatically that performance often deteriorates. In your own athletic or coaching experience, you have probably perceived a racing heartbeat, a dry mouth, butterflies in your stomach, trembling muscles, or an inability to clearly focus thoughts. In these situations you may have told yourself that you were too tight or tense or that you couldn't think straight. Common expressions like these often prompt practical questions concerning whether the athlete should be "fired up" as much as possible or relaxed as much as possible before an important competition. Or perhaps there is some in-between state that should be sought.

These concerns are generally related to the topic of motivation and, more specifically, the concept of arousal. Understanding arousal and its effects on athletic performance, finding ways to estimate the arousal demands of a particular sport, and assessing arousal levels of individual athletes form the focus of this chapter. In the first section we will describe arousal and its effects and outline a model for understanding its influence

163

on athletic performance. In the second section we will describe the major hypotheses and research evidence for the arousal–performance relationship. Finally, in the third section we will describe a method whereby the coach or sport psychologist can estimate the optimal arousal level for a particular sport and for specific individuals within that sport.

THE NATURE OF AROUSAL

Before considering how arousal is related to performance, it is necessary to clarify the nature of the arousal construct. This will be done by first defining arousal, followed by a discussion of its origin and how it is generated. Finally, various techniques for measuring arousal will be presented.

Defining Arousal

For our purposes, *arousal* will be viewed as an energizing function that is responsible for the harnessing of the body's resources for intense and vigorous activity (Sage, 1984). An individual's state of arousal is seen as varying on a continuum ranging from deep sleep at one end (as in a comatose state) to extreme excitement at the other (e.g., a panic attack) (Malmo, 1959).

An analogy used by Martens (1974) may be helpful in describing the concept of arousal. Imagine arousal as being equated with the engine speed of a stationary automobile. The engine may run very fast, or just idle slowly. The intensity of the engine can be measured in revolutions per minute, whereas the intensity of the human engine is assessed by measuring the person's arousal level. The ideal intensity should match the requirements for the desired task outcome (e.g., quick acceleration) in order to produce the greatest performance efficiency. Sometimes, however, this is not the case. The human engine, just like the automobile, can be running very fast, but because it is in neutral or "park" gear, its effects may not be observed. At other times, the engine may be racing with the car in forward gear but with the emergency brake on. This unnatural state is akin to what we will refer to later as a performance "disregulation," where extraneous influences (e.g., the brake or anxiety brought about by negative, self-defeating thought processes) interfere with the natural coordinative action of the skill being performed. The human engine refers to both the activation of the brain and the innervation of different physiological systems.

Unlike the car engine, our human engine cannot be turned off—at least while we are alive! Even as you sleep, there is electrical activity in your brain as well as small amounts in the muscles. Thus, arousal is a natural, ongoing state. However, when arousal levels become extremely high, you may experience unpleasant emotional reactions associated with the autonomic nervous system. This maladaptive condition is often referred to as stress or state anxiety. As we will see in a later section of this chapter, anxiety reactions to competition can result in ineffective performance, faulty decision making, and inappropriate perception. Helping athletes harness arousal so that it will not become an uncontrollable anxiety response is one of the major preoccupations of sport psychologists. It is important to bear in mind that sport psychologists do not seek to make people unemotional zombies but instead attempt to teach skills that will enable the athlete to better control arousal and, thereby, more effectively cope with anxiety.

Origin of Arousal States

The structures for controlling arousal are located in the brain and primarily involve the cortex, reticular formation, the hypothalamus, and the limbic system. These centers interact with the adrenal medulla and the somatic and autonomic systems to determine overall arousal. We can demonstrate the integration of these different systems in an athletic situation by means of the following example.

A field hockey goalie sits in the dressing room minutes before an important match. She is worried about the upcoming game because she doubts her ability to play well in the biggest match of the season. These thoughts lead to anxiety about performance. Her worrying may not be realistic, but to her body, that does not matter. The cortex sends signals to the hypothalamus, which in turn releases hormones that activate the pituitary gland. The pituitary gland releases a hormone (ACTH) that triggers the adrenal glands to pour epinephrine and norepinephrine (also called adrenaline and noradrenaline) into the bloodstream (Krahenbuhl, 1975). These hormones, together with increased activity of the autonomic system, prepare her body and mind for an emergency "fight or flight" situation. Heart rate, blood pressure, and breathing increase, and muscles in general begin to tighten. Blood vessels in the hands and feet close down, and their blood supply is shunted to the larger, deeper muscles. The hockey goalie is now in an overly aroused or anxious state. Needless to say we would not expect this athlete to perform well in this condition.

How Arousal Is Generated

From the foregoing example, we can see that the athlete's initial appraisal of the situation was the starting point of a chain reaction that ultimately led to the overly aroused state. This chain reaction along with the host of other

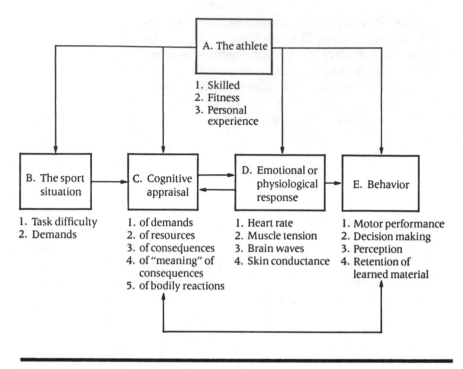

FIGURE 12.1
A Model Illustrating Factors That Affect the Arousal–Performance Relationship

factors involved in the arousal–performance relationship are outlined in Figure 12.1.

Our hockey goalie appraised the situation negatively and decided that her capabilities did not meet the demands of the upcoming game. This combination of an important, meaningful event and doubts about her ability was responsible for generating anxiety and worry. This is usually the first part of the arousal process,* which unless stopped will inevitably lead to the physiological reactions described in Figure 12.1 (see D.1–4). Once these physiological responses start to occur, she begins to appraise the feelings as well (C.5). Not knowing how to cope with the physiological reactions can create even more worry and apprehension (C.1–4). Notice also that, once performance begins, aspects of the athlete's behavior (see

* Although mental appraisal usually precedes the emotional reaction, it can sometimes follow it. This occurs in startle responses that can subsequently be interpreted to evoke an anger or a good-natured response. It can also occur when the athlete is unknowingly doing something (e.g., stringing a bow before an archery competition) that may increase the level of psychological arousal.

E.1 – 4) are fed back for cognitive appraisal (C.1 – 5) that may further intensify anxiety. As we shall see later, this process can be influenced by individual difference variables such as skill level, personality, physical and
psychological fitness, and competitive experience.

Measurement of Arousal

Since arousal affects so many bodily functions, it appears to be an easy
construct to measure. Unfortunately, this is not the case. We will discuss
three areas of arousal measurement (see Table 12.1) and highlight the
advantages and disadvantages of each.

Physiological measures In sport psychology research, much frustration
has resulted from the lack of consistent agreement among different physiological variables and questionnaire measures of arousal. This situation has
prompted investigators (e.g., Martens, 1974) to abandon physiological
measures in favor of questionnaires. Indeed, in the last decade, research
concerning the relationship between arousal and sport performance has
almost exclusively relied upon questionnaires despite evidence favoring
physiological measures (Landers, Wang, & Courtet, 1985; Light & Obrist,
1983).

The low correlations found among physiological measures has been
explained by Lacey, Bateman, and Van Lehn's (1953) principle of "autonomic response stereotypy." For example, in the same stressful situation,
athlete A might display an elevated heart rate, while athlete B might show
an increase in gastrointestinal activity. This principle suggests that averaging one physiological variable (e.g., heart rate) across a group of subjects
may conceal individual arousal reactions.

To overcome this problem, Duffy (1962) has recommended the use of
multiple measures as an index of the arousal response. She suggests that if
investigators derive mathematical combinations of many variables, then
greater validity of the autonomic indicators of arousal will be brought
about.

The current view concerning physiological measures is that they are far
more complex than first thought. However, with increased understanding
of physiological processes and the continuing trend of cheaper, more sophisticated equipment, physiological measures have much potential as reliable indicators of the arousal response.

Biochemical measures The adrenal glands are responsible for the release of epinephrine and norepinephrine into the bloodstream in times of
stress. Also a variety of corticosteroids enter the blood during high arousal

T A B L E 1 2 . 1
Some Common Physiological, Biochemical, and Questionnaire Measures of Arousal

---

Measure and Description

A. Physiological
  1. Central
     Electroencephalography (EEG). Changes occur in brain wave patterns
        from an alpha or relaxed state (8–13 Hz) to beta or a more aroused state
        (14–30 Hz).
  2. Autonomic
     Electrical properties of the skin. This measure assesses either the amount
        of skin conductance or resistance to an electric current. Elevations in
        arousal cause increased perspiration, which increases the flow of the
        current.
     Heart rate. Increases in heart rate, the pattern of beats, and heart rate
        variability can all be indices of arousal.
     Blood pressure. Increases in blood pressure are also associated with
        increased arousal levels and can be measured by cannulation or by the
        stethoscope and pressure-cuff method.
     Muscle activity. Muscle tension can be measured by electromyography
        (EMG), which measures the firing rate of motor units by means of
        surface electrodes attached to the muscle.
B. Biochemical
     Epinephrine. Epinephrine is released from the adrenal medulla during
        times of stress. This hormone can be measured in the urine and blood.
     Norepinephrine. Levels of this hormone are also elevated during stressful
        activities and can be measured by the same techniques used for
        analyzing epinephrine.
C. Questionnaires
  1. Unidimensional measures
     State-Trait Anxiety Inventory (Spielberger, Gorsuch, & Lushene, 1970)
     Somatic Perception Questionnaire (Landy & Stern, 1971)
     Activation Deactivation Adjective Checklist (Thayer, 1967)
     Sport Competitive Anxiety Test (Martens, 1977)
  2. Multidimensional measures
     Cognitive-Somatic Anxiety Questionnaire (Schwartz, Davidson, &
        Goleman, 1978)
     Competitive State Anxiety Inventory-2 (CSAI-2). (Martens et al., 1983)

---

states. Increases in hormonal levels have been examined chiefly by analyzing either the blood or urine. Blood analysis usually involves drawing blood
from the subject by syringe or catheter. The analysis is complex and requires
sophisticated equipment. Another disadvantage is that the drawing of the
blood can be traumatic to certain subjects, thus confounding the results of
the study. Urine analysis is less evasive but suffers from the same cost and

time disadvantages as blood analysis. At this point, it is also unclear how accurately these measures reflect the brain's overall hormonal levels.

Questionnaires Many questionnaires are designed to assess the different effects of increased arousal. Some measure cognitive variables, some assess physiological responses, and others assess both dimensions in the same questionnaire (see Table 12.1). The advantages of questionnaires are that they are quick and easy to administer and relatively easy to analyze. One disadvantage is that they may be insensitive to changes in arousal levels by being susceptible to unwanted effects such as the social desirability response. Thus, athletes may complete a questionnaire with responses they perceive the coach or sport psychologist would like to see. Another disadvantage is that questionnaires usually necessitate large samples to offset the inherent variability among subjects. This is often impossible with teams or small groups of athletes.

Many questionnaires are designed to assess both trait and state forms of anxiety. Trait anxiety is a *general* predisposition to respond across many situations with high levels of anxiety. To assess trait anxiety, subjects are asked to rate how they generally feel. State anxiety is much more specific, referring to a subject's anxiety at a particular moment. People who are high in trait anxiety are expected to respond with higher levels of state anxiety, or situationally specific anxiety. The State-Trait Anxiety Inventory (Spielberger, Gorsuch, & Lushene, 1970) is a popular example of a well-researched questionnaire that assesses both dimensions of anxiety. Whereas the questions on the Spielberger et al. (1970) scales are of a general nature, the Sport Competitive Anxiety Test by Martens (1977) has both trait and state scales that are specifically designed to assess anxiety in competitive situations.

A new development in the construction of anxiety questionnaires is the trend toward more multidimensional instruments. Two questionnaires, one general (Schwartz, Davidson, & Goleman, 1978) and the other competition specific (Martens, Burton, Vealey, Smith, & Bump, 1983), have subdivided anxiety into the components of somatic and cognitive aspects. Somatic or bodily anxiety is assessed by questions such as "How tense are the muscles in your body?" Cognitive anxiety would be indicated by affirmative responses to questions such as "Do you worry a lot?" It is believed that by subdividing anxiety into its component parts more will be understood about its nature and more effective therapies can thus be designed. However, compared to many of the unidimensional measures, at this time there is relatively little research to support these multidimensional instruments.

THE RELATIONSHIP BETWEEN AROUSAL AND MOTOR PERFORMANCE

In the motor behavior literature two hypotheses have been advanced to explain the relationship between arousal and performance. We will first consider the drive theory hypothesis and then the inverted-U hypothesis.

Drive Theory Hypothesis

Although this is not a consistently held view among all psychologists, for our purposes we will equate the term *drive* with *arousal*. In other words, drive and arousal convey what we referred to earlier as the intensity dimension of behavior.

Drive theory, as modified by Spence and Spence (1966), predicts that performance (P) is a multiplicative function of habit (H) and drive (D): $P = H \times D$. The construct of "habit" in this formulation refers to the hierarchical order or dominance of correct or incorrect responses. According to this hypothesis, increases in arousal should enhance the probability of making the dominant responses. When performance errors are frequently made, as in the early stages of skill acquisition, the dominant responses are likely to be incorrect responses. Conversely, when performance errors are infrequent, the dominant response is said to be a correct response. Increases in arousal during initial skill acquisition impair performance, but as the skill becomes well learned, increases in arousal facilitate performance.

For example, a novice basketball player shooting foul shots only sinks three shots out of ten; therefore, the incorrect response (a miss) is dominant. The drive theory hypothesis would predict that given greater pressure, the novice player is likely to miss more than seven shots out of ten. By contrast, the all-star basketball player may average eight successful shots for every ten attempted. In this case, because the dominant response is a correct response, an increase in arousal should enhance the player's chance of sinking more than eight shots out of ten.

It is questionable whether a linear relationship between arousal and performance can be found for accuracy tasks such as foul-shooting. However, Oxendine (1984) argues that linear relationships, as depicted in Figure 12.2, do exist for gross motor activities involving strength, endurance, and speed. These types of activities are typically overlearned with strongly formed habit patterns. It seems likely, therefore, that a very high level of arousal is desirable for optimal performance in these types of gross motor skills. Anecdotal evidence regarding "superhuman" feats performed in emergency situations where unexpected physical strength, speed, or endurance was required (e.g., a mother lifting a station wagon off her trapped child) supports this view.

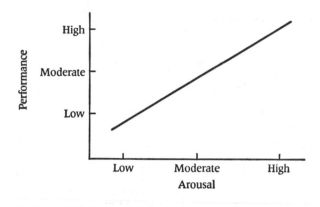

FIGURE 12.2
The Linear Relationship Between Arousal and Performance as Suggested by
Drive Theory

At first glance, these examples seem to provide ample evidence to support a drive theory explanation for sport skills involving strength, speed, and endurance. Contrary to Oxendine's analysis, however, we would like to argue on conceptual grounds that the "fight or flight" arousal responses produced in these emergency situations are not appropriate comparisons to the sport situation. The sport setting is highly structured, often involving complex decision-making and perceptual strategies, in addition to the performance of a motor skill. The surge of epinephrine resulting from an emergency situation may enhance strength in an uncontrolled manner, but this may actually be detrimental in actual sport performances. For example, there are many instances of overaroused sprinters recording false starts in intense competition. Similarly, many superenergized weight lifters have forgotten to chalk up or have lifted the barbell in a biomechanically inefficient way in major competitions. Thus, on experiential grounds, it appears that even among weight lifters, sprinters, and long- or middle-distance runners there are limits to the amount of arousal the athlete can tolerate without suffering performance decrements.

The drive theory hypothesis has not fared much better when the experimental evidence from the motor behavior literature has been examined. For example, Freeman (1940) has shown that with high levels of arousal, reaction times are slower than when arousal levels are in the moderate range. Furthermore, in other arousal-producing situations (e.g., audience effects) where the drive theory hypothesis has received extensive support, it is now known that these effects were so small as to be of trivial practical significance (Bond & Titus, 1983; Landers, Snyder-Bauer, & Feltz, 1978).

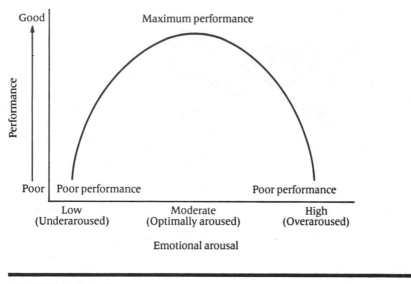

FIGURE 12.3
The Inverted-U Relationship Between Arousal and Performance

Thus, it appears that other hypotheses, such as the inverted-U, need to be considered as a more plausible explanation for the relationship between arousal and athletic performance.

Inverted-U Hypothesis

The inverted-U relationship between arousal and performance is shown in Figure 12.3. The inverted-U hypothesis predicts that as arousal increases from drowsiness to alertness, there is a progressive increase in performance efficiency. However, once arousal continues to increase beyond alertness to a state of high excitement, there is a progressive decrease in task performance. Thus, the inverted-U hypothesis suggests that behavior is aroused and directed toward some kind of balanced or optimal state.

Although the exact shape of the curve does not exactly match the idealized pattern in Figure 12.3, the decrement in performance at high levels of stress does occur across studies with considerable regularity. For example, Martens and Landers (1970) found greater motor steadiness at intermediate levels of arousal as measured with a physiological measure. Wood and Hokanson (1965) have observed a similar inverted U-shaped pattern for performance when arousal has been experimentally produced by varying muscle tension. Babin (1966) and Levitt and Gutin (1971) have also found reaction-time performance curves resembling an inverted-U that were produced during total body exercise on a treadmill or bicycle ergometer of varying work-load intensities and durations.

Inverted-U relationships have even been found in research studies that have used real-world sport skills. Fenz and Epstein (1969) have reported such relationships among physiological measures, self-report measures, and jumping efficiency of sport parachutists. Finally, Klavora (1979) found inverted-U performance patterns among high school basketball players as measured by coaches' performance ratings and self-reported anxiety measures by players for each game.

Of course, some experiments do not show inverted-U curves (Murphy, 1966; Pinneo, 1961), but the weight of the evidence seems to support the inverted-U hypothesis. Overall, the findings suggest the following conclusions. First, the inverted-U hypothesis seems to generalize across field and experimental situations. Second, the same performance patterning generally exists for arousal induced psychologically or physically through drugs, exercise, or muscle tension.

Task characteristics From an arousal perspective the characteristics of a skill or activity are essential determinants of performance. As early as 1908 it was known that the optimal level of arousal varied among different tasks. Using laboratory animals, Yerkes and Dodson found that on more complex tasks, the decrement in performance under increasing arousal conditions occurred earlier than it did for less complex tasks. The interaction of task complexity with arousal level is clearly illustrated in Broadhurst's (1957) experiment (see Figure 12.4). In this experiment arousal was created by holding rats underwater for zero, two, four, or eight seconds prior to allowing them to swim underwater to complete a two-choice maze. In one condition the choice was made easier by making the correct escape door more obvious (brightly painted lines), whereas in the more difficult condition the doors were very similar. As shown in Figure 12.4, decrements in time to negotiate the maze occurred much earlier (after two seconds of submergence) in the more complex decision-making situation. Thus, higher levels of arousal can be tolerated on less complex tasks before performance is curtailed.

What does all of this mean for the performance of sport skills? Basically, the complexity characteristics of the motor skill need to be analyzed to determine how much arousal is optimal. A number of factors that must be considered appear in Table 12.2. Take for example the precision and steadiness characteristics required for successful execution of a skill. (See Figure 12.5.) For very precise fine motor skills that involve steadiness or control of unwanted muscle activity (e.g., golf), very little arousal can be tolerated without accompanying performance decrements. However, for tasks such as weight lifting that involve minimal fine motor precision, a much higher level of arousal can be achieved before performance is impaired.

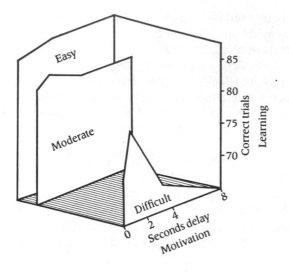

FIGURE 12.4
A Three-Dimensional Model Illustrating the Yerkes–Dodson Law. Rats were held underwater and deprived of air for varying numbers of seconds after which they were allowed to escape by selecting the correct door. The optimal level of motivation for learning depended on task difficulty.

Source: Broadhurst, 1957.

   In addition to considering factors associated with the motor act itself, it is important to consider the decisional and perceptual characteristics of the task. The underwater swimming of the rats in Broadhurst's (1957) experiment was an example of inverted-U performance curves when the complexity of alternative *decisions* was varied. Generally speaking, tasks with

TABLE 12.2
The Complexity of Motor Performance

Decision	Perception	Motor Act
Number of decisions necessary	Number of stimuli needed	Number of muscles
Number of alternatives per decision	Number of stimuli present	Amount of coordinative actions
Speed of decisions	Duration of stimuli	Precision and steadiness required
Sequence of decisions	Intensity of stimuli	Fine motor skills required
	Conflicting stimuli	

Source: Based on Billing, 1980.

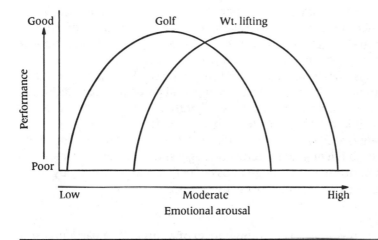

FIGURE 12.5
Sport-Specific Optimal Levels of Arousal

higher decisonal demands require lower arousal levels for optimal performance compared to tasks with lower decisional demands.

The relationship of perception to the inverted-U hypothesis has been
primarily studied in situations where subjects are attending to potentially
conflicting stimuli. A number of studies (see Landers, 1978, 1980, for reviews) have shown that when dual tasks are performed subjects will generally allocate more attention to one of them in order to maintain or better
their performance. This strategy is typically chosen because it is believed
that humans have very limited spare capacity for focusing attention on
task-irrelevant cues when they are performing complex motor skills.

There are many examples of attention being shifted from secondary
tasks to enhance the concentration necessary to perform the primary task.
The experimental situation, called the dual-task paradigm, involves creating differing levels of arousal while subjects are performing a primary task
and at the same time periodically reacting to a tone or a visual stimulus
(Landers, Wang & Courtett, 1985; Weltman and Egstrom, 1966).

From similar studies in which the dual-task paradigm has been used,
Bacon (1974) offers the generalization that arousal effects depend upon the
degree of attention the stimuli attract, with "sensitivity loss systematically
occurring to those cues which initially attract less attention" (p. 86). Other
investigators (e.g., Easterbrook, 1959) suggest that arousal acts to narrow
the range of cue utilization, which results in the inverted-U function described above. The underaroused performer, for example, has a broad perceptual range and, therefore, either through lack of effort or poor

selectivity, accepts irrelevant cues uncritically. Performance in this case is understandably poor. When arousal increases to a moderate or optimal level, perceptual selectivity increases correspondingly and performance improves, presumably because the performer tries harder or is more likely to eliminate task-irrelevant cues. Arousal increases beyond this optimal point result in further perceptual narrowing, and performance deteriorates in accord with the inverted-U hypothesis. For instance, in a highly anxious state, a football quarterback's attention may be focused too narrowly to detect task-relevant cues such as secondary receivers open in the periphery. The ideas of both Bacon and Easterbrook suggest that the effects of arousal impair one's performance through a loss of perceptual sensitivity by interfering with one's capacity to process information.

Individual differences   The optimal level of arousal for a particular task is also dependent upon factors that are unique to the individual. People differ in the amount of prior experience with a task as well as the amount of practice they have had. As we discussed earlier, the strength of the correct habit response varies from one person to the next. The person who is more skillful — that is, has a stronger habit hierarchy — is more likely to offset the detrimental effects of increased arousal more effectively than the individual who is less skillful and possesses a weaker habit strength.

Of course, habit patterns may not always be appropriate. Landers (in press) has indicated that subtle changes in habit patterns may lead to "disregulations," which are defined as a physiological measure of arousal that either negatively correlates with performance or creates some degree of discomfiture for the performer. For example, in our work with a world champion archer, we found that he developed a habit of tightly squinting his nonsighting eye following the release of the arrow. At the end of several hours of shooting, this resulted in a tension headache. With the archer having to concentrate so much on the act of shooting, it was difficult for him to focus on the source of his problem. To correct this, it was necessary for us to bring the disregulation to his conscious awareness by providing an EMG signal of the electrical activity around his nonsighting eye. After several shots with this type of biofeedback, the squinting, which lasted for several seconds, was reduced to a blink and the headaches disappeared.

Perhaps the greatest individual difference factor is one's personality. The most relevant personality variable affecting one's optimal arousal level is the level of trait anxiety. As shown in Figure 12.6, if an athlete is high-strung, even a small amount of arousal can put him or her over the top on the inverted-U curve. On the other hand, if the athlete is calm, cool, and collected, he or she will be able to tolerate much higher levels of arousal without suffering a performance impairment.

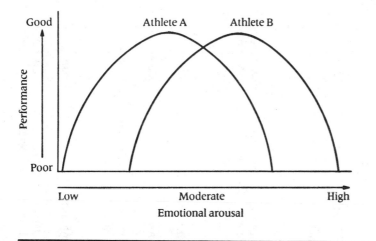

FIGURE 12.6
Athlete-Specific Optimal Levels of Arousal

ESTIMATING THE RELATIONSHIP BETWEEN AN ATHLETE'S OPTIMAL AROUSAL AND PERFORMANCE

As indicated above, the optimal arousal level will depend on task characteristics as well as individual difference factors. To help the athlete learn to regulate arousal during the competition, it is important that the coaches or sport psychologists compare the arousal demands of the sport task to the athlete's typical competitive arousal state. We recommend the following guidelines. Select a specific task such as playing the quarterback position in football. Avoid global activities such as gymnastics, football, or basketball, and be as task specific as you can! Once you zero in on the task, answer the questions in Table 12.3. For example, high scores (3s and 4s) in the sport of archery on motor act characteristics (C.1–4) would produce high total scores. In short sprints, however, the decision/perceptual processes would in general receive low values (1s and 2s), and the gross motor nature of sprinting would keep the overall task score at a relatively low level. When using this table, bear in mind that it is only a rough guideline for estimating the complexity of your sport.

Total your scores and see where your chosen skill falls on the range in Table 12.4 (page 180). If the skill has a low score, this indicates that the average athlete can be psyched up to a greater extent and still perform optimally. If an athlete performing this task is low trait anxious and typically responds to competition in a consistently laid-back fashion, you may

TABLE 12.3
Estimating Complexity of Motor Performance

	0	1	2	3	4
A. Decision Characteristics of Skill					
1. Number of decisions necessary	None	Few	Some	Several	Many
2. Number of alternatives per decision	None	Few	Some	Several	Many
3. Speed of decisions	Not relevant	Very slow	Slow	Fast	Very fast
4. Sequence of decisions	Not relevant, only one decision	Sequence of 2	Sequence of 3	Sequence of 4	Sequence of 5 or more
B. Perception Characteristics of Skill					
1. Number of stimuli needed	None	Few	Some	Several	Many
2. Number of stimuli present	Very few	Few	Some	Several	Many
3. Duration of stimuli	More than 20 sec	More than 10 sec	More than 5 sec	More than 2 sec	Less than 2 sec
4. Intensity of stimuli	Very intense	Intense	Moderately intense	Low intensity	Very low intensity
5. Clarity of correct stimulus among conflicting stimuli	Very obvious	Obvious	Moderately obvious	Subtle difference	Very subtle difference

C. Motor Act Characteristics of Skill

	0	1	2	3	4
1. Number of muscle actions to execute skill	1–2	3–4	5–6	7–8	9 or more
2. Amount of coordination of actions	Minimal	A little	Some	Several coordinative actions	A great deal
3. Precision and steadiness required	None	Minimal	Some	Considerable	A great deal
4. Fine motor skill required	None, only gross motor skill	Minimal	Some	Considerable	A great deal

TABLE 12.4
Optimum Arousal Level, Complexity Scores, and State Scores for a Variety of Typical Sport Skills

Level of arousal	Complexity score range	Sport skills	Spielberger et al. state scores	Martens competitive state anxiety scores
5 (extremely excited)	0–10	Football blocking, running 200 meters to 400 meters	50–60	30–34
4 (psyched up)	11–16	Short sprints, long jump	45–49	25–29
3 (medium arousal)	17–21	Basketball, boxing, judo	35–44	20–24
2 (some arousal)	22–31	Baseball pitching, fencing, tennis	30–34	15–19
1 (slight arousal)	32+	Archery, golf, field goal kicking	20–29	10–14

Source: Based on Oxendine, 1984, and Billing, 1980.

need to supplement normal psych-up procedures by teaching the athlete some of the energizing techniques presented in Chapter 13. However, if the athlete scores over 32 in the task you have selected, he or she can tolerate very little arousal. It is particularly important in the latter case to pay heed to the relaxation, imagery, and cognitive coping strategies presented in Chapters 13, 14, and 15. Athletes who display consistent, high-level performance during practice or unimportant competition but then fail to perform efficiently in major competitions will have even more need to practice these coping techniques regularly.

Also note that Table 12.4 contains scores from Spielberger, Gorsuch, and Lushene's (1970) state anxiety scale as well as the Competitive State Anxiety Inventory (Martens, 1977). Obtaining objective anxiety data for individual athletes on these scales is a valuable supplement to the coach's and sport psychologist's assessment of the athlete's anxiety level. The Spielberger et al. scale ranges from 20 to 80 for extremes in low and high anxiety, respectively. Martens' (1977) scale ranges from 10 to 40. To perform optimally in skills that are highly complex (number 1), a very low level of self-reported anxiety is desirable. In skills with low complexity scores (number 5), the athlete can safely achieve above-average but not excessively high anxiety scores (less than 60) without incurring a decrement in performance. It is important to remember that at all levels (1 through 5) inverted-U relationships between arousal and performance can occur if arousal levels are inappropriate for the skill being performed. That is, poorer performance may result from the athlete's being underaroused or overaroused.

Armed with the information in this chapter and the techniques described in Chapter 11, you and the athletes with whom you work, will be better equipped to select, develop, and use the arousal self-regulation skills presented in Chapter 13.

Identifying Athletes Who Are Overaroused

Often coaches and sport psychologists want to identify athletes with appropriate arousal levels for the tasks they are performing. Figure 12-1 suggests some areas that will serve as a guide in the identification process. The situation (B) of greatest interest, of course, is competition. The cognitive (C), physiological (D), and behavioral (E) response of athletes in the competitive situation can be compared to responses in noncompetitive situations (i.e., practice conditions). Marked discrepancies in these responses, accompanied by a poor competitive performance, may provide clues that the athlete is overaroused.

At the level of cognitive appraisal (C) the coach or sport psychologist should look for signs of distraction before competition. This is usually indicated by an athlete who is not paying attention to coaches' pregame instructions. The athlete may express more concern than is normal by making statements that indicate a certain degree of self-doubt about his or her ability to meet the competitive demands. This identification process is often simplified at a cognitive appraisal level when the athlete recognizes the excessive worry and comes to the coach or sport psychologist for help.

Even without this self-disclosure, many times it is possible to detect physiological or emotional responses (D) that relate to cognitive appraisal (C) in the way described in Figure 12-1. Where there is a consistent shift to poor performance from practice to competition, the coach or sport psychologist should look for obvious signs of emotional reactivity (i.e., flushed face, sweaty palms, dilated pupils, etc.). Another way of getting more direct verification of the arousal mismatch is to administer various measures of arousal throughout the competitive season through use of unidimensional- or multidimensional-state anxiety measures (Table 12-1.C). All the questionnaires include questions that assess cognitive appraisal, physiological/emotional and behavioral aspects. The use of state anxiety measures has been employed by Klavora (1979) to determine inverted-U patterns for each athlete. Some physiological measures are also quite easy for a coach or sport psychologist to use. For instance, Tretilova and Rodimiki (1979) tracked the heart rates of 22 top Soviet shooters and found an optimal heart rate increase above resting values where best performance scores were fired. Similarly, Jones (1978) has used skin resistance deflections above baseline levels to identify high arousal in shooters.

Finally, at a behavioral level (Figure 12-1.E.) much can be gained from careful observation of the athlete's motor activity, actions, and speech characteristics. Hyperactivity before a performance can be gleaned from erratic behaviors, such as pacing, fidgeting, and yawning. An unusually high or low energy level before or during competition may also indicate an inappropriate level of arousal. Rapid speech that sounds abnormal for a particular athlete may provide a reason for the coach or sport psychologist to inquire further into an athlete's arousal state.

The above-mentioned cognitive, physiological and behavioral manifestations of arousal should not be the last step of the identification process. These factors are only indicators or clues that can serve as a basis for discussions with the athlete. Don't mistake fidgeting because the athlete needs to go to the bathroom as a sign of overarousal. Check out these possible signs of arousal to see what meaning the athlete gives to them. This interpretation is essential in the final determination of overarousal. As we will see in Chapters 13, 14, and 15, the interpretation is also important for designing interventions to help bring arousal levels under control.

SUMMARY

In this chapter we have attempted to provide a basic understanding of arousal/performance relationships. The drive theory and inverted-U hypotheses were presented; the latter hypothesis is considered to provide the better explanation for the relationship between arousal and performance. According to this hypothesis, optimal performance occurs at moderate levels of arousal. To determine optimal arousal levels, several task characteristics must be considered as well as individual differences in state anxiety. We have provided guidelines to assist coaches and sport psychologists to estimate the arousal demands in reference to the complexity of the task to be performed. Finally, we have made suggestions to help in identifying athletes who are overaroused. We anticipate that, by increasing their understanding of arousal/performance relationships, coaches and sport psychologists will be able to use this knowledge to better assess the task demands and more accurately determine appropriate arousal levels for their athletes.

REFERENCES

Babin, W. (1966). *The effect of various work loads on simple reaction latency as related to selected physical parameters.* Unpublished doctoral dissertation, University of Southern Mississippi, Hattiesburg.

Bacon, S. J. (1974). Arousal and the range of cue utilization. *Journal of Experimental Psychology, 103,* 81–87.

Billing, J. (1980). An overview of task complexity. *Motor Skills: Theory into Practice, 4,* 18–23.

Bond, C. F., & Titus, L. J. (1983). Social facilitation: A meta-analysis of 241 studies. *Psychological Bulletin, 94,* 265–292.

Broadhurst, P. L. (1957). Emotionality and the Yerkes–Dodson Law. *Journal of Experimental Psychology, 54,* 345–352.

Duffy, E. (1962). *Activation and behavior.* New York: Wiley.

Easterbrook, J. A. (1959). The effect of emotion on cue utilization and the organization of behavior. *Psychological Review, 66,* 183–201.

Fenz, W. D., & Epstein, S. (1969). Stress in the air. *Psychology Today, 3* (4), 27–28, 58–59.

Freeman, G. L. (1940). The relationship between performance level and bodily activity level. *Journal of Experimental Psychology, 26,* 602–608.

Jones, R. S. (1978). *Rifle accuracy as a function of electrodermal activity.* Unpublished master's thesis, Tennessee Technological University.

Klavora, P. (1979). An attempt to derive inverted-U curves based on the relationship between anxiety and athletic performance. In D. M. Landers and R. W. Christina (Eds.), *Psychology of motor behavior and sport.* Champaign, Ill.: Human Kinetics.

Krahenbuhl, G. S. (1975). Adrenaline, arousal and sport. *Journal of Sports Medicine, 3,* 117–121.

Lacey, J. I., Bateman, D. E., & Van Lehn, R. (1953). Autonomic response specificity: An experimental study. *Psychosomatic Medicine, 15,* 8–21.

Landers, D. M. (1978). Motivation and performance: The role of arousal and attentional factors. In W. Straub (Ed.), *Sport psychology: An analysis of athletic behavior.* Ithaca, N.Y.: Mouvement Publications.

Landers, D. M. (1980). The arousal–performance relationship revisited. *Research Quarterly, 51,* 77–90.

Landers, D. M. (in press). Psychophysiological assessment and biofeedback: Applications for athletes in closed skill sports. In J. H. Sandweis and S. Wolf (Eds.), *Biofeedback and sport science.* New York: Plenum.

Landers, D. M., Snyder-Bauer, R., & Feltz, D. L. (1978). Social facilitation during the initial stage of motor learning: A reexamination of Marten's audience study. *Journal of Motor Behavior, 10,* 325–337.

Landers, D. M., Wang, M. Q., & Courtet, P. (1985). Peripheral narrowing among experienced and inexperienced rifle shooters under low- and high-stress conditions. *Research Quarterly, 56,* 57–70.

Landy, F. J., & Stern, R. M. (1971). Factor analysis of a somatic perception questionnaire. *Journal of Psychosomatic Research, 15,* 179–181.

Levitt, S., & Gutin, B. (1971). Multiple choice reaction time and movement time during physical exertion. *Research Quarterly, 42,* 405–410.

Light, K., & Obrist, P. A. (1983). Task difficulty, heart rate reactivity, and cardiovascular responses to an appetitive reaction time task. *Psychophysiology, 20,* 301–312.

Malmo, R. B. (1959). Activation: A neuropsychological dimension. *Psychological Review, 66,* 367–386.

Martens, R. (1974). Arousal and motor performance. In J. H. Wilmore (Ed.), *Exercise and sport science reviews.* New York: Academic Press.

Martens, R. (1977). *Sport competitive anxiety test.* Champaign, Ill.: Human Kinetics.

Martens, R., Burton, D., Vealey, R., Smith, D., & Bump, L. (1983). *The development of the Competitive State Anxiety Inventory-2 (CSAI-2).* Unpublished manuscript.

Martens, R., & Landers, D. M. (1970). Motor performance under stress: A test of the inverted-U hypothesis. *Journal of Personality and Social Psychology, 16,* 29–37.

Murphy, L. E. (1966). Muscular effort, activation level and reaction time. *Proceedings of the 74th Annual Convention of the American Psychological Association* (p. 1).

Oxendine, J. B. (1984). *Psychology of motor learning.* Englewood Cliffs, N.J.: Prentice-Hall.

Pinneo, L. R. (1961). The effects of induced muscle tension during tracking on level of activation and on performance. *Journal of Experimental Psychology, 62,* 523–531.

Sage, G. (1984). *Motor learning and control.* Dubuque, Iowa: Wm. C. Brown.

Schwartz, G. E., Davidson, R. J., & Goleman, D. (1978). Patterning of cognitive and somatic processes in the self-regulation of anxiety: Effects of meditation versus exercise. *Psychosomatic Medicine, 40,* 321–328.

Spence, J. T., & Spence, K. W. (1966). The motivational components of manifest anxiety: Drive and drive stimuli. In C. D. Spielberger (Eds.), *Anxiety and behavior.* New York: Academic Press.

Spielberger, C. D., Gorsuch, R. L., & Lushene, R. E. (1970). *Manual for the State-Trait Anxiety Inventory (STAI).* Palo Alto, Calif.: Consulting Psychologists Press.

Thayer, R. E. (1967). Measurement of activation through self-report. *Psychological Reports, 20,* 663–679.

Tretilova, T. A., & Rodmiki, E. M. (1979). Investigation of emotional state of rifle shooters. *Theory and Practice of Physical Culture, 5,* 28.

Weltman, A. T., & Egstrom, G. H. (1966). Perceptual narrowing in novice divers. *Human Factors, 8,* 499–505.

Wood, C. G., & Hokanson, J. E. (1965). Effects of induced muscle tension on performance and the inverted-U. *Journal of Personality and Social Psychology, 1,* 506–510.

Yerkes, R. M., & Dodson, J. D. (1908). The relation of strength of stimulus to rapidity of habit formation. *Journal of Comparative Neurology of Psychology, 18,* 459–482.

13

Relaxation and Energizing Techniques for Regulation of Arousal

DOROTHY V. HARRIS

Noll Laboratory, University Park, Pennsylvania

Somehow the misconception persists that if one practices and trains hard enough physically for a competition, everything else will magically come together. In fact, during a given competition, or between two competitions that closely follow each other, there is usually no marked change in an athlete's skill level, physiological capacity, or biomechanical efficiency. The fluctuation in performance is generally caused by the fluctuation in the athlete's mental control. The athlete simply does not lose and gain stamina, skill, strategy, or conditioning during the ebb and flow of a competition. What the athlete does lose is control of cognitive factors such as the ability to concentrate, to process relevant cues, to focus on positive self-talk, etc. In the final analysis, the athlete is inappropriately aroused.

Consistent high-level performance begins with the discovery of those factors and conditions that accompany superior performance. (See Chapter 11 for suggestions on how to discover what mental and bodily states are typically associated with an athlete's superior performance.) Beyond that, acceptance of the fact that each of us has control over our own behavior and arousal allows the athlete to learn and develop skills and strategies necessary to consciously regulate his or her responses in order to maintain an optimal level of performance.

Elmer and Alyce Green (1977) have studied the effects of the mental control of the so-called autonomic functions, including the muscular and hormonal changes that occur in sport performance. In their experiments measuring the influence of the mental control of bodily functions, they studied yogis from India. The Greens found that yogis were voluntarily able to alter their brain waves, heart rate, breathing, blood pressure, body temperature, and other bodily processes that are generally regulated by the autonomic nervous system. The researchers also discovered that the ability to voluntarily control these processes could be taught to others with ease in a relatively short period of time. The Greens concluded that each of us possesses a highly complex, sophisticated, and effectively integrated network between the mind and body. They further concluded that every change in the mental–emotional state is consciously or unconsciously accompanied by an appropriate change in the bodily state. This conclusion provides strong support for the idea that we think with our entire body. Accepting this, we can learn to exercise much greater mastery and control over all of our functions and responses. Our bodies tend to do what they are told to do; the trick is to learn how to communicate with our bodies. This is the principle of learning how to regulate arousal and relaxation. The same principle applies to activating and "psyching" ourselves up to reach an optimal level of performance. Once an athlete has learned to identify which mental–emotional and bodily states and feelings accompany superior performance, he or she can learn to "program" these responses voluntarily to set the stage for another superior performance. Basically, that is all sport psychology is trying to do for the athlete.

Readiness, being psyched, energized, wired, activated, aroused, or whatever is an integration of the mind–body feelings and thoughts that provide the athlete with a feeling of confidence, of mastery and control. The athlete can learn to reach this state voluntarily by practicing the skills and strategies included in this book; learning to regulate arousal level, the subject of this chapter, is one important part of the process. Once an athlete has identified his or her optimal level of arousal for maximizing performance, the athlete can use appropriate relaxation or energizing techniques and strategies to reduce or increase that arousal as needed. See Chapter 12 for ways of determining optimal level of arousal for consistent, high-level performance and a discussion of the factors that influence optimal arousal level.

Obviously, all athletes need a certain amount of arousal or motivation to accomplish a task; however, some need more than others to perform at the same level. Too much arousal is detrimental; that is more often the problem than needing a "win one for the Gipper" speech to psych up a team. Some athletes will respond positively to a highly charged motivational speech whereas others will become overaroused. Most coaches and athletes have tended to emphasize the "psyching up" aspect of preparation for performance; most sport psychologists have focused on lowering arousal.

As noted in the preceding chapters, a combination of physiological, psychological, and behavioral responses occurs when an athlete is worried and afraid that he or she will not perform as desired. Each athlete has to learn his or her particular pattern of overarousal resulting from worry and anxiety about performance. Learning to relax is essential to regulating these responses to avoid any detrimental effects on performance. When a muscle tenses up, as it does with worry and anxiety, it contracts or is shortened. This contraction involves nerves as well. Approximately one half of the nerves alert the muscles to respond to the messages from the brain, and the other half carry the messages back to the brain. Human nerve circuits have no automatic regulators; there are no signals to alert one to too much tension.

Muscle tissue only works in one direction; it can only pull, which it does by shortening and thickening. Consequently, the voluntary muscles in humans (and animals) are arranged in pairs. When a muscle tightens, its opposite sets up a counter tension to hold the segment of the body in place. The double pull can build up formidable heights of tension over much of the body yet remain unidentified by most people. This double pull explains why a person can be scared stiff, become rigid with anger, be unable to move because of stage fright, and so forth. It also explains why an athlete shoots air balls, blows a short putt, passes with too much force, overhits a tennis ball, etc. The principle of the double pull, sometimes referred to as bracing, has great significance for the athlete. When muscular tension occurs with anxiety and worry, it interferes with performance because many of the nerves needed for coordinated movement messages are taken up with worry messages. Proper form in any movement involves using just the right amount of tension in the muscle; too much tension interferes with the execution of the skill. We can learn to spend only those energies necessary to accomplish our purposes without waste. This is called differential relaxation.

Excessive muscular tension can be triggered by mental input generated by worry and anxiety about not performing well. When the nerve pathways are occupied by impulses alerting the system to "fight or flee," the impulses necessary for skillful, coordinated movement are inhibited to some degree. The more muscular tension in the body, the more difficult it is to execute good form or the proper coordination in any type of movement task. The following is an excellent technique for illustrating how excessive tension disrupts speed and coordination. Have your athletes rest their dominant forearm and hand palm down on a desk or tabletop. Now have them tense all the muscles in their hand and fingers and then try to alternately tap their index and middle fingers back and forth as quickly as possible. Then have them relax the muscles of the hand and fingers and repeat the exercise. Athletes quickly discover how too much tension makes their movements clumsy and slow!

To learn to avoid too much tension, athletes need to be taught how to relax. Total relaxation means letting go and doing absolutely nothing with the muscles so that no messages are traveling either to or from the brain.

As a coach or sport psychologist, you may be wondering why any athlete would want to be completely relaxed. Athletes need muscular tension and arousal to perform; some need maximal tension to accomplish their sport. However, in learning to train the muscles to relax totally, athletes develop a much greater sensitivity to their bodily feelings and responses. Once athletes become aware of bodily responses and learn to associate them with certain types of behavior and performance, they can learn to regulate different levels of tension to deal with the environment actively and effectively.

Once trained in relaxation, athletes can use this skill to lower general muscular tension under any condition. Relaxation can assist in removing localized tension such as that occurring with headaches or lower back pain or that surrounding injuries. Relaxation can facilitate recovery when athletes have only a short time between events or when they are fatigued. Relaxation also promotes the onset of sleep and reduces insomnia problems that plague many athletes prior to competition. Probably the most important contribution that relaxation can make to athletes is to teach them the regulation of muscular tension so that nerve pathways to the muscle are never overcharged.

In general, the techniques of relaxation can be divided into two categories. The first category includes techniques that focus on the bodily aspects, the "muscle to mind" techniques. Jacobson's (1930) scientific neuromuscular relaxation or progressive relaxation falls into this category. The objective is to train the muscles to become sensitive to any level of tension and to be able to release that tension. The second category of techniques includes the cognitive or mental approaches to relaxation; these work from "mind to muscle." Benson's relaxation response (1975), meditation, autogenic training, and imagery all approach relaxation from the mind-to-muscle perspective. Either approach is effective; the point is to disrupt the stimulus – response pattern of half of the nerves leading to the brain or away from the brain. It is immaterial whether the athlete focuses attention on the brain-to-muscle efferent portion of the central nervous system or the muscle-to-brain afferent portion, which reduces the stimulation to the brain. Learning to reduce the sensation in either half of the circuit will interrupt the stimulation necessary to produce unwanted muscular tension.

Relaxation skills must be practiced on a regular basis just as any sport skill. When teaching relaxation to athletes, it is more effective to begin the training after a workout because it is easier to "let go" after having had some exercise. It is more difficult to hold muscular tension when physically fatigued. In addition, exercise is nature's best tranquilizer and tends to lower general anxiety and tension. Once the athletes are trained in relaxation skills, they should begin the practice workout with a brief period of relaxation to eliminate all unwanted muscle-brain-muscle stimulation so that they can focus their complete attention on the practice. When practices are conducted in this manner, their quality increases so that the amount of time necessary to reach the same level of accomplishment is reduced considerably.

Some athletes take longer to develop relaxation skills than others, but most should observe improvement after a few weeks of regular practice. Emphasize the fact that it takes time to develop the skills, and encourage the athletes to continue to practice for several weeks even though they will not detect immediate improvement.

The degree of relaxation attainable varies to some extent. Within that variation, athletes should learn how to relax and withdraw completely from the environment as well as to relax momentarily. The ability to relax completely serves a different function from relaxing momentarily. After a hard training session, before falling asleep at night, when fatigue sets in, or when an athlete is worried, sick, or under emotional stress, deep, complete relaxation is desirable. Learning to relax completely provides a reference point as the athlete learns what a "zero arousal" level feels like. It also provides an opportunity to increase awareness of both mental and physical responses and how integrated they are. In the process, the athlete learns to recognize patterns of feelings, thoughts, and behaviors and how they affect performance. As a result, the athlete can develop procedures for changing behaviors that interfere with performance. The athlete can learn through deep relaxation how to become detached from the environment and be in full control without interference. The ability to relax completely produces a positive, pleasurable, and beneficial experience that provides the central nervous system with a rest. That, in turn, allows regeneration of physical, mental, and emotional states with the athlete in control.

Finally, the ability to relax completely provides the foundation for learning the skill of "momentary" relaxation during practice or competition. Learning to relax momentarily is extremely important for athletes so that they can reduce overarousal at any point. When the nerves are carrying worry messages instead of the stimuli for smooth coordinated, integrated efforts, the performance suffers. With momentary relaxation, worry and anxiety stimuli are removed, resulting in an enhanced kinesthetic awareness. The momentary respite also allows the athlete to return to a point of controlled balance. Every aspect of performance is enhanced: concentration, attentional focus, awareness, confidence, precision, speed, and so on.

Momentary relaxation can be used just before and during warm-up. In fact, during stretching in preparation for competition is a good time to utilize the strategies of momentary relaxation and to focus on the upcoming game. The more uptight the athlete is prior to performance, the longer the session of momentary relaxation should be. After the competition, this type of relaxation can be used to return to the controlled, balanced state. During the competition, depending on the specific sport and/or position within the sport, brief periods or lapses in play allow for momentary relaxation as needed. The athlete must learn to become aware of tension and arousal levels and adjust them as necessary.

The learning of skills and strategies for a sport is enhanced when one is in a relaxed state, particularly if periods of learning are alternated with periods of relaxation. This is true for academic learning as well as athletic learning. Relaxation preparation is also necessary for concentration and imagery practice because it reduces and eliminates other thoughts and stimulation that interfere with the single-minded focus necessary for imagery practice.

MUSCLE-TO-MIND RELAXATION SKILLS AND STRATEGIES

Most athletes respond positively to muscle-to-mind techniques, perhaps because of their more physical life-style. When learning these relaxation techniques, athletes should be in a comfortable position and in a quiet, warm environment. Once athletes are trained, they should be able to relax in any environment under any condition. Learning, however, should occur under ideal conditions.

Breathing Exercises*

Breathing properly is not only relaxing, it facilitates performance by increasing the amount of oxygen in the blood. This carries more energy to the muscles and facilitates the removal of waste products. Unfortunately, many individuals have never learned deep, diaphragmatic breathing, and those that have often find their breathing pattern disrupted under stress. Athletes who get uptight during a high-pressure performance situation find their breathing is usually affected in one of two ways—they either hold their breath or they breathe rapidly and shallowly from the upper chest. Both of these adjustments create even more tension and impairment of performance. A good technique for making athletes aware of what shallow, chest breathing feels like is to have them raise their shoulders way up and notice what happens to their breathing.

Fortunately, with practice, breathing is also one of the easiest physiological systems to control. Learning to take a deep, slow, complete breath will usually trigger a relaxation response. This relaxing, complete breath is the basis for a variety of breathing exercises. Suggestions for specific exercises for breathing control to increase relaxation follow. Depending on the exercise and how it is practiced, these techniques can be used for both deep and momentary relaxation. Some coaches and sport psychologists even "choreograph" specific breathing times into the performance of certain skills such as gymnastic and figure skating routines.

* Several of these exercises are adaptations from Mason, 1980.

Complete breath Proper breathing comes from the diaphragm, the thin muscle that separates the lung and abdominal cavities. During inhalation the diaphragm should move down slightly, thus pushing the abdomen out and creating a vacuum in the lungs. This fills up the lungs from the bottom. For practicing a deep, complete breath, have the athletes imagine that the lungs are divided into three levels or parts. Have the athletes concentrate on filling the lower section of the lungs with air, first by pushing the diaphragm down and forcing the abdomen out. Have them continue by filling the middle portion of the lungs by expanding the chest cavity and raising the rib cage and chest. Finally, have the athletes fill the upper portion of the lungs by raising the chest and shoulders slightly. All three stages should be continuous and smooth. The athletes should hold the breath for several seconds, then exhale by pulling the abdomen in (which pulls the diaphragm up) and lowering the shoulders and chest to empty the lungs. Finally, instruct the athletes to pull the abdomen in further to force out the last bit of air from the lungs. They should let go of all muscular action at the end of the exhalation so the abdomen and chest are completely relaxed.

Stress to your athletes that during the exhalation they should feel as if the air drains out of the bottom of the lungs, first emptying the upper part, then the middle, and finally the lower part. Repeat this exercise many times with instructions. Once athletes are comfortable with the sequential complete breath, emphasize that on the inhalation they should take a long, slow, deep inhalation through the nose, inhaling as much air as possible. Emphasize that the exhalation should be slow and complete and that the athletes should try to feel all tension leaving the body as the air is exhaled.

After learning the procedure, the athletes should take at least 30 to 40 deep breaths each day. Associating deep breathing with events that naturally occur during the day will facilitate practice. Suggest to the athletes that each time the phone rings, they should take a deep breath, exhaling fully and completely before answering. Some stress therapists suggest affixing to a person's wristwatch dial a tiny colored paper disc so that each time the person looks at the watch, he or she is reminded to relax by taking a deep breath. Another good time for athletes to practice this breathing exercise is during the time they are waiting for class to begin or when they need momentary relaxation, such as before a free-throw shot, tennis serve, or golf putt.

Sighing with exhalation Sighing aids in reducing tension. Instruct the athletes as follows: "Inhale slowly and then hold your breath for 10 seconds, feeling the tension building in the throat and chest. Exhale through the mouth with a slight sigh as you let go of the tension in the rib cage. Do nothing about inhaling, let that happen naturally. Hold your breath and repeat the sigh with the exhalation as you force the air out of the lungs."

The quietest or calmest time of the breath is between the exhalation and inhalation. Stress that athletes feel the stillness at the moment directly after fully exhaling and sighing. If athletes can feel this quietness, they are learning how to relax. Practice again, but without holding the breath. As athletes exhale fully and completely, they should feel all the tension leaving the body. Be aware of the quiet time during the breath. Whenever athletes feel themselves getting too tense, they should try to recreate this moment of peace and calm by momentarily practicing this exercise.

Rhythmic breathing   Have the athletes inhale to a count of four, hold for a count of four, exhale to a count of four, and pause for a count of four before repeating the sequence. You can alter the rhythm of their breathing by changing the count.

1:2 ratio   Have the athletes take a deep, full breath and then exhale fully and completely. Have them breathe again, only this time to a count of four on the inhalation and a count of eight on the exhalation. If the athletes run out of breath before reaching eight, suggest that next time they take a deeper breath and exhale more slowly. Stress awareness of a full inhalation and exhalation. With more practice and deepened relaxation on the part of the athletes, you may need to change the count to 5:10 or 6:12. This exercise is a very powerful relaxer if done properly.

5-to-1 count   Instruct the athletes as follows: "Say to yourself and visualize the number 5 as you take a deep, full, slow breath. Exhale fully and completely. Mentally count and visualize the number 4 with your next inhalation. As you begin the exhalation, say to yourself, 'I am more relaxed now than I was at number 5.' Do not rush the thought. Inhale while mentally counting and visualizing the number 3. With the exhalation, say to yourself, 'I am more relaxed now than I was at number 4.' Allow yourself to feel the deepening relaxation. Continue until you reach number 1. As you approach number 1, you should feel totally calm and relaxed."

The complete exercise takes one to two minutes. If done properly, it should lead to more relaxation than practicing a single complete breath. This exercise can be used before or during practices and competition, depending on how much time is available and how much relaxation is needed.

Concentration breathing   Have the athletes concentrate on focusing their attention on their breathing rhythm. Tell them that if their mind wanders to some other thought between inhaling and exhaling to redirect their attention back to their next breath, letting the intruding thought disappear. Instruct them to think of becoming more relaxed with each exhalation. This is a good exercise for athletes to practice when they are having problems with distracting thoughts.

Progressive Relaxation (PR) Exercises

Working under the assumption that an anxious mind cannot exist within a relaxed body, Jacobson (1930) developed the concept of progressive relaxation (PR), another muscle-to-mind approach to relaxation. PR consists of a series of exercises that involve contracting a specific muscle group, holding the contraction for several seconds, then relaxing. The exercises progress from one muscle group to another. The purpose of the contraction of the muscle is to teach an awareness and sensitivity to what muscular tension feels like. The letting go, or relaxation phase, teaches an awareness of what absence of tension feels like and the acknowledgment that it can voluntarily be induced by passively releasing the tension in a muscle. The initial training program devised by Jacobson required much more time in training each muscle group than many of the modifications that have been developed over the years.

Approximately 30 minutes per instructional period is needed during initial practices. Once skill is acquired, shorter practice sessions can be used. The coach or others knowledgeable about relaxation should give the instructions. Tape recordings of instructions are available, but coaches and sport psychologists can make the instructions more relevant to a particular sport and situation. Encourage athletes to practice outside of the teaching session on their own to improve their skills. Be sure to mention that practice should not occur within an hour after eating a meal. Providing athletes with tapes or written handouts of relaxation exercises will facilitate their likelihood of practicing. With increased experience, these will not be needed.

As you read the PR instructions, maintain a quiet unaccentuated voice pattern, pacing the instructions by doing the exercises with the athletes. Pause about 20 to 30 seconds after each contraction so relaxation can continue for brief periods. Tense larger muscle groups longer than the smaller ones. Repetition is the key to learning so continue to practice the same muscle groups until the athletes can relax quickly without producing additional tension. Before you begin, explain to the athletes exactly what they will be doing and what they can expect. For example, feelings of warmth and heaviness are common as the relaxation response increases. Also explain that muscle twitches and spasms are to be expected as muscle fibers begin to let go. If there is a great deal of tension, an entire muscle group may let go, producing involuntary movement. On occasion, this happens just before one falls asleep if there is a tremendous buildup of muscular tension. The flexor pair lets go before the extensors and they take up the slack, resulting in a sudden jerk throughout the body.

Restlessness is a signal to let go and relax further. If you are working with a single athlete or a small group, have the participants signal by raising a finger to indicate when they have followed instructions and accomplished the task. As they become proficient in relaxing, there is a tendency to not follow instructions. Emphasize the importance of following instructions passively. This is particularly true during the relaxation phase. Just let the relaxation happen, don't force it. Relaxation requires no effort. Any effort to relax causes tension.

PR can be done in either a sitting or lying posture. The latter is usually more conducive to relaxation, but athletes should sit up if they tend to fall asleep. The lying down position is on the back with the head, neck, and trunk in a straight line. The legs should be straight and slightly apart with the heels pointing inward and the toes pointing outward. The arms should be comfortably at the side with the hands a little away from the thighs, palms up, and fingers comfortably bent. A small pillow (rolled up "sweats" are a good substitute) can be put under either the knees or neck (not both) for additional comfort. If a chair is being used for the sitting position, athletes should sit upright, hips against the backrest, with the arms and legs uncrossed and the feet flat on the floor. The hands rest comfortably on the thighs (palms down). If no chairs are available, athletes can lean against the gymnasium wall.

Athletes wearing hard contact lenses can either remove them or keep their eyes open while practicing PR. They should also remove or loosen any constrictive clothing such as belts, shoes, etc. The body should be completely supported by the chair, floor, mat, or whatever is being used. Regardless of which PR exercise is being practiced, the preceding protocol is a good one to follow.

Active PR   Read or tape the following directions: "Sit or lie down in a comfortable position and try to put yourself in a relaxed state. Close your eyes and take a long, slow, deep breath through your nose, inhaling as much air as you can. Then exhale slowly and completely, feeling the tension leaving your body as you exhale. Take another deep breath and let the day's tensions and problems drain out of you with the exhalation. [Pause.] Relax as much as possible and listen to what I say. Remember not to strain to relax, just let it happen.

"Begin by bending the hand of the dominant arm back as hard as possible as though you are trying to place the back of your hand on your forearm, hold for 5 to 10 seconds and identify where tension is felt, relax and let go, slowly releasing the tension. Notice the difference between tension and relaxation [pause 20 to 30 seconds]. Tense again [pause 5 to 10 seconds] and relax. Just let the relaxation happen; don't put out any effort [pause 20 to 30 seconds].

"Now bend the hand as though you are trying to touch the fingers to the underside of the forearm, hold 5 to 10 seconds, identify the tension, let go. . . . Tense again . . . slowly release the tension. . . . Be aware of the difference between tension and letting go into relaxation.

"Let's repeat that sequence with your other arm. Bend your hand back as far and hard as you can, note the tension . . . and slowly relax, draining all of the tension out. . . . Bend back again . . . and relax; note the difference between the feelings of tension and relaxation. . . . Now bend your wrist toward your body and hold the tension. . . . Relax and let it go, just let it happen. . . . Bend inward again . . . and relax; notice the decrease in tension, drain it all out, and enjoy the feelings of relaxation. . . .

"Turn your attention back to your dominant arm. Flex your elbow and tightly contract your bicep muscle. . . . Slowly release and relax. Remember to tense completely and relax fully. Notice any difference in sensations for each new muscle group. Flex your elbow and tense the biceps again . . . and relax. . . .

"With your nondominant arm, bend your elbow and tense the biceps muscle. . . . Let the tension slowly drain out. Notice the decrease in tension but also concentrate on the tension that still remains. . . . Tense again . . . and relax completely . . . enjoy the spreading sensation of relaxation.

"Reach both arms straight out in front of you so you feel tension and pulling in both arms. Stretch way out tightening your triceps muscles. Hold this taut position for a few moments, and then relax your arms, completely letting them go limp at your side. . . . Stretch them out again, hold . . . and relax. . . . Notice the sensations you now have in the muscles of both arms and hands. . . . Perhaps there is a sort of flow of relaxation—perhaps a feeling of warmth and even heaviness in these muscles. Notice and enjoy this feeling of relaxation.

"Wrinkle your forehead by raising your eyebrows; note the tension in the entire forehead area and scalp [pause for only a 3- to 5-second contraction with these smaller muscle groups], and relax. . . . Frown and lower your eyebrows . . . and relax. Release all the tension. . . . Your forehead should feel smooth as glass. . . .

"Clench your jaws but not so tightly that it hurts your teeth. Note the tension in the jaws and cheeks. Relax. . . .

"Bring your tongue upward and press it against the roof of your mouth. Note the tension in and around your tongue. Relax. . . .

"Press your head backward. . . . Roll way to the right . . . roll to the left . . . and straighten. Relax; drain all the tension from the muscles in the neck and scalp. . . . Repeat.

"Bend your head forward so your chin presses against the chest. Note the tension in the neck and jaws. Straighten and relax. . . . Bend forward again . . . and relax.

"Raise your shoulders upward toward your ears and hold. Note that familiar tension sensation. Most athletes raise their shoulders when they are uptight. Relax; just let your shoulders droop. Drain all the tension from your shoulders and neck. . . . Raise them again, hold . . . release the tension, and relax. Let your shoulders drop completely. Enjoy the spreading sensation of relaxation. . . .

"Take a deep breath and hold it for 15 seconds. Note the tension slowly building in the entire chest area and shoulders. . . . Slowly exhale fully and completely. Feel the relaxation that comes with the exhalation. . . . Take another deep breath, hold . . . and exhale. . . .

"Tighten your abdomen as though you expect a punch. Hold the tension and study it . . . and then relax, letting your stomach stick out slightly. . . .

"Tighten your lower back and consider the tension. Do not strain too hard, particularly if you have back problems. . . . Feel the tension, and relax. Drain all the tension out; just let it happen. . . .

"Tighten the buttocks as though you were squeezing these muscles together. . . . Relax. . . .

"Turn your attention to your right leg. Now tighten the muscles in your right thigh. Try to localize the tension only to your thigh. . . . Note the sensation and relax. . . .

"Turn your attention to your right foot. Flex your ankle as though you are trying to touch your toes to your shin. Be aware of the tension in your toes, foot, ankle, and calf. . . . Release the tension; let go of any remaining tension. . . .

"Turn your attention to your left leg. Tense only the thigh. . . . Relax. . . .

"Flex your left ankle as though you are trying to touch the toes to your shin. . . . Relax; drain all the tension from your toes, foot, ankle, and calf. . . .

"Now keeping both thighs as relaxed as possible, curl the toes of both feet so you feel as though you are digging your toes into the bottom of your shoes. Relax. . . . Curl your toes again, and note the tension. . . . Relax completely. . . .

"Now relax all the muscles of your body—let them all go limp. You should be breathing slowly and deeply. Let all last traces of tension drain out of your body. Scan your body for any places that might still feel tension. Wherever you feel tension, do an additional tense and relax. You may notice a sensation of warmth and heaviness throughout your body, as though you are sinking deeper and deeper into the chair or floor. Or you may feel as though you are as light as air, as though you are floating on a cloud. Whatever feelings you have, go with them. . . . Enjoy the sensation of relaxation. . . .

"Before opening your eyes, take a deep breath and feel the energy and alertness flowing back into your body. Stretch your arms and legs if you wish. Open your eyes when you are ready."

After taking your athletes through their first few PR practices, take several minutes to discuss their reactions. Get them to identify what it felt like and how successful they thought they were at relaxing. For those who had difficulty in relaxing, stress again the importance of the absence of efforting, of being passive and just letting it happen. Also remind them of the need to practice regularly. Just like any physical skill, PR takes practice. See if any of the athletes became aware of places in their body where they tend to hold tension. The goal is now to spot this tension and release it before it causes any pain, such as headaches and backaches, or performance problems.

Have the athletes practice this lengthy active PR exercise daily for one to two weeks. If less time is available, do only one repetition of each muscle group. Once athletes have achieved some skill in being able to relax at will, you can have them practice one of the following modifications or abbreviations.

Differential active PR The differential active PR exercise is performed with the same sequence of muscle groups as the preceding exercise. The difference is in the amount of tension generated. Rather than doing an all-out contraction twice for each muscle group, do an initial all-out contraction, then generate half as much tension, and then just enough tension to identify and let it go. If time is limited, use the preceding routine but combine the arms in the arm exercises and the legs in the leg exercises. You can also delete some of the smaller, less important muscle groups. Throughout the exercise, stress that tension should only occur in the muscle group being contracted.

This exercise is an important way to help athletes become aware of differential relaxation. As noted earlier, relaxing all muscle groups as completely as one can almost never occurs in sport. Neither does only total muscle contraction. Differential relaxation is far more common. Differential relaxation involves learning to relax all of the muscles except those that are needed for the task at hand. The muscles that are used should only be tensed to the level needed. Learning appropriate differential relaxation not only leads to better performance but also to less fatigue. With proper training in the active PR exercise, followed by practice of this exercise, athletes can better accomplish differential relaxation because they become more sensitive to tension in different muscle groups and more confident in their ability to control the level of tension.

Abbreviated active PR Once the athletes have learned the PR technique, you can have them use a shorter procedure to achieve deep muscle relaxation quickly. Whole muscle groups can be simultaneously tensed and then relaxed; tense each group for 5 to 10 seconds and relax each for 20 to 30 seconds. Read the following directions:

"Make a tight fist with both hands, tighten the biceps and forearms, hold, and relax for 20 to 30 seconds.

"Wrinkle the forehead, press head against floor or wall, turn head as far to right and left as possible. . . . Relax. . . .

"Now wrinkle the muscles of the face, making a big grimace or frown, close eyes tightly, purse lips, press tongue against roof of mouth, hunch shoulders, HOLD, relax and let go. [Give the instructions quickly so the tension buildup is continuous.]

"Next arch the back, take a deep breath and hold, relax and let go. Repeat, taking a deep breath and pushing the stomach out as you inhale.

"Pull feet and toes back toward the shin bone, tighten shin muscles, hold, relax. Curl toes, tighten calf muscles, thighs and buttocks, and then let go.

"A shortened version of this exercise is to put as much tension as you can in all muscle groups simultaneously, hold for 10 seconds, and let go, trying to maintain that tension-free, let-go position. Repeat this several times."

Passive PR   Once the athletes have learned the skill of deep muscle relaxation, they can relax the muscles without first tensing them. Many people find this passive form of relaxation more effective than the active form. With passive PR, the participant merely lets go from whatever level of muscular tension is in the muscle group. There is a slow progression from one part of the body to another as the participant relaxes each body part more deeply by letting go of any remaining tension. The same sequence of body parts can be used for passive PR as for active PR. (Some people prefer to progress from the feet up or from the head down.)

After a general lead-in to the exercise, progress through the specific body parts with directions such as the following: Turn your attention to your dominant hand. Just tune in to how this hand feels. Become aware of any tension that might be in it and let go of the tension — even more and more. Let go of all the muscles in your dominant hand. Allow it gradually to become looser and heavier. Think about letting go further. Now go to your nondominant hand. Think of your nondominant hand getting looser, heavier, just letting go of the muscles in your nondominant hand. Let go further, more deeply, and now feel the relaxation coming into your left and right forearms. Feel your forearms getting looser and heavier. Enjoy the relaxation that is now coming into your forearms. . . .

Quick body scan   The quick body scan is an abbreviated passive PR technique that is a helpful momentary muscle relaxation exercise best used during performance, such as just before serving, shooting a free throw, or batting. Quickly scan the body from head to toe (or toe to head). Stop only at muscle groups where the tension level is too high. Release the tension and continue the scan down (or up) the body.

Neck – shoulder check It is very common for athletes to carry excessive tension in the neck and shoulders when they are worried or anxious. Once they have learned to spot tension and relax, instruct your athletes to scan their neck and shoulders periodically for any undue signs of tension. If they feel tension in the neck, they should release it passively or roll the neck around the shoulders. If the tension is in the neck, the athletes can drop (slump) the neck and shoulders. Releasing excessive tension in these two areas tends to spread relaxation to the rest of the body; it may also have a calming effect on the mind.

MIND-TO-MUSCLE RELAXATION TECHNIQUES

The majority of additional relaxation techniques and strategies focus on efferent nerve control, or the stimulation from the brain to the muscles. Among these techniques are meditation, visualization, and autogenic training. The techniques should be initially practiced in a comfortable position in a quiet environment. Any of the positions suggested for progressive relaxation practice can be used.

Meditation

The regular practice of meditation not only helps one teach a state of deep relaxation, it facilitates concentration by disciplining the mind. Four basic components are common to most types of meditation: a quiet environment, a comfortable position, a mental device, and a passive attitude. A mental device, such as a mantra or fixed gazing at an object, helps to shift the mind from logical, externally oriented thought by providing a focus of attention on something that is nonarousing and nonstimulating. A mantra is a nonstimulating, meaningless rhythmic sound of one or two syllables that a person regularly repeats while meditating.

It is critical that athletes not worry about how well they are performing the technique because this disrupts effective meditation. Stress their adopting a "let it happen" attitude. The passive attitude is perhaps the most important element in learning to meditate. Distracting thoughts or mind wandering may occur, but this is to be expected and does not mean that the technique is being performed incorrectly. When these thoughts occur, simply redirect attention to the mental device, focusing on this cue and letting all other thoughts move on through consciousness with a passive attitude, making no attempt to attend to them.

The "relaxation response" developed by Herbert Benson (1975), a physician at Harvard Medical School, is an excellent meditative technique to teach athletes. This technique is a generalized version of a variety of Eastern and Western religious, cultic, and lay meditation practices. It has the advantage, however, of being a noncultic technique, with all reference to mysticism and unusual postures eliminated. In fact, the technique does not even need to be called meditation. For a mental device, Benson recommended the word *one*. However, *one* is a very arousing, stimulating word for achievement-oriented athletes. A better word might be *calm* or *warm*. The following are directions for meditation based upon a variation of Benson's relaxation response:

1. Sit quietly in a comfortable position.
2. Close your eyes.
3. Deeply relax all your muscles, beginning at your feet and progressing up to your face. Keep them relaxed.
4. Breathe through your nose. Concentrate on your breathing. As you breathe out, say the word *calm* or *warm* silently to yourself. For example, breath IN . . . OUT, *calm;* IN . . . OUT, *calm;* and so forth. Breathe easily and naturally.
5. Continue for 10 to 20 minutes. You may open your eyes to check the time, but do not use an alarm. When you finish, sit quietly for several minutes, at first with your eyes closed and later with your eyes open. Do not stand up for a few minutes.
6. Do not worry about whether you are successful in achieving a deep level of relaxation. Practice the technique once or twice daily, but not within two hours after any meal, since the digestive processes seem to interfere with the elicitation of the relaxation response.

Visualization

If athletes have been trained in imagery and can visualize easily, visualizing being in a place conducive to relaxation is another successful technique for eliciting relaxation. For example, an athlete might visualize lying on a beach in the warm sun listening to the continuous rhythm of breaking waves. Other images might be sitting in the midst of a beautiful mountain scene or lying in a grassy valley by a gentle, gurgling stream. Whatever image provides the athlete with a sense of calm and relaxation is the one he or she should use.

Autogenic Training

Autogenic training was developed in Germany in the early 1930s by Johannes Schultz and has been used extensively with European athletes. The training consists of a series of exercises designed to produce two physical sensations, warmth and heaviness. Basically, it is a technique of autohypnosis or self-hypnosis. Attention is focused on the sensations one is trying to produce. As in meditation, it is important to let the feeling happen in a very passive manner. There are six stages in the training (see the summary below). Have the athletes learn each stage before progressing to the next stage. Some people suggest that trainees spend two weeks at each stage. However, the progression can be modified to suit the athletes' learning rate as well as the training program and length of season of the sport. It usually takes several months of regular practice of 10 to 40 minutes, one to six times per day to become proficient enough to experience heaviness and warmth in the limbs and to produce the sensation of a relaxed, calm heartbeat and respiratory rate accompanied by warmth in the abdomen and coolness in the forehead. Once athletes have reached that level of training and can attain a relaxed state, they can use imagery to increase the depth of relaxation.

The first autogenic stage involves focusing attention in a passive manner on the dominant arm while silently saying, "My right (left) arm is heavy," three to five times during one minute. Have the athletes flex the arms and move the body about, then repeat the sequence with the nondominant arm, then with the dominant leg, followed by the nondominant leg. A sense of heaviness should take over the body. If the mind wanders, emphasize passively redirecting attention back to the task at hand. Some athletes may be able to produce a sense of heaviness immediately; others may take one or two weeks of three or more times of practice daily to accomplish the sensation. Instructions should follow the same format for the warmth stage, which may take longer to achieve. Regulation of the heartbeat is the third stage after mastering the heaviness and warmth exercises. Repeat the instruction, "my heartbeat is calm and regular" three to five times during one minute. Take a brief break from the focus of concentration and then repeat the instruction again three to five times during one minute. Do a total of four repeats for the exercise. Follow the same procedures for the fourth, fifth, and sixth stages.

In summary, the stages for autogenic training are as follows:

Stage 1: Heaviness
       My right arm is heavy.
       My left arm is heavy.
       Both arms are heavy.
       My right leg is heavy.

My left leg is heavy.
Both legs are heavy.
My arms and legs are very heavy.

Stage 2: Warmth
Follow instructional format of stage 1.

Stage 3: Heart rate
My heartbeat is regular and calm.

Stage 4: Breathing rate
My breathing rate is slow, calm, and relaxed: "It breathes me."

Stage 5: Warmth in the solar plexis
My solar plexis is warm (hand placed on upper abdominal area).

Stage 6: Coolness of the forehead
My forehead is cool.

It may take anywhere from two months to a year to master these skills. As one becomes more proficient, the six stages can be combined by going through the above directions once, completing the entire series in a matter of minutes. Regular daily practice for several minutes three or four times a day is recommended during training.

Autogenic Training with Visualization

After athletes have mastered the six stages of autogenic training and can induce the desired state in a few minutes and sustain it for 30 minutes to an hour, they are ready to move to the next phase of training, which combines autogenic exercises with visualization. The progression goes from first imagining the entire visual field being filled with one color to visualizing colors in movement or formations to holding an image of a particular object in a static position to visualizing some abstract concept such as happiness or confidence to reexperiencing through imagery some chosen state or feeling such as "flow," winning, or a peak experience when everything goes just right. The fourth and fifth elements of the progression enable athletes not only to practice self-regulation of arousal but also to reexperience thoughts, feelings, and states that led to optimal performance. The sixth and final element of the progression includes visualizing other people such as the coach, teammates, and/or opponents. However, the athlete should begin visualizing neutral individuals first. This phase can ultimately lead to imagining successful sport performance in the competitive setting with all of the individuals involved.

As indicated earlier, autogenic training takes a relatively long time to master. As a result, it is less popular in the United States because athletes seldom train under the same coach for such long periods of time. In addition, the competitive seasons are frequently too short to introduce and learn autogenic training. However, it is used extensively in many European countries where athletes are housed in sport training centers for several years working with a relatively stable staff of coaches and sports medicine personnel. Despite the time required to become proficient in autohypnosis, many athletes find it a satisfactory means of training for relaxation and imagery. This approach will be particularly appealing to those athletes who respond to autosuggestion.

SKILLS AND STRATEGIES FOR LEARNING HOW TO INCREASE ACTIVATION AND ENERGY

Once athletes have been taught how to slow down the heart rate and respiration rate and to increase blood flow and temperature in the extremities, they can also learn to develop skills to speed up the heart rate, respiration rate, etc., and to get the physiological systems ready for action. These skills are essential for generating energy on short notice or when brief bursts of energy are needed.

Just as there are a variety of effective techniques for decreasing arousal, there are many techniques for energizing or increasing arousal. Such skills and strategies should be used to build appropriate arousal when athletes are not psyched up enough for practice or for competition. They can also be used to reduce fatigue during practice and competition. The coach should encourage athletes to practice and develop these skills and strategies. Not only should athletes identify primary energizing techniques that tend to work for them, but they should also have backup techniques in the event that the effectiveness of the primary techniques diminishes over time.

First, the athletes need to identify when energizing is generally needed in their particular sport or in specific positions or situations within the sport. The coach and sport psychologist should try to become sensitive to each athlete's optimal level of arousal; some athletes are much more likely than others to need energizing. The athletes also need to learn how to recognize signs and symptoms of low energy and activation and where they are located in the body. As an example, a track athlete may need to learn how to energize "dead legs" during a race. Or a weight lifter may want to put all available energy into the legs and arms to attain a particular lift.

We turn now to nine specific skills and strategies that athletes can use to increase their activation and energy.

Breathing

Breathing control and focus work as effectively in producing energy as in reducing tension. Instruct your athletes to focus on a regular, relaxed breathing rhythm. Now have them consciously increase that rhythm and imagine with each inhalation that they are generating more energy and activation. With each exhalation, the athletes should imagine that they are getting rid of any waste products or fatigue that might prevent them from being at their best. Ask them to feel in full control, supplying sufficient oxygen and energy for any task that they have to perform. Have the athletes increase their breathing rate as they increase their level of energy generation. Along with the accelerated breathing rate, athletes may want to say "energy in" with each inhalation and "fatigue out" with each exhalation.

Using Energizing Imagery

Using imagery skills, have the athletes imagine that they are machines capable of generating energy at will. As an example, have them imagine that they are a train that is just beginning to move, building up steam, momentum, and power with each deep breath. There are literally hundreds of images that can be conjured up as cues for generating energy: animal images, machine images, forces of nature, etc. Instruct the athletes to develop a supply of imagery cues that work for them in various situations encountered in their particular sport. Instruct them to establish a plan for using these cues ahead of time and to practice and prepare to use them on a regular basis. Some sports have lapses in action that are much more conducive to using cues for activation and energizing than others. Help your athletes to become aware of and to plan for the times when they can use these strategies with self-talk, concentration, and imagery. They are particularly effective when fatigue is beginning to set in, when a series of points have been lost, when a sudden burst of energy is needed to finish a play.

Formulating Energizing Verbal Cues

In the midst of a performance, depending on the sport or position, there are many occasions when the athletes do not have enough time to prepare imagery techniques to generate energy. In preparation for such times, think of word cues and images with which they can quickly associate energy buildup. Words such as explode, charge, psych up, go, and the like, as well as any image representing energy, can be used. Then have the athletes select the cues that are appropriate to their sport and to the tasks that they perform during competition. Athletes need to get to know themselves well enough to learn what types of thoughts, images, and cue words serve to activate and energize them during practice and competitive performance.

Transferring Energy

Help your athletes learn to convert energy from other sources into a positive and useful force for athletic performance. Activation and arousal that result from aggression, anger, frustration, or some other emotion that tends to interfere with performance need to be converted into energy to accomplish performance goals.

Storing Excess Energy for Later Use

Many athletes have found that the strategy of storing excess energy that is frequently generated just prior to competition accomplishes two purposes: It provides them a means of transferring that energy somewhere else, and it provides a well of energy from which to draw upon at some later point. If an athlete has a problem with overarousal, suggest that the athlete store away that energy and use it later when he or she feels fatigued or discouraged.

Using the Environment

Some athletes have learned how to draw energy from the spectators to use for their own performance. This type of strategy provides the home team with an advantage. Athletes need to learn how to take all types of energy available in the sport environment and put it to their own use through imagery, word cues, self-talk, etc. They can even draw energy from their opponents, particularly when it appears that the opponents have the momentum going for them.

Listening to Music

Music is often a good energy provider. With the availability of cassette players and headphones, athletes can readily select and listen to the music that works best for them. However, the coach should ensure that the practice or competitive environment is not saturated with loud music that may detract from the optimal level of arousal for many athletes.

Improving Pacing

Athletes become underaroused in some sports because of fatigue. This tiredness is often caused by inappropriate pacing and unnecessary sources of energy drain. The alert coach can spot athletes who have difficulty in rationing out their energy over time. Appropriate physical practice plus teaching the athlete to become more sensitive to physical signs and symptoms can improve pacing. Pacing is also improved when unnecessary sources of energy drain are eliminated; these sources include too much muscle tension for a particular skill or situation, anger, frustration and undue response to officiating calls, and anxiety or worry over one's own performance or that of teammates.

Using Distraction

Another way to deal with underarousal caused by fatigue is to focus one's attention away from the state of fatigue being experienced. Most athletes do just the opposite; the more fatigued they become, the more they tune into it. This just increases the sense of fatigue as well as its detrimental effects on performance. Instead, suggest to the athletes that they apply their concentration skills and focusing ability on what is happening and about to happen within the performance setting. Remind the athletes to think about what they are doing rather than about how they are feeling.

SUMMARY

It is the coach's and sport psychologist's responsibility to teach the athlete strategies and techniques for achieving an optimal level of arousal for practice and competition. Acquiring the ability to self-regulate arousal not only enhances one's learning and performance of athletic skills but also one's functioning in many nonathletic situations.

It is important for coaches to know that poor performance during competition is more frequently a consequence of overarousal than underarousal. All too often coaches assume the opposite and partially contribute to the continuation of the problem by berating athletes to try harder when intervening with some calming strategy would be much more appropriate. This chapter has described techniques for achieving total relaxation and momentary or partial relaxation. Such techniques rid the muscles of disruptive tension that interferes with performance and help "quiet" the rest of the body and the mind. They also promote confidence in the athlete's ability to lessen or eliminate the effects of undesirable thoughts and feelings.

Energizing skills and strategies that can be used to increase arousal and lessen the effects of fatigue are also described in this chapter.

No single control strategy is effective or desirable for all athletes. Consequently, coaches and sport psychologists will need to teach their athletes a variety of techniques. Athletes should be encouraged to identify and practice the primary techniques that tend to work best for them as well as some backup techniques in the event that the primary ones lose their effectiveness.

REFERENCES

Benson, H. (1975). *The relaxation response.* New York: Avon Books.
Green, E., & Green, A. (1977). *Beyond biofeedback.* New York: Dell Publishing Co.
Jacobson, E. (1930). Progressive relaxation. Chicago: University of Chicago Press.
Mason, L. J. (1980). *Guide to stress reduction.* Culver City, Calif.: Peace Press.

14 Imagery Training for Performance Enhancement

ROBIN S. VEALEY

Miami University

Julie, a collegiate varsity tennis player, lacks consistency in her performance. In certain matches she plays brilliantly, yet in other matches she repeatedly commits unforced errors. When asked about her inconsistency, Julie shrugs and replies, "Some days you have it, and some days you don't."

John is a world-class cross-country skier. His performance is suffering because he is unable to concentrate effectively throughout the entire race. He seeks the help of a hypnotist to correct his problem.

Sue is the starting point guard for a major college basketball team. She does a fine job of handing out assists and running the team offense, but she is shooting poorly. Sue shoots well during practice, but in games she tends to freeze up. When Sue asks her coach what she can do to avoid "choking," her coach replies, "Just don't think about it! It'll come."

Julie, John, and Sue are physically gifted athletes. Yet their lack of psychological skill prevents them from performing well in sport. Like many athletes, they have no idea how to solve their problems. Julie believes she has no control over psychological factors that influence her performance. John hopes to find a quick and easy way to learn to concentrate. Sue's coach seems to feel that her performance slump will disappear by magic.

In this chapter we suggest an alternative to magic: the use of imagery as a psychological tool to facilitate sport performance. Imagery is a mental technique that "programs" the human mind to respond as programmed. All athletes possess the ability to use imagery to improve their performance. Imagery is not magic. Evidence supports the effectiveness of imagery in improving sport performance, but like physical skill the psychological skill of imagery requires systematic practice to be effective.

Thus, the purpose of this chapter is to guide you, the coach and sport psychologist, in the systematic use of imagery in sport. We begin by presenting the basic concepts of how and why imagery works and then cite experiential and experimental evidence to allow you to judge the effectiveness of imagery in performance enhancement. Next we outline four easy steps to enable you to set up a sport imagery program. These steps involve introducing imagery to athletes, evaluating their imagery ability, training them in basic imagery skills, and implementing a systematic imagery program. These steps are followed by an "imagery cookbook" containing "ingredients" such as ways to use imagery and times, methods, and tips for using imagery. Finally, we present three sample imagery programs as examples of how to integrate different ingredients into a systematic imagery program.

UNDERSTANDING IMAGERY

Imagery involves using all the senses to recreate or create an experience in the mind. This definition contains three keys to understanding imagery.

Using All the Senses

First, imagery can and should involve all the senses. Although imagery is often termed visualization or "seeing with the mind's eye," sight is not the only significant sense. In sport, the visual, auditory, olfactory, taste, tactile, and kinesthetic senses are all important. *Auditory* refers to sound. *Olfactory* refers to smell, such as a swimmer smelling chlorine. *Tactile* is the sensation of touch, such as feeling the grip of a golf club or the sensation of diving into water. *Kinesthetic* sense is the feel or sensation of our body as it moves in different positions. Using all appropriate senses may help the athlete create more vivid images. The more vivid the image, the more effective it is.

Let's use the example of a wide receiver in football to stress the importance of using different senses. The receiver uses his visual sense to read the defense and focus on the ball before catching it. He uses his auditory sense to listen to the snap count barked by the quarterback. He uses his tactile and kinesthetic senses to run his pattern, jump in the air, catch a hard thrown ball, and touch both feet in bounds. He may also smell freshly mown grass and the sweat of his opponent's jersey when he is tackled. He may even taste the saltiness of his own sweat.

The emotions associated with various sport experiences are also important in the practice of imagery (Martens, 1982). In using imagery to help control anxiety, anger, or pain, athletes must be able to recreate these emotions in their minds. For example, athletes must recreate the thoughts and feelings they experience during competition to understand how and why anxiety hurts their performance.

Imagery as Recreating or Creating

Through imagery we are able to recreate as well as create experiences in our mind. We *recreate experiences* all the time. Have you ever watched someone perform a flashy basketball move and then gone out and done it yourself? Or maybe you've perfected your serve after watching a professional tennis player for a few hours? We are able to imitate the actions of others because our mind "takes a picture" of the skill that we use as a blueprint for our performance. In essence, this is imagery. Imagery is based on memory, and we experience it internally by reconstructing external events in our mind.

Similarly, we can use imagery to *create new events* in our mind. Although imagery is essentially a product of memory, our brain is able to put the pieces of the internal picture together in different ways. As the programmer of your own imagery program, you are able to build an image from whatever pieces of memory you choose.

Fran Tarkenton used imagery to create offensive game plans. He viewed film of the opponent's defense and through imagery directed successful offensive patterns against that defense. Although Tarkenton may not have previously played that particular opponent, he was able to create images by combining his offensive plays with the defensive alignments he viewed on film.

Before the 1976 Summer Olympics, representatives from the Soviet Union shot pictures of the Olympic facilities in Montreal. These pictures were returned to the Soviet Union and studied by the athletes. Although the Soviet athletes had not been to Montreal, they used the pictures to create images of themselves performing in those facilities. Creating these types of images served to familiarize the athletes with the Olympic environment before they arrived.

Building a Mental Machine

On the basis of our definition of imagery, we have discussed how senses and emotions are important in the practice of imagery and how imagery may be used to recreate past sport experiences as well as create future experiences. The final key to understanding imagery involves an analysis of how it works. How can a sensory experience in our mind enhance our ability to perform in sport? How can imagining clearing a high-jump bar, skiing a cross-country course, or kicking a field goal help us to do these things better? Sport psychologists have advanced two theoretical explanations to explain the imagery phenomenon.

Psychoneuromuscular theory We know that as athletes engage in various sport movements, the brain is constantly transmitting impulses to the muscles for the execution of the movements. The psychoneuromuscular theory suggests that similar impulses occur in the brain and muscles when athletes imagine the movements without actually performing them. Scientific evidence supports the notion that vivid, imagined events produce innervation in our muscles that is similar to that produced by the actual physical execution of the event.

Jacobson (1931) first supported this phenomenon. He demonstrated that the imagined movement of bending the arm created contractions in the flexor muscles of the arm. Jacobson's work was later replicated and supported by Hale (1982). Eccles (1958) presented evidence that the slight firing of neural pathways puts down a mental blueprint that helps the individual execute the movement later on. Richard Suinn (1980) tested this phenomenon by having a downhill skier recreate a race by using imagery. Suinn monitored the electrical activity in the skier's leg muscles as he imagined the downhill run. Suinn found that the printout of muscle firings mirrored the terrain of the ski run. Muscle firings peaked at certain points during imagery that corresponded to times in which extra muscle involvement would be expected because of turns and rough sections on the run.

Thus, whether athletes actually perform movements or vividly imagine performing them, similar neural pathways to the muscles are used. Although the muscle activity is far less during imagery as compared to actual movement, this phenomenon is enormously significant. Through imagery, athletes may actually *strengthen* the neural pathways for certain movements in their sport. Think of it as *building a machine*. When athletes continuously practice a sport skill over and over, in essence they are attempting to build a machine. Basketball players are coached to get into a groove when shooting free throws and shoot the same way each time. Divers attempt to fine-tune their body to make the muscles react flawlessly in a dive. Shot-putters work hours refining their technique in order to uncoil their body in maximum thrust.

The objective in performing any sport movement is to make that skill flawless and automatic, to build a machine. Coaches and athletes spend a great deal of time using drill and repetition attempting to build a flawless, automatic machine. Why not use imagery to help? By systematically practicing their sport techniques through imagery, athletes can actually make their body believe they are practicing the skill!

Symbolic learning theory   The second explanation of how imagery can facilitate sport performance suggests that imagery may function as a coding system to help athletes acquire or understand movement patterns. All movements that we make must first be encoded in our central nervous system—we must have a blueprint or plan for this movement. The symbolic learning theory suggests that imagery facilitates performance by helping individuals to blueprint or code their movements into symbolic components, thus making the movements more familiar and perhaps more automatic. For example, a gymnast can use imagery to cue herself on the temporal and spatial elements involved in performing a balance beam routine.

This theory was first proposed by Sackett (1934), who stated that imagery enables performers to rehearse the sequence of movements as symbolic components of a task. This theoretical position has been supported by studies that have demonstrated greater performance improvement through imagery on movement tasks that required cognitive coding as opposed to pure motor tasks (Feltz & Landers, 1983; Ryan & Simons, 1981; Ryan & Simons, 1983; Wrisberg & Ragsdale, 1979). This theory has also been supported by research showing improved free throw shooting (Hall & Erff-meyer, 1983) and motor performance (Housner, 1984) by using imagery to mentally encode modeled movement behaviors.

Like the neuromuscular theory, this theoretical explanation may also be thought of as a way to *build a machine* to enhance sport performance. When athletes physically practice sport skills, they use feedback from their muscles and senses to encode the proper cognitive elements of the skills. Through mental practice or imagery, athletes may also use this cognitive encoding of feedback to help strengthen the mental blueprint (symbolic cognitive code), make the skills more automatic, and build a flawless machine.

BELIEF IN IMAGERY

The evidence supporting the positive influence of imagery on sport performance is impressive. Both scientifically controlled studies and experiential accounts of the use of imagery to enhance performance report positive results.

Scientific Evidence

Richardson (1967a, 1967b) and Corbin (1972) conducted extensive reviews of studies that evaluated the effects of imagery training on motor performance. Although these reviews were qualified with certain conditions, the researchers concluded that imagery is valuable in learning and performing sport skills. As a follow-up, Martens (1982) reviewed the imagery research related to sport and motor behavior from 1970 to 1982. He concluded that imagery is an effective technique to improve performance and documented improvement in the following sport skills through imagery practice: basketball free throw shooting, football place kicking, swimming starts, dart throwing, alpine skiing, karate skills, volleyball serving, tennis serving, and golf. Feltz and Landers (1983) conducted an extensive review of the imagery literature using meta-analytic procedures to provide some definitive answers to previous contradictory findings. Although these researchers identified several factors that serve to influence the relationship between imagery and sport performance, they concluded that using imagery to practice sport skills influences performance better than no practice at all.

Anecdotal Evidence

Perhaps it would be helpful to learn firsthand from athletes themselves how imagery works for them. Several athletes who have at one time been the best in the *world* at their sport advocate the use of imagery. Dwight Stones, a three-time Olympian in the high jump, has used imagery throughout his career. If you have ever watched Stones compete, you will notice that he stands and stares intently at the bar before he begins his approach. Stones believes in the power of imagery and practices it before every jump.

Jack Nicklaus, one of the greatest golfers of all time, says that playing the ball to a certain place in a certain way is 50% mental picture. Nicklaus "goes to the movies" before every shot by using imagery to see three things: First, he sees the ball land in the target area. Second, he pictures the flight path of the ball to the target area. Finally, he vividly imagines himself using the appropriate swing for that particular shot. Certainly, Jack Nicklaus is successful because of his enormous physical talent. Yet experts feel that his concentration skills have carried him to a level above all other golfers. Nicklaus's systematic practice of imagery may facilitate the concentration that is the key to his success.

Greg Louganis reached the pinnacle of his magnificent diving career at the 1984 Summer Olympics by winning gold medals in both the springboard and platform events. Louganis believes in the power of imagery. He speaks of using imagery to practice each dive and of his particular technique of setting his dives to music as he practices them in his head.

The list goes on. Fran Tarkenton, Chris Evert-Lloyd, Jean Claude Killy, O. J. Simpson—all of these athletes attest to using imagery to facilitate their performance. Coaches and teachers believe in the power of imagery, too. Tennis coaches are implementing imagery in their programs on the basis of the recommendations of Gallwey (1976) in his book *Inner Tennis*. Peter Karns, the 1976 U.S. Olympic biathlon coach, credited a relaxation and imagery program for improving his team's performance. Several U.S. national teams in various sports practice imagery as part of their training.

SETTING UP THE IMAGERY PROGRAM

There are four phases in setting up an imagery program. First, coaches must sell the idea of using imagery to athletes. Second, coaches must evaluate the imagery ability of the athletes in order to develop the most appropriate type of program. Third, coaches must train athletes in basic imagery skills. Fourth, coaches must monitor and implement a systematic program of imagery practice.

Introducing Imagery to Athletes

Imagery only works for athletes if *they believe in it.* It is your job to sell the product. However, you should avoid unnecessary hype or unrealistic claims. Make sure your athletes understand that imagery will not guarantee success. It is simply a training technique that has been shown to enhance sport performance.

Basically, you should go over these main points with the athletes: (a) what imagery is, (b) evidence that imagery does work, (c) why imagery works, (d) why athletes should use imagery, and (e) how you will implement an imagery program. When talking to the athletes, use phrases such as "building a mental machine" instead of "strengthening neural pathways." It is also very important to talk about well-known athletes and elite programs that practice imagery.

In addition, taking your athletes through the following two exercises will help most athletes immediately experience the power of imagery. If correctly done, these exercises are extremely helpful in convincing skeptical athletes of the merits of practicing imagery.

String and bolt Give each athlete a string approximately 14 to 16 inches long threaded through a heavy bolt (a neck chain or heavy ring will also work). Stabilizing the elbow, ideally on a tabletop, each athlete should lightly hold the two ends of the string between the thumb and forefinger with the weight suspended directly below. Focusing on the weight, each athlete in his or her mind's eye will imagine the weight moving right and left like the pendulum of a clock. Once most of the athletes have at least some movement right and left, have them change the image so the weight swings directly away from and then toward the chest. Again, once successful, change the image so that the weight moves in a clockwise circle and finally in a counterclockwise circle. In discussing this exercise, you will find most athletes absolutely amazed at how just imagining the movement ultimately translated to the actual physical movement.

Arm as iron bar Pair the athletes with partners of similar height and strength. While directly facing each other, one partner extends his or her dominant arm straight out, palm up, so the back of the wrist is resting on the partner's opposite shoulder. The other partner cups both of his or her hands above the bend in the partner's elbow. The person whose arm is extended then maximally tightens all the muscles in the arm, trying to make it as strong as possible. Then, the partner tests for strength by pushing down at the elbow with both hands, trying to see how much strength it takes to bend the arm. Next the partners switch roles and perform the exercise. Afterward, the partners resume their initial positions. This time to create strength, the partner is to close everything out of his or her mind and imagine that the arm is a thick steel bar and also that it extends out through the opposite wall. Once the partner has created the image of an unbendable, strong steel bar, he or she indicates such by raising one of the fingers of the opposite hand. This signals the partner to again test for strength. Again, the partners switch roles and perform the exercise. In follow-up discussion, you will find that most athletes are amazed at how much stronger their arm is with the iron bar image.

Evaluating Athletes' Imagery Ability

Before implementing an imagery program with your athletes, you must evaluate their imagery ability. As discussed earlier, athletes need to be able to use all appropriate senses and their emotions when practicing imagery. Thus, it is important to have some idea of athletes' abilities to experience each of these through imagery.

One method of evaluation is to take the athletes through some of the imagery exercises in basic training (see next section). By discussing their images with them, you can determine whether certain areas need to be strengthened. A better idea is to administer the sport imagery questionnaire designed by Martens (1982) to measure athletes' abilities to experience the various senses when imaging. There are other inventories designed to measure imagery, but Martens's instrument seems to be most useful to the coach/practitioner. This questionnaire appears on pages 232–234.

Just as they differ in physical skills, athletes will differ in their ability to develop vivid images. For best results, direct athletes through the exercises in the questionnaire. Encourage athletes to answer honestly on the basis of their imagery ability. Administering the questionnaire should take approximately 10 minutes.

Basic Training

Imagery is a skill. Athletes differ in their ability to develop vivid and controllable images, just as they differ in physical ability. But as with physical ability, athletes can increase their imagery ability through training. Basic training is similar to a preseason conditioning program. By developing a foundation of strength and endurance, athletes are better equipped to fine-tune their physical skills when the season begins. By strengthening their "imagery muscle" in basic training, athletes are more likely to benefit from the use of imagery during the season.

Basic training includes three sets of imagery exercises. First, athletes need to develop *vivid* images. Like a fine-tuning control on a television set, increasing the vividness of images sharpens the details of the image. The vividness set includes exercises designed to strengthen the senses we have identified as important in sport performance. Second, athletes must be able to *control* their images. Controllability exercises involve learning to manipulate images by will. Third, athletes need to increase their *self-perceptions* of their sport performance. It is a skill to be able to stand back and look at yourself through imagery. This type of imagery enables athletes to practice being detectives investigating their own behavior in sport. This set of exercises will also increase athletes' vividness of emotional imagery as they try to recreate graphically their thoughts and feelings during competition.

It is important for athletes to gain proficiency in the type of exercises in each set. The following example exercises purposely use vague descriptors to encourage you to develop your own imagery exercises that are appropriate for your athletes. It is also helpful to develop additional exercises in areas in which athletes are having trouble. For example, kinesthetic imagery is usually the most difficult so you should create kinesthetic imagery exercises based on the particular movements in your sport.

Vividness *Exercise 1.* Pick a close friend or someone that you are around quite often. Have the person sit in a chair in front of you. Try to get a sharp image of the person. Try to visualize the details of the person: facial features, body build, mannerisms, clothes, etc.

Now imagine that person talking. Still focusing on the person's face, try to hear his or her voice. Imagine all of the person's facial expressions as he or she talks.

Think about how you feel about the person. Try to recreate the emotions you feel toward him or her whether they be warm friendship, deep love, or admiration and respect.

Exercise 2. Place yourself in a familiar place where you usually perform your sport: the gym, pool, rink, field, track, etc. It is empty except for you. Stand in the middle of this place and look all around. Notice the quiet emptiness. Pick out as many details as you can.

Now imagine yourself in the same setting, but this time with many spectators present. Imagine yourself getting ready to perform, and focus on the sights, sounds, smells, and feelings you experience when getting ready to perform in front of the crowd.

Exercise 3. Choose a piece of equipment in your sport such as a ball, pole, racquet, club, etc. Focus on this stationary object. Try to imagine very fine details of the object. Turn it over in your hands and examine every part of the object. Feel its outline and texture.

Now imagine yourself performing with the object. First, focus on seeing yourself very clearly performing an activity. Visualize yourself repeating the skill over and over. Next, try to hear the sounds that accompany this particular movement. Listen carefully to all of the sounds that are being made as you perform this skill. Now put the sight and the sound together. Try to get a clear picture of yourself performing the skill and also hear all of the sounds involved.

Exercise 4. Pick a very simple skill in your sport. Perform the skill over and over in your mind and imagine every feeling and movement in your muscles as you perform the skill. Concentrate on how the different parts of your body feel as you stretch and contract the various muscles associated with the skill. Think about "building a machine" as you perform the skill flawlessly over and over again.

Now try to combine all the sensations, particularly those of feeling, seeing, and hearing yourself perform the skill over and over. Do not concentrate too hard on any one sense. Instead try to imagine the total experience using all of your senses.

Once the athletes have mastered these exercises, you might consider follow-up variations to imagine more complex skills, grouping skills together, or placing the skill in the context of competition (for example, as reacting to certain defenses, executing strategy, etc.).

Controllability   *Exercise 1.* Imagine again the person you selected for the first exercise in vividness. Concentrate on the person's face and notice all of the different features. Now imagine this person getting up from the chair and walking about a room full of people. Watch the person walk about the room greeting and talking to different people. Continue watching as the person walks up and greets you. Create a conversation with this person.

Exercise 2. Choose a simple sport skill and begin practicing it. Now imagine yourself performing this skill, either with a teammate or against an opponent. Imagine yourself executing successful strategies in relation to the movements of your teammate or opponent.

Exercise 3. Choose a particular sport skill that you have trouble performing. Recreate the experiences in which you have not performed the skill well. Take careful notice of what you are doing wrong. Now imagine yourself performing the skill correctly. Focus on how your body feels as you go through different positions in performing the skill correctly. Repeat this exercise using slow motion to find and correct mistakes.

Self-perception   *Exercise 1.* Think back and choose a past performance in which you performed very well. Using all your senses, recreate the situation in your mind. See yourself as you were succeeding, hear the sounds involved, feel your body as you performed the movements, and reexperience the positive emotions. Try to pick out the characteristics that made you perform so well (e.g., intense concentration, feelings of confidence, low anxiety). After identifying the characteristics, try to determine why they were present in this situation. Think about the things you did in preparation for this particular event. What are some things that may have caused your great performance? Repeat this exercise imagining a situation in which you performed very poorly.

Exercise 2. Think back to a sport situation in which you experienced a great deal of anxiety. Recreate the situation in your head, seeing and hearing yourself. Especially recreate the feeling of anxiety. Try to feel the physical responses of your body to the emotion, and also try to recall the thoughts going through your mind that may have caused the anxiety. Now repeat this exercise imagining a situation in which you experienced a great deal of anger.

Exercise 3. The purpose of this exercise is to help you to become more aware of things that happen during competition that bother you when you perform. Think about the times when your performance suddenly went from good to bad. Recreate several of these experiences in your mind. Try to pinpoint the specific factors that negatively influenced your performance (e.g., officials, teammates, opponents' remarks, an opponent started to play really well). After becoming aware of the cues that negatively affected your performance, take several minutes to recreate the situations, develop appropriate strategies to deal with the negative cues, and imagine the situations again but this time imagine yourself using your strategies to keep the negative factors from interfering with your performance.

Implementing a Systematic Program

After basic training, athletes should be fairly proficient at experiencing vivid images, controlling these images, and using imagery to become more self-aware. They should also be proficient at using all senses and emotions when imaging and being able to integrate these types of imagery into a total sensory experience.

Athletes are now ready to begin a systematic program of imagery. Keep in mind that imagery practice must be systematic to be effective. Your first concern is to build the imagery program into the athletes' routine. The imagery program must *not* be something extra but should instead be an integral part of training and practice.

Another key is to fit the needs of the athlete. The imagery program does not need to be long and complex. In fact, when first starting the program, keep it concise and simple. Initially, choose a sport skill or strategy that is easy to control. That is, choose a movement in which the environment is stable rather than reactive. For example, in basketball you could start with free throw shooting and in racquet sports with the serve. As your athletes become more proficient and accepting of the program, you can increase the variety of the program.

IMAGERY COOKBOOK FOR COACHES AND SPORT PSYCHOLOGISTS

It is impossible to design an imagery program appropriate for all sports. For that reason, this section is designed as a "cookbook" in which the necessary "ingredients" of an imagery program are itemized. The ingredients include ways to use imagery, times in which imagery may be practiced, methods of practicing imagery, and helpful tips to enhance the effectiveness of an imagery program. It is up to you to choose which ingredients are most relevant for the needs of your athletes.

Uses

Athletes can use imagery in a number of ways to enhance overall sport experience. In this section we offer nine suggestions.

Practicing sport skills   Often termed mental practice, imagery is used to perform a specific sport skill repetitively in the mind. Examples include using imagery to shoot free throws, execute a takedown, sprint over a set of hurdles, swing a golf club, hit a baseball, or perform a routine on the balance beam.

Practicing strategy   Using imagery to practice strategies involves imagining types of team concepts or individual strategies. Examples of this include athletes using imagery to go through the options in a basketball offense, ski over a particular course to plan which techniques they will use, practice throws from the outfield based on where the runners are on base, and plan the type of shots they will play against a particular tennis opponent. As discussed earlier, Fran Tarkenton used imagery in this way to prepare offensive game plans against specific opponents.

Learning sport skills   Imagery can also be used to aid beginners in learning sport skills. Imagery can help develop the appropriate mental blueprint to be followed in learning the skill (Feltz & Landers, 1983). It is a way of "building a machine" from scratch. It is advisable to have athletes combine imagery of this type with verbal triggers (discussed in a later section) to emphasize that correct technique is being imagined.

Learning strategy Anyone who has ever walked through a basketball pattern 101 times ·in learning a team offense can appreciate the use of imagery to learn strategy. Although imagery can never take the place of physical practice, it is a useful technique to learn new strategies. It is helpful in learning, both cognitively and physically, the appropriate actions.

For example, imagery could be used to help quarterbacks learn the different options of new plays or to help soccer players learn their positions in certain team patterns. Lou Henson, men's basketball coach at the University of Illinois, admits that his team learned their offensive patterns more quickly and thoroughly as a result of a systematic imagery program.

Problem solving It may be helpful for athletes to use imagery when they are mired in a slump or having problems with certain aspects of their performance. Imagery should be used in this way to examine critically all aspects of performance to uncover what may be creating the problem.

Practicing psychological skills Imagery can be used to practice various psychological skills. Psychological skills that are usually practiced through imagery include attentional control, stress management, energizing, goal setting, self-confidence, and interpersonal skill. For example, athletes can use imagery to "program" goals by repeatedly imagining achieving their goals in competition. Athletes can practice the interpersonal skill of confrontation by imagining how they will approach the coach about a lack of playing time. Other contributors to this book have provided specific examples of how imagery may be used as a tool to develop the psychological skills discussed in their chapters.

Increasing sport perception By systematically practicing imagery, athletes can become more aware of what is taking place within and around them. Just as an art teacher brings the subtle effects of shading to students' attention, imagery can help athletes relax and pay attention to sensory details. A runner may learn much about a previously run race by vividly recreating it in her mind.

A member of the U.S. Nordic Ski Team was having problems sustaining the level of concentration she needed throughout her races. By imaging her past races, she became aware that she was shifting attention to the wrong things toward the end of the race. All athletes can learn more about themselves or their sport if they "tune to the imagery channel."

Controlling physiological responses Scientists are providing evidence that imagery can influence body functions previously thought beyond conscious control such as heart rate, respiration, blood pressure, and skin temperature (Blakeslee, 1980; Schwartz & Beatty, 1977). Martens (1982) cites the example of the Indian yogis who are able to alter their heart rate, respiration, and brain waves through the practice of imagery.

Why is this important in sport? Performance can be enhanced in many sports through the control of physiological responses. Biathletes must be able to reduce their body responses after strenuous cross-country skiing to achieve the static relaxation important in shooting. Jacque Mayol broke the world underwater diving record by using imagery and relaxation to reduce his autonomic body processes. Athletes can also use imagery to control and optimize arousal prior to competition. We are only beginning to scratch the surface with regard to understanding the power of imagery in controlling our bodies.

Recovery from injury Imagery can be used to cope with pain, speed up recovery of the injured area, and keep physical skills from deteriorating. The injured athlete who attends practices and competitions but cannot physically practice should imagine running through all the drills and workouts just as though he or she were actually physically experiencing them. There are numerous stories of athletes who have used imagery and had remarkable recovery from injury and a quick return to their former skill level.

Times

You now know some specific uses for imagery. But when is the most effective time to use imagery? Staying with our "cookbook" design, we offer three suggestions about when to use imagery.

Daily practice A recurring theme throughout this chapter is the systematic use of imagery. To be systematic, daily imagery practice is advised. As you will see in the sample programs at the end of the chapter, this may only require 10 minutes per day.

First, you can have athletes do imagery practice *before actual physical practice sessions.* This fits imagery into the athletes' routine and may get them into the proper frame of mind for practice.

It may also be appropriate for athletes to practice imagery *after actual physical practice sessions.* This has been successful with groups in reaffirming the points emphasized in practice that day. Also, athletes are more relaxed at the end of practice and may be more receptive to imagery at that time.

There are certain times when imagery may be beneficial *during practice.* For example, if a basketball coach implements an imagery program to practice free throws, he or she may build in time for imagery practice prior to shooting free throws in practice.

Preperformance routine It is helpful for athletes to go through a preperformance imagery routine *before every contest.* The routine should be individualized for each athlete and practiced in noncompetitive situations. Suggestions about the content of these routines appear with the sample programs at the end of the chapter.

Also, certain skills in sport may be conducive to a preperformance imagery routine *before actually performing the skill.* This is the type of routine that Jack Nicklaus practices before hitting each shot. "Closed" skills such as shooting free throws, kicking field goals, ski jumping, volleyball serving, and gymnastic vaulting are more easily practiced in this way as opposed to "open" skills such as broken field running in football or executing a fast break in basketball.

Postperformance review Another appropriate time to use imagery is *after competition.* Again, this should be an individual exercise, but coaches can monitor the exercise by having the athletes complete *postcompetitive evaluation sheets* on the basis of their postperformance imagery. Using imagery at this time facilitates increased awareness of what actually happened during the competition.

Methods

Now that we have examined some specific uses of imagery and suggested when to use it, we turn our attention to methods of practicing imagery.

Individual vs. group practice It is beneficial to individualize imagery programs to fit the specific needs of each athlete. However, do not assume that this means giving athletes the information and letting them set up their own programs. Only the most conscientious athlete will take time to design an imagery program without the guidance (and gentle prodding) of a coach or sport psychologist. If there is time, meet with each athlete to implement individual imagery programs.

For team sports, group imagery exercises are most practical. Coaches or sport psychologists can use the group setting to introduce imagery to athletes, evaluate their imagery ability, go through basic training, and then incorporate some of the ways of using imagery into a systematic program. If certain athletes want to do more (such as set up an individual program to be practiced on their own), so much the better.

Cassette tapes Some athletes find it useful to buy commercially produced imagery tapes or make their own imagery tapes. Several tapes now on the market utilize imagery to enhance psychological skills such as relaxation and concentration. Coaches and sport psychologists can make tapes for the practice of specific physical skills and strategies. The actual imagery practice should be preceded by a three- to five-minute relaxation exercise. This is normally followed by "guided" imagery practice and then unguided practice. If a sport psychologist records the tape, he or she should incorporate the coach or athlete's verbal cues to describe the technique points during physical practice into the guided imagery section of the tape. Again, athletes differ in their preference for tapes. Some find them limiting; others like the structure.

Imagery logs To monitor imagery practice and progress in the program, it is useful for athletes to keep a log or written record. The log should contain different types of imagery exercises and self-evaluation forms to monitor individual progress in the program. The postperformance review exercise discussed in the preceding section could be included in the log. This is a means of emphasizing systematic practice and provides a way to monitor that practice.

Triggers Triggers are words or phrases that help athletes focus on the correct cues during imagery. The key to a trigger is its ability to program the proper image.

Sam Snead used the word *oily* to describe his fluid swing. A famous female golfer kept the word *oooom-PAH* written on her driver to program the image of a easy slow backswing and a vigorous downswing. A basketball player struggling with his shooting used the trigger *straight up* to perfect the image of his jump shot. A cross-country skier having trouble with her uphill technique used the word *quick* to symbolize the quick, short kick technique needed on hills. U.S. biathletes use the trigger *Rock of Gibraltar* to program the steady body state they need to shoot effectively.

Researchers advise the use of triggers by beginners when using imagery to emphasize the basic elements of the skill (Lane, 1980). As discussed earlier, imagery can be useful in teaching and learning sport skills, but triggers should be used to ensure that the correct technique is being imaged.

Pregame uses of imagery As suggested earlier, one good time to use imagery is before a competition. To facilitate this, it is helpful to have a dark, comfortable room available to all athletes before a game. However, if no room is available, imagery can be practiced anywhere. It is unwise to force athletes into precompetitive imagery as a group except to quickly run through a particular strategy or technique to be used in the particular contest. As a general rule, precompetitive imagery should be a private affair.

Tips

Here are a few additional tips that you may find helpful in promoting the use of imagery among your atheletes.

1. *Relaxation should usually precede imagery practice.* Research indicates that imagery combined with relaxation is more effective than imagery alone (Kolonay, 1977; Suinn, 1972; Weinberg, Seabourne, & Jackson, 1981). Be sure that every imagery session begins with some type of relaxation technique such as passive progressive relaxation, relaxing images (favorite place, in bed, lying on a beach), or slow, deep breathing. It is not important to use high-powered relaxation or hypnotic techniques but to start off with a pleasant image that will relax the athletes and clear their minds.

2. *Athletes should probably practice imagery from an internal perspective.* Although Jacobson (1931) was the first to study differences in imagery perspective, Mahoney and Avener (1977) first classified imagery as either internal or external. From an internal perspective athletes see the image from behind their own eyes as opposed to an external perspective from which they see the image from outside their body as with a movie camera. Mahoney and Avener found that elite athletes reported a higher frequency of internal (as opposed to external) images. Hale (1982) found that an internal imagery perspective produced more electrical activity in the biceps muscle than an external imagery perspective when subjects imagined flexion of the arm.

It seems that an internal perspective may allow more realistic images than an external perspective. Why practice a golf swing from an external perspective? An internal perspective would seem to help a golfer become more aware of how the body feels during the swing and how the various parts of the swing look while he or she is making the shot. However, if some athletes tend to naturally imagine externally or if they are not comfortable imagining internally, they should use an external perspective. Other athletes may prefer to alternate between an internal and external perspective.

3. *Athletes should practice imagery with realistic expectations.* Imagery is not a magic power. It is a vitamin supplement that can complement physical practice. Unrealistic fantasizing is not the same thing as practicing imagery. Imagery cannot get a 5'9" player into the NBA or a 128-pound defensive back into the NFL. Emphasize to athletes that imagery will not allow them to go beyond their physical limits.

4. *Athletes should practice imagery in a quiet setting.* As mentioned before, relaxation and concentration usually facilitate imagery. Therefore, athletes should practice imagery in a quiet, comfortable setting that is free of distractions.

SAMPLE PROGRAMS

You now have the ingredients necessary to put together an effective imagery program. It is up to you to analyze the needs of your group and decide which ingredients will work best in your situation. To aid you in that endeavor, three specific imagery programs are outlined here as examples. The first program is for a team sport and suggests types of group exercises. The second program is for individuals in less structured situations. The third program is an example of teaching golf by using imagery. Remember: these are only sample programs. You should develop your own program on the basis of the ingredients discussed earlier and the samples outlined here. Good luck!

Program 1: Team Imagery Program

First two weeks of preseason: (each day for 10 minutes at end of practice)

1. Introduce program
2. Evaluate athletes' imagery ability
3. Basic training [Begin basic training with the exercises suggested in this chapter, then add exercises that are appropriate for your team and sport (team patterns and strategies)]

Rest of season: (each day for 10 minutes at beginning, end of, or during practice) Imagery session following this outline:

* Relaxation imagery
* Simple sport skills
* Advanced sport skills
* Game strategies
  Recreate past success experience
  Goal programming

The imagery exercises marked with an asterisk should be included in *all* sessions. They are a form of warm-up for the other types of imagery. After these initial warm-up exercises, any types of exercises can be used. Other suggestions of items to insert include:

Fulfilling roles on the team

Concentration
Using triggers
Arousal control
Correcting mistakes
Pregame imagery routine (practice at least twice a week)

Pregame imagery routine: Incorporate the first six steps listed under "Rest of Season" into individual pregame routines. Encourage each athlete to develop his or her own routine, and make available a pregame imagery room or specified area in which the athletes can practice imagery.

Postgame imagery review: Devise an event evaluation sheet that athletes will complete after each game. This sheet should ask the athletes to evaluate their performance in the following areas: physical skills, strategies, fulfillment of role, achievement of goals, arousal level throughout game, concentration throughout game, self-confidence throughout game, areas that need improvement, and strategies to improve these areas. Make the sheet concise and objective so the athletes will find it easy to complete (see Chapter 11 for a sample evaluation sheet). Then ask the athletes to replay the game through imagery and complete the evaluation form. They can either keep the forms in a log book or turn them in to you after each game.

Program 2: Individual Imagery Program

1. Evaluation of imagery ability
2. Basic training
3. Regular imagery sessions

Prepractice (10 minutes):
technique work
goal programming for practice

Postpractice (10–15 minutes):
go over practice performance
problem solving
psychological skill practice (according to individual need)
practice preevent imagery program

4. Competition day

Preevent imagery (10 minutes):
use format suggested in Program 1: Team Imagery

Postevent review (10 minutes):
design personal event evaluation sheet or log

Program 3: Golf Skill Acquisition Program

Skill acquisition exercises:

1. Set up in the correct address position. Stay there for a moment and concentrate on the *feeling* of your body and *how it looks* from where you stand. Be very sensitive as to how your body feels in this position. Repeat the setup five different times, and work to develop a pattern each time you set up so that it will become automatic.

2. In slow motion take your swing to the top and hold. Be aware of the overall coiled feeling of your body and the tension in each body part. Repeat your swing 10 times, attempting to replicate the arc of your clubhead each time. Build a machine!

3. Swing freely 10 times. Concentrate on the rhythm and feel of the swing as you come through each time. As you follow through with your hands high, track the imaginary ball you have hit in its flight.

Activity: Hit 10 balls, concentrating on swingly freely through each shot.

Triggers for full swing:

1. Firm left side (proper setup technique)
2. Stake through your body (around which the body should rotate during the swing)

Imagery practice with triggers: Use each trigger to program the proper technique of the golf swing. Imagine performing the full swing five times, using each trigger as a guide to proper technique.

Routine for each shot:

1. Before lining up, view your target area and imagine the ball there.
2. Visualize the flight path of the ball.
3. As you set up in the address position, use the trigger's "firm left side" and "stake through your body" to reaffirm proper swing technique.
4. Imagine the perfect swing as described by the triggers.
5. Hit the ball.

Imagery exercise: Imagine this routine for each different golf shot.

A FINAL WORD

A story is told of a basketball player who was fouled in the closing seconds of a game in which his team was behind by one point. When the opposing team called time out, the player's coach advised, "Now is the time to use your imagery." The player frantically looked at his coach and exclaimed, "Not now, coach! This is *important!*"

Many athletes will humor their coaches and themselves by going through the motions of practicing imagery. Yet deep inside these athletes really doubt that it can improve their performance. Besides being skeptical, many athletes are afraid of using imagery. They say that thinking too much will hurt their performance. That seems analogous to an ostrich putting its head in the sand. The practice of imagery enables athletes to program proper technique, achieve optimal psychological skills, and correct problems and mistakes instead of hoping that things will work out by magic.

Imagery can only hurt performance if athletes build the wrong machine. That is, imagery will hurt performance if athletes imagine themselves choking at the free throw line, blowing game-winning field goals, or falling off the balance beam. Such negative images do occur in athletes at times, but with practice athletes can easily learn to control their images. Athletes must gain confidence in the effectiveness of imagery and learn to harness its powers. By believing in the power of imagery and implementing the programs discussed in this chapter, coaches, sport psychologists and athletes can work together to elevate sport performance to new heights.

SUMMARY

Imagery involves using all the senses to recreate or create an experience in the mind. It is a mental technique that "programs" the human mind to respond as programmed. The evidence supporting the positive influence of imagery on sport performance is impressive. Both scientifically controlled studies and experiential accounts of the use of imagery to enhance sport performance report positive results.

Two theories suggest how imagery may enhance performance. The *psychoneuromuscular theory* states that vivid, imagined events produce innervation in the muscles that is similar to that produced by physical execution of the event. Through imagery, then, athletes may actually strengthen the neural pathways for certain movements in their sport. The *symbolic learning theory* suggests that imagery facilitates performance by helping individuals blueprint or code their movements into symbolic components, thus making the movements more familiar and perhaps more automatic. Both theories have been supported by research.

All athletes possess the ability to use imagery to improve their performance. However, like physical skill the psychological skill of imagery requires systematic practice to be effective. To set up a systematic imagery program, four steps are advocated: First, athletes should be educated about imagery and convinced about the merits of practicing imagery. Exercises are helpful to convince athletes of the power of imagery. Second, coaches must evaluate the imagery ability of the athletes in order to develop the most appropriate type of program. Just as athletes differ in physical skills, they will differ in their ability to develop vivid images. Third, coaches must train athletes in basic imagery skills. It is important for athletes to use all appropriate senses and their emotions when practicing imagery. In basic training, athletes practice imagery exercises designed to develop their ability to mentally experience the sensations and emotions that are important in their sport. Fourth, coaches must monitor and implement a systematic program of imagery practice. Major concerns here are building the imagery program into the athletes' routine and fitting the program to the needs of each athlete. Coaches and athletes can incorporate many uses of imagery and different methods of practicing imagery into this four-step program.

REFERENCES

Blakeslee, T. R. (1980). *The right brain.* New York: Anchor Press.

Corbin, C. B. (1972). Mental practice. In W. P. Morgan (Ed.), *Ergogenic aids and muscular performance* (pp. 93–118). New York: Academic Press.

Eccles, J. (1958). The physiology of imagination. *Scientific American, 199,* 135.

Feltz, D. L., & Landers, D. M. (1983). The effects of mental practice on motor skill learning and performance: A meta-analysis. *Journal of Sport Psychology, 5,* 25–57.

Gallwey, W. T. (1976). *Inner tennis.* New York: Random House.

Hale, B. D. (1982). The effects of internal and external imagery on muscular and ocular concomitants. *Journal of Sport Psychology, 4,* 379–387.

Hall, E. G., & Erffmeyer, E. S. (1983). The effect of visuo-motor behavior rehearsal with videotaped modeling on free throw accuracy of intercollegiate female basketball players. *Journal of Sport Psychology, 5,* 343–346.

Housner, L. D. (1984). The role of visual imagery in recall of modeled motoric stimuli. *Journal of Sport Psychology, 6,* 148–158.

Jacobson, E. (1931). Electrical measurements of neuromuscular states during mental activities. *American Journal of Physiology, 96,* 115–121.

Kolonay, B. J. (1977). *The effects of visuo-motor behavior rehearsal on athletic performance.* Unpublished master's thesis, Hunter College, The City University of New York.

Lane, J. F. (1980). Improving athletic performance through visuo-motor behavior rehearsal. In R. M. Suinn (Ed.), *Psychology in sports: Methods and applications* (pp. 316–320). Minneapolis: Burgess.

Mahoney, M. J., & Avener, M. (1977). Psychology of the elite athlete: An exploratory study. *Cognitive Therapy and Research, 1,* 135–141.

Martens, R. (1982, September). *Imagery in sport.* Unpublished paper presented at the

Medical And Scientific Aspects of Elitism in Sport Conference, Brisbane, Australia.

Richardson, A. (1967a). Mental practice: A review and discussion (Part 1). *Research Quarterly, 38,* 95–107.

Richardson, A. (1967b). Mental practice: A review and discussion (Part 2). *Research Quarterly, 38,* 263–273.

Ryan, D. E., & Simons, J. (1981). Cognitive demand, imagery, and frequency of mental rehearsal as factors influencing acquisition of motor skills. *Journal of Sport Psychology, 3,* 35–45.

Ryan, D. E., & Simons, J. (1983). What is learned in mental practice of motor skills: A test of the cognitive-motor hypothesis. *Journal of Sport Psychology, 5,* 419–426.

Sackett, R. S. (1934). The influences of symbolic rehearsal upon the retention of a maze habit. *Journal of General Psychology, 13,* 113–128.

Schwartz, G. E., & Beatty, J. (1977). *Biofeedback: Theory and research.* New York: Academic Press.

Suinn, R. M. (1972). Behavioral rehearsal training for ski racers. *Behavior Therapy, 3,* 519.

Suinn, R. M. (1980). Psychology and sports performance: Principles and applications. In R. M. Suinn (Ed.), *Psychology in sports: Methods and applications* (pp. 26–36). Minneapolis: Burgess.

Weinberg, R. S., Seabourne, T. G., & Jackson, A. (1981). Effects of visuo-motor behavior rehearsal, relaxation, and imagery on karate performance. *Journal of Sport Psychology, 3,* 228–238.

Wrisberg, C. A., & Ragsdale, M. R. (1979). Cognitive demand and practice level: Factors in the mental rehearsal of motor skills. *Journal of Human Movement Studies, 5,* 201–208.

APPENDIX

SPORT IMAGERY QUESTIONNAIRE*

As you complete this questionnaire, remember that imagery is more than just seeing or visualizing something in your mind's eye. Vivid images may include not only visualizing but experiencing all the senses — hearing, feeling, tasting, smelling. Along with these sensations, you may also experience emotions, moods, or certain states of mind.

Below you will read descriptions of four general sport situations. You are to imagine the general situation and provide as much detail from your imagination as possible to make the image just as "real" as you can. Then you will be asked to rate your imagery on four dimensions:

1. How vividly you saw or visualized the image.
2. How clearly you heard the sounds.
3. How vividly you felt your body movements (kinesthetic sense) during the activity.
4. How clearly you were aware of your state of mind or mood or felt the emotions of the situation.

After you read each general description, think of a specific example of it — e.g., the skill, the people involved, the place, the time. Next close your eyes and take a few deep breaths to become as relaxed as you can. Put aside all other thoughts for a moment. Keep your eyes closed for about one minute as you try to imagine the situation as vividly as you can.

There are, of course, no right or wrong images. Use your imagery skills to develop as vivid and clear an image of the general situation described as possible. Your accurate appraisal of your images will help you to determine which exercises you will want to emphasize in the basic training exercises.

After you have completed imagining the situation described, please rate the four dimensions of imagery by circling the number that best describes the image you had.

1 = no image present
2 = not clear or vivid, but a recognizable image
3 = moderately clear and vivid image
4 = clear and vivid image
5 = extremely clear and vivid image

* Adapted from Martens, 1982.

Practicing Alone

Select one specific skill or activity in your sport, such as shooting free throws, performing a parallel bar routine, executing a takedown, throwing a pass, hitting a ball, or swimming the butterfly. Now imagine yourself performing this activity at the place where you normally practice the activity (gymnasium, pool, rink, field, court) without anyone else present. Close your eyes for about one minute and try to see yourself at this place, hear the sounds, feel your body perform the movement, and be aware of your state of mind or mood.

a. Rate how well you saw yourself doing the activity.   1   2   3   4   5
b. Rate how well you heard the sounds of doing the activity.   1   2   3   4   5
c. Rate how well you felt yourself making the movements.   1   2   3   4   5
d. Rate how well you were aware of your mood.   1   2   3   4   5

Practicing with Others

You are doing the same activity but now you are practicing the skill with the coach and your teammates present. This time, however, you make a mistake that everyone notices. Close your eyes for about one minute to imagine making the error and the situation immediately afterward as vividly as you can.

a. Rate how well you saw yourself in this situation.   1   2   3   4   5
b. Rate how well you heard the sounds in this situation.   1   2   3   4   5
c. Rate how well you felt yourself making the movements.   1   2   3   4   5
d. Rate how well you felt the emotions of this situation.   1   2   3   4   5

Watching a Teammate

Think of a teammate or acquaintance performing a specific activity unsuccessfully in a contest such as missing a field goal, being passed by other runners, falling from the rings, etc.

Close your eyes for about one minute to imagine as vividly and realistically as possible watching your teammate performing this activity unsuccessfully in a critical part of the contest.

a. Rate how well you saw your teammate in this situation.   1 2 3 4 5

b. Rate how well you heard the sounds in this situation.   1 2 3 4 5

c. Rate how well you felt *your own* physical presence or movement in this situation.   1 2 3 4 5

d. Rate how well *you* felt the emotions of this situation.   1 2 3 4 5

Playing in a Contest

Imagine yourself performing the same or a similar activity in a contest, but imagine yourself doing the activity very skillfully and the spectators and teammates showing their appreciation. Now close your eyes for about one minute and imagine this situation as vividly as possible.

a. Rate how well you saw yourself in this situation.   1 2 3 4 5

b. Rate how well you heard the sounds in this situation.   1 2 3 4 5

c. Rate how well you felt yourself making the movements.   1 2 3 4 5

d. Rate how well you felt the emotions of the situation.   1 2 3 4 5

Scoring

Now let's determine your imagery scores and see what they mean. First, sum the ratings for your four answers to part a in each section, your four answers to part b in each section, and so on, recording them in the proper place below. Next total the score for the four rating dimensions to obtain a total score and record it where indicated.

Dimension   *Score*

a. Visual   _____

b. Auditory   _____

c. Kinesthetic   _____

d. Mood   _____

TOTAL   _____

15 Cognitive Techniques for Improving Performance and Building Confidence

LINDA BUNKER

University of Virginia

JEAN M. WILLIAMS

University of Arizona

The most consistent finding in peak performance literature is the direct correlation between self-confidence and success. Athletes who are truly outstanding are self-confident. Their confidence has been developed over many years and is often the result of positive thinking and frequent experiences in which they have been successful. Coaches and sport psychologists can probably identify many confident players with whom they have been associated. They are the people you would like to have come to bat when the game is at stake. They are the people whom you do not give up on even when they have lost the first set in a tennis match, fallen behind in a race, or been penalized in a competition.

Confident athletes think about themselves and the action at hand in a different way than those who lack confidence. What athletes think or say is critical to performance. Unfortunately, the conscious mind is not always an ally. We all spend vast amounts of time talking to ourselves. Much of the time we are not even aware of this internal dialogue, much less its content. Nevertheless, thoughts directly affect feelings and ultimately actions. Inappropriate or misguided thinking usually leads to negative feelings and poor performance just as appropriate or positive thinking leads to enabling feelings and good performance.

THOUGHTS → FEELINGS → BEHAVIOR

Confident athletes think they can and *they do.* They never give up. They typically are characterized by positive self-talk, images, and dreams. They imagine themselves winning and being successful. They say positive things to themselves and never minimize their abilities. They focus on successfully mastering a task rather than worrying about performing poorly or the negative consequences of failure. They are still in touch with reality, knowing their capabilities as well as their limitations. It is no wonder that confident athletes are usually winners. Their confidence has programmed successful performance.

If confidence is so critical to successful performance and personal growth, what can coaches and sport psychologists do to help promote self-confidence within their athletes? Many of the earlier chapters in this book have provided, either directly or indirectly, some answers to this question. For example, seeing improvement in physical skill is an obvious way to build confidence. Providing for a history of successful experiences builds both confidence and the expectation of future success. Coaches who observe the learning and performance guidelines outlined in Chapters 2 and 3 will be more likely to maximize successful skill development in their athletes. Effective coach–athlete interactions, as illustrated in Chapters 5, 6, 7, and 8, are likely to enhance each athlete's sense of self-worth and self-esteem. Practices that maximize such growth in athletes, whether the growth be in physical skills or personal development, lead to a more positive self-concept and increased self-confidence.

In this chapter we discuss techniques for improving confidence and performance by learning to use and control thoughts or cognitions appropriately. It is important that athletes understand how the mind works, how it affects their feelings and actions, and ultimately how it can be disciplined. Initially, thoughts may appear to occur spontaneously and involuntarily — thus, beyond control. With the skills of "intentional thinking," athletes can control their thoughts. They can learn to use self-talk to facilitate learning and performance. They can also learn to replace self-defeating thoughts with positive ones — thoughts that build confidence and the expectation of success. Such positive thought processes can become self-fulfilling prophecies.

SELF-TALK

The key to cognitive control is self-talk. The frequency and content of thoughts vary from person to person and situation to situation. Anytime you think about something, you are in a sense talking to yourself. Self-talk becomes an asset when it enhances self-worth and performance. For example, such talk can help the athlete stay appropriately focused in the present, not dwelling on past mistakes or projecting too far into the future. Self-talk gets in the way when it is negative, inappropriate, or so frequent that it disrupts the automatic performance of skills.

Before we address the matter of how specific types of self-talk can be used in different situations to help achieve excellence in learning and performance and to promote confidence, we want to remind you that the interview research reported in Chapter 9 found many athletes stating that their best sport performances occurred when they had no thoughts at all. The athletes were so immersed in the action that it just seemed to happen without conscious thought. Tim Gallwey, author of *The Inner Game of Tennis* (1974), and others have stressed that peak performance does not occur when athletes are thinking about it. Gallwey emphasizes learning to turn performance over to unconscious or automatic functions — functions that are free from the interference of thought.

It may be desirable to strive for such thought-free performance, but athletes usually *do* think both before and during most competitions. They also think during practices and outside of practices. Their thoughts affect their self-concept, self-confidence, and behavior. Therefore, it is important that coaches and sport psychologists teach athletes to recognize and control their thoughts. We concur with Keith Bell, author of *Championship Thinking* (1983), who supports this concept by emphasizing that it is not thinking itself which leads to substandard performance but inappropriate or misguided thinking. If used properly, thinking can be a great aid to performance and personal growth. The question should not be whether to think but what, when, and how to think.

The uses for self-talk are almost as varied as are the different types of sports. The effective coach and sport psychologist can use self-talk to aid athletes in learning skills, correcting bad habits, preparing for performance, focusing attention, creating the best mood for performance, and building confidence and competence.

Self-Talk for Skill Acquisition

The nature of thoughts and self-talk should change as performers become more proficient. During early learning, skill acquisition is usually aided when self-instructional talk is used to remind the performer of certain key aspects. For example, cue words might be used to describe a particular movement phase or to help in learning the appropriate sequencing of actions. Simple cues such as "step, swing" in tennis, "step, drop, step, kick" for a soccer punt, and "arms straight, elbows in" for the golf address are designed to foster cognitive associations that will aid the athlete in learning proper physical execution. Even on the beginning level, self-talk should be kept as brief and minimal as possible. Oververbalization, by the coach or athlete, can cause paralysis by analysis. As skills are mastered, talk becomes shorter, less frequent, and more likely to be focused on strategies and optimal feelings than technique cues. With learning, the goal is to reduce conscious control and promote the "automatic" execution of the skill. For most athletes, this means less "technique" self-talk. A simple verbal cue may still be used to trigger the automatic action.

The effectiveness and content of self-talk while the athlete is learning skills also depends on the nature of the task. Skills that are self-paced — i.e., initiated by the performer when he or she is ready — are positively influenced by thoughts just prior to performance. Examples include skills such as pitching, riflery, bowling, archery, golf, free throw shooting, and any kind of serve. Successful execution can be "programmed" by positive thoughts and images just prior to physical execution. If the skills are well learned, the nature of the self-talk should focus on what the performer is trying to achieve rather than the physical mechanics of the act. For example, in the book *Mind, Set and Match*, Bunker and Rotella (1982) suggest that a server in tennis should think or see "deep outside corner" to specify the landing area of the serve. Similarly, a pitcher might think "high and inside," or a free throw shooter might simply say "arch and swish." There is less time for this type of direct verbal-mental programming in reactive, externally paced skills such as spiking in volleyball, fast breaking in basketball, or volleying in tennis. With externally paced skills the performer needs to rely more on being able to respond correctly automatically. Sometimes this can be aided by preprogramming performance, but programming usually does not take place right before execution.

Self-Talk for Changing Bad Habits

Experienced athletes may wish to use "technique" self-talk when they want to change a well-learned skill or habit. In such cases, the athletes must unlearn an automatic response that is no longer effective and replace it with a new one. In order to change a bad habit, it is usually necessary to intentionally force conscious control over the previously automatic execution. Self-talk can be an effective way to "deautomatize" the old skill and make way for a new response.

The more drastic the change, the more detailed the demands of self-talk in the relearning phase. For example, if a tennis player is attempting to change from a two-handed to a one-handed backhand, considerable *self-instruction* may be required. In this case, the athlete must verbally redirect the entire swing motion. However, if the change is merely to get behind the ball and hit it a little bit earlier with more weight on the front foot, then a simple cue may be all that is necessary.

When an athlete uses self-talk to redirect technique or strategy, it is essential that the content of the statements focus on the desired outcome rather than on what the athlete is trying not to do. If a coach or athlete fails to focus on the desired goal and instead talks about avoiding the undesirable, the head is merely filled with the negative image. For example, saying,

"Don't stay on your back foot" when hitting a backhand gives no direction to the swing pattern, and it emphasizes the negative. Effective self-talk would be using a cue such as "step-hit." In short, athletes should be trained to focus on what they want to happen, not what they want to avoid. An additional bonus with this type of self-talk is that it reinforces the habit of making thoughts positive.

Attention Control

Self-talk can also help athletes control their attention. It is often easy to be distracted during competition and practice. By using a specific set of verbal cues, athletes can keep their minds appropriately focused. Attentional control is particularly important in helping athletes stay in the present. After all, the only important point or shot is the one that's about to happen! The future cannot be controlled, and the past cannot be erased or replaced. It is essential to remain in the present. If athletes allow themselves to wander into the past tense (e.g., "If I had only made that last putt") or focus on the future (e.g., "If I birdie the next hole, I'll be leading the field"), they will have difficulty executing the present shot. Several books, including *Mind Mastery for Winning Golf* (Rotella & Bunker, 1981), have emphasized the importance of remaining in the present tense. (For further elaboration and specific examples, see Chapter 17.)

Creating "Affect" or Mood

Researchers have found that affective cues can produce significant changes in performance. For example, runners who say "fast" or "quick" have been found to increase their speed (Meichenbaum, 1975). Golfers who use swing thoughts such as "smooth" or "oily" produce swings that appear smoother and more controlled (Bunker & Owens, 1985). Power words such as "blast," "hit," and "go" are important aids in explosive movements. A runner in the starting blocks should not be thinking about hearing the gun. It is much more effective to be saying "go" or "explode" so that when the gun sounds, it will directly trigger the desired movement (Silva, 1982). Otherwise, the athlete must process the fact that the gun went off and then start. For a long distance run, an athlete may wish to shift word cues throughout the race. During the initial portion, words that encourage consistent pace and energy conservation may be most appropriate. During the middle portion of the run, words that encourage persistence and tuning in to the body are important, while the final portion requires speed and power. Corresponding cues might be "easy," "responding," and "sprint." Each word has an emotional quality that is linked to the movement quality or content (Meichenbaum,

1975). Use of the right affective cues can ultimately help lead to the best potential for peak performance.

Controlling Effort

Self-talk can be an effective technique to help maintain energy and persistence. It may be difficult for some athletes to get started in the morning, at practice, or in the first few moments of a contest. Others may have difficulty changing tempo or maintaining effort. Phrases such as go for it, easy, pace, pick it up, cool it, hold onto it, push, stay, and so forth can be very effective in controlling effort (Harris & Harris, 1984).

Sustaining effort over a long training period is a typical problem for athletes. If practices become boring or fatigue sets in, athletes may begin to question their commitment or the value of that commitment. Athletes can use self-talk not only to direct action but also to sustain it. Such emphasis on effort control is essential because it helps athletes recognize the importance of hard work in achieving success. And, if by chance the athletes do not succeed, they are more likely to attribute failure to insufficient effort and therefore want to work harder in the future. Coaches should note that this is a much more productive "attribution" strategy than blaming lack of success on factors such as luck, poor officiating, or the weather.

Affirmations for Building Confidence

The way in which athletes think about themselves reflects the degree of their self-confidence and ultimately their behavior. Believing in oneself is enabling because it frees people to use their full talents. People are only able to do what they think they can do. One type of self-talk that evokes positive feelings and behavior is the use of affirmation statements. Affirmations are statements that reflect positive attitudes or thoughts about oneself. If used frequently, they promote confidence in the ability to do whatever action is being affirmed. Muhammed Ali and Martina Navratilova might say, "I'm the greatest!" They believed it, and so did millions of others.

The most effective affirmations are both believable and vivid. They are also often spontaneous and thus capture the feelings of a particularly satisfying and successful experience (Syer and Connolly, 1984). "I am as strong as a bull," "I will fly down the finish line," and "I really come through under pressure" are all good examples of positive affirmations.

Team slogans can also serve as affirmations: "Winners think they can and they do"; "See it, think it, believe it, do it"; "Say yes to success." Each slogan can become a recipe or formula for success provided it is internalized.

IDENTIFYING SELF-TALK

Appropriate use of the preceding kinds of self-talk will enhance self-worth and performance, but the same cannot be said for all types of self-talk. More specifically, negative or self-defeating self-talk will produce undesirable effects on performance (Rotella, Gansneder, Ojala & Billing, 1980).

The first step in gaining control of self-talk is to become aware of what you say to yourself. Surprisingly enough, most people are not aware of their thoughts, much less the powerful impact they have on their feelings and behavior. By getting athletes to review carefully the way in which they talk to themselves in different types of situations, both the athlete and coach or sport psychologist will identify what kind of thinking helps, what thoughts appear to be harmful, and what situations or events are associated with this talk. Once athletes develop this awareness, they usually discover that their self-talk varies from short cue words and phrases to extremely complex monologues, with the overall content ranging from self-enhancing to self-defeating. The key is to know both when and how to talk to yourself.

It is particularly helpful if athletes are instructed to identify specifically the type and content of thought associated with particularly good and particularly bad performances. For example, are there any usual thought patterns or common themes during different situations? Most athletes find different thinking during successful and unsuccessful performance. Identifying the thoughts that typically prepare an athlete to perform well and to cope successfully with problems during performance can provide a repertoire of cognitive tools for the enhancement of performance. The use of these same thoughts in future performance environments should create similar feelings of confidence and direct performance in much the same way.

During unsuccessful performance, most athletes discover that their mind actually programmed failure through self-doubt and negative statements. The body merely performed what the mind was thinking. Examples include an athlete's thinking before a competiton, "I never swim well in this pool" or "I always play poorly against this opponent" and then going on to swim or compete exactly as prophesied. Obviously, future performance would be enhanced if athletes could eliminate dysfunctional and self-defeating thoughts that lead to worry and poor performance. Before such thoughts can be eliminated, they need to be identified. Three of the most effective tools for identifying self-talk are retrospection, imagery, and keeping a self-talk log.

Retrospection

By reflecting back to situations in which someone performed particularly well or particularly poorly and trying to recreate the thoughts and feelings that occurred prior to and during these performances, many athletes are able to identify typical thoughts and thought patterns associated with both good and bad performance. It is also beneficial to recall the specific situation, or circumstances, that led to the thoughts and resulting performance. Viewing videotapes of actual past performances helps the athlete recount the action by heightening the memory of the event. If this technique is used, not only should the actual performance be taped but, ideally, the time before the contest begins, the time-outs or "breaks" during the contest, and even the time right after the contest ends. Thoughts during all of these times play a major role in performance, one's expectations regarding future performance, and even one's feelings of self-esteem or worth.

Imagery

Another technique is to have athletes relax as deeply as possible and then try reliving a past performance through visualization. This technique is much more effective if athletes have been previously trained in imagery (see Chapter 14 for suggestions). Athletes who are effective at imagery can usually describe exactly what happened during the competition and what thoughts and feelings preceded, accompanied, and followed the performance. After athletes have relived past performances through imagery, it may be helpful to have them write down the recalled thoughts, situations, and outcomes. If it is not disruptive, the athletes may even want to transcribe into a tape recorder as they are imaging.

Self-Talk Log

Not all athletes can use retrospection and imagery to remember accurately how they thought and felt or what circumstances triggered their thoughts and feelings. Even athletes who are comfortable using these tools run the risk of time and personal impressions distorting the actual thoughts and circumstances. Keeping a daily diary or self-talk log of thoughts and performance situations is an excellent tool for accurately creating awareness of self-talk. Thoughts should be transcribed as soon after they occur as possible. Athletes in sports such as golf, archery, rowing, and running have found it beneficial to have a tape recorder present while they perform so they can directly tape their thoughts and a description of the situation as they occur.

When keeping a log, the athlete should address such questions as, "When I talk to myself, what do I say? What thoughts precede and accompany my good performances? Not only what thoughts, but how frequently am I talking to myself? When playing poorly, do I deprecate myself as a person? Do I call myself names and wish I were still sitting on the bench? Are my comments about how I feel about myself, about how others will feel about me, about how I may let down my friends and teammates, or about how unlucky I am?"

If there is a problem in thinking, the goal is to identify the problem and its boundary points in very specific terms. This means that each athlete must be able to answer questions such as, "When do I have negative thoughts? Do I begin doubting myself even before I have a chance to perform? For example, when a whistle blows, do I automatically assume it is directed at me? If I have been fouled, do I start worrying from the moment the whistle blows until after I have shot the free throw or do I begin worrying only after I walk to the free throw line?" Athletes must be able to specify the initial cue that caused them to start worrying or thinking negatively. Also, when do they stop saying self-defeating things? Such detailed knowledge will help in planning an effective intervention. For instance, if worry begins with the referee's whistle, then this is the cue with which an alternate thought pattern should be linked.

It is as important to monitor self-talk during practice as it is during competition. The thoughts typically occurring prior to, during, and after practice play an important role in developing typical thought and behavior patterns. More specifically, the athlete should identify what is said after making mistakes, after teammates perform poorly, after having difficulty performing a new skill or strategy, when fatigued, and after the coach criticizes performance. Oftentimes the pattern of thoughts found during competition is merely a reflection of what occurs during practices. Learning to recognize and control the nature of self-talk during practices becomes the foundation for effective thinking during competition.

TECHNIQUES FOR CONTROLLING SELF-TALK

Using the preceding self-monitoring tools is an essential first step in the process necessary for producing performance-enhancing thoughts and eliminating disabling thoughts. However, the mere act of monitoring thoughts is usually not enough. In fact, paying too much attention to negative thoughts or thoughts associated with poor performance can be detrimental if they are not linked to some action or change process. Once awareness of negative talk and feelings is heightened, the coach or sport psychologist should immediately instruct the athlete in how to start dealing with these thoughts. Similarly, when good performance is analyzed, it should be with the intent of capitalizing on the state of mind that existed during that performance in the hope of being able to purposefully duplicate it in the future. In this section we present techniques for controlling self-talk.

Thought Stoppage

If an athlete talks too much or if the talk produces self-doubt, it must be terminated. Getting rid of negative thoughts often makes it possible to break the link that leads to negative feelings and behaviors just as stopping excessive or task irrelevant talk facilitates the athlete's regaining a more appropriate attentional focus. The technique of thought stoppage provides one very effective method for eliminating negative or counterproductive thoughts (Meyers & Schleser, 1980). The technique requires *briefly* focusing on the unwanted thought(s) and then using a "trigger" to interrupt or stop the undesirable thought. The trigger can be a word such as *stop* or a physical action such as snapping the fingers or clapping one hand against the thigh. Each athlete should choose the most natural "trigger" and use it consistently. (Most athletes who use a verbal cue prefer the word *stop,* but almost any cue is acceptable if it is used consistently.)

Thought stoppage will not work unless the athlete recognizes undesirable thoughts and is motivated to stop them. This is not as easy for the coach and sport psychologist to accomplish as it sounds. For example, even after using the typical tools for creating awareness of thoughts, one young professional golfer would not admit negative statements were affecting her golf. As a method to convince her of the severity of the problem, she was asked to empty a box of 100 paper clips into her pocket. Each time she had a negative thought, she had to move a clip to her back pocket. At the end of the golf round she had shot an 84 and had 87 paper clips in her back pocket! The process of actually counting paper clips, each of which represented a negative thought, made her dramatically aware of her problem and motivated her to try thought stoppage (Bunker & Owens, 1985).

Thought stoppage should be used initially outside of practices or during practice rather than in actual competition. An effective way to practice thought stoppage is to combine it with imagery. Athletes should be instructed to select a typical negative thought, or thought pattern, they would like to eliminate. Next they should close their eyes and as vividly as possible imagine themselves in the situation in which they usually have the negative thought. Once they have "recreated" the situation and negative thought, they should practice interrupting the thought(s) with whatever trigger they have selected for thought stoppage. They should do this over and over until the negative talk and accompanying feelings of worry and anxiety have been eliminated entirely.

It is suggested that during the earlier stages of "physical" thought stoppage practice, athletes should "visibly" use their trigger. Saying "stop" out loud not only makes athletes even more conscious of their wish to stop excessive or negative talk but serves several additional functions. It helps the coach to monitor whether athletes are doing what they were instructed to do. If an athlete's body language is showing frustration or disgust with play, his or her thoughts probably are too. The coach who sees no visible thought-stoppage trigger during these circumstances should directly confront the athlete by asking him or her what thoughts are occurring. This will serve to reinforce awareness and the need to stop negative talk immediately. The other advantage of visibly practicing the technique is that athletes realize they are not alone in their need to deal more effectively with self-talk. The technique is particularly effective when becoming more positive is a team effort and responsibility. Thus, this is a good time to encourage athletes to be supportive of one another rather than critical. When one high school basketball coach instituted such a program halfway though his season, he was so impressed with the outcome that he attributed a losing season's turning into a winning season to the athletes' learning to control negative talk and body language and becoming supportive rather than critical of one another.

Thought stoppage takes time to learn, particularly when negative thought patterns have become the dominant mode of response. Cautela & Wisocki (1977) have emphasized the importance of learning to turn off negative thoughts. Frustration over the recurrence of negative thoughts may be lessened if the coach or sport psychologist draws the parallel of trying to eliminate negative thoughts with trying to unlearn some well-established error in physical technique. Old habits change slowly whether they are physical or cognitive, and they only change with considerable motivation and practice. The more practice an athlete employs, the less likely negative thought patterns are to recur.

Even with practice it may not always be possible to avoid negative thoughts. When such thoughts do occur, good advice would be not to allow the mind to focus or dwell on them. Just let them pass on through and instead concentrate on some positive thought or some specific cue that can serve to trigger what the athlete wants to do next. This leads to the next technique for controlling thoughts—changing self-defeating thoughts to self-enhancing thoughts.

Changing Negative Thoughts to Positive Thoughts

Not only should negative thoughts be stopped, there is obvious merit in turning them into positive thoughts that either provide encouragement and support or appropriately direct attention. The coach or sport psychologist should instruct athletes to extinguish unwanted thought as soon as it is recognized and then immediately practice switching to a positive or more appropriate thought.

Another advantage for teaching this technique along with thought stoppage is that it takes some pressure off athletes who initally doubt their ability to control their thoughts. Perhaps these athletes think they cannot control what thoughts enter their head, but they will accept their ability to control the last thoughts they have. For example, for the professional golfer who through use of the "paper clip" technique finally accepted that she had many negative thoughts that adversely impacted on her performance, the initial goal in working with cognitions was simply to reduce the negative statements that were not followed by self-enhancing statements. Not having to worry about the occurrence of a self-defeating statement took considerable pressure off of her. Each day she was able to reduce the number of paper clips that stood for negative thoughts not followed by positive thoughts, and in time she was able to get rid of the recurring pattern of negative talk.

Changing self-talk from negative to positive works best if coaches and sport psychologists have their athletes individually make a list of typical self-defeating things they say and would like to change. Often athletes can generate this list from the self-talk log discussed earlier. Meichenbaum (1977) has emphasized that it is important for athletes to specify when they make these self-defeating statements and what causes them to make such statements. The goal is to recognize what the situation involved and why the negative thought occurred. Athletes should then design a substitute positive statement. It may be helpful to make a table with the self-defeating thoughts on one side and the preferred self-enhancing statements on the other side, directly opposite the negative thought (see Table 15.1).

Notice that the self-enhancing statements in the table always bring the athlete back to the present time and personal control of the situation. The positive self-talker sees a possibility in every problem, not a problem in every possibility.

The coach or sport psychologist may also want to couple relaxation techniques with changing self-defeating thoughts to self-enhancing ones. Most negative thoughts occur when an individual is under stress and therefore usually overly aroused physiologically. Instruct athletes to stop their negative thought and then take a deep breath. As they feel relaxation spreading with the long, low exhalation, they should repeat the substitute self-enhancing thought.

There is nothing unusual about having negative thoughts, but winners do not store them away—they stop them and replace them with positive thoughts. The key is never to leave the negative thought in place.

Countering

Changing negative to positive self-statements probably will not achieve the expected behavioral outcome if the athlete still believes in the negative statements. For example, an athlete might change his or her talk from "I

TABLE 15.1

Self-defeating thoughts	Change to self-enhancing thoughts
I can't believe it's raining. I have to play in the rain.	No one likes the rain, but I can play as well in it as anyone else.
You dumb jerk.	Ease off. Everyone makes mistakes. Sluff it off and put your mind on what you want to do.
There's no sense in practicing. I have no natural talent.	I've seen good players who had to work hard to be successful. I can get better if I practice correctly.
This officiating stinks; we'll never win.	There's nothing we can do about the officiating so let's just concentrate on what we want to do. If we play well, the officiating won't matter.
Why did they foul me in the last minute of play—I'm so nervous, I'll probably choke and miss everything.	My heart is beating fast. That's ok, I've sunk free throws a hundred times. I'll take a deep breath to relax and then visualize the ball going in the basket "swish."
We'll win the meet only if I get a 9.0 on this routine.	Stop worrying about the score; just concentrate on how you're going to execute the routine.
The coach must think I'm hopeless. He never helps me.	That's not fair. He has a whole team to coach. Tomorrow I'll ask what he thinks I need to work on the most.
I don't want to fail.	Nothing was ever gained by being afraid to take risks. As long as I give my best, I'll never be a failure.
I'll take it easy today and go hard next workout.	The next workout will be easier if I go hard now.
Who cares how well I do anyway?	I care, and I'll be happier if I push myself.
This hurts; I don't know if it's worth it.	Of course it hurts, but the rewards are worth it.

will never be able to run this offensive pattern; I'm just not quick enough" to "I can too; I'm as quick as anyone else." The athlete is merely going through the outward motions of being positive if the real belief system is still saying, "No I can't; I really am too slow." Dysfunctional thought patterns will keep recurring if they have strong underlying bases that are not identified and refuted.

Heyman and Rose (1980) discussed the fact that athletes will rarely be able to accomplish something if they truly believe they cannot. Further, the motivation to even try will be eroded if there is no belief that one's efforts will ultimately yield success. Bell (1983) proposes that in such instances, merely directing one's thoughts toward desired actions may not be enough. Instead, the athlete may have to identify and build a case against the negative self-statements that are interfering with effective performance. Bell suggests using the tool of countering under these circumstances. *Countering* is an internal dialogue that uses facts and reasons to refute the underlying beliefs and assumptions that led to negative thinking. Rather than blindly accepting the negative voice in the back of the head, the athlete argues against it.

When learning to use counters, it is important that the athlete actually describe the evidence necessary to change an attitude or belief. In the preceding example, the coach or sport psychologist might try helping the athlete identify issues such as "What makes me think I am slow? Have I ever in the past played with good speed? Am I as fast as any of the other athletes? If yes, are they successful at running this offense? What might be causing my slowness, and can I do anything to change it? If I am not quite as fast as some of my teammates, do I have any other talents that might compensate for this, such as using my good game sense to read the situation faster so I can react more quickly? What other skills do I have that might help me learn this offensive pattern?"

Any or all of the preceding approaches should lead to some evidence for refuting either the athlete's slowness or the importance of only speed in being successful at the offensive pattern. The more evidence and logic there is to refute the negative belief structure, the more effective the counters will be in getting the athlete to accept the positive statement; and the more firmly the athlete believes in the counters, the less time it will take to turn the thinking around. Later it may be possible for the athlete to identify the negative or irrational thought and simply dismiss it with such phrases as "No, that's not right," "Who says I can't?" or just plain "bull."

In his discussion of countering, Bell (1983) makes another excellent point. Sometimes thinking is neither right nor wrong—it cannot be verified. Under such circumstances, Bell suggests challenging the utility of the thoughts in helping athletes reach their goals. Get the athletes to ask themselves, "Is this thinking in my best interest? Does this thinking help me feel the way I want to or does it make me worry and be tense? Does this thinking help me perform better?" If the answer is no, advise the athletes to use the tool of thought stoppage when they identify counterproductive statements and follow the thought stoppage with statements such as "This thinking is not useful; it isn't helping me feel the way I need to feel to perform well."

Reframing Irrational and Distorted Thinking

In addition to dealing with negative talk and self-doubt, athletes need to realize that they may also be engaging in cognitive distortions and irrational thinking. Such thinking is counterproductive because it negatively influences self-concept, self-confidence, and performance. Once identified — a task that may take considerable soul-searching — these self-defeating cognitions need to be modified. According to Gauron (1984), the best way to cope with these thoughts is to look for different interpretations, contexts, and possible meanings. The world is literally what we make it. Gauron encourges athletes to cultivate the skill of reframing, that is, creating alternative frames of reference or different ways of looking at the world. Following are some irrational thoughts and cognitive distortions that are common among athletes (Gauron, 1984).

> **Irrational and Distorted Thinking**
> Perfection Is Essential
> Catastrophizing
> Worth Depends on Achievement
> Personalization
> Fallacy of "Fairness"
> Blaming
> Polarized Thinking
> One-Trial Generalizations

Perfection is essential One of the most debilitating irrational ideas for an athlete is that he or she must be competent and near perfection in everything attempted. No one can consistently achieve perfection. Athletes who believe they should be perfect will blame themselves for every defeat. Their self-concept will likely be lowered and they may start a fear-of-failure syndrome. Further, they will put such pressures upon themselves to do well that both their enjoyment and performance will likely suffer. There is always value in *striving* for perfection, but nothing is gained by *demanding* perfection. The same can be said for the thinking of the coach.

Catastrophizing Catastrophizing often accompanies perfectionistic tendencies as the athlete believes that any failure will be a humiliating disaster or that pleasing others (especially friends and parents) is the number one priority. Catastrophizers expect the worst possible thing to happen. Consequently, expecting disaster often leads to disaster! Individuals become plagued by "what ifs." "What if I lose today?" "What if my parents are embarrassed when I strike out?" "How will I ever be able to compete again?"

Perfectionistic thinking and catastrophizing can be combatted by realistic evaluations of the actual situation and the setting of appropriate goals.

A careful assessment of the actual odds of success or failure as well as the objective nature of the possible outcomes or consequences is essential.

Worth depends on achievement   Another problem for some athletes is the belief that their worth depends on their achievements. Many young athletes believe that they are only as good as what they win. Correspondingly, they think they must excel in order to please others. Try asking an athlete or coach to describe who he or she is without mentioning his or her sport or success rate! Athletes must learn to value themselves for more than what they do; worth as a human being is based on factors other than achievement outcome.

Personalization   The concept of personal worth is often linked with the self-defeating tendency to personalize everything. Unfortunately, some athletes believe that every time they walk past a crowd that is laughing, the crowd is laughing at them. This essentially egocentric attitude does little to help focus attention on personal effort or performance. Instead it diverts attention to external events that are outside the athletes' control and often not related to anything the athletes did or said.

Fallacy of fairness and ideal conditions   Some athletes believe they are entitled to fair treatment and ideal conditions. "Fair" is usually a disguise for just wanting one's personal preferences versus what someone else sees as being in the best interests of all concerned. "Ideal conditions" means that coaches should carve out the easiest possible path for athletes to follow. Athletes need to realize that it is irrational to think that things will come easily or that they will not need to be self-disciplined and to work hard. Rarely will athletes achieve any valuable gain without effort, pain, and sacrifice.

Blaming   Any feeling of unfair treatment can also produce blaming or external attributions. Nothing is gained by making excuses and/or assigning faults to others. This type of thinking allows the athletes to abdicate all responsibility—an absolutely nonproductive form of cognition. Athletes must learn to replace external attributions with attributions that are within their control: "Success comes from effort and working hard to develop my full potential whereas failure comes from lack of effort or insufficient practice of key fundamentals." Athletes often learn their attributions from coaches. If coaches usually blame failure on external factors, athletes will too. This subtly leads athletes to expect failure under similar future circumstances, e.g., bad weather, poor officiating. However, if coaches and sport psychologists provide appropriate internal attributions for individual athlete and team successes and failures, they will help athletes eliminate some of their feelings of external control and inappropriate, superstitious thinking. The more athletes realize they are personally responsible for and in control of their performance, the more their confidence will grow after good performance and the more confidence they will have in turning current failures into future successes.

On the other hand, if athletes accept complete responsibility for everything, they may be equally nonproductive. For example, some players are prone to taking sole responsibility for the entire team's performance. "We lost because I missed that last free throw." Accepting such irrational blame can lead to many potential problems, including further irrationalizations: "The coach and my teammates must really hate me." The answer to this kind of irrational thinking lies in helping athletes to be realistic and honest in evaluating performance outcome.

Polarized thinking Polarized thinking is the tendency to view things and people in absolute terms. All-or-nothing thinking can lead an athlete to categorize everything as either successful or unsuccessful, good or bad rather than learning from each and every experience. Such thinking often leads to judgmental labeling—the identification or description of something or someone with a single evaluative word or phrase such as choker, butterfingers, airbrain, loser. Athletes, and people who work with athletes, need to recognize that such negative labeling is very detrimental because labels are often internalized and become, in a more or less permanent way, a part of self-concept and future expectations. Once established, labels are difficult to erase. Coaches and sport psychologists should instead stress the avoidance of any kind of negative evaluative language, judgmentalism, and absolute thinking. The personal behavior of the coach and sport psychologist should set the example for what they expect from their athletes.

One-trial generalizations Perhaps the most dangerous cognitive distortions come from one-trial generalizations or superstitions. These are also among the easiest to desensitize. Overgeneralizations occur when a single incident causes athletes to link the situation with the outcome. Examples include statements such as "I never swim well in a pool without gutters" and "I can't golf well in the rain." If these conclusions are based on only one or two experiences, then some careful analysis can usually lead athletes to negate them. If they are based on many experiences, then they should merely be used to direct practice to overcome the apparent obstacle to performing well. Practicing under perceived negative conditions until success is achieved will often produce effective evidence to repudiate the initial negative generalization.

Constructing Affirmation Statements

Confidence and feelings of personal control will be enhanced if coaches and sport psychologists assist athletes in constructing personal affirmation statements. As noted earlier, a good source of affirmations is positive statements that might naturally have occurred with previous successful performance. Another way to build affirmations is to have each athlete make a self-esteem list and a success list (Gauron, 1984). The self-esteem list contains all of the athlete's positive attributes—all of his or her perceived assets, strengths, and positive qualities. The success list contains all of the athlete's successes thus far. The goal is to use one's own personal history in an enabling way by reviewing, reexperiencing, and visualizing previous success experiences.

The self-esteem and success lists serve to remind the athlete of how capable he or she is and how deserving of being successful. This is not the time for modesty but for honest reflection on all of one's positive qualities and successes. Rushall (1979) has emphasized that once this positive frame of reference is established, the athlete should write specific affirmation statements that are *positive action-oriented* self-statements affirming his or her capabilities and what he or she would like to do. A positive action-oriented affirmation statement might be "I play well under pressure" rather than "I know I can play well under pressure." Affirmations should be in the present tense and worded in a way that avoids perfectionist statements that may be impossible to live up to, such as "I always . . ." or "I never. . . ."

Once formulated, how can these statements be maximally used to foster confidence and the desired goal of the affirmation? Gauron suggests having a number one affirmation to work on each day, especially when feeling "bummed" or going into a slump. An athlete may want to write the statement 10 to 20 times each day on a piece of paper or on a card that can be carried around and pulled out and read during free moments. Once the affirmation becomes so integrated into the conscious mind that it is completely believed and made automatically, the athlete can select another affirmation to work on. Other techniques for utilizing affirmations are to post them (singularly or in combination) in places such as one's bedroom, bathroom, or locker. There is also merit in recording affirmations on cassette tape and playing them whenever possible, such as between classes or before going to bed.

Designing Coping and Mastery Self-Talk Tapes

Every individual has the capacity to program his or her mind for successful thoughts. Some athletes do it naturally; others must learn how to be effective thinkers. Helping athletes design coping and mastery self-talk tapes is another strategy that coaches and sport psychologists can use to program confidence. According to Bell (1983), confident athletes focus their thoughts and images on coping with the environment and the opponent, on mastering the task, and the rewards of success rather than worrying and catastrophizing about performing poorly and the consequences of failure. Rotella, Malone, and Ojala (1985) have provided an excellent description of designing coping and mastery tapes.

Coping tapes should allow the athlete to practice dealing with negative and anxious thoughts and situations. The athlete rehearses the strategies needed to regain control and confidence. To make a coping tape, an athlete should imagine all of the potential problems to be faced and how they might be handled successfully. Concern over such things as practice time, physical conditioning, environmental conditions, performance situations, pressures from other people, lack of sleep, unfriendly officials, and tough competition should all be considered. The coping tape includes a description of the negative situation(s) and initial negative self-talk followed by rehearsal of an appropriate strategy and self-statements for dealing effectively with the situation(s). Listening over and over to this type of self-talk will help create a sense of well-being because if the same situations occur in real life, the athlete will already have practiced coping with them successfully. Once the athlete learns the skill of imagery, he or she can listen to the tape and actually visualize himself or herself successfully coping with what is described on the tape.

The ideal situation on a mastery tape is always to be playing perfectly and always to be in complete control. The athlete records all of the positive thoughts and phrases that might occur if he or she were performing perfectly in some imagined situation that is progressing exactly as the athlete would wish. If feasible, the mastery tape should be approximately the same length as the actual performance. For example, if an athlete is trying to master a perfect routine for free throw shooting in basketball, he or she would want a segment of tape about 15 to 30 seconds long. If the athlete needs to build confidence in the ability to handle time-outs being called before shooting, the tape might include the length of a time-out and possible desirable self-talk for both this time and the preparation time before actually shooting. Listening over and over to a mastery tape rendition of the perfect performance should "program" the conscious and subconscious mind for success by helping the athlete become comfortable with positive statements and associating these statements with his or her own voice and performance.

SUMMARY

There is a direct correlation between self-confidence and success. Confident athletes think about themselves and the action at hand in a different way than those who lack confidence. The positive thinking of confident athletes is likely to lead to enabling feelings and good performance just as the inappropriate or misguided thinking of athletes lacking in confidence is likely to lead to negative feelings and poor performance. Athletes can learn to use self-talk to build confidence and to facilitate learning and perform-ance. The first step in an athlete's gaining control of thinking is to monitor self-talk to become aware of what kind of thinking helps, what thoughts are occurring that appear to be harmful, and what situations or events are associated with the talk. Three of the most effective tools for identifying self-talk are retrospection, imagery, and keeping a self-talk log.

Once awareness of self-talk and feelings is heightened, particularly negative talk, the coach or sport psychologist can instruct the athlete in how to start dealing with these thoughts. Techniques such as thought stoppage, changing negative thoughts to positive thoughts, countering, reframing of irrational and distorted thinking, and constructing affirmation statements are all discussed as possible tools for producing performance enhancing thoughts and eliminating disabling thoughts.

REFERENCES

Bell, K. F. (1983). *Championship thinking: The athlete's guide to winning performance in all sports.* Englewood Cliffs, N.J.: Prentice-Hall.

Bunker, L. K., and Owens, N. D. (1985). *Golf: Better practice for better play.* West Point, N.Y.: Leisure Press.

Bunker, L. K., & Rotella, R. J. (1982). *Mind, set and match.* Englewood Cliffs, N.J.: Prentice-Hall.

Cautela, J. R., & Wisocki, P. A. (1977). Thought stoppage procedure: Description, application and learning theory interpretations. *Psychological Record, 27,* 255–264.

Gallwey, W. T. (1974). *The inner game of tennis.* New York: Random House.

Gauron, E. F. (1984). *Mental training for peak performance.* Lansing, N.Y.: Sport Science Associates.

Harris, D. V., & Harris, B. L. (1984). *The athlete's guide to sports psychology: Mental skills for physical people.* West Point, N.Y.: Leisure Press.

Heyman, S. R., & Rose, K. G. (1980). Psychological variables affecting SCUBA per-formance. A reconsideration of methodological questions and data. *Journal of Sport Psychology, 4,* 295–300.

Meichenbaum, D. (1975). Toward a cognitive theory of self-control. In G. Schwartz & D. Shapiro (Eds.), *Consciousness and self-regulation: Advances in research.* New York: Plenum.

Meichenbaum, D. (1977). *Cognitive behavior modification: An integrative approach.* New York: Plenum.

Meyers, A. W., & Schleser, R. A. (1980). A cognitive behavioral intervention for improving basketball performance. *Journal of Sport Psychology, 2,* 69–73.

Rotella, R. J., & Bunker, L. K. (1981). *Mind mastery for winning golf.* Englewood Cliffs, N.J.: Prentice-Hall.

Rotella, R. J., Gansneder, B., Ojala, D., & Billing, J. (1980). Cognitions and coping strategies of elite skiers—an exploratory study of young developing athletes. *Journal of Sport Psychology, 1,* 350–354.

Rotella, R. J., Malone, C., and Ojala, D. (1985). Facilitating athletic performance through the use of mastery and coping tapes. In L. K. Bunker, R. J. Rotella, & A. S. Reilly, *Sport psychology: Psychological considerations in maximizing sport performance.* Ithaca, N.Y.: Mouvement Publications.

Rushall, B. S. (1979). *Psyching in sports.* London: Pelham.

Silva, J. (1982). Performance enhancement through cognitive intervention. *Behavior Modification, 6* (4):443–463.

Syer, J., & Connolly, C. (1984). *Sporting body sporting guide: An athlete's guide to mental training.* New York: Cambridge University Press.

16 Concentration and Attention Control Training

ROBERT M. NIDEFFER

President, Enhanced Performance Associates

The ability to control thought processes, to *concentrate* on a task (e.g., to "keep your eye on the ball") is almost universally recognized as the most important key to effective performance in sport. Mental control is typically viewed as the deciding factor in competition in both individual and team sports. In spite of the tremendous importance of concentration to performance, very little has been done either to define concentration or to systematically train athletes to concentrate more effectively.

One of the major roles of sport psychologists in the future will be to define "operationally" constructs such as concentration and arousal for both coaches and athletes. This chapter represents the beginning of the process. Only by operationally defining these concepts can we reach the point of being able to test scientifically our knowledge and the validity and utility of our training and counseling techniques. To define concentration operationally, we must define what it is behaviorally. In addition, we must begin to define those factors or conditions that affect the ability to concentrate. We must describe the conditions that affect concentration, and we must predict the behavioral effects (e.g., what specifically will happen to the ability to concentrate and to one's behavior or performance as a consequence).

Attention control training (ACT) is a set of training procedures that developed as a result of operationally defining attentional (or concentration) processes as they relate to performance. Although the training procedures are based on "operational" constructs, considerable research still needs to be conducted to evaluate and refine further both the attentional constructs and the training procedures.

OPERATIONALLY DEFINING CONCENTRATION

How many times have you heard someone say, "concentrate" or "don't choke" and wondered just what that person was telling you to do or not do?

When a coach tells an athlete to pay attention to the game, what is the coach really saying? Very often it isn't just the athlete who is confused; a great many coaches cannot even tell you what they mean. If they are asked for a definition of concentration, they sometimes get defensive. The thought of explicitly and behaviorally defining just what one should attend to does not seem to occur. Most coaches simply assume that an athlete is concentrating effectively if he or she is winning. Likewise, they assume that concentration is ineffective if performance is below their expectations. It is small wonder that it takes most people a very long time to develop good concentration skills and consistent performance under pressure! How can coaches possibly teach something that they have not thought about enough even to define?

In the next section we present a summary of the hypothetical principles that underlie attention control training. These principles begin the process of behaviorally and operationally defining concentration in sport.

ATTENTION CONTROL TRAINING

The eight principles that underlie attention control training are outlined here and elaborated upon in the subsections that follow.

1. Athletes need to be able to engage in at least four different types of attention.
2. Different sport situations will make different attentional demands on an athlete. Accordingly, it is incumbent upon the athlete to be able to shift to different types of concentration to match changing attentional demands.
3. Under optimal conditions, the average person can meet the attentional demands of most sport situations.
4. There are individual differences in attentional abilities. Some of the differences are learned, some are biological, and some are genetic. Thus different athletes have different attentional strengths and weaknesses.
5. As physiological arousal begins to increase beyond an athlete's own optimal level, there is an initial tendency for the athlete to rely too heavily on the most highly developed attentional ability.
6. The phenomenon of "choking," of having performance progressively deteriorate, occurs as physiological arousal continues to increase to the point of causing an involuntary narrowing of an athlete's concentration and to the point of causing attention to become more internally focused.

7. Alterations in physiological arousal affect concentration. Thus, the systematic manipulation of physiological arousal is one way of gaining some control over concentration.
8. Alterations in the focus of attention will affect physiological arousal. Thus, the systematic manipulation of concentration is one way to gain some control over arousal (e.g., muscle tension levels, heart rate, respiration rate).

Different Types of Concentration

When a coach tells an athlete to concentrate, the athlete is more likely to respond to the instruction if the coach specifically defines the type of concentration that he or she would like the athlete to engage in. To do this, it is necessary to think of attention as requiring at least two different types of focus. First, the athlete will need to control the width of his or her attentional focus. Certain sport situations require a fairly broad focus of attention because the athlete must be sensitive to several different cues. Other sport situations require a narrower type of concentration. Hitting a baseball, for example, requires a very narrow type of concentration. The second type of focus that needs to be controlled relates to the direction of the athlete's attention. In some situations, attention must be directed internally toward the athlete's own feelings and/or thoughts. At other times, attention must be focused externally, on the opponent, the ball, etc. Table 16.1 presents the four different types of concentration that are required by different sport

TABLE 16.1
Four Different Types of Attentional Focus

Broad–external	Broad–internal
Used to rapidly assess a situation (e.g., the type of attention initially required on a fast break in hockey or basketball).	Used to analyze and plan (e.g., the type of attention used to develop a game plan or strategy).

Narrow–external	Narrow–internal
Used to focus in a nondistractible way on one or two external cues (e.g., the ball).	Used to systematically mentally rehearse a performance situation, or to monitor and/or control physical arousal (e.g., mentally rehearse golf putting or focus on taking deep breaths to relax).

situations and that result when both width and direction of attention are controlled.

Shifting Attention

Recall from page 258 the second principle underlying attention control training: different sport situations make different attentional demands on athletes. Thus, a position such as quarterback in football places a greater demand on an athlete to be able to develop a broad–external focus of attention (e.g., to be aware of the entire field) than a position such as guard, which requires a narrower type of concentration (e.g., to block a particular athlete on the other team). Beyond this difference, however, there are demands for shifting attention within a particular sport. An example from golf will illustrate the point.

When golfers step up to the ball prior to hitting a shot, they start off with a fairly broad–external type of attention. Golfers need to take in several different kinds of information. They need to be aware of the placement of hazards (trees, sand traps, out-of-bounds markers, water, etc.) and course conditions (dryness of the grass, amount and direction of wind). Once they have gathered this external information, golfers shift attention to a broad–internal focus to plan their shot. At this time, they should try to recall past similar situations, remembering how they played them and what the results were. Then they must think about any changes they may have made in the meantime, changes that might modify how they should now play this similar situation (e.g., have they changed their swing, gotten new clubs; are they in a different tactical position such as needing to be conservative or to take a risk). Analyzing all of this information allows golfers to select a particular club and to determine how they want to hit the ball.

Once golfers have formulated a plan, they shift to a narrow–internal type of concentration to monitor their own tension (e.g., making sure they are not too tight or too relaxed) and to mentally rehearse the shot. They may picture in their mind what they want to feel and see as they execute the shot. Finally, golfers shift attention to a narrow–external focus as they address the ball and begin their backswing. At this time concentration is on the ball; to attend to other external or internal cues would only interfere with their execution of the shot.

This basic model can be applied to a great many sports. Thus, athletes are continually required to shift attention across the different dimensions listed even though some sports require more of one type of attention than others. In addition, in some sport situations coaches and/or other athletes can make up for attentional deficiencies of some players. As an illustration, in football the coach can select the plays for the quarterback. This limits the need for the quarterback to be able to develop a broad–internal type of attention.

It is essential during physical instruction and practice that coaches communicate to their athletes what type of concentration is appropriate. Then, when the coach tells an athlete to concentrate, the athlete will at least know what is expected. This knowledge, combined with attention control training, will lead to better concentration.

Individual Differences

The third and fourth principles underlying attention control training deal with an individual's ability to shift attention. The third principle indicates that if individuals are appropriately motivated and trained and if they have control over their level of arousal (so that it is neither too high nor too low), they are capable of effective concentration. They can control the width and direction of attention enough to be effective. The actual attentional demands of most sports are not so extreme that the average person cannot meet them! This means that there is hope for most athletes.

At the same time, the fourth principle indicates that it will be easier for some athletes to meet a given sport's attentional demands than for others. Just as we are willing to concede that there are physiological and biological differences among athletes, we should be willing to concede that there are attentional differences. As mentioned earlier, some of the differences seem to be learned (e.g., the result of social and environmental factors), whereas others seem to be genetic and/or biological. Research on attentional processes suggests the following differences among others.

1. Different individuals have different capacities for developing a broad–internal type of attention. Thus, some individuals are better suited to analyzing large amounts of information than others.
2. Certain individuals appear to be more sensitive to environmental (external) information than others. The former read and react to other people more effectively.
3. Some individuals are more capable of developing a narrow, nondistractible type of attention.

Some superstars in sport seem to have been born for their particular event. There are sprinters with more fast-twitch muscle fibers than most other people, divers with a greater kinesthetic awareness, etc. Likewise, some athletes are more attentionally suited to their sport. Their ability to focus narrowly makes it easier for them to be "dedicated" to follow-through on a task, to be as selfish as they must be to make it to the top. Some athletes have the ability to deal with a great deal of information and not become overloaded and confused; this helps them to be more resistant to pressure and makes it easier for them to perform in critical situations.

Although a small percentage of the world's athletes may indeed have been born "dedicated" and resistant to "choking," the majority have to learn to focus attention in order to achieve these goals. An increasingly important role for the sport psychologist and coach will be assisting athletes in recognizing the attentional demands of their sports, as well as helping athletes identify their own relative attentional strengths and weaknesses. The systematic assessment of attentional abilities and of the ability to shift from one type of attention to another will play a major role in the development of training programs. This assessment will aid the majority of athletes in developing concentration skills and/or compensating for any attentional problems they may have. Early attempts at this type of assessment have already begun and are described in the suggested readings at the end of this chapter.

Playing to One's Attentional Strength

The fifth principle underlying attention control training indicates that athletes have a tendency to play to their strengths as pressure increases. This is true of almost all of us. We have an unerring capacity to become our own worst enemies, to turn what are normally strengths into weaknesses. For example, outgoing people who are normally appreciated because they also have enough sensitivity to know when to leave other people alone occasionally lose their sensitivity and become pests.

There is an unproven assumption in sport that good coaches do not make good athletes and vice versa. If this is true, one of the reasons might be that coaching makes a very heavy demand on an individual to be able to think and analyze. Coaches must be able to develop a broad–internal type of attention. In contrast, a great many sporting situations require athletes to shut off their analyzing. If they do not, we see the "paralysis by analysis" that coaches are so fond of talking about. The athletes think too much and fail to react to the sport situation. They are "in their head" at an inappropriate time. Athletes who ultimately become coaches are often the ones who were continually analyzing; they are not the brilliant broken field runners who reacted instinctively.

Take the pressure off most coaches and athletes and they can be either analytical or instinctive. Put them under pressure, however, and they play to their strengths. Analytical coaches become too analytical. They go inside their head and lose sensitivity to the athletes and the game situation. Often they attempt to communicate their analysis to the athletes, overloading them with information, getting them to think too much.

Instinctive athletes have a tendency to react too quickly. They may fail to analyze and plan when they need to. They lose their capacity to make adjustments, getting faked out by the same moves time and time again, not learning from their own mistakes. If arousal reaches the point of causing narrowing of attention and of increasing internal distractions, then the athletes' ability to process information deteriorates. At this time, coaches should be minimizing the amount of information that they are giving their athletes. The coaches should be providing as much structure and support as possible. If coaches are playing to their own strength, they fail. Instead of calling the play for their athletes, unsuccessful coaches ask the athletes what they think or give them several possibilities.

Another role of sport psychologists is to "team build" with coaches and athletes to get them to maintain effective communication under pressure. Sport psychologists do this by sensitizing coaches and athletes to their own and others' "relative" strengths and weaknesses. Sport psychologists help coaches and athletes identify the specific situations in which communication is likely to break down and help them plan alternative ways to behave. When no sport psychologist is available to help, coaches need to be sufficiently knowledgeable and aware to do this on their own.

As an example of the team-building process, consider a situation in which a coach tends to be more analytical and more assertive than the athletes (a normally ideal situation). As pressure increases, the coach becomes more analytical and more assertive and the athletes less so. At a certain point the athletes should be confronting the coach with the fact that they are being overloaded with instructions; they may behave in an even more outwardly compliant way, nodding their head to show agreement even when they are not hearing or when they are confused. The coach, thinking that he or she has a willing, even enthusiastic audience, feels encouraged to give still more information. The sport psychologist helps the athletes recognize their feelings of confusion and provides them with the support they need to confront the coach. Then all work together to develop ways of minimizing the problem. Perhaps insight is all the coach needs to decrease the amount of information he or she gives. Perhaps the coach's insight and an initial confrontation with the coach (e.g., "Coach, I can't take all of this right now") will provide all the encouragement the athletes need to be able to be honest with the coach in the future. The sport psychologist can usually give the coach suggestions for communicating the same information in a more simplified and structured way.

Operationally Defining Choking

Before we can examine the sixth principle underlying attention control training, we must define operationally the term *choking*. (Unfortunately, there is little agreement between most coaches and athletes regarding the definition of as critical a term as *choking*. Thus, when a coach tells an athlete not to choke, the athlete may have no idea of what he or she is supposed to avoid.)

Given what we do know about the interaction between thought process (what we attend to) and physiological process, it is possible to come up with a definition of *choking* that can be very useful to coaches, athletes, sport psychology practitioners, and researchers alike.

Behaviorally, we can infer that athletes are choking when their performance seems to be progressively deteriorating and when they seem incapable of regaining control over performance on their own, that is, without some outside assistance—for example, the baseball player who follows a bobbled catch with a throwing error, or the diver or gymnast who lets an early mistake (e.g., on a dive or particular move) upset him or her to the point of making additional errors on other maneuvers.

Figure 16.1 illustrates the interaction that occurs between physiological and attentional processes under highly stressful conditions. The figure also shows how the changes that occur affect performance. By using Figure 16.1 and the description that follows, coaches should gain a more useful understanding of the choking process—an understanding that can help increase their ability to understand, predict, and control behavior in sport situations.

Situations that result in an athlete's choking may be highly individual-

Situations Leading to Choking

The "big game"
Fears (e.g., of injury)

Physiological Changes ←——————→ **Attentional Changes**

1. Increases in muscle tension (bracing).
2. Increases in heart rate and respiration.

1. Narrowing of attention.
2. Internal focus of attention.

Performance Problems

1. Disturbances in fine muscle coordination and timing.
2. Rushing.
3. Inability to attend to task relevant cues.
4. Fatigue and muscle tightness.

FIGURE 16.1
Interaction Between Physiological and Attentional Processes Under Highly Stressful Conditions

ized. At the same time, it is generally accepted that the more emotionally important an event is to an athlete, the greater the potential for choking to occur. Thus, athletes who find themselves in championship games for the first time or who have to make the critical shot in order to win frequently perform well below their capabilities. This is one reason why the quality of play in championship games (e.g., the Superbowl or World Series) is often well below the level of play that got the teams there in the first place.

Suppose that an athlete whom we will call Jim is playing in a conference championship game for the first time. Jim is only a sophomore in college, and because of his relative lack of experience and the importance of the game, he is very nervous. To add to the pressure, Jim did not have a particularly good game the last time he played. Furthermore, the championship game is being played at home. Jim knows that his girlfriend and family will be there to see him play. Finally, he has been called aside and told, "You are the key to the team's success."

All of these factors make the game very important to Jim, and as a result he experiences the physical and attentional changes presented in Figure 16.1. Physiologically, Jim experiences tightness in his neck and shoulders. Sitting on the bench and waiting to go up to bat, he keeps turning his head and hunching his shoulders trying to relax the muscles. The added pressure causes him to brace, to tense muscles that will be antagonistic to his hitting the ball. He will find when he goes to bat that he is working against himself, and this will interfere with his timing and coordination.

The changes in Jim's muscle tension are accompanied by changes in his breathing and heart rate. Jim begins to breathe more rapidly and shallowly. This combination of changes creates the feeling that things are happening more quickly than usual. Jim begins to feel that he is being rushed, that he must move more quickly than usual to keep up. This feeling of being rushed will result in his swinging at the ball before it reaches the plate. This same feeling will cause him to attempt to throw the ball before he has finished catching it. As a result, he will either drop it or make a throwing error.

Attentionally, Jim's concentration narrows and becomes more internally focused. He is having difficulty listening to the coaches' instructions and starts to get confused. At key times (e.g., when he should be watching the coaches for signs), he is distracted by his own feelings of tension and his thoughts. He is negatively interpreting his tension and begins to subvocalize the negativism: "Whew, I'm pretty tight. Sure hope I don't blow it in front of my family."

Sure enough, as the game starts Jim's worst fears are realized. An easy ground ball is hit to shortstop. Jim gets in front of it, but because of the muscle tightness, his hands are not as "soft" as they usually are. The ball bounces off his glove, and Jim scrambles to pick it up. Although the ball is right in front of him and he has plenty of time, Jim feels as if he must hurry.

He dives for the ball, picking it up and throwing off balance. The ball lands in the opposition's dugout, and the runner advances to second base.

Now Jim has an actual failure to focus on in addition to the fears and feelings that have been distractors. That failure adds to his tension and leads to further attentional distractions. His own negative thoughts start increasing his tension and his tension increases the negative thoughts. His performance goes from bad to worse, and we have a classic example of choking.

The same basic process occurs when an athlete fears an injury. Susan hurt herself earlier on the balance beam. Now as she enters a competition, she is thinking about the previous injury. Her fear causes the physical and attentional disturbances outlined in Figure 16.1. As she starts her routine, she is muscularly tight and begins to rush. She has difficulty maintaining her balance because of the tension, and she makes simple errors that cause slight deductions from her score. Although she recovers from the first couple of mistakes, these errors serve to reinforce her fear. Her tension and fears increase, and ultimately she falls from the beam.

Prevention and Treatment of Choking

The seventh and eighth principles underlying attention control training suggest that by creating changes in what is going on either physiologically or attentionally, athletes can break the downward spiral associated with choking. Thus, if they eliminate the physical feelings associated with excessive tension (tight muscles, pounding heart), they will reduce the number of attentional distractors and improve their ability to concentrate. Likewise, if coaches can get the athletes to either ignore or reinterpret their physical feelings (e.g., if they give a positive interpretation to being aroused, such as "I'm ready"), gradually the physical changes will be reduced and tension levels and heart rate will return to "normal" for the competitive conditions.

Under ideal conditions, we would be able to prevent choking from ever occurring. One of the unrealistic goals of many sport psychology programs is to prevent choking by teaching athletes some type of relaxation and/or rehearsal procedure. In truth, we probably can reduce the frequency of choking through better training and through some type of relaxation and rehearsal process. We can reduce the tendency to choke, but we cannot eliminate it. In addition, we are likely to be successful only if our program has a performance-specific focus. That is, we should teach the athletes to use the relaxation at a particular time (e.g., at bat) and we should train them to rehearse a particular performance situation (e.g., hitting under certain conditions).

By teaching athletes to relax, to monitor their own muscle tension levels, and to use their tension levels as a signal to employ some brief type of relaxation procedure, we can help them improve the consistency of their performance. By getting them to mentally simulate anticipated performance conditions and to systematically rehearse what they will see and feel, we can begin to desensitize them, to reduce the newness of the experience, and to increase the likelihood that tension will not reach a level that will cause them to choke.

With a specific training focus, we can reduce the frequency of choking and "season" athletes more quickly. Simulation and rehearsal can make up for some lack of experience. Nevertheless, there will always be unanticipated situations that we could not prepare for. If we tried to think of every contingency, we would overload ourselves and never make any progress. As a result, we must begin to train athletes to recover quickly from the unexpected. Learning to recover once tension has already gotten out of control or once a mistake has been made is even more critical than trying to eliminate choking altogether.

Process vs. Outcome

Once athletes have made a mistake or once they become aware of the tension and the attentional distractions that are likely to interfere with performance, what they attend to becomes critical. In the prevention strategy outlined above, emphasis was placed on training the athlete to recognize and reduce physical tension, thereby improving concentration. Once mistakes have been made, however, many athletes find it difficult to directly challenge what is going on in their bodies.

Imagine a situation in which you have just double-faulted away a game in a critical tennis match. You know you are tight and you try to counter it by saying, "It's all right, just relax; the game isn't that important anyway," and a little voice inside of you immediately counters with, "Oh yes it is, you blew it, you can't do it."

Your lack of confidence created by the feelings and the failure causes you to doubt your own ability. Attempting to pick yourself up by your bootstraps, to take control directly only creates more distractions and frustration. If you had a great deal of confidence in yourself, you could do that. You could challenge and confront yourself, using your frustration and anger to help you concentrate on the task. When you lack confidence, however, you must focus your attention on something else. You must become "process" focused rather than "outcome" focused.

During practice, especially in sports that require a great deal of training and sacrifice on the part of the athlete, individuals motivate themselves by thinking about outcome: "If we win the championship, I'll be a hero." "I am working this hard because I want to win a gold medal." "By making these sacrifices I can get the recognition and financial rewards I want."

Once the competition begins, however, an outcome focus can become very negative.

To be thinking about how important the outcome of a contest is or about what one can win or lose during the actual competition typically generates additional physical and attentional changes that interfere with performance. One of the biggest contributors to choking is thinking about the outcome or the importance of a contest while involved in it. To break out of this thinking, sport psychologists are training athletes to recognize their tendency to place too much importance on outcome (during the competition) and to use those thoughts, when they occur, as signals to attend to "process." Coaches need to do the same thing. Process cues are related to the process of performing as opposed to the outcome. For example, a swimmer might attend to some technical aspect of her stroke or to the feeling of her body moving through the water. Often the focus is on generating a rhythm. Over time, people learn that if they maintain this type of focus, the outcome will take care of itself. Then as they have success and as confidence builds, they can begin to attend to outcome in order to motivate themselves to try harder. Thus, the athlete who has a lot of success and who becomes a little lazy or too relaxed needs to think about outcome to get the arousal up and to keep going.

Crisis Intervention

Although sport psychologists and coaches can do a great deal to teach athletes to prevent and control their own arousal and concentration, there will still be times when the individual athlete needs outside assistance. The choking phenomenon has gone too far, the athlete can no longer stop it. On these occasions, the coach or sport psychologist provides assistance by giving the athlete structure and something simple to concentrate on. For example, the coach calls a time-out and breaks into the athlete's internal wheel spinning. The coach makes eye contact with the athlete and talks in a tone that demands attention; the coach may even make physical contact with the athlete. Once the athlete is attending, the coach directs the athlete's attention toward neutral nonperformance related matters or process cues. In other words, the coach gives the athlete simple instructions to attend to a particular cue or stimulus; this task prevents the athlete from thinking about outcome. The coach or sport psychologist should not ask questions such as "What's going on?" The athlete could not answer a question like that and would only become more confused if he or she tried to figure it out. Instead, the coach or sport psychologist must provide support and structure to facilitate the redirection of the athlete's attention.

Additional readings regarding the research, theory, and practice outlined in this chapter are presented at the end of the chapter. Specific techniques that coaches and sport psychologists can use to help train better concentration in athletes appear in Chapter 17.

SUMMARY

We are reaching the point in sport psychology where it is possible to begin to define operationally terms such as *concentration* and *choking*. Several different types of attention or concentration are required in athletic situations. One of the roles of coaches and sport psychologists is to teach athletes how to control concentration and arousal. As we develop systematic training programs, we can improve athletes' level and consistency of performance.

Although most athletes are capable of developing the different types of concentration required by sport situations, individual differences do exist. There may be a few attentional superstars, but most athletes have relative attentional strengths and weaknesses. By learning what their own strengths and weaknesses are, athletes can be encouraged to develop programs either to overcome their weaknesses or to compensate for them.

ADDITIONAL READINGS

Nideffer, R. M. (1976a). *The inner athlete: Mind plus muscle for winning.* San Diego: Enhanced Performance Assoc.

Nideffer, R. M. (1976b). Test of attentional and interpersonal style. *Journal of Personality and Social Psychology, 34,* 394–404.

Nideffer, R. M. (1981). *The ethics and practice of applied sport psychology.* Ithaca, N.Y.: Mouvement Publications.

Nideffer, R. M. (1985). *Enhanced performance in sport.* Champaign, Ill.: Human Kinetics.

17 Techniques for Training Concentration

ANDREA SCHMID and ERIK PEPER

San Francisco State University

Concentration is essential for performing one's best. The major component of concentration is the ability to focus one's attention on the task at hand and thereby not be disturbed or affected by irrelevant external and internal stimuli. External stimuli may include an audience booing, music, certain officiating calls, and unsportsmanlike behavior from the opponents. Internal stimuli include distracting body sensations and thoughts and feelings such as, "I'm really tired," "Don't be nervous," and "I blew it!" Although external and internal stimuli appear to be separate categories, they continually affect each other. Almost every external event will trigger a cognitive and emotional shift in the athlete. Because this interaction occurs all of the time, coaches and sport psychologists must train athletes to cope with these events under pressure situations such as a major competition. Unless this training has occurred and been mastered, performance will almost always suffer.

For example, one 16-year-old U.S. rhythmic gymnast lost her poise and concentration and performed very poorly when a loud teenage voice yelled a lewd comment as she walked toward the mat to compete in an international meet. During the fifth game of a critical intercollegiate volleyball match, the visiting team completely lost its composure when the home crowd began stamping feet and clapping in unison whenever the away team was serving the ball. A closely contested game with an 8–8 score ended 8–15 in favor of the home team. These examples illustrate the potential for distractions in a competitive environment. The ability not to react to or be disturbed by distractions such as these is achieved when athletes learn how to control their thoughts and focus their attention appropriately.

This learned mental control was demonstrated by Zoltan Magyar, the Olympic gold medalist, during the twentieth gymnastics world championship in 1979. At the finals of the pommel horse competition, Magyar was up after Nikolai Adrianov, the Olympic all-around champion. Adrianov missed two elements in his routine, and 10,000 spectators verbally reacted. Magyar was able to tune out all sound and distractions. He was also able to shut out defeating thoughts and to synchronize and harmonize the forces of his mind and body to defend his Olympic gold medal. According to the team

271

physician, Magyar did not even realize that Adrianov had missed! Magyar was able to channel all of his energy into a productive performance. He had achieved the highest level of single-mindedness and exclusive concentration and attention (Schmid. 1982).

Many other performers such as surgeons, artists, writers, and musicians can often achieve this kind of high level of concentration. For example, Walsh and Spelman (1983) reported that conductor Carlos Kleiber was concentrating so intently when conducting Strauss's *Der Rosenkavalier* at La Scala that he never noticed the earthquake that rattled a giant chandelier! The preceding examples illustrate how elite performers tend not to be disturbed by external factors, a skill not yet acquired by many developing performers.

Paradoxically, trying to concentrate is also not concentrating. By *concentration* we mean focusing, not forcing, one's attention on the task. At times this may be perceived as shielding ourselves from stimuli that might penetrate and disturb our focus of attention. Active shielding by itself would be a distraction. Thus, concentration is the learned skill of passively not reacting to or being distracted by irrelevant stimuli. Concentration also means being totally in the here and now, in the present. When our minds drift into the past or future, we are not as effective in our present performance. The ability to concentrate is a skill, and like any other skill, it can be developed and improved through practice. We either learn to decrease attention to irrelevant stimuli or increase attention to relevant stimuli. In this process, we learn selective awareness — the skill of selectively paying attention to relevant stimuli and ignoring irrelevant stimuli. In addition, when we lose concentration, previous concentration training enhances our ability to rapidly refocus our attention on the task at hand without continuing to think about or feel some momentary distraction.

In Chapter 16 Nideffer identified the different types of attention or concentration that seem to be required in athletic situations. These types were described along two dimensions: broad versus narrow and internal versus external. The most appropriate type of focus, or attentional style, depends upon the sport skill and the demands of the specific situation. In concentration training, knowing what to focus on is as critical as knowing how to control one's focus. An athlete may have excellent concentration skills, but if he or she is focusing on the wrong things, the skills will not be very helpful!

In addition to providing athletes with techniques that help train better control of concentration, coaches and sport psychologists need to assist athletes in identifying different attentional styles and the most appropriate focus for their specific sport involvement. An excellent technique for helping athletes experience the different attentional styles is an "expanding awareness" exercise developed by Gauron (1984). Athletes can practice this exercise in its entirety or break the various segments into separate exercises. When practicing, athletes should sit or lie in a comfortable position.

1. First have the athletes focus on their breathing while continuing to breathe normally. For the next minute have them breathe more deeply and slowly while keeping the chest, shoulders, and neck relaxed. Return to normal breathing for 3 – 4 breaths and then back to deep breathing until the deep breathing is comfortable, easy, and regular.

2. Now have the athletes pay attention to what they hear by taking each separate sound, identifying it, and then mentally labeling it such as footsteps, voices, a cough. Next, simultaneously listen to all the sounds without attempting to identify or label them. Listen to the blend of sound as you would to music while verbal thinking drops away.

3. Now become aware of bodily sensations such as the feeling of where the chair or floor supports your body. Mentally label each sensation as you notice it. Before moving on to another sensation, let each sensation linger for a moment while you examine it; consider its quality and its source. Next, experience all these sensations simultaneously without identifying or labeling any particular one. This necessitates going into the broadest possible internal body awareness.

4. Attend now only to your emotions or thoughts. Let each thought or emotion appear gently, without being forced. Identify the nature of your thoughts and feelings. Remain calm no matter how pleasant or unpleasant they may be. Feel one, then another, then another. Now try to empty yourself of all thoughts and feelings. If this is not possible, tune in to only one and hold your attention there.

5. Open your eyes and pick some object across the room and directly in front of you. While looking directly ahead, see as much of the room and the objects in the room as your peripheral vision will allow. Simultaneously observe the entire room and all the things in it. Picture now a broad funnel into which your mind is moving, and centered in the middle of the funnel is the object directly across the room from you. Gradually narrow your focus by narrowing the funnel so the only thing at the small end of the funnel is the object across from you. Expand your focus little by little, widening the funnel until you can see everything in the room. Think of your external focus as a zoom lens; practice zooming in and out, narrowing or broadening according to your wishes.

Besides helping athletes experience different attentional styles, the preceding exercise illustrates what it is like to keep focus in one place and then to change across the internal to external dimension and the specific to panoramic focus. This type of experience provides an excellent foundation for clarifying the most appropriate focus for specific athletic skills and situations.

In the remainder of this chapter, we provide specific strategies and techniques that coaches and sport psychologists can use to train better concentration control in athletes. These strategies are divided into two sections: strategies to control distracting external factors and strategies to control internal distractions. The categorization is somewhat arbitrary, however, because external and internal stimuli continually affect each other. Because of this interaction, strategies in one category may be equally effective in correcting apparent lack of concentration in the other category.

EXTERNAL FACTORS: STRATEGIES TO KEEP CONCENTRATION

Athletes need to be trained not to react (orient) to irrelevant external stimuli. In a competition, these stimuli are the situational factors that coaches often expect the athletes to have learned to control by trial and error in previous competitive experiences. This "previous experience" strategy has obvious limitations and false assumptions. Coaches need to realize that athletes can be systematically trained before a competition to be situationally independent. The concept underlying training is based upon Pavlovian conditioning. The novelty of the competitive environment, compared to the practice environment, tends to reduce performance. Through training, the novelty of the competitive environment can be eliminated. In short, athletes need to experience simulated competition training in which they practice their physical skills while being exposed to all possible external stimuli that can occur during a real competition. This training follows similar procedures by which NASA and the U.S. Air Force train their astronauts and pilots to cope with emergencies. For example, in flight training, beginning pilots practice dead stick landings, pulling out of a spin, recovering from a stall, and so forth. For athletes, strategies that reduce the novelty effect upon performance by conditioning an appropriate response include "dress rehearsal" practice, general simulation of competition experiences, and mental rehearsal of concentration training.

Strategy 1: Dress Rehearsal

Dress rehearsal is a particularly effective strategy for sports such as gymnastics, diving, synchronized swimming, and figure skating. Dress rehearsal is based upon the concept that ease in skillful competitive performance is unconsciously conditioned by the external and internal stimuli that surround the athletes during practice. The greater the number of different stimuli present during competition compared to practice, the more performance tends to decrease. Stimuli can include things such as the athletes' uniforms and background sounds such as announcers' voices and music. Ironically, in order to make a good impression during the competitive event, athletes usually wear uniforms different from the ones they wear during practice. This means that an unconscious stimulus (the practice uniform) associated with the performance of the skill is absent during the competition. Wearing the clean or new uniform tends to be a new stimulus, which may inhibit performance. This may be one reason why some athletes tend to perform better during practice than during competition. Such athletes need to practice their complete competitive routine during practice in the same uniform they wear during actual competition. Dress rehearsal needs to be conducted frequently after the athletes have learned a new skill and are practicing the whole routine for performance. This strategy can also be applied when an athlete is in a slump. In this case the athlete ceremoniously discards his or her uniform and thereby symbolically disconnects from the slump associations and now practices with a new uniform; thereby, the athlete is metaphorically and ritualistically reborn.

Strategy 2: Rehearsal of Simulated Competition Experiences

Simulated competition experiences enable the athlete to become so familiar with the stimuli associated with competition that they are no longer distracting. This is the same concept that underlies dress rehearsal practice. The athletes are trained to concentrate and dissociate from the disruptive stimuli. For example, in gymnastics athletes might rehearse their routines in practice while a loud tape recording of a previous meet is played over the public-address system. This tape would include another gymnast's floor exercise music, audience applause, and so on. A similar example for team sports such as football, basketball, and volleyball would be holding the week's practice before an away game with the public-address system loudly playing hostile crowd noises and the opposing team's fight song. Such exercises reduce the effect of "meet-induced novelty," which tends to interfere with performance, and make the competitive experience seem just like practice workouts.

When using this strategy, coaches and sport psychologists should overtrain athletes by including simulated practice of the worst possible scenario, such as having a basketball player ready to take a free throw shot and then having to wait the length of a time-out before shooting. "Wet ball" drills in football are based upon the same concept. Many psychologically astute coaches turn the sprinklers on before practice and then soak the ball between plays when preparing for a football game during which rain is likely. Just as learning a physical skill takes time, learning the mental control of concentrating on the task while not reacting to external stimuli takes many hours of training.

Strategy 3: Mental Rehearsal

Using mental rehearsal to practice concentration and to learn not to react to purposely induced external distractions is another useful strategy for athletes. Obviously, athletes can only benefit from this strategy after they have learned imagery skills (see Chapter 14). Such a strategy might involve having athletes form pairs in which one member of the pair relaxes and mentally rehearses his or her sport while the other member attempts to distract the performer from the mental rehearsal. The distraction can be anything except touching. After this type of mental rehearsal, the coach or sport psychologist might have the athlete rate his or her achieved concentration on a zero-to-six scale. Thereafter the athletes reverse roles. In a study involving members of the United States national rhythmic gymnastic team (Schmid & Peper, 1982), the gymnasts practiced the preceding exercise daily for five days. On the first and fifth days, they were asked to rate their concentration while mentally rehearsing their routine and being disturbed by their partner. They reported a significant increase in their concentration from the first day to the fifth day. Through this type of exercise, athletes learn how to detach and dissociate themselves from external distractions and resulting unwanted internal stimuli while instead focusing on the task of mentally rehearsing their sport.

Just as the coach or sport psychologist can train athletes to use mental rehearsal to attain concentration, he or she can also train athletes to use mental rehearsal to regain concentration. For example, as soon as athletes realize their concentration has been disrupted by external factors such as crowd noises, they should stop themselves, take a deep breath to relax, and then bring their attention back by mentally rehearsing what they should be doing next.

The three strategies we have just outlined can be employed during regular physical practice sessions. Athletes are responsive to them and especially enjoy being involved in generating the distracting stimuli.

INTERNAL FACTORS: STRATEGIES TO STAY CENTERED

The coach or sport psychologist must train the athlete's mind to exert control because concentration inhibits distraction. Lapses in concentration invite fear and self-doubt, and the resulting worry and anxiety lead to further increases in lack of concentration, thus creating a vicious circle that ultimately leads to failure. The effect of internal factors becomes more pronounced in high-pressure situations. As an analogy, consider what would happen if someone were to ask you to walk on a board, 4 inches wide, 15 feet long, and 9 inches above the ground (like a practice beam in gymnastics). You would be able to do this without hesitation just by concentrating on the task of walking across the board. On the other hand, if the board were 60 feet off the ground you might become paralyzed by the fear of falling. Such fear inhibits performance and increases the possibility of falling. Ironically, there is no difference in the physical skill required. The difference is in your psychological response to the perceived stressful event, and as a result your attention is on trying not to fall instead of on walking across the beam. In addition, if you had previously fallen off a beam, then every time you thought about it or related the experience to someone, you might have unknowingly rehearsed all of the cognitive and motor events that led to failure.

Similar psychological processes occur during competition. For example, a field-goal kicker who normally hits his short kicks during practice may react quite differently during competition when he goes to kick a short field goal and there are only a few seconds left on the clock and his team is behind by two points. He is even more likely to fear "blowing it" if he has recently missed a kick in similar circumstances. One professional football player, while kicking under such a high-pressure situation, described the goal posts as looking as though they had narrowed to less than a foot apart. It does not take much insight to figure out what happened to his kick!

One way to improve concentration is to reduce self-doubt and resulting competitive anxiety. Arousal and cognitive control techniques appear in Chapters 13 and 15. Unless an athlete has control over internal dialogue, his or her focus of attention will not be congruent with good performance, let alone peak performance. In addition to the specific arousal and cognition techniques found in preceding chapters, in our work with performers we have found the following strategies helpful in controlling internal dialogue and facilitating concentration and performance.

Strategy 1: Attentional Cues and Triggers

In addition to using certain cues to trigger appropriate arousal, athletes can use verbal and kinesthetic cues to focus their concentration and to retrigger concentration once it has been lost. These cues can help athletes center their attention on the most appropriate focus within the task at hand, and thus help them to avoid distracting thoughts and feelings (Schmid, 1982). Generally speaking, it is best to find cues that focus on positives rather than negatives, the present (current or upcoming moment) rather than the past or future, and the process (proper form or execution) rather than the score or outcome. During a television interview on September 1, 1984, Greg Louganis, the Olympic diving champion, gave some excellent examples of effective attentional cues. He said, "I picture my dive as the judge will see it, then as I see it." In his forward three-and-one-half somersault dive, he uses the following word cues: "Relax, see the platform, spot the water, spot the water, spot the water, kick out, spot the water again." This helps him to concentrate and focus on the dive. Consequently, with his power to concentrate, he obtains a maximum result with a minimum of apparent effort. Coaches and sport psychologists should work with athletes to help them establish effective verbal and kinesthetic cues for triggering concentration. Such cues must be individualized, however. What is effective for one athlete may not be effective for another. Similarly, some athletes perform best with frequent cues and others with very few cues.

Strategy 2: Turning Failure into Success

Many athletes report that they commonly lose concentration after making a mistake. One way to deal with this problem is to train your athletes to turn failure into success. This is a cognitive habit by which athletes mentally rehearse successful performance after a failure. As soon as possible after making an error (learning is only possible when errors occur), athletes should mentally rehearse executing the same skill perfectly rather than dwell on the error. The purpose of this strategy is to avoid self-judgment and self-blame, which disrupt concentration, and to condition successful performance. Also, each time the athletes recite (verbally or mentally) a previous failure, they condition the mind to make *that* the preferred motor pattern. The verbal retelling to others or the chronic rumination on why one made a mistake is a type of global visual motor behavior rehearsal in which one is training the mind to perform the same failure behavior again. Instead of reciting the error, the athletes might ask: "What was the problem?" "How could I have performed differently in the same situation?" or "What other skills do I need?" Then the athletes can mentally rehearse the previous conditions leading to the error but now change their behavior so that they perform the skill perfectly.

The coach or sport psychologist can also encourage athletes to do the same thing after an injury. When a concerned friend asks what happened, instead of recounting the accident, the athletes should explain how they will correct the mistake and give a perfect performance the next time. After a 16-year-old downhill skier ran off the course and was seriously injured, her skiing improved remarkably when she stopped telling other people how she got injured. Whenever people asked her what happened, she described how she would now ski the race successfully. (When she felt herself going too fast, she would sink down into her skis and continue to breathe while setting the edges as she was going through a gate.) As she talked, she unconsciously rehearsed how to react successfully to the conditions under which she had previously fallen.

Strategy 3: Use of Electrodermal Feedback

The coach or sport psychologist can use electrodermal feedback devices in conjunction with peak performance training to (1) illustrate how thoughts affect the body and performance, (2) monitor physiological relaxation, (3) identify stressful components of the athletic performance during imagery rehearsal, and (4) facilitate concentration training (Peper & Schmid, 1983 – 1984). Such devices are available from biofeedback companies and businesses like Radio Shack.

An electrodermal activity (EDA) feedback unit measures and feeds back changes in skin conductance. Skin conductance measures the changes in sympathetic arousal as produced in the perspiration of the palmar surface of the hand. These changes correlate highly with the triggering of the fight or flight response. An increase in autonomic arousal usually results in an increase in skin conductivity. The feedback device reflects this change by increasing the pitch of the sound when conductivity and arousal increase and decreasing the pitch when conductivity and arousal decrease. The latency of the EDA response is about two seconds. It is important to note that EDA is a useful biofeedback tool with many athletes. However, some athletes do not respond in this physiological way. Instead, they may respond cardiovascularly, gastrointestinally, or muscularly (Peper & Williams, 1981).

Technique A: Thoughts affect body EDA feedback can be used to show that thoughts and feelings affect our performance. That is, each thought has a corresponding physiological effect—a concept that many athletes are unaware of. We often illustrate this concept in a group meeting in which one of the athletes is attached to a portable EDA feedback device. After the device is turned on, we ask the athlete to think of an anxiety-provoking event or we whisper something to him or her such as, "You just blew your routine." Each time the person thinks of an embarrassing or anxiety-provoking situation such as imagining a difficult move, the pitch of the sound increases. After demonstrating the EDA feedback device, we ask the athletes to use it to experience how their thoughts and feelings affect their physiological state. This helps them to identify and stop disturbing thoughts and feelings, as well as to restructure their self-talk from negative to positive.

Technique B: Facilitating mental rehearsal   The athletes can use small portable EDA feedback units while they mentally rehearse their routine. These small feedback units fit in the palm of the hand and the athletes receive the auditory feedback.

With the help of the EDA feedback, athletes can more rapidly identify stressful, anxiety-provoking events or cues during imagery rehearsal of their routine or athletic event. In the case of the rhythmic gymnasts we worked with, some of their subjective experiences associated with the EDA feedback occurred

> during a hoop routine: on a toss or catch that was risky
>
> just when I was about to do a toss that I frequently miss
>
> right before a toss, when I thought, "You've got to make it!" so I tensed up
>
> just before the routine began.

During a final assessment, most of the gymnasts reported that EDA feedback was helpful in learning to reduce their arousal during mental rehearsal. In fact, many of the gymnasts reported that within two weeks they had learned to inhibit the EDA feedback tone during imagery rehearsal.

Technique C: Enhancing concentration training   EDA feedback can be used to facilitate concentration learning in an enjoyable dyadic practice similar to the one described earlier (see page 276). In this practice, athletes again form pairs with one member of each pair mentally practicing the competitive routine while receiving EDA feedback. Simultaneously, the other partner attempts to distract and arouse him or her so that there will be a change in the EDA feedback signal. After two to five minutes of practice, the athletes reverse roles. Athletes enjoy this competitive practice and at the same time learn awareness of their own internal cues of anxiety, as well as strategies to control their EDA response through passive attention. Through this competitive practice, they learn the ability to detach and dissociate from external distractions and unwanted internal stimuli while focusing on the task.

Strategy 4: Increasing Focusing Skill

Focus training teaches performers to gently hold their attention on a predefined task and if the attention wanders, to gently bring the attention back. The dynamics of this strategy are similar to those of meditative practices such as Raja yoga meditation in which a person focuses on a mantra, and each time the attention wanders from the mantra, the person gently guides the attention back to the mantra. Using a similar approach, the following exercises can help performers improve their focusing skills.

Exercise A Sit quietly, close your eyes, and see how long you can focus on a single thought.

Exercise B Look at an action photo or an object from your sport. For example, if your sport is baseball, softball, or tennis, you might focus on the ball. If distracting thoughts enter your mind, bring your attention back to the ball; neither shut out the thoughts nor continue to explore the disruptive thoughts or feelings. Just gently bring the attention back to the ball.

Have athletes practice these two exercises daily for five minutes and chart their progress. Get them to time how long they can focus their attention on a single thought or on the picture. It is our experience that these home practices help athletes eliminate their concentration-breaking thoughts. Another similar exercise to practice focus training is Benson's relaxation response described in Chapter 13.

Exercise C Another training exercise for practicing focusing ability is the grid exercise (Harris & Harris, 1984). This exercise necessitates having a 10″-by-10″ block grid with each block containing a two-digit number ranging from 00 to 99 (see Figure 17.1 for a sample grid). The purpose of this exercise is to scan the grid and within a given time (usually one minute) find and put a slash through as many numbers as possible in numerical sequence starting with number 00. The same form can be used several times by starting with a number just higher than the highest number reached on the first attempt. New grids can be developed easily by simply relocating the numbers. According to Harris and Harris, athletes who have the ability to concentrate, scan, and store relevant cues will usually score in the upper 20s and into the 30s during a one-minute timed trial. Those who cannot disregard everything except the task at hand do much more poorly. After initial practice, you can increase the difficulty of the exericse by creating distractions such as loud noises and verbal harassment to see if the performer can block out everything and concentrate fully on the grid.

Besides training focusing skills, Harris and Harris report that this exercise has been used extensively in Eastern Bloc countries as a precompetition screening device for current level of concentration ability. Athletes are selected for competition on the basis of their performance.

GRID CONCENTRATION EXERCISE

Directions:
Beginning with 00, put a slash through each number in the proper sequence.

84	27	51	78	59	52	13	85	61	55
28	60	92	04	97	90	31	57	29	33
32	96	65	39	80	77	49	86	18	70
76	87	71	95	98	81	01	46	88	00
48	82	89	47	35	17	10	42	62	34
44	67	93	11	07	43	72	94	69	56
53	79	05	22	54	74	58	14	91	02
06	68	99	75	26	15	41	66	20	40
50	09	64	08	38	30	36	45	83	24
03	73	21	23	16	37	25	19	12	63

Comments:

FIGURE 17.1
Sample Grid Exercise Form for Training and Assessing the Ability to Concentrate

Strategy 5: Developing Performing Protocols

Many athletes develop the ability to tune in to their ideal performance state by associating concentration with certain performance rituals. Preset behavioral protocols should be established during warm-ups, practice, and the actual competition. These protocols should be designed to cue both the body and mind. It will take time to help each athlete identify his or her own ideal protocol. Once a definite routine is developed, it should be practiced consistently. Over time, with such practice, these protocols will serve to automatically trigger the focused concentration athletes need for good performance.

"Reactivating" such protocols is also an excellent tool for regaining concentration once it has been lost.

CONCLUSION

The ability to control thoughts, arousal, and attentional focus appears to be the common denominator in the concentration of winning competitors. For example, the Canadian gold medal winner in rhythmic gymnastics at the 1984 Olympics reported that her goal was to perform to her best ability. Specifically, she reported, "I went out to perform and not worry about my scores. In fact, it helped me more not to know my scores at all. That way I didn't have anything to worry about . . . I didn't care what anyone else was doing and I didn't want to know at all" (Botkin, 1984). She won by 0.050 of a point because she did not focus on winning. She was able to hold onto the present and to focus on her routine while the Romanian girl who had led the competition all three days lost her composure and made major faults in her last routine.

Many other athletes also report that peak performance occurred when they eliminated all thoughts about winning and their focus was instead on the process, the task at hand. This type of mental control allows athletes to be in the present. They do not ruminate over past performances, judge present performance, or anticipate future performances. To achieve consistency in performance, the athletes need to develop and practice these mental skills in special practice sessions and then practice them throughout all physical workouts. Such a mental preparedness program should follow these steps to better concentration in order to achieve peak performance:

1. Learn personal strategies to attain optimal arousal for performance.
2. Learn to practice with a positive attitude versus self-doubt and negative talk.
3. Learn what attentional focus is best.
4. Associate concentration with certain triggers such as cue words or feelings.
5. Become aware of the competitive environment and practice exercises that will help one "habituate" to it.
6. Practice dissociation.
7. Develop protocols or rituals to trigger concentration.

In summary, concentration is the ability to direct one's full attention to appropriate cues in the present task instead of being controlled by irrelevant external or internal stimuli. Most top athletes have developed their own mental strategies for doing this. These strategies are often perceived as a component of natural athletic ability. In fact, they are not innate. They are skills that the athletes acquired through regular practice of attention control training. The consistent control over one's attentional focus before and during competition is thus learned through practice, just as any difficult physical skill is learned.

REFERENCES

Botkin, M. (1984). Olympic gold makes topping oh so sweet. In *The 1984 four continents rhythmic sportive gymnastics championships program* (pp. 4–5). Indianapolis, Ind.: USGF.

Gauron, E. F. (1984). *Mental training for peak performance.* Lansing, N.Y.: Sport Science Associates.

Harris, D. V., & Harris, B. L. (1984). *The athlete's guide to sports psychology: Mental skills for physical people.* New York: Leisure Press.

Peper, E., & Schmid, A. B. (1983–1984). The use of electrodermal biofeedback for peak performance training. *Somatics,* IV (3), 16–18.

Peper, E., & Williams, E. A. (1981). *From the inside out: A self-teaching and laboratory manual for biofeedback.* New York: Plenum.

Schmid, A. B. (1982). Coach's reaction to Dr. A. B. Frederick's coaching strategies based upon tension research. In L. D. Zaichkowsky and W. E. Sime (Eds.), *Stress management for sport* (pp. 95–100). Reston, Va.: AAHPERD.

Schmid, A. B., & Peper, E. (1982). *Mental preparation for optimal performance in rhythmic gymnastics.* Paper presented at the Western Society for Physical Education of College Women Conference, Asilomar, California.

Walsh, M., & Spelman, F. (1983, June 13). Unvarnished symphonies. *Time,* p. 75.

18 Self-Hypnosis

LARS-ERIC UNESTÅHL

Örebro University, Sweden

Many years ago a rumor was spread that hypnosis was one reason for the high standard of swimming in Australia. According to the rumor, one particularly effective method was to give the swimmers the posthypnotic suggestion that they were being chased by sharks. A top American swimmer heard the rumor and went to a lay hypnotist to receive the same advantage. In the next competition he swam very fast—for one length, no more: He never turned.

This story illustrates one important point about hypnosis: the effects may be good or bad, depending on how hypnosis is used. If hypnosis is used to relax an athlete who needs more pep or to psych up an athlete who needs to relax, the results will naturally be bad.

A STATE OF MIND BUT NOT A METHOD

Hypnosis is not a method or a technique; it is a special state of mind that can be combined with all kinds of techniques and can be applied to many different areas. Its application in medicine is called medical hypnosis; in psychotherapy, hypnotherapy; in dentistry, hypnodonti, etc. Nonclinical applications comprise areas such as educational hypnosis and hypnosis in physical and creative performance. What hypnosis primarily does is augment the effects of the different techniques being used in conjunction with hypnosis, the good and appropriate ones as well as the bad and inappropriate ones. These include techniques such as imagery and affirmation statements.

Hypnosis as an Alternative State of Consciousness

Often referred to as an altered state of consciousness, hypnosis might better be called an alternative state of consciousness, which emphasizes that it is a natural alternative state of mind. Other natural alternatives are the 20 to 25 years of sleep and the 6 to 7 years of dreams that the typical person experiences throughout a lifetime. The "normal" waking state of consciousness is not a specific and consistent one. It contains many quantitative and qualitative variations. We all slip into hypnosis and hypnoticlike states now and then. In these states we are more susceptible to and more influenced by words, thoughts, and images — good as well as bad ones, others' as well as our own. Lack of control over these changes in mind state indicates considerable risk for negative programming. Thus, hypnotic treatment often contains "dehypnotizing" from problems that have their origin in earlier spontaneous hypnotic states. This points to the importance of learning to be more aware of and more in control of these variations.

Criteria for Hypnosis

To find criteria for hypnosis, it is necessary to ask the following questions:

1. What are the reported and measurable changes in a hypnotic state?
2. Which of these changes are related to hypnosis per se and which deal with other factors such as induction method, specific suggestion, and so forth?
3. Which of these changes can be removed by suggestion?

There have been many reported changes during hypnosis for physiological parameters such as heart rate, breathing, blood flow, EDA, nystagmus, pupil size, and so forth (Uneståhl, 1975). However, none of these changes reflects the hypnotic state as such. Instead, they reflect what the hypnotized person is doing or feeling.

It can also be difficult to identify hypnotic behavior, especially if "active hypnosis" is induced. On a live TV program, I asked a hypnotized patient, Karen, to "open her eyes and behave as usual, but to remain in the hypnotic state." After a while the program moderator raised a question: "But if we can't see any differences between Karen and other people, how can we then know that she is in hypnosis?" I demonstrated the differences through decreased reality testing and increased suggestibility by inducing pain detachment in Karen and the moderator. The latter did not react in spite of hearing my instructions and understanding what they meant. Karen, however, reacted very efficiently to the instructions and suggestions. I also pointed out that my presence was not at all necessary and that Karen could do the same thing on her own, which she also demonstrated.

D Mode and A Mode

In recent years hypnosis has been popularly defined as a "hemispheric shift," an activation of the right hemisphere and a corresponding deactivation of the left hemisphere of the brain. This definition is easy to grasp and make sense of because the hypnotic state is characterized by changes in perception (time and space), thought processes (less analysis, logic, and reality testing and more "trance logic," creativity, and suggestibility), other forms of expression (images instead of words), and other ways of processing information (parallel or simultaneous processing instead of linear processing). The cerebral location of many human functions is still questionable, so it is too early to equate hypnosis with a hemispheric shift. Instead it may be more relevant to speak about two distinct and different modes of consciousness—the D-dominant mode and the A-alternative mode. See Figure 18.1 for specific characteristics of these two modes of consciousness.

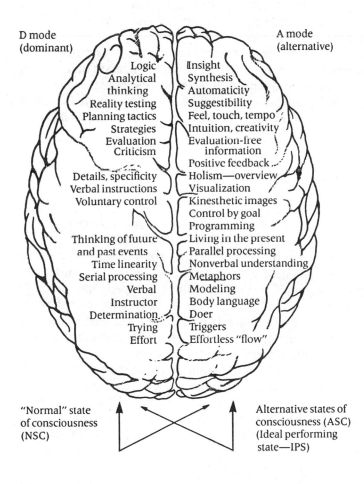

D mode
(dominant)

A mode
(alternative)

D mode	A mode
Logic	Insight
Analytical thinking	Synthesis
	Automaticity
Reality testing	Suggestibility
Planning tactics	Feel, touch, tempo
Strategies	Intuition, creativity
Evaluation	Evaluation-free information
Criticism	
	Positive feedback
Details, specificity	Holism—overview
Verbal instructions	Visualization
Voluntary control	Kinesthetic images
	Control by goal
	Programming
Thinking of future and past events	Living in the present
	Parallel processing
Time linearity	Nonverbal understanding
Serial processing	Metaphors
Verbal	Modeling
Instructor	Body language
Determination	Doer
Trying	Triggers
Effort	Effortless "flow"

"Normal" state
of consciousness
(NSC)

Alternative states of
consciousness (ASC)
(Ideal performing
state—IPS)

FIGURE 18.1
Modes of Consciousness and Sport

The A Mode and the Ideal Performance State

The striking similarities between the ideal performance state (IPS) — when we perform at our best — and a hypnotic state have been described in earlier publications (Uneståhl, 1983). Good performance seems to imply changes in thinking (less paralysis by analysis), memory (amnesia), perception (slow motion, enlargement of objects), dissociation (pain detachment), and information processes (parallel processing) in very much the same way as hypnosis does. This ideal state, where self-imposed limitations are momentarily forgotten, has various nicknames. A basketball player talks about a "hot night," a tennis player about "playing out of his head." An Australian football player is reaching for the "purple patch," and Jimmy Connors is trying to "go into the tunnel."

The frequency of this trance state varies among sports and athletes. It seems to be somewhat related to the degree of automatization of the sport. However, a common opinion among athletes is that IPS appears too seldom. Another concern among athletes is that most of them cannot predict when IPS will come. Thus, one purpose of self-hypnotic training is to increase personal control over IPS.

WHO IS HYPNOTIZABLE?

Hundreds of experiments have investigated the relation between interpersonal variations in hypnotic depth and factors such as age, sex, IQ, personality traits, attitudes, suggestibility scores, etc. The results, in general, have been both confusing and contradictory. There are at least two possible explanations for this: (1) There exist different operational definitions of hypnotic depth — for example, subjective ratings of experienced depth or number of passed tasks on a standardized scale of hypnotic susceptibility. (2) A person's hypnotic susceptibility is often measured during the first hypnotic session. This means that the result obtained is often far from the person's maximal hypnotic susceptibility.

Systematic and long-term hypnotic training could provide substantial quantitative and qualitative improvements in hypnotic capacity. Thus, there actually may be no ultimate differences in people's hypnotic susceptibility as such. The differences may be only in the time it takes to learn to use hypnotic skills in such a way that each person reaches effective self-control and self-mastery.

ALL HYPNOSIS IS SELF-HYPNOSIS

Questions such as "Could you hypnotize me?" should be answered in the following way: "No, there is only one person who could do that and that is you, yourself. The only thing I could do is to teach you the way. I cannot give you anything that you do not already have. My role is to be the teacher, an instructor who shows you the way, or various ways, to enter into a hypnotic state. It is your trance, not mine, and the sooner you can take over completely, the better.''

The popular notion that hypnosis implies a decrease of the subject's control and an increase in control from some external source derives from misinterpretations of hypnotic phenomena. Stage hypnosis is, unfortunately, still legally permitted in some countries, including the United States, and such shows contribute to misunderstandings. For example, a hypnotized subject gets instructions that his hands are glued together and that he cannot separate them. He uses all his voluntary effort, but in vain; his hands are inseparable. It is understandable that he, as well as the audience, gets the impression that the hypnotist has the control. What is really happening is that the subject, by accepting the instruction, creates an image of his hands being glued together. This image, in combination with the hypnotic state, can be more effective than his voluntary effort.

Thus, the statement that all hypnosis is self-hypnosis requires two qualifiers to be true. A person must know (1) that *he or she* has the control and (2) *how* to take control.

Learning by Effortless Receiving

Doing and trying, effort and overmotivation make it more difficult to enter a hypnotic state. The same is true of going to sleep, concentrating, relaxing, and so forth. The same is often true of trying to improve sport performance even though coaches and athletes often relate competitive sport to effort, struggle, and trying harder. Self-hypnosis is easier to learn if the subject can concentrate on the process instead of having to provide his or her own instructions. Self-instructions are related to reality testing and planning functions and tend to disturb the hypnotic process (the experiencing ego).

Different Learning Paths

Learning self-hypnosis is enhanced by instructions from outside. This does not mean, however, that someone else has to be physically present. Experiments by Unestâhl (1973) and others have shown that no differences in hypnotic depth (measured with standardized tests) could be found between hypnotic induction given by a physically present hypnotizer compared with induction by means of a tape recorder.

Different ways of learning self-hypnosis can be distributed along two axes, degree of outside guidance and degree of obtained self-control, as shown in Figure 18.2 (Unestâhl, 1982).

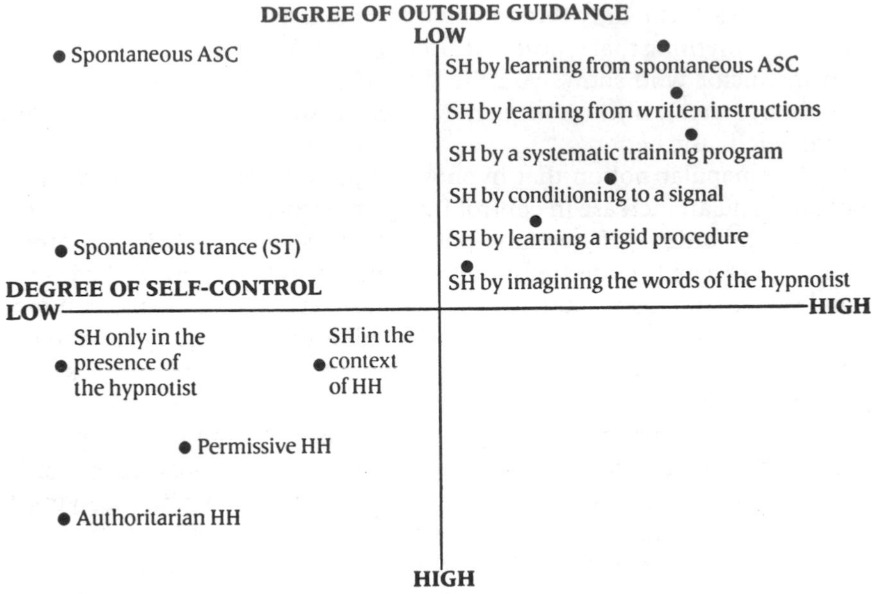

DEGREE OF OUTSIDE GUIDANCE
LOW

● Spontaneous ASC   ●
                                                     SH by learning from spontaneous ASC
                                                                 ●
                                                     SH by learning from written instructions
                                                                       ●
                                                     SH by a systematic training program
                                                             ●
                                                     SH by conditioning to a signal
                                                         ●
● Spontaneous trance (ST)   SH by learning a rigid procedure

DEGREE OF SELF-CONTROL   ●
LOW——**HIGH**
                                                     SH by imagining the words of the hypnotist

    SH only in the   SH in the
  ● presence of   ● context
    the hypnotist   of HH

           ● Permissive HH

  ● Authoritarian HH

                              HIGH

FIGURE 18.2
Self-Hypnosis (SH)

SELF-HYPNOSIS THROUGH PROFESSIONAL AND PERSONAL HELP

Hypnotic treatment should be combined with teaching the athlete self-hypnosis. This may start during the first session when a qualified professional teaches the athlete to wake up. Knowing how to terminate the hypnotic trance creates a feeling of security and self-control. A natural continuation of this is to hand over the induction to the athlete after only a few sessions, sessions in which the athlete has learned the "teacher's" way of inducing hypnosis. As a transition to self-instruction and self-pacing, the athlete may prefer to imagine the teacher's being there, telling him or her the same words as before.

Another way for the teacher or therapist to turn over control to the athlete is to condition the induction to a signal or trigger and then hand over the signal to the athlete. When this works efficiently, the athlete can trigger the whole induction process by just activating the signal.

The next step consists of teaching the athlete to combine the self-hypnotic state with positive and effective techniques.

SELF-HYPNOSIS THROUGH SYSTEMATIC SELF-TRAINING: INNER MENTAL TRAINING

One procedure for learning self-hypnosis was developed by the author and is called inner mental training (IMT) (Uneståhl, 1979, 1982). In this procedure, self-hypnosis is learned by regular and systematic self-training that consists of the steps outlined in Figure 18.3. The procedure requires training five days a week, with a training session lasting an average of about 15 minutes. Tape recordings provide the necessary instruction.

In the first training program, the athlete's perception is directed to the differences between tension and relaxation. In muscle after muscle, contraction is induced, maintained, and released in order to obtain the contrasting effect of physical relaxation. By concentrating on the feelings of local muscle tension release, the athlete (trainee) can gradually experience and learn the meaning and content of total body relaxation. (See Chapter 13 for a similar progressive relaxation exercise.) Each successive program starts with a prolonged contraction of the left fist in conjunction with a deep inhalation and breath hold, followed by exhalation and relaxation. This will later act as a physical trigger to increase the induction spread of the relaxation process.

Along with the perception of the differences between tension and absence of tension due to the muscular contractions and release, the athlete's attention is also directed to other dimensions in the state of relaxation that accompanies exhalation. These are associated psychological states such as calmness, security, confidence, certitude, and comfort that often accompany the warm, heavy sensations of physical relaxation. The exhalation is later used as another trigger to induce relaxation and the psychological states that have been associated with it.

The second week of training is also directed to physical relaxation but in an abbreviated form. The athlete induces the body to relax simply by thinking of the body parts in a progressive order. The tape recording directs the athlete's attention to the feelings that accompany the physical relaxation. The induced state of relaxation is facilitated both through the effects of practice and by the suggestions given on the audiotapes. Soft music especially composed for the relaxation, provides a supporting background to the athlete's sense of physical and mental well-being.

Mental Relaxation

By using the triggers learned and conditioned during the first two weeks, the athlete quickly induces and deepens the state of physical relaxation. The attention of the athlete trainee is then directed more to the psychological

	TRAINING CONTENT	SPECIFIC PROGRAM	WEEK
IMT-I SKILL ACQUISITION	Psychotonic training	Muscular relaxation (1)	1
		Muscular relaxation (2)	2
	Self-hypnosis	Mental relaxation (1)	3
		Mental relaxation (2)	4
	Activation	Activation training	5
	Concentration	Meditation	6
		Attention release	7
		Dissociation, detachment	8
IMT-II MOTIVATION TRAINING	Goal setting	Goal-awareness inventory	9
		Goal-analysis selection	10
		Goal-formulation contracts	11
	Goal programming	Ideomotor training	12
		Career goals	13
IMT-III APPLIED MENTAL TRAINING	Problem solving	Reconditioning	14
		Systematic desensitization	15
		Thought stopping	16
	Attitude training	Cognitive restructuring	17
		Autonomic restructuring	18
		Mastery training	19
		Self-confidence training	20

A. CAREER TRAINING

INNER MENTAL PREPARATION

B. **COMPETITIVE PREPARATION**
- Model training
- Preseasonal training
- Precompetitive rehearsal
- Countdown preparation
- Competitive strategies

C. **SPECIFIC APPLICATIONS**
- Information retrieval
- Group dynamics
- Rehabilitation after injuries

FIGURE 18.3
Inner Mental Training (IMT)

effects of the relaxation by means of reassuring verbal cues such as "calm," "certain," "comfortable," and so forth. The use of images of descending staircases, sinking, and so on also induce and deepen the self-hypnotic state. The athlete notices a melting of barriers between mind, body, and surroundings, and feelings of liberation, floating, and gliding away from time and space are emphasized.

The induced self-hypnotic state is anchored to an "inner mental room," an enticing image of a warm, comfortable inner room that provides the athlete trainee with an inner locale in which to carry out the rest of the mental training procedures.

During the fourth week of training, the athlete attains the self-hypnotic state with increased speed and depth. The inner mental room is now equipped with a screen, a blackboard, and an energy machine to be used respectively for mental rehearsal, self-suggestions, and activation control. Thus, during this week the self-hypnotic state is combined with the special techniques (images, suggestions) that the athlete will use for self-control and self-programming. Toward the end of the session, the athlete uses the blackboard to decide how he or she wants to feel upon awakening.

Concentration and Disassociation Training

Hypnosis is sometimes defined as a state of increased concentration, sometimes as a state of increased disassociation. It may seem as though these definitions are contradictory. In reality, however, they represent two sides of the same coin. We can view concentration as a more intense attention to a smaller number of stimuli. Relevant stimuli may come from a narrow arc of attention (focusing) or from a broad area (defocusing). (See Chapter 16 for further discussion of the specific sport skills and situations in which a narrow or broad focus of attention is considered desirable.) Thus, in the sixth to the eighth week of training, the self-hypnotic state is used to train concentration. The increased concentration skill will, in turn, have an enhancing effect on the depth and the quality of the self-hypnotic state.

Because concentration may be looked upon as a ratio between attention to a signal (relevant stimulus) and attention to noise (irrelevant stimulus), the training combines the increase of signal values (attention release) with decreased noise values (disassociation training). In the latter the induction of self-hypnosis is attempted in nonprotected environments in which distractions occur. The training is carried out in noisy situations, with other people watching, or in uncomfortable body positions. The training is intended to provide the trainee with experiences in which he or she can obtain and maintain physical and mental self-control in every possible environment.

Self-Control

Research on learned helplessness has shown the devastating effects of lack of control. To increase the athlete's feeling of self-control, alternative systems of control are developed during the training. These systems, which are alternatives to the voluntary control related to effort and struggle, are based on self-hypnosis.

Trigger control   As an example of situations in which feelings of helplessness easily occur, consider the situation of trying to go to sleep. Any conscious effort and struggle to sleep keeps us awake longer. Sleep is a passive process that will come sooner or later whether we want it to or not. Thus, if we are distracted from active attempts to go to sleep, the onset of sleep is more likely to occur. The distraction is normally induced by doing something else. Hundreds of distraction methods exist for enhancing the onset of sleep. In addition to distraction, we can also use what is known as the trigger effect. There already exists a connection in our mind between what we are doing and the onset of sleep. Our method, whatever it is, "triggers" the sleep process.

Triggers are effective means of inducing such passive processes as sleep, relaxation, concentration, hypnosis, emotions, and so forth. Before the attention release training (week 7), the athlete chooses a trigger that is a natural part of his or her normal preparation for a competition. For example, the trigger might be placing the feet in a certain position, gripping the club, or adjusting the skis before going downhill. During self-hypnosis this trigger is conditioned to the athlete's formal experience of total concentration. This means that the athlete does not have to do anything different before competition. He or she can follow his or her normal routines, but they will trigger a better concentration.

A bowler described the effect like this: "When I stick my fingers into the ball [his trigger], I can notice how the lights in the room go down. After some seconds there exists only one light corridor, which is my own alley with the marks and the pins. This lasts until the ball hits the pins. Then the light comes back and I become aware of what's happening on the other alleys. This gives me a very good feeling of control. I can relax and rest between my hits because I know that as soon as I stick my fingers into the ball, the total concentration will be there."

Imagery control   Diametrically opposed to expending effort and "conscious determination" are trying to relax and trying to go to sleep. In order to experience the effects of these activities on performance, you might have your athletes perform the following two experiments:

1. Measure a distance of 60 to 100 meters. Then run it twice under two sets of conditions: First, try as hard as you can. Consciously push yourself all the way, every step, from the start to the finish so that you use every ounce of strength and speed that you have. The second time start by deciding that you are going to have a good run. In your mind, picture yourself running very fast. While your body is running, watch how it flies over the ground easily, lightly and quickly. You have now told your body what you want it to do, so leave the rest to your body.

2. Try to bend another person's arm at the elbow while this person uses all of his or her strength to prevent you from bending the elbow. The person is facing you with the arm extended, palm up, and the back of the wrist resting on your shoulder. Next ask the other person to make an image of his or her arm as unbendable. One way is to imagine the arm as an iron bar that extends into the wall. Perform the experiment again, and compare how much of your effort it takes to bend the arm in the first and second situations.

The effects of images will increase if they are combined with a self-hypnotic state. In hypnosis athletes were asked to imagine their arm as an iron bar. They were then asked to try as hard as possible to bend *their own* arm; they could not do it. Physiological data indicated that there was considerable muscle activity in the biceps and triceps, indicating that the athletes expended a high degree of effort. However, the image of the iron bar was so strong that the voluntary effort was not enough to bend the arm. Appropriate use of imagery, therefore, is one powerful tool for controlling concentration.

Motivation Training

A study of 5,500 widows in England showed a 45% increase in the mortality rate within six months after a husband's death compared with a control group in the same age bracket. When life motivation goes down, the rates of illness and mortality seem to increase. Motivation is like both the engine and the wheel on a car. It gives energy and force as well as direction. Training in motivation ought to consist of two parts: goal setting and goal programming (weeks 9–13 in IMT, as shown in Figure 18.3). The first part is an analytical one related to the D mode, whereas the integration of goals relates to the A mode.

Unfortunately, many "motivators" work only with the goal-setting part. This may lead to goal fixation, looking at goals as a burden instead of a source of power. If the goals are not integrated in such a way that we can become more process oriented, enjoying the route to the goals, they can become another stress factor in life. The self-hypnotic state facilitates the effective programming and integration of short-term, long-term, and life goals. (More specific goal-setting guidelines appear in Chapter 10.)

Problem Solving

The earlier section on concentration and dissociation training illustrated the power of images. The only problem is that negative images have as powerful an effect on the body as do positive images. Negative images and problem images can become so effective that voluntary effort and struggle are inadequate and insufficient. For example, a soccer team in the first division had not lost on its home field for one year. The problem was that the team had not won on an away field for one and a half years! In spite of being the same team made up of the same players, the athletes could not use their resources on an away field. They were highly motivated and struggled hard, but as long as they had the image of bad play on an away field they could not win.

Situation-related problems like the preceding one are very common, not only in sport but also in everyday life. They can take different forms, including impaired performance and a conditioned negative emotion. For example, more than 50% of any given population typically shows phobic reactions when they have to speak in public. Weeks 14 – 16 of IMT address problem-solving concerns.

Neutralizing Images

Phobic reactions, uncontrollable fear in nondangerous situations, illustrate another problem in the way of increased self-control. Imagery control requires control of the content of images. The ability to think positive decreases if we are afraid of various negative alternatives. Thoughts such as "This must not happen" or "I'm afraid of what could happen" will catch other thoughts like a magnet. It seems that the emotional content of various images tends to direct control. Because negative emotions are often stronger than positive ones, we have a tendency to imagine fearful outcomes.

Neutralizing images are a requisite for increased control. We can neutralize images by means of various cognitive strategies or by learning procedures such as systematic desensitization. With systematic desensitization, some relaxation technique such as progressive relaxation or self-hypnosis is used to induce and maintain feelings of calmness, safety, and security while the mind is directed to the fearful images. (See Chapter 15 for cognitive strategies that can prove useful in neutralizing images.)

Attitude Training

One of my books (Uneståhl, 1983) contains a chapter about a girl born with one arm. She developed an attitude in life that is in accord with the title of the chapter: "Everything Is Possible." She never saw having one arm as a handicap. She participated in all kinds of activities, including competitive sport. Her friends tried to teach her that competition is a fight between people and, therefore, she should not have higher goals than qualifying for the school gymnastics team. The girl, however, chose to define competition as a fight between herself and her goals — goals that she set and controlled, goals related to her own improvements. By means of a combination of such goals and her general attitude toward herself and the world, the girl ended up in second place in two of the NCAA's four gymnastic events. No one had thought it was possible for a one-armed person to beat the American elite in such a sport as gymnastics.

Many of the failures, shortcomings, and limitations that we face in life have to do with self-imposed mental limitations that we often develop early in life. Self-imposed mental limitations are a part of an athlete's self-image as well as his or her goal setting and goal programming. One of the main characteristics of the hypnotic state is a loss or decrease in reality testing. This opens up the possibility of changing negative parts of the perceived reality to positive ones. Outside of hypnosis it is considerably more difficult to "take" someone into better confidence. The logical arguments will be resisted by the individual athlete's frame of reference and by his or her sense of reality testing. In an hypnotic state, the battery of positive and ego-strengthening suggestions and images will be accepted and integrated. Thus, the use of self-hypnosis for confidence building, ego strengthening, and assertiveness training can be very important for an athlete. Weeks 17–20 in IMT are spent practicing various techniques that have proved helpful in attitude training.

Another part of attitude training is mastery training. A good athlete will experience mistakes but not failure. Both coaches and athletes want to develop an attitude toward sport and life in which mistakes are seen as learning opportunities to develop, improve, and grow. Everything that happens, if used appropriately, can be regarded as learning for the future.

Because there are as many realities as people in the world, it is impossible to find criteria for true or false realities. It is easier to agree on criteria for "better realities." I define a better reality as a reality which helps the individual to act, react, perform, and function better. Athletes and coaches can learn such reinterpretation or retraining in a quicker and more efficient way through self-hypnosis because the decreased reality testing makes such retraining possible.

Life Training

The 20-week inner mental training procedure we have been examining is designed to be done just once in a lifetime. The total amount of training time does not exceed 25 hours. However, because the nature of the training (lying down instead of moving around) differs from physical training, it takes a motivated and receptive mind to master the training.

The training can be continuous across the 20-week time frame, or it can be divided into various steps. The first step, the basic mental training, can begin with children as young as five years of age. In comparison with an adult, a child naturally has more of the basic qualities that the basic training is designed to teach. A child is more relaxed, has more imaginative capability and involvement, and is more process oriented. Unfortunately, we lose many of those positive childlike qualities when we grow older. Instead of having to learn these again as an adult, early training can help people maintain and preserve childlike skills. These ideas have led to a project to introduce basic mental training into the Swedish school system (Setterlind & Uneståhl, 1981), a project that has been so successful that Sweden is the first country to include relaxation in the curriculum at all schools.

Mental Preparation

Many of the learned skills in inner mental preparation (see the lower portion of Figure 18.3) will affect performance in a spontaneous and natural way. However, there are also procedures for obtaining additional control over performance situations. As shown in the figure, inner mental preparation (IMP) consists of the following parts:

1. Model training (the psychological and qualitative part of every training session)
2. Mental preparation for the coming season
3. Long-term competitive preparation
4. Countdown preparation
5. Competitive strategies (preplanned and pretrained strategies to be used, if needed, during competition)

Many of the training components are designed to induce and maintain the ideal performing feeling (IPF). See Figure 18.4. By hypnotic conditioning of past good experiences to future situations, the IPF will be "waiting" when the athlete comes to the competition.

The purpose of some of the preceding preparatory procedures is to translate external images into internal ones — to start with visual rehearsal

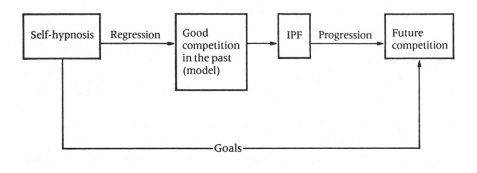

FIGURE 18.4
Technique for Inducing and Maintaining the Ideal Performing Feeling (IPF)

and then go into kinesthetic feelings. Many of the competitive strategies have the purpose of maintaining IPF by immunization to potentially disturbing elements in the competitive environment. Strategies to cope with mistakes and unwanted or unexpected elements play an important role here.

CONCLUSION

Many systematic programs can be used to facilitate the mental training of athletes. Inner mental training includes the components of the other programs plus the special feature of self-hypnosis. Self-hypnosis can help make the effects of the specific techniques used in mental training even more powerful. Although IMT can be used by any athlete under the supervision of a coach or sport psychologist, it is essential that all parties realize that hypnosis is merely a natural, alternative state of mind or consciousness that every athlete is capable of learning to control.

The effects of IMT have been evaluated in laboratory and field settings. The subjects have come from diverse backgrounds and include athletes, artists, executives, schoolchildren, and cancer patients. The reported results are excellent. The effects of IMT increase with training and are clearest and most evident after a long, regular training period. At this time the changes have been integrated in such a manner that they have become a natural and automatized way of thinking, feeling, and behaving.

Peak performance is not only a goal for athletes but for every person seeking to reach his or her potential in life. Thus, the general goal of IMT is to help athletes, coaches, sport psychologists, and others achieve self-control and excellence in sport and life.

REFERENCES

Setterlind, S., & Uneståhl, L. -E. (1981). *Introducing relaxation in Swedish schools.* Örebro, Sweden: Veje.

Uneståhl, L. -E. (1973). *Hypnosis and posthypnotic suggestions.* Örebro, Sweden: Veje.

Uneståhl, L. -E. (Ed.) (1975). *Hypnosis in the seventies.* Örebro, Sweden: Veje.

Uneståhl, L. -E. (1979). *Självkontroll genom mental träning (Inner control by mental training).* Örebro, Sweden: Veje.

Uneståhl, L. -E. (1982). *Hypnos i teori och praktik (Hypnosis in theory and practice).* Örebro, Sweden: Veje.

Uneståhl, L. -E. (1982). Inner mental training for sport. In J. Salmela, J. Partington, & T. Orlick (Eds.) *Sport learning.* Ottawa, Ontario, Canada: Coaching Association of Canada.

Uneståhl, L. -E. (Ed.) (1983). *The mental aspects of gymnastics.* Örebro, Sweden: Veje.

19 Integrating and Implementing a Psychological Skills Training Program

JEAN M. WILLIAMS

University of Arizona

The authors of Chapters 9 through 18 have discussed peak performance characteristics, psychological theory, and exercises for training specific psychological skills. Many questions still remain. How old and skillful should athletes be before beginning psychological skills training? Who should conduct the training program — the sport psychologist or the coach? Is there an ideal time during the year for implementing a psychological skills training program? How much time is needed for psychological skills training? What specific components should be incorporated in training, and how should those components be sequenced and integrated? Are there any general guidelines for teaching psychological knowledge and training exercises other than those already provided in earlier chapters? What ethical considerations should the person implementing the program be aware of? In this chapter we address these questions and others, but first we must recognize serious limitations in our ability to offer definitive answers.

Most comprehensive mental training programs stress the development of comparable psychological skills. However, there is no one way to integrate all of the components; nor is there agreement on how much time should be spent on the various components. There is not even a consensus about what techniques are best for achieving certain objectives. Circumstances and time do not always permit the implementation of a comprehensive mental training program and thus make it necessary to plan an abbreviated program. What should be done in this type of situation is even more uncertain.

Unfortunately, there are no ready-made solutions to questions of how coaches and sport psychologists can integrate and implement a psychological skills training program. The data base available is very limited, and there are few references on the subject. Nonetheless, if the training program is to be effective, strategies for putting all of the different components into place

301

must be planned. In this chapter we offer some suggestions and practical pointers for implementing mental skills training and for integrating various psychological skill components. Unless otherwise noted, these guidelines are the same for either the coach or sport psychologist. We caution you to view these recommendations only as suggested guidelines. They are not firmly established principles that have arisen from an extensive research base, and they have not been empirically tested over time.

WHO WILL BENEFIT FROM PSYCHOLOGICAL SKILLS TRAINING

Many coaches and athletes misunderstand peak performance sport psychology. They think mental training strategies are only applicable to elite athletes or that these techniques can only fine-tune the performance of the already skilled. In actuality, mental skills training can be beneficial for people of any skill level and age-group. If beginning athletes are taught to set realistic goals, increase self-confidence, visualize success, react constructively to mistakes and failure, and handle the pressure of competition, surely we can expect their performance and personal development to progress faster than the performance and development of athletes who fail to receive similar mental training. Special adjustments may be needed for very young athletes, such as fewer goals, shorter training sessions, and simpler verbal instruction, but these athletes will still benefit from mental skills training provided they are interested in receiving it. Regardless of the age or skill level of the athletes, the individuals who will benefit the most from the training are probably those who have the weakest psychological skills, that is, athletes lacking in confidence and emotional control.

The ideal time for initially implementing training may even be when individuals are just beginning to participate in sport. As any experienced teacher or coach knows, it is far easier to develop proper physical technique in a beginner than it is to modify poor technique in a more experienced athlete. Although never tested, the same phenomenon may be true for psychological skills. Furthermore, early implementation assures the laying of a psychological skills foundation that will facilitate future achievement of full athletic potential, enjoyment, and benefit.

WHO SHOULD CONDUCT THE PSYCHOLOGICAL SKILLS TRAINING PROGRAM

Ideally, a psychological skills training program should be planned, implemented, and supervised by a qualified consulting sport psychologist. The sport psychologist has the advantage of having more extensive special training and experience than the coach. Also, athletes may be more open in discussing difficulties with the psychological aspects of play because the sport psychologist does not sit in judgment regarding who stays on the team and who gets to play. Even though it is desirable to have a sport psychologist administer the program, this is rarely feasible except perhaps at the highest levels of competition. This does not mean that psychological skills development should be reserved only for an elite setting. The basic premise of this book is that it is also the responsibility of the coach to provide mental skills training. The coach can be one of the most effective people in providing training and reinforcing optimal psychological states; after all, who knows the athletes better and who works more closely with them? Thus, there are advantages to having mental skills training provided by the consulting sport psychologist or the coach.

When the mental training program is to be implemented by a sport psychologist, the selection of that person is critical. Who is qualified to be a sport psychologist? Unfortunately, there are no clearly identified standards for the training and certification of a sport psychologist (see Chapter 1 for a more thorough discussion of this issue). Until such time as there are established standards, the following questions may help coaches decide whether they would like a particular individual to work with their team. What is the person's educational background? That is, has he or she had specific training in psychology or counseling and the sport sciences, particularly sport psychology? What personal experience has the person had in athletics and working with athletes in sport psychology? Does the person have references from other people or teams with whom he or she has worked? How does the person view his or her role with the team? Will the person's focus be on dealing with personal, emotional problems or teaching mental skills for enhancing performance? How does the person plan to determine what needs to be done? How much time would he or she like to work with the athletes?

If a sport psychologist conducts the program, we recommend that the coach, or coaching staff, attend at least most of the initial group training sessions. There are a number of reasons for this recommendation. First, the coach's presence tells the athletes that he or she thinks the sessions are important. Second, the sport psychologist will not be present during most of the physical practices and competitions; therefore, a knowledgable coach can be a key person in assuring the effectiveness of mental skills training by seeing that appropriate application of such training occurs. Ideally, the sport psychologist and coach should have special meetings to discuss ways for the coach to apply and reinforce whatever the sport psychologist emphasizes in mental skills training sessions. Third, misunderstandings regarding what the sport psychologist is doing will not occur because the coach will know exactly what is happening and will be providing feedback regarding what he or she perceives needs to be done.

WHEN TO IMPLEMENT A PSYCHOLOGICAL SKILLS TRAINING PROGRAM

The least desirable time to implement a psychological skills program is after the competitive season has started and there is concern because athletes are doing poorly. At this time mental training usually amounts to no more than a quick-fix, Band-Aid approach and consequently is rarely, if ever, effective. Even if there are benefits, the influence is probably only that of a short-term placebo — the athlete expects the psychological intervention to improve performance, and therefore it does. As soon as the novelty wears off, the athlete usually slips back into old ways of thinking, feeling, and performing. Another reason for not beginning a mental skills training program well into the competitive season is that making athletes aware of psychological aspects of competition when there is not sufficient time to provide for learning the skills needed to control the mental game can actually be harmful. For these reasons, many sport psychologists believe that the best time to initially implement psychological skills training is during the off-season or preseason. There is more time to learn the skills, and it is easier to try new ideas because this is the time of year when athletes are not so pressured.

WHEN TO PRACTICE PSYCHOLOGICAL SKILLS

The rudiments of most psychological skills should first be taught and systematically practiced during special training sessions. The first or last 15 to 30 minutes of practice is often a good time for training. The content of the particular session will determine whether it is better held at the beginning or end of practice (see earlier chapters for suggestions on which training exercises are better practiced before or after physical workouts). Homework assignments also can be given; but unless the athletes are self-directed, it is better to have most mental training practice occur under someone's supervision.

As soon as possible, the psychological skills practice should be integrated with physical skills practice. When integrating the two, the rehearsal of mental skills should have a performance-specific focus. For example, once athletes have learned the skill of relaxation and recognizing tension, they should be instructed while performing to scan their muscles for harmful tension and to practice appropriate differential relaxation. Specific performance times should be identified — for example, always scan and relax before pitching, shooting a free throw, serving a tennis ball, or taking a shot in golf. Once relaxation skills have been effectively integrated into physical workouts, they should be tried during simulated or practice competition and later during actual competition. The same stepwise building of competence should occur for introducing and practicing other mental skills such as imagery and concentration.

This progressive method of practice is psychologically sound from a learning standpoint because it allows the athletes to gain knowledge and competence in using each mental skill as environmental demands slowly become more variable, challenging, and applicable. The ultimate goal is for the practice of mental skills to become such an integral part of all physical practices that the training program does not appear to be something extra. This type of systematic, consistent practice of mental skills is likely to achieve lasting optimal results rather than short-term placebo effects.

HOW MUCH TIME SHOULD BE SPENT IN MENTAL TRAINING

By now it should be obvious that the time needed for practicing mental skills varies according to what is being practiced and how well it is learned. If a new mental skill is being introduced, special 15- to 30-minute training sessions three to five days per week may be needed. Some weeks no special sessions are needed because all practice can occur along with physical workouts. The more proficient athletes become, the fewer the special training sessions. However, special sessions still may be advisable for individual athletes who are experiencing difficulty in learning the mental skills. Even when separate time is not being designated solely for mental training, the coaching staff or sport psychologist needs to provide verbal reminders for integrating mental skills practice with physical skills practice, as well as appropriate reinforcement for observance or lack of observance of the mental side of performance.

The time frame we have just recommended may not be desirable if a sport psychologist is implementing the training, particularly when the sport psychologist has to spend time traveling to reach the team. Under such circumstances, fewer and longer mental training sessions are usually held. Most of these should be group sessions in order to optimize the use of the psychologist's time. It is particularly critical that athletes be assigned training exercises to practice between sessions led by the sport psychologist. Successively longer intervals should be scheduled between psychologist-led sessions to allow for mastery and absorption of the techniques and coping strategies. The same stepwise building of competence that we described earlier should be observed here.

The "traveling" sport psychologist must design practice exercises in such a way that maximum feedback occurs from participation and that adherence to training is likely to occur. In the absence of the sport psychologist, the coach can play a major role in ensuring compliance and feedback if he or she assumes responsibility for personally conducting the training exercises or at least provides the time for athletes to practice. If this is not possible, the coach should remind athletes of their homework assignments and briefly discuss the athletes' reactions to the exercises once the homework has been completed.

When can athletes stop mental skills training? In the truest sense, mental skills training continues as long as athletes participate in sport. In this sense, mental skills are no different from physical skills. Retention will not occur without continued practice. Athletes who during physical practice allow their concentration to be sloppy, their mental attitude to be negative, or their arousal level to be too high or low invariably find the same behaviors occurring during competition.

If athletes never stop mental skills training, what is the ideal length of time for their first exposure to a "formal" mental skills training program? Most sport psychologists would recommend an average of between three and six months. The specific sport, time available, existing mental skills, and commitment of individuals are all factors that should be considered in determining actual length of time.

ASSESSING PSYCHOLOGICAL NEEDS

The first step in planning any mental skills training program should be to determine psychological skill objectives. A needs assessment helps reveal those psychological skills that are deficient or appear to be having the most adverse effect on performance and personal satisfaction. If a sport psychologist is planning the program, it is essential that the coach be thoroughly involved in the needs assessment because he or she is more likely to know a team's mental strengths and weaknesses. There is also merit in involving the athletes, particularly if they are relatively mature and experienced. When possible, the sport psychologist should observe practices or competition. Training should be based upon the results of the assessments. For example, quite different psychological needs would probably be perceived for a team with a long history of losing compared to a team that climbed to the top and was currently experiencing the pressure of trying to maintain number-one status. The person working with the losing team might determine that primary emphasis should be on developing a positive mental attitude. In such a case, systematic planning and strategies might be directed at getting the athletes to stop feeling like losers and begin thinking and feeling like they could win. Techniques for building confidence, monitoring and replacing self-defeating talk, and setting realistic goals might prove quite beneficial. On the other hand, the coach or sport psychologist working with the highly successful team might perceive a primary need to develop skills for regulating arousal and maintaining concentration. Techniques would need to be planned for coping with the stress of being expected to win consistently, even when playing against excellent competitors who are always up for the defending champions, and for keeping sufficiently energized and focused in concentration when playing against clearly inferior competitors. An obvious implication of this needs assessment guideline is that the coach should be wary of anyone, or any product, that presents a "canned" mental training program that does not provide for the specific needs of a given group of athletes. Although such a program may be better than nothing, optimal benefits for the investment in time will only come from training designed to meet the specific needs, maturation, and experience of the given group. This also means that the beginning sport psychologist should not attempt to deliver the same mental skills training to all of the different groups and individuals with whom he or she initially works.

DETERMINING WHAT SKILLS TO INCLUDE AND HOW TO SEQUENCE THOSE SKILLS

Once the assessment is complete and all needed psychological skills have been listed, the coach or sport psychologist must decide how many of these skills to emphasize. This decision should be based upon when the program is first being implemented (e.g., preseason, practice season, competitive season) and how much time the athletes and coach are willing to devote to mental skills training. Several questions are pertinent at this point: How much practice time will be given up on the average each week for mental skills training? How many weeks of practice are available? Will there still be time to practice mental skills after the competitive season starts, or after the first couple of losses? How interested are the athletes in receiving mental skills training? The answers to these questions will help provide a realistic perspective on the commitment to mental skills training and the time available for accomplishing psychological skill objectives. When there is not adequate time and/or commitment for a comprehensive training program, it is better to prioritize objectives and emphasize a few with which to work on initially rather than work superficially on all of the needed skills. The coach or sport psychologist may even wish to develop a two-to-three-year plan (Gould, 1983).

When there is time, interest, and need for providing a comprehensive

TABLE 19.1
Possible Sequence for a Comprehensive Mental Skills Training Program

---

Lay foundation for program
Increase awareness of each athlete's own ideal performance state
Establish goals: Physical and mental
Self-regulation of arousal
Imagery training
Thought control training: Emphasis on performance cues and being positive and confident
Concentration training
Ultimately integrate psychological skills into systematic specific applications:
   1. Specific performance or mental skills problems such as reactions to mistakes and coping with fatigue or pain
   2. Countdown to competition preparation
   3. During competition preparation
   4. Postcompetition review

---

mental training program, how should the coach or sport psychologist sequence the teaching of all of the different psychological skill components? Although it is arbitrary to take the general state of psychological readiness for peak performance and divide it into separate facets such as concentration, confidence, and self-regulation of arousal, the division does help athletes better understand the mental states and skills and the practice techniques designed for developing them. Any progression for teaching the psychological skill components is also very arbitrary, but in the interest of assisting the person who might be implementing a comprehensive mental skills training program for the first time, Table 19.1 presents one possible sequence for teaching and integrating psychological components.

The implementer should examine whatever his or her present situation is and make appropriate modifications in the progression. For example, if improving confidence is the most primary objective, work on thought control might precede imagery and arousal training because athletes do not need skill in imaging and regulating arousal before examining self-talk and cognitive techniques for improving performance and building confidence. Skill at relaxation, however, should precede imagery training because research findings indicate that imagery is more effective if a person first assumes a relaxed state. Similarly, techniques for controlling concentration often involve regulation of arousal state, controlling thoughts, and using imagery to focus attention. We therefore suggest that detailed attention to concentration training not occur until athletes have been taught the preceding skills. When this is done, most athletes can easily learn effective concentration protocols that integrate many psychological skills.

Regardless of the psychological component being developed, it is desirable to integrate psychological skills and make specific performance applications as soon as it is possible and appropriate to do so. This may mean that some of the integrated applications suggested as the last step in the training program in Table 19.1 may better occur earlier in the program. For example, if a basketball player's free throw shooting is suffering because of a performance slump, the player should be instructed to practice momentary relaxation and visualize successful performance before each shot as soon as relaxation and imagery training has occurred. Later, when thought control skills and the use of positive affirmation statements have been introduced, these too might be integrated into the athlete's mental skills training ritual for enhancing free throw shooting.

Regardless of whether a comprehensive or abbreviated training program is being planned, it will be more effective if psychological objectives appropriate to the athletes are identified (Silva, 1982; Seabourne et al., 1985). These objectives need to be defined in easily understood and measurable terms (see Table 19.2 for examples). Such definitions help clarify exactly what is meant by the objective and what outcomes are expected once the objective is achieved. The definitions also provide a clear foundation for planning strategies to accomplish the objectives and for assessing how effective the strategies were in achieving the objectives.

ESTABLISHING WITH ATHLETES A FOUNDATION FOR MENTAL SKILLS TRAINING

When meeting with athletes in a psychological training program, the sport psychologist or coach should first convince the athletes of the need for systematic mental training and create a positive belief structure regarding the effects of mental training. This can be done in many ways. One way to start is to have athletes identify how important state of the mind is in achieving success by having them decide what percentage of their game is mental. Then compare this percentage to the actual percentage of practice time spent training mental skills. The disparity between the two figures will usually provide enough incentive for their taking the time to practice mental skills. Providing anecdotes regarding the importance of mental preparation from well-known amateur and professional athletes is another effective way to increase receptivity. The extensive coverage of the 1984 Olympics and other sport literature provide many personal stories of the positive effects of mental training. Such anecdotes are usually much more

TABLE 19.2
A Sample of Psychological Skills Objectives and Outcomes*

Objective 1 Positive Mental Attitude	Objective 2 Coping with Mistakes and Failures	Objective 3 Handle the High-Stress Situation
Don't make negative statements at games or practices.	Accept the fact that mistakes and failures are a necessary part of the learning process.	Learn to interpret the situation as a challenge rather than a threat.
Change "I can't" statements to "I can" statements.	Don't make excuses. Appropriately accepting responsibility will help turn failures into successes.	Recognize too much tension. Achieve appropriate differential relaxation.
Always give 100% effort.	Stay positive even after a stupid mistake.	Keep thoughts positive and focused on the task at hand.
Don't talk while coaches talk.	Be supportive of teammates—even when they are making mistakes.	Image goal of performing well under high-stress situations.
Hustle during all plays and drills.	Keep focused concentration rather than dwelling on preceding mistakes.	Focus concentration on appropriate cues.

* Modified from Gould, D. (1983). Developing psychological skills in young athletes. In N. Wood (Ed.), *Coaching science update*. Ottawa, Canada: The Coaching Association of Canada.

motivating than a recitation of the results of research studies on mental training.

Fortunately, the popularity of applied sport psychology has evolved to the point that it is not very difficult to sell a mental skills training program to most athletes. Nevertheless, you should still expect some athletes to refuse to accept mental skills training. Most sport psychologists recommend not forcing unreceptive athletes to participate. There can also be problems with athletes who are highly enthusiastic about mental training. Occasionally this enthusiasm leads to unreasonable expectations. Athletes, coaches, and sport psychologists must realize that no amount of mental training will substitute for poor mechanics or lack of physical aptitude. Also, good psychological skills cannot replace hard physical conditioning and training. Another problem may come from an athlete's expecting miracles from only a small investment of time. Excellent physical skills did not develop overnight and neither do mental skills. Once athletes recognize that good mental skills are acquired in the same way as good physical skills, i.e., through long-term consistent practice, the foundation has been laid for appropriate mental skills training and practice.

PRACTICAL POINTERS FOR TEACHING MENTAL SKILLS

In the preceding chapters on mental skills training, the authors present many excellent pointers for teaching specific mental skills. The following pointers apply either to the entire psychological training program or to many of its components.

Provide the What, Why, When, and How of Training

For mental skills to be of maximum value, the athlete must consciously and continually choose to utilize mental training methods. This necessitates a high level of commitment, an understanding of proper execution, and ultimately the ability to be self-sufficient in mental preparation. This can be accomplished in a number of ways. Athletes who are taught the what, why, when, and how of mental skills training are much more likely to acquire the necessary knowledge base to become self-sufficient in mental training and the motivation to do so. At the beginning of each special mental training session, the coach or sport psychologist should outline for the athletes the purpose, content, and approximate length of the session. Similarly, before initiating practice on a new exercise or technique, the coach or sport psychologist should first explain the entire procedure so athletes know exactly what to expect and any questions can be answered. It is also a good idea to allot time for discussion and questions after practicing each exercise and at the end of each session. This type of learning atmosphere encourages open discussion and forthright self-examination. In addition to enhancing the learning process, such sharing often improves communication and understanding among teammates and leads to better group support and more team cohesiveness.

Structure the Environment to Complement Your Purpose

The coach or sport psychologist may even want to plan the seating arrangement of athletes during mental training sessions. For example, if the purpose of the session involves a group discussion, lining up the athletes in rows in front of you—particularly if you are standing and they are sitting—is counterproductive. It is almost inevitable that the athletes will say little and whatever they do say will be directed strictly at you. A group discussion is much more likely to occur when everybody, including the leader, is sitting in a circle and all participants can see one another. During discussion encourage all athletes to participate. There may be merit in intentionally drawing out the younger and less-experienced athletes first because they are often hesitant to say something after one of the team leaders or starting players has spoken.

Stress Personal Responsibility

When it comes to performance, some athletes have the attitude, When you're hot, you're hot, and when you're not, you're not. These athletes view peak performance as more a consequence of fate than something under their own personal control. Implementers of mental skills training should teach the opposite attitude. Peak performance is not mysterious; it is a product of the body and mind, both of which can be controlled. This is why, with the right physical and mental training, athletes can learn to repeat their best performances more consistently. This means learning to be in control of oneself versus letting the environment or others do the controlling. The athlete must ultimately accept the fact that only he or she can take responsibility for being physically and mentally ready to compete; but it is the responsibility of the coach and sport psychologist to teach the athlete the skills that are needed to get ready for performance. Therefore, no matter what mental skills are being taught or practiced, the coach and sport psychologist must continually emphasize that athletes assume personal responsibility for their thoughts, feelings, and actions.

Be Flexible, Eclectic, and Individualized

When teaching mental skills to a group of athletes, the best approach is to be flexible, eclectic, and individualized. All athletes do not learn mental skills in the same way and at the same pace any more than they do physical skills. Within reasonable time constraints, a variety of techniques should be introduced and practiced. Do not force everyone into a fixed pattern. Instead, encourage athletes to modify or combine techniques until they derive the most effective method for them. A back-up technique should also be identified and practiced for those times when the preferred one fails to accomplish its objective. As indicated earlier, ultimately these techniques should be applied within a performance-specific focus. Once a basic foundation of mental skills has been established, it is critical that the application of these skills be individualized on the basis of the specific psychological skill needs of the athlete and the requirements of his or her performance situation. Thus, the most effective coaches and sport psychologists will be those who can work simultaneously with the group and with individuals within the group.

Providing handouts and cassette recordings of exercises and specific concepts is another way to assure that athletes have a variety of exercises with which to work and the knowledge base for making modifications and application. You might even consider making handouts or recordings of some of the material in the chapters of this book. Many of the exercises are presented in such a way that they need only be photocopied or read into a cassette recorder. Although many athletes like to use recordings and handouts in their practice, be sure they do not become so dependent upon them that they cannot practice the mental skills without such props.

Use Goal Setting and Journal Assignments

You can also enhance and individualize the teaching of specific mental skills by using goal setting and journal assignments. This is one reason why many sport psychologists suggest that athletes be encouraged to keep journals and be taught how to set goals early in a training program. The following is an example of their use. After athletes have been taught to recognize tension and to relax, have them monitor muscle tension while performing and record in their journals any muscle groups that tend to carry too much tension and when this is most likely to occur. Then instruct them to record in the journal a specific goal for getting rid of the disruptive tension and strategies for achieving the goal. Finally, on each following day, they should record the progress they have made in achieving the goal.

In illustration, a runner identifies that he grimaces and his neck and shoulder muscles tighten when he is running under poor weather conditions, after experiencing the first signs of fatigue and when a steep hill is coming up. He records this in his journal. Next, the runner sets a reasonable goal for correcting the problem; e.g., "In one week I will run a workout over hilly terrain keeping my face, neck, and shoulder muscles relaxed throughout the run." After he records the goal, he plans and records a strategy for reaching the goal; e.g., "(1) Do five minutes of progressive relaxation (PR) each day on just the face, neck, and shoulder muscles. (2) After PR practice, visualize running fluidly over hilly terrain. (3) When running, frequently scan the face for tension—if. needed, relax the face so the forehead is smooth as glass and the jaw is slack. When face is relaxed, scan neck and shoulders for unwanted tension. If tense, relax by slowly rolling the head and/or dropping the shoulders." Each day the runner records his progress in achieving the goal. Once the runner feels he has consistently achieved the goal, he may want to establish a slightly more difficult goal and repeat the process.

Although the preceding example refers to developing appropriate differential relaxation, the creative coach or sport psychologist can use the tools of goal setting and journal keeping to facilitate the learning and performance of almost any psychological skill.

Encourage a Passive State of Mind Versus a Forcing Attitude

It is essential that coaches and sport psychologists help athletes understand that maintaining a passive state of mind facilitates the learning of most of the mental skills addressed in earlier chapters. A passive state of mind is not an active control. Rather, it is as if the person intends to move toward a certain effect, or objective, yet remains detached from his or her actual progress. Trying too hard, exerting effort to the point of trying to force it, is the opposite. In Chapter 18, Ünestahl provides a common example of the counterproductiveness of a forcing attitude: "Any conscious effort and struggle to sleep keeps us awake longer. Sleep is a passive process . . . if we are distracted from active attempts to go to sleep, the onset of sleep is more likely to occur" (p. 294). Schmid and Peper make the same point in Chapter 17 when discussing concentration: "Thus, concentration is the learned skill of passively not reacting to or being distracted by irrelevant stimuli" (p. 272). Active attempts at forcing concentration, e.g., "I will not let myself be distracted by the spectator's booing," are usually ineffectual. A more effective, passive approach to a distracting audience is to focus instead on the desired goal, e.g., shooting a free throw, by keying on cue words that trigger the desired skill and/or by imaging the performance.

Unfortunately, the typical athlete's past athletic environment has done little to foster skill in using a passive state of mind to correct a problem. When they are failing or having difficulty performing, most athletes are admonished to try harder. Thus, excessive effort often becomes the conditioned response when one is having performance difficulties. A coach will be more effective if he or she first assesses the motivation level of the athlete having difficulty and then, unless there is reason to believe the athlete is undermotivated, give the athlete direction in how to focus in a positive way on cues or images for performing the task at hand. This more passive approach will lead to better learning and performance of both mental and physical skills.

Plan Precompetition Preparation Rituals

The ultimate goal of psychological skills training is for each athlete to learn how to create consistently at competition time the ideal performance state (thoughts, feelings, bodily responses) typically associated with his or her peak performance. Rarely will this occur if precompetition preparation and competition behaviors are left to chance or good and bad breaks. Each athlete gets ready for competition in some way, but more often than not he or she does not have a consistent pattern in readying procedures. Performance is likely to be enhanced if an athlete's preparation becomes more systematic. Implementers of psychological skills training programs can help athletes plan effective behavioral protocols or preparation rituals that can be used regularly as precompetition and competition readying procedures. The authors of the preceding chapters have already recommended many outstanding mental training protocols that can be used during competition. Therefore, in this section we will address only the planning of precompetition preparation rituals.

One of the objectives of precompetition preparation is to arrange the external and internal world in a way that maximizes the athlete's feelings of control. The athlete's external world consists of the actual physical surroundings, what is happening in these surroundings, and the physical things the athlete does. The internal world is the athlete's thoughts, feelings, and mental images. The greater the familiarity, routine, and structure in the external environment, the easier it is for the athlete to be in control of his or her internal world. The external world can be stabilized in a number of ways: for example, eating similar meals and with the same time lapse before each competition, always arriving at the contest site with an equal amount of time for precompetition preparation, establishing a set dressing ritual, and following the same equipment check, taping, and warm-up procedures.

Maintaining a constant and familiar external world is even more critical with away competitions. This is more easily accomplished when athletes diligently adhere to elaborate and consistent precompetition rituals before both home and away games. The coach can also increase familiarity with the site of away games by taking the athletes to the site before the competition begins, ideally at least a day before. Some coaches and sport psychologists even advocate getting films of the away facility, including the locker rooms, and showing these films to their athletes well before a competition (see Chapters 13 and 16 for further elaboration on how such films can be used and why they are effective in improving performance).

The best preparation or countdown to competition rituals consists of procedures that get the athlete physically and mentally ready for competition. Most coaches already prepare their athletes well physically for competition by tapering heavy workouts on the days prior to competition and conducting warm-up exercises and technique drills before the start of a competition. However, these physical preparations must be supplemented with emotional and cognitive readying procedures if athletes are to maximize their chances of being ready to peak at competition time. This entails planning procedures for monitoring and controlling thoughts so that they are positive and progressively narrowing in focus to the task at hand as competition nears. It also means monitoring and controlling emotions so that the energy and excitement for competing slowly builds, but without the athlete's becoming energized too soon or becoming so overenergized that feelings of anxiety and worry rather than excitement and challenge occur.

Mental monitoring and readying procedures should be integrated with certain external markers such as waking up the morning of competition, traveling to the competition, arriving at the competition site, getting dressed, doing warm-up exercises and technique drills, and dealing with the short time between physical warm-ups and the beginning of competition. For example, some athletes have found it effective to wake up slowly in the morning and then, before getting out of bed, to relive through imagery a previous best performance. These athletes believe that this type of imagery starts the competition day with a winning feeling and expectancy of success. When some athletes arrive at a competition site, they like to find a quiet place where they can practice 5 to 10 minutes of relaxation exercises such as deep breathing or passive progressive relaxation. Such athletes believe that these relaxation procedures have the benefit of bringing them to the same starting point prior to each competition before they begin the rest of their on-site preparation. Other athletes combine their dressing ritual with cognitive focusing techniques designed to narrow attentional focus to what the athletes want to do during the competition. Oftentimes athletes end their dressing ritual or precede their physical warm-up with a 5- to 10-minute visualization of performing exactly the way they want to perform during competition. Some athletes even use all of the preceding readying procedures.

The most effective readying procedure is individual; this means that the length, content, and sequencing of behavioral protocols vary greatly from one player to another — even when the players are on the same team. Such variability stems partly from different needs in creating an ideal performance state and different preferences for the mental training exercises. Much trial-and-error experimentation, accompanied by consultations with a coach or sport psychologist, may be necessary before each athlete identifies the most effective precompetition ritual for performing well.

Ultimately, it is important that each athlete develop a definite routine that he or she systematically goes through for every competition. The particular routine should be the one that best helps the athlete to get in touch with thoughts, feelings, and bodily responses and to make whatever adjustments are necessary so that when the time for competition arrives, the athlete is as near his or her ideal performance state as possible. A good starting point in developing a routine is to examine what athletes are already doing in their precompetition preparation. The more experienced, successful athlete may already have an effective preparation ritual, although it may not be identified as such or be used systematically. It may be best to leave this athlete alone, except to have him or her consciously identify existing preparation behaviors that are effective and then commit to using these procedures consistently before each competition. The less experienced or less effective athlete will need more assistance and experimentation until the most effective readying procedures are identified.

No athlete should be forced to use precompetition or competition readying procedures. Although most athletes find such structured rituals to be an effective way to enhance level and consistency of performance, some athletes are not comfortable with such techniques or feel they are not beneficial. Other athletes may need only a very abbreviated readying procedure. For example, Jimmy Connors has said, "Because I'm familiar with the games of most players on tour, I never think far ahead about what I'm going to try to do in a match. . . . Before playing a tournament match, I just like to go off by myself somewhere private for five minutes or so to collect my thoughts." (Connors, 1984, p. 34). One important implication of the diversity in effective readying preferences is that many coaches may need to allow athletes a great deal more flexibility in precompetition preparation procedures than is currently observed in many sports.

Stress Application to Other Life Pursuits

One tremendous bonus that comes from implementing a mental training program is that the skills learned are applicable to life in general as well as to athletics, and the benefits last long after the competitive years are over. The implementer of the training program can assist athletes in applying their new mental skills by suggesting relevant uses in nonathletic settings. For example, suggest that athletes learn to do their homework more quickly by using mental training concentration skills. With these skills, athletes can sooner become aware of when their mind is wandering and can bring their focus of attention back to the task at hand. If an athlete gets so uptight before tests that he or she cannot remember what was learned, the same relaxation and positive thinking skills that athletes are taught to control competitive anxiety can be used for test-taking anxiety and every other stressful situation people face in life. Another application of mental training is to visualize a speech or an important job or TV interview in advance to give oneself confidence. The potential benefits that come from increased self-control, confidence, mastery, and so on are limitless. When athletic programs offer both physical and mental skills training, no one can argue that participating in competitive sport is not a valuable educational experience.

Practice It Before Teaching It

Before teaching any of the mental training exercises to athletes, take the time to practice each technique yourself. Not just one time but many times. Personally experiencing an exercise is an excellent way to increase your qualification for teaching the techniques and for answering any questions athletes may have. An additional bonus of practicing the exercises, particularly if the practice is systematic and long-term, is that the practitioner will accrue psychological benefits similar to those athletes receive from the practice. After all, athletes are not the only people who can benefit from learning skills such as effectively setting goals, planning strategies for goal achievement, handling stress, and maintaining concentration and confidence under even the most demanding situations.

Teach by Example

In regard to psychological control, or any type of behavior, good coaches and sport psychologists teach and lead by example. If the person leading the mental training program does not exemplify what he or she is teaching, it is highly unlikely the athletes will. The coach who appears calm, confident, and in control during a competition usually has athletes who act the same way. Players are more likely to offer encouragement and support toward one another when they have a leader who models encouragement (Wescott, 1980). But research on modeling need not be cited to illustrate the importance of teaching by example. All one has to do is watch a ball game. The next time you see athletes consistently losing control and concentration after poor officiating calls, look to the bench and you probably will see the coach behaving similarly. Watch how athletes react to poor performance. Athletes who become negative or rattled after mistakes are often led by coaches who react similarly. For psychological training to be maximally effective, the coaches and sport psychologists must exemplify in practice and competition the behavior they expect from athletes.

SUGGESTIONS AND ETHICAL CONSIDERATIONS FOR THE COACH AND SPORT PSYCHOLOGIST

The following general suggestions should help the coach and sport psychologist become more effective implementers of mental skills training. Also presented are important ethical issues and guidelines that all implementers need to be aware of and observe in their own practices.

Emphasize Strengths as Competition Nears

Behavior by the coach and sport psychologist prior to and during competition is particularly critical. The nearer the time is to competition, the more important it is that you are reassuring and complimentary toward athletes. This is not the time to be critical of technique or anything else. Besides, it is too late to change weaknesses so there is no reason to focus on them. Instead, if at all possible, get athletes to think they are looking great and will perform accordingly. In short, now is the time to build from what is positive, to play to strengths rather than weaknesses. Such behavior by the coach and sport psychologist will help the athletes build and maintain confidence rather than self-doubt prior to competition. This usually means better performance.

Most coaches automatically do this, even if they do not know why. They just know it works. Unfortunately, some coaches naturally tend to be critical right up to and through game time. Often these coaches are not even aware of their unsupportive behavior and its potential negative impact on players' self-confidence, self-esteem, and enjoyment. Other coaches succeed in staying positive in pregame preparation and during a game until something goes wrong. They then jump all over the athletes (often because they have lost emotional control) rather than being reassuring and directing behavior in a positive way toward what needs to be done. Using the self-monitoring and/or outside monitoring described in the next section should help coaches and sport psychologists assess behavior prior to and during competition.

Monitor Your Behavior

In Chapter 11 Ravizza suggests that athletes become more aware of their behavior, thoughts, and feelings through self-monitoring. The same awareness on the part of the coach and sport psychologist can help these leaders become more effective in working with athletes. For example, by means of self-monitoring, the coach and sport psychologist can become more conscious of how they communicate with athletes during different situations. Monitor what you say as well as what you communicate with your body language. How is your behavior likely to change in certain situations? Are you a good role model for the mental discipline and psychological control you wish to teach? Also, if you are a coach, does your behavior exemplify the principles proposed in Chapters 2 through 8 for improving coaching effectiveness? In your self-monitoring, the underlying question should always be "Am I behaving in a way that facilitates the personal growth and performance of my athletes or is my behavior toward them disabling?" Identify how you act in a disabling way and when this behavior is most likely to occur. The awareness created by conscientious and objective self-monitoring is a necessary first step in becoming more effective in working with athletes.

There is also merit in having someone else observe and evaluate your behavior. For example, if you are a coach and a sport psychologist is working with the team, he or she would be an ideal person to observe your behavior during practices and games. The coaching behaviors should be analyzed on the basis of the principles for desirable behavior elaborated in earlier chapters. Evaluation would be facilitated if special forms were designed (see Tharpe & Gallimore and Smith, Smoll & Hunt for examples). The information presented in earlier chapters can be used to help plan a specific strategy for modifying a coach's behavior in a direction that is more likely to facilitate the performance and personal growth of his or her athletes. A prospective sport psychologist's behavior could be assessed through a supervised internship of working with athletes on mental skills training.

Behave Ethically

Sport psychology is a relatively young profession and there are no universally accepted ethical guidelines; members are nonetheless obligated to be responsive to ethical issues. The purpose of this section is to call attention to some basic ethical concerns involved in implementing mental skills training. This brief discussion should not be construed as a complete presentation of the many complex ethical issues and interrelationships involved in psychological skills training. A more thorough discussion of these topics can be found in Danish & Hale (1981, 1982), Nideffer (1981, 1984), Nideffer, Feltz, & Salmela (1982), Heyman (1984), and Rotella & Connelly (1984).

Associations for sport psychology (NASPSPA and CSPLSP) have developed a modification of the American Psychological Association's Ethical Standards as standards that should guide the conduct of sport psychologists. At the core of these standards is the general philosophy of the preservation and protection of fundamental human rights. The essence of this philosophy is that the athlete's welfare must be foremost. To this end, the sport psychologist must always attempt to act in the best interest of both the athlete and the team in such ways as the following:

1. Accurately present your credentials and those of your profession to avoid any misunderstanding. Do not make unsubstantiated claims regarding the benefits of psychological skills training.

2. Inform the athletes and coaches about the nature and purpose of the training procedures, making certain that all parties understand the ground rules.

3. Recognize the potential and limits of the techniques you use. Many of the mental skills training techniques are very powerful and should not be abused or used with athletes who are not stable.

4. Recognize limitations based upon your training, being careful to differentiate between performance problems that are responsive to mental skills training and serious personal problems that may need professional clinical or counseling intervention. Although most athletes are psychologically stable, the small percentage (5% to 10%) of athletes you encounter who are not emotionally stable should be helped to obtain professional assistance from those capable of providing therapy.

5. Safeguard confidentiality. Do not talk about one athlete to another or discuss with others (including the coach) what you say during individual sessions unless the athlete chooses otherwise.

6. Respect the orientations and prerogatives of those for whom you work. It is the coach's team. The sport psychologist is only a facilitator and should not permit his or her own ego to supersede to the extent of taking credit for the athlete's performance, stepping on the coach's ego, or doing anything that might undermine the coach's authority and decisions.

Evaluate the Psychological Skills Training Program

It is not easy to evaluate the impact of a psychological skills training program, yet evaluation is essential for improving a training program and the skills of the person in charge of the program. Evaluation should be a continuous process. After each mental skills training session, the implementer should assess the strengths and weaknesses of the content and delivery of the content. Address questions such as the following: Did the session accomplish its objective(s)? Were explanations of psychological concepts and directions for practicing the training exercises adequate? What techniques appeared to work best? Was time allotted appropriately during the session? Are any additions or deletions warranted? How responsive did the athletes appear to be? Athletes' reactions might also be sought and included in the critique. Writing a critique is more beneficial than simply trying to remember strengths and weaknesses. Plans for future sessions may need to be modified on the basis of the results of each session evaluation.

A more formal, total evaluation should occur at the end of the mental skills training program. This evaluation might include team and individual discussions, written evaluations by the athletes (the coach, too, if a sport psychologist administers the program), and assessment of any changes in performance (e.g., Did performance level improve? Did the improvement last? Did athletes who were inconsistent in performance become more consistent? If there were improvements in performance, were they greater than one would expect from physical practice alone? How frequently did the athletes who improved in performance use the mental training strategies and techniques?). In addition to assessing changes in the physical performance of athletes, evaluate the program's psychological skill objectives and how many athletes appeared to be successful in achieving the expected outcomes (see Table 19.2 for examples of observable and measurable outcomes). Ask athletes, among other things, what they saw as the major strengths and weaknesses of the mental skills training, what mental skills improved the most, what exercises were the most helpful, and what they perceived as needing the most work in the future. The information gained from a thorough evaluation process is invaluable in helping make future mental skills training even more effective.

Continue to Learn and Improve

We suggest that you periodically reread many of the preceding chapters. Rereading will refresh your memory regarding basic psychological concepts, the variety of techniques available for mental training, and how these concepts and techniques can best be applied to the needs of a specific athlete or situation. It is particularly beneficial to reexamine the chapters after your first attempt at implementing mental skills training because you can learn still more with the insights gained from experience in implementing mental skills training. Additionally, you should read other books and articles on mental skills training and, if possible, attend sport psychology workshops.

Do not be discouraged if your initial attempts at psychological skills training are not as effective as you had hoped. The ability to teach mental skills and apply psychological constructs improves with practice. If you are an experienced coach, think back to your first coaching season and the kind of coach you were then compared to now. Experience and further study will improve your effectiveness in teaching mental skills just as it did teaching physical skills and strategies. The rewards that ultimately come from effectively teaching psychological skills are as numerous and exciting as those that come from effectively teaching physical skills.

SUMMARY

In this chapter we have addressed many general issues relating to the integration and implementation of a psychological skills training program. In summary, (1) there are advantages to having either a coach or a sport psychologist implement a psychological skills training program, (2) athletes of all age and skill levels can benefit from mental training, (3) mental skills training should continue for as long as an athlete participates in sport, (4) the initial mental skills training program should probably be three to six months in length and start in the off-season or preseason, (5) a psychological skills needs assessment should be made in order to determine the specific components to be incorporated in training and the psychological objectives to be achieved, (6) there is no one best way to sequence and integrate psychological components even though one was proposed, (7) once basic mental skills are acquired they should have a performance specific focus and be integrated with practice of physical skills, and (8) real benefits from psychological skills training will only occur with long-term systematic practice.

We have also suggested practical teaching pointers that apply to either the entire psychological training program or to many of its components: Stress that athletes accept self-responsibility for their mental state. Be flexible, eclectic, and individualized in planning training techniques. Emphasize employing a passive state of mind when learning psychological skills. Stress personal growth and how to use mental skills in nonathletic settings. Practice techniques before teaching them. Teach by personally exemplifying the mental skills being taught.

Finally, we concluded the chapter with ethical considerations that all psychological training implementers need to be aware of and observe in their own behavior.

This chapter and the earlier chapters on psychological skills training have emphasized that the rewards are many for those who choose to teach and practice mental training in their dedication to the pursuit of excellence. Benefits will accrue not only in athletic performance but in performance outside of the athletic setting and, perhaps more importantly, in general personal growth and an enhanced sense of self-worth.

REFERENCES

Connors, J. (1984, December). *Tennis,* pp. 33–35.

Danish, S. J., & Hale, B. D. (1981). Toward an understanding of the practice of sport psychology. *Journal of Sport Psychology, 3,* 90–99.

Danish, S. J., & Hale, B. D. (1982). Let the discussions continue: Further considerations on the practice of sport psychology. *Journal of Sport Psychology, 4*(1), 10–12.

Gould, D. (1983). Developing psychological skills in young athletes. In N. Wood (Ed.), *Coaching science update.* Ottawa, Canada: The Coaching Association of Canada.

Heyman, S. R. (1984). Cognitive interventions: Theories, applications, and cautions. In W. F. Straub & J. M. Williams (Eds.), *Cognitive sport psychology* (pp. 289–303). Lansing, N.Y.: Sport Science Associates.

Nideffer, R. M. (1981). *The ethics and practice of applied sport psychology.* Ithaca, N.Y.: Mouvement Publications.

Nideffer, R. M. (1984). Current concerns in sport psychology. In J. M. Silva & R. S. Weinberg (Eds.), *Psychological foundations of sport* (pp. 35–44). Champaign, Ill.: Human Kinetics.

Nideffer, R., Feltz, D., & Salmela, J. (1982). A rebuttal to Danish and Hale: A committee report. *Journal of Sport Psychology, 4*(1), 3–6.

Rotella, R. J., & Connelly, D. (1984). Individual ethics in the application of cognitive sport psychology. In W. F. Straub & J. M. Williams (Eds.), *Cognitive sport psychology* (pp. 102–112). Lansing, N.Y.: Sport Science Associates.

Seabourne, T. G., Weinberg, A. S., Jackson, A., & Suinn, R. M. (1985). Effect of individualized, nonindividualized, and package intervention strategies on karate performance. *Journal of Sport Psychology, 7,* 40–50.

Silva, J. M. (1982). Performance enhancement in competitive sport environments through cognitive intervention. *Behavior Modification, 6,* 443–463.

Smith, R. E., Smoll, F., & Hunt, E. (1977). A system for the behavioral assessment of athletic coaches. *Research Quarterly, 48,* 401–407.

Tharpe, R. G., and Gallimore, R. (1976, January). What a coach can teach a teacher. *Psychology Today,* pp. 75–78.

Wescott, W. L. (1980). Effects of teacher modeling on children's peer encouragement behavior. *Research Quarterly, 51,* 585–587.

Part Three

Psychological Considerations: Burnout, Injury, and Termination from Athletics

20 Athletic Staleness and Burnout: Diagnosis, Prevention, and Treatment

KEITH P. HENSCHEN

University of Utah

"Fatigue makes cowards of us all!" (Vince Lombardi)

The phenomenon of fatigue, burnout, staleness, or whatever label is used to identify it is very real. Picture, if you will, a team that performs very well from the beginning of the season through the third quarter of the schedule, then just seems to be going through the motions. Physically, each player is in peak shape, but something is lacking. There is no excitement, no feeling, no motivation, just a lackluster performance. While other teams seem to be peaking, this team becomes proficiently stagnant. Eventually a team with much less talent but more "heart," defeats our talented team. Why? What has happened? How can individuals with so much physical talent become so apathetic during performance? The answers to these questions are as complex as the phenomenon itself.

Athletic staleness occurs frequently, and most coaches and players appear to be at a loss in terms of diagnosing, preventing, and treating this malady. Considering the high demands placed upon today's athletes and the length of most sport seasons, it is not surprising that many athletes and coaches have difficulty avoiding performance slumps and, at times, total burnout. In this chapter we will discuss what causes staleness, what physiological and psychological factors are typically associated with periods of athletic staleness, and what techniques are available to diagnose, prevent, and treat it.

DEFINITIONS AND DIAGNOSIS

What do we mean by the terms *burnout, staleness,* and *slump?* What do they have in common and how do they differ? The term *burnout* first appeared in the literature concerning job stress. *Burnout* was defined as a state of mental, emotional, and physical exhaustion brought on by persistent devotion to a goal, the achievement of which is dramatically opposed to reality (Freudenberger & Richelson, 1981; Maslach, 1982; Pines, Aronson, & Kafry, 1981). Burnout afflicts overly dedicated, idealistic men and women who are motivated toward high achievement and who work in unrewarding situations (Maslach & Pines, 1977; Pines, Aronson, & Kafry, 1981). Considering the type of person susceptible to burnout, it is easy to understand why many athletes may also be at risk. Feigley (1984) noted that the circumstances of job stress and athletic stress show remarkable parallels even when comparisons involve children as young as age 10.

Burnout's devastating states of physical, mental, and emotional exhaustion result in the development of negative self-concepts; negative attitudes toward work, life, and other people; and a loss of idealism, energy, and purpose (Freudenberger & Richelson, 1981; Maslach, 1982).

Burnout represents the long-term end result of striving without reward; staleness may be described as a symptom of ensuing burnout, an early warning sign of the negative state to come. If athletic staleness is ignored, burnout will eventually follow. However, if staleness is recognized by the athlete, coach, and sport psychologist, the devastating path to burnout may be averted.

A slump may occur along with staleness or may be a result of staleness. The term *staleness* refers to an overall physical and emotional state, whereas the term *slump* indicates a more specific performance-related phenomenon. Harris and Harris (1984) defined slumps as "periods when the athlete fails to maintain the usual consistency in performance without any detectable mechanical failure in execution" (p. 170). Furthermore, the cause is frequently related to the athlete's mental perception. The skill is performed and the execution seems right, but the actual outcome does not feel right. Once this feeling establishes itself within the athlete, it is likely to recur again and again. An uneasiness, a negative feeling toward performance, or a predisposition toward mediocrity is the outcome. What results is a vicious cycle — almost a self-fulfilling prophecy. The athlete will begin to worry about his or her performance, which can contribute to sustaining the slump and staleness. The end result may become serious enough to be classified as burnout.

According to Feigley (1984), certain personality characteristics and behavioral patterns increase an individual's susceptibility to burnout. Shank (1983) identified the following characteristics and behaviors as predisposing certain people to burnout: (1) perfectionism, (2) being other-oriented, and (3) lack of assertive interpersonal skills. Perfectionists are at risk because they are overachievers who tend to set high standards for themselves and others (Freudenberger & Richelson, 1981). They also may tend to invest more time and effort on a task than is necessary. Other-oriented people have a strong need to be liked and admired and are often extremely sensitive to criticism. They tend to be generous with everyone but themselves. People who lack assertive interpersonal skills find it difficult to say no or express negative feelings such as anger without feeling extremely guilty.

Feigley also noted that, ironically, coaches often find quiet, concerned, energetic perfectionists to be ideal athletes. Care must be taken to make sure burnout does not cause these people to quit their sport before they can reach and enjoy their full potential. Coaches and sport psychologists should not persuade these athletes to curtail their commitment to athletics but persuade them to achieve a better balance. "While dedication to a sport is essential for high-level success, if one's focus is too narrow, too intense, or too prolonged at too early an age, the likelihood of burnout increases dramatically" (Feigley, 1984, p. 112).

Slumps and staleness, or periods of poor performance, can also be caused by a multitude of psychological or environmental factors and physical problems. Athletes who attempt too much, worry continually, and adhere to poor health habits (especially poor nutrition) frequently manifest the staleness syndrome. Also, many athletes who experience staleness attribute the situation to attitudinal problems or a general lack of motivation. Factors such as chronic fatigue, anxiety, and boredom are normally precursors to staleness. Physical symptoms such as minor body aches, stomach upsets, headaches, and eating disorders usually accompany staleness. Thus, both physiological and psychological characteristics contribute to and are manifestations of athletic staleness. Assessment of staleness should take into account both types of manifestations.

From a physiological point of view, Kereszty (1971) listed the following characteristics when discussing staleness and overtraining:

Higher resting heart rate

Higher systolic blood pressure

Delayed return to normal heart rate

Elevated basal metabolic rate

Elevated body temperature

Weight loss

Impeded respiration

Subcostal aching

Bowel disorders

When athletes manifest any combination of these physiological disorders to any magnitude, the coach or sport psychologist should consider the possibility of staleness.

The psychological factors may be more difficult to detect than the physiological ones and are much more difficult to treat. Psychologically, staleness is normally characterized by the following:

Sleep disturbances

Loss of self-confidence

Drowsiness and apathy

Quarrelsomeness

Irritability

Emotional and motivational imbalance

Excessive weariness that is prolonged

Lack of appetite (anorexia)

Fatigue

Loss of vigor

Depression

Anxiety

Anger/hostility

Confusion

Kashiwagi (1971) introduced into industry a psychological rating scale of human fatigue that appears to be readily adaptable to assessing staleness in the athletic setting. The fatigue rating (FR) scale is a questionnaire that consists of 20 items, 10 of which indicate "weakened activation" and 10 of which indicate "weakened motivation." To utilize the scale, a coach or sport psychologist would rate each athlete on a five-point Likert-type scale according to the following descriptive statements:

Weakened Activation	*Weakened Motivation*
1. Too lazy to work	1. Many misstatements
2. Unsteady voice	2. Avoids others' eyes
3. Absentminded	3. Difficult to speak
4. Hollow-cheeked	4. Sluggish
5. Avoids conversation	5. Restless
6. Sulky face	6. Anxious about other things
7. Spiritless eyes	7. Pale face
8. Irritable	8. Stiff face
9. Dull	9. Trembling fingers
10. Confused	10. Unable to listen and concentrate

Another psychological tool that the coach or sport psychologist can use to diagnose the onset of staleness in sports is the Profile of Mood States (POMS) (McNair, Lorr, & Droppleman, 1971). The POMS measures six transitory affective states (tension, depression, anger, vigor, fatigue, and confusion) by rating 65 adjective states on a five-point scale ranging from "not at all" to "extremely." Successful athletes have been found to differ psychologically from unsuccessful athletes. Psychological mood states typically associated with top-level athletic performance form what Morgan has called an iceberg profile (Morgan & Johnson, 1977, 1978). That is, more successful athletes tend to score high on vigor and low on anxiety, depression, anger, fatigue, and confusion.

In carefully documented research with swimmers, Morgan (1984; Morgan & Brown, 1983) found that the psychological mood state profile of "stale" athletes was the opposite of successful athletes. Specifically, as the season progressed, the iceberg profile of stale swimmers "inverted." There was a stepwise increase in the group's mood disturbance that coincided directly with increases in swimming training, and decreases in the training regimen (i.e., tapering) were associated with improvements in mood state.

These findings suggest that astute coaches and sport psychologists should be cognizant of mood swings in their athletes because these swings can indicate the possible onset of athletic staleness. Workout modifications such as tapering in swimming and making practice less intense or allowing time off in other sports might be dictated if athletes appear to be "flattening" or "inverting" on their optimal psychological mood state profile. Additional suggestions for avoiding undesirable shifts in psychological states appear in the next section.

Sport psychologists, coaches, and athletes should learn to recognize the initial signs associated with staleness. By the time many of these signs are in full bloom, the battle is half lost. The most important challenge is to eliminate the possibility of staleness ever securing a firm foothold. A word of caution: When an athlete consistently experiences most of the psychological characteristics of staleness, simultaneously and at high levels, with or without accompanying physical symptoms, the coach should consider referring the athlete to a professionally certified counselor or psychologist. Under such circumstances, the coach should not try to play amateur psychologist.

PREVENTION

To understand how to prevent athletic staleness one needs to know how the causes of this phenomenon are associated with training and competition. Innumerable factors contribute to athletic staleness. Suffice it to say, prevention must be a planned program.

Obviously, there are a few main contributors to staleness or burnout that coaches can help eliminate. Possibly the most significant factor promoting staleness is the length of the season. Most high school and college sport programs have seasons that are virtually year-round. This hurts the athlete. The length of a season is dictated by high school activity associations and the National Collegiate Athletic Association (NCAA); but many coaches ignore or circumvent these time constraints. An example of this occurs in college basketball. The NCAA states that practice cannot begin officially until October 15 of each year. In any major college in the country, practice typically (officially) begins on the first day of school (around the first week of September). After six weeks of illegal "conditioning," practice begins legally. By the first week in March of the following year, a basketball team has practiced for approximately 25 weeks. After the season is over, most teams informally condition, weight train, and illegally practice until the following September, when the cycle is repeated. No wonder staleness occurs. Many college athletes spend more time at their sport activities than do their professional counterparts.

Another prime contributor to athletic staleness is the monotony of training. Far too many athletes are *forced* to participate in practice situations that resemble pure drudgery. Many coaches are guilty of embracing the philosophy of "the more the better." If one hour of practice is sufficient, then two hours would be more beneficial, four hours would be even better, and so on. Motor learning research unequivocally refutes this practice, but these coaches ignore the research findings and continue to adhere to their mistaken philosophy. Staleness is frequently the final outcome.

Other environmental factors present during practice can also hasten the onset of staleness. Feelings of being locked in with no other place to go, a constant lack of positive reinforcement, abusiveness from those in authority, and unreasonable institutional rules are factors that predispose an athlete to staleness. All of these factors interact to structure a situation in which the athlete feels out of control or trapped in a hopeless circumstance. The logical result is going through the motions, a characteristic of staleness.

When the preceding factors are combined with high levels of emotional stress and the typically young age of the athlete, a volatile no-win situation often develops, the end result being staleness. Sport competition involves a great deal of emotional stress, and young athletes are often unequipped to handle it effectively. Unless the athlete achieves constant success, or a variable ratio of success, a common outcome is staleness.

What can be done to prevent this ailment before it begins to occur? Obviously, the coach should keep the season's length in proper perspective and formulate practice sessions that eliminate boredom. He or she can also take five additional steps to prevent staleness:

1. Schedule time-outs
2. Allow athletes to make some choices
3. Control outcomes
4. Plan mental practice periods
5. Handle postcompetition tension

Time-outs

It is essential for our mental wellness to experience periods of time away from a continual stressor. Athletes are no exception. They need time away from competition and practice. Business has realized this concept by providing for vacations, holidays, and even weekends away from the work environment. Many people in the athletic establishment have yet to realize the value of time-outs in regard to performance. Many teams practice or compete every day from the beginning to the end of the season. It is hard to understand why some coaches believe that a break is a sign of weakness. A time-out period used appropriately will refresh and invigorate the athletes.

There are some very creative ways to use time-out periods. Once in my high school basketball-playing days, our coach did something very unusual. We had, as a team, been practicing from the start of the season for about four weeks. Our first game was approximately one month away. We were a veteran team and thought all of the practice was a waste of time. Consequently, our commitment to practice was not great. After going through the motions of practicing the first month, we found that our coach had posted a message on the locker room door stating that there would be no practices until further notice. All of the players felt this was a little strange, but we enjoyed the first few days away from practice. We spent considerable time socializing. At the end of the first week of no practice, with our season opener only three weeks away, our concern began to turn into panic. Players at the other high schools in our area were practicing daily and, in our minds, were getting far ahead of us. Something had to be done quickly. Even our parents became concerned. Some of us were candidates for college scholarships. The following Monday morning every player was in the locker room the minute the school opened (one hour before the first class). Still no practice was called.

By now we were sure that our coach had lost his mind. The team voted to send the captains to talk to the coach. The captains tried to talk to him, but he would not see them until Friday! By then we had missed two entire weeks of practice. On Thursday of the second week of no practice, the coach called a general team meeting for the next day. We didn't know what to expect. When the meeting started, the coach asked us if we had enjoyed our two-week vacation and if we were ready to start practice again. We all emphatically assured him that we were ready, eager, and willing to do anything he wanted. The season's first game was only two weeks away. Needless to say, our practices from then on were crisp, sharp, and intense. As players, we were convinced that we were behind the other teams who had continued to practice while we vacationed. Actually, that season was one of the best basketball seasons our school ever experienced. Years later I asked the coach what his rationale was for our not practicing for those two weeks. His explanation was very enlightening:

> That team was as stale as any team I had ever coached. You guys were a veteran team who needed shaking up. Your practices were lousy, and I needed to do something to get you recommitted to our program. You were all good kids, but the spark of enthusiasm was

missing. I probably could have waited until we lost a game and then somehow got you back into my way of thinking, but I decided to gamble a little. I just felt you boys needed a break to get your heads screwed back on. Boy, did you guys come back. I look back at that as one of my finest decisions.

This example is evidence of what happens after a time-out period. Staleness is replaced by enthusiasm.

Choices

Another procedure that is effective in alleviating staleness is allowing the athletes to participate in some of the decision making. By permitting input from the athletes and using their suggestions, the coach helps to solidify the players' commitment. This procedure allows the athletes to make their involvement on the team a primary instead of a secondary commitment. When the team becomes a primary force in the lives of its players, the team members will do almost anything to ensure its success. If, on the other hand, a secondary association is formed, the resultant commitment will be partial and sporadic. A person actively participating in any endeavor does not have the time or energy to dwell on the negative for long. When a person's decisions or choices are being utilized and subsequently evaluated, he or she will do everything possible to ensure success. One way to involve athletes in making decisions is to have them form committees to decide which offenses or defenses they should use in upcoming games. Have the players demonstrate to other team members what the opponent will be doing and how to nullify the opponent's strengths. Again, providing an atmosphere in which the athletes' choices are considered important is crucial to eliminating staleness. (See Chapters 6, 7, and 8 for more detailed suggestions on when and how to do this.)

Control of Outcomes

Research on overtraining and burnout indicates that a prime contributor to these conditions is the feeling of no control over what is happening (Morgan, 1984). When athletes perceive a hopeless situation in which they are physically present but not totally involved, staleness is normally inevitable. Provide an environment that allows the athletes to feel that they have some control over their own destiny, and you will diminish the likelihood of staleness. (This procedure is similar to the previous one.)

Mental Practice Periods

Another way to prevent staleness is to add variety to practice and training in order to increase motivation and interest. One technique that you can use to accomplish this is to incorporate periods of mental practice within the physical training sessions. This accomplishes two things: (1) it breaks up the monotony of the practice session, and (2) it allows the body to recuperate physically without jeopardizing practice time. Even though the body might be fatigued, the mind can continue almost indefinitely. By alternating periods of physical practice and mental practice during training sessions, the likelihood of fatigue is greatly lessened. The University of Utah's women's gymnastics team (which as of this writing has won four consecutive NCAA championships) has used this technique for the past five years. Three or four times each day the team (as a group) takes 10 minutes to relax and mentally rehearse individual routines. When these mental practice periods are completed, the gymnasts continue their physical training in a much more refreshed state. (See Chapter 14 for suggestions on how to develop mental rehearsal skills and the different ways in which mental rehearsal can be used.)

Postcompetition Tension Management

What is postcompetition tension? How are contemporary coaches handling this psychological phenomenon, and what is its relationship to staleness? Many coaches may not even be aware that this phenomenon exists, but an understanding of the relationship between postcompetition tension and athletic staleness is crucial to preventing staleness.

For years researchers have been accumulating evidence which indicates that some ingredient is lacking in the psychological training and treatment of athletes (Henschen, 1973). Postgame quarrels, fights, drinking binges, and so forth are instigated by athletes who have pent-up emotions that the end of the game has failed to relieve. Other responses include withdrawal and depression. The final buzzer does not stop or ease many of the intense psychological variables that a sporting contest evokes. Many coaches seem to spend unlimited hours preparing athletes psychologically to compete but at the conclusion of the contest leave it to the athletes to devise a means of relieving the excess emotion caused by the competition. Coaches should have a similarly intensive program for dealing with postcompetition tension as they do for precompetition preparation because athletes who remain constantly frustrated will eventually experience burnout.

Research indicates that most athletes experience one of three emotional states at the conclusion of a contest regardless of the outcome: (1) depression, (2) euphoria, or (3) intrapunitive or interpunitive aggression (Henschen, 1973). Any of these emotions left unchecked for a period of time will rapidly contribute to a state of staleness. These emotions can quickly drain an athlete of any and all available energy.

Handling postcompetition tension is as important for the reserves as it is for the starters. In fact, the athletes for whom the coach should be most concerned are probably the substitutes who have not received an opportunity to play. These athletes experience increased frustration because they have not seen any game action.

Because postcompetition tension and its relationship to staleness is a relatively new area of concern within the athletic establishment, you may find the following suggestions useful in your attempts to alleviate this situation.

1. The coach must be able to provide a supportive atmosphere immediately following a contest. Many coaches, in satisfying their own feelings, ignore their players when the athletes need them the most. The coach should be with his or her team after a contest.

2. While the players are showering and dressing, the coach can converse individually with each competitor. During this conversation the coach can provide the player with his or her perception of that player's performance. Providing an unemotional yet realistic assessment of the performance will help the athletes deal with their own emotions. This is an opportunity for the coach to encourage some players and verbally chastise others for the immediate past performance. The coach also needs to converse with all the team members who did not participate in the game.

3. Once the athletes have dressed, provide the whole team with some type of group activity. Possibilities include (a) a postgame meal instead of a pregame training meal, (b) a team swimming or bowling party, (c) a postgame movie. A group activity can provide the athletes with an opportunity to think about and do something other than the sport in which they are involved. Such an activity can also keep the athletes temporarily away from their parents and peers, who are usually very critical or overly praising right after a contest; this can aggravate latent emotions and produce detrimental effects for the future. A group activity further aids in developing cohesion and comradery.

4. The coach should get on with the program. The coach cannot permit team members to gloat indefinitely over a success or exhibit prolonged depression over a loss. Long-standing emotions drain energy and serve to frustrate athletes. Preparation for the next opponent should begin with the first practice after a previous contest.

Prevention and the Concept of Enjoyment

A few final thoughts concerning the prevention of staleness seem to be in order. All of the prevention procedures we have just reviewed basically boil down to the concept of enjoyment. Possibly the best way to prevent stale-ness is to ensure that the athletes are having *fun*. Years ago the Western Electric studies convinced psychologists that any type of change would increase productivity of assembly-line workers (Roethlisberger & Dickson, 1947). Behaviorists embraced the concept that if an activity is followed by a pleasurable feeling or reward, it is likely to be repeated (Rotter, Chance, & Phares, 1972). People continue to do things that they enjoy. Far too many coaches, through improper reinforcement and motivational techniques, make athletics pure drudgery and work. When this is the perception, then athletes become bored, stale, or burned out. Something does *not* have to hurt to be good. No gain without pain is a myth.

TREATMENT

By this time you should be able to recognize the symptoms of staleness and also be aware of a variety of techniques that you can use to prevent it. Now comes the real test. How do you treat a team or individual who has already demonstrated a degree of staleness?

Remember: Each case is unique and should be treated as such!

As a general rule, the most effective means for treatment of athletic staleness is a psychological reprogramming. Initially, the coach needs to reassess his or her entire season, determine the most likely contributors to the staleness syndrome, and progress from that point. Realistically, only two courses of action are available: (1) Remove the athletes from the situa-tion; have them withdraw completely from the activity for an appropriate period of time. (2) Devise a program that will alleviate the staleness syn-drome. The first course of action can provide some great benefits, but it is not a feasible solution in most athletic situations. Therefore, only repro-gramming holds any real promise in sports. You might try any or all of the following suggestions to reprogram an individual, but be aware that not all of these procedures will work for every athlete; so do not become discour-aged if one method is not always successful.

The best method of eliminating, or at least reducing, staleness is to digress a few steps and reestablish *goals* for both practice and competition (O'Block & Evans, 1984). Good goal setting keeps us on the road to success. The type of goal setting needed to treat staleness is very simple. Set short-term goals and provide rewards or incentives every time a goal is accom-plished. For many athletes experiencing staleness, the only meaningful goal they have is just getting through the season. New, meaningful, exciting goals will take their minds off the long, sometimes dreary season and put some pizzazz back into playing. Each sport is different; but having *fun goals* in the late stages of a season is very beneficial. The key point here is to set fun goals for practice as well as competition. Almost all goals seem to be competition oriented. Most coaches and players appear to forget that nine tenths of participation time in sports is spent in practicing, not competing in games. Performance goals are necessary, but enjoyable practice and training goals are essential to mental well-being. Be sure that the rewards for attaining goals are meaningful to the athletes and that the rewards are greater toward the end of the season than at the beginning.

Another procedure for treating staleness is to teach the athletes how to relax themselves. As noted earlier, one of the prime contributors to staleness is frustration. A common remedy for frustration is self-relaxation. Every athlete should be taught a variety of self-control techniques. Relaxation is just one of these techniques. Whether you select autogenic training, modified autogenic training, self-hypnosis, or progressive relaxation is irrelevant. The important point is that each athlete has one of these techniques at his or her command. Athletes who can control themselves usually do not demonstrate staleness. For many athletes a simple progressive relaxation technique is quite useful. (Review the progressive relaxation exercises in Chapter 13.)

You can also use a couple of other methods to aid in the mental reprogramming. The objective is to "eliminate any physical causes and then learn to disregard mental distractions" (Harris & Harris, 1984). A simple procedure is to teach athletes the method of self-talk. This has the sobering effect of putting things back into a proper perspective. Self-talk should always be positive and concerned with the correct maneuver or skill. Far too many athletes seem to concentrate on mistakes or errors instead of good performances.

An example of self-talk is as follows: A golfer has had difficulty putting lately. She seems to be concentrating on what not to do rather than on a positive perspective. As she addresses the ball, she tells herself exactly what she expects the ball to do (correctly). She ignores any negative thought and dwells only on positive thoughts.

Self-talk will become almost automatic if practiced diligently. Stopping the negative thoughts and only concentrating on the positive can change an athlete's outlook and thus lessen the effects of staleness.

One final suggestion for the treatment of athletic staleness through reprogramming is the use of imagery. A perceptive coach will turn inward to an athlete's thoughts to treat staleness rather than resort to more physical overtraining, which just compounds the situation. Every person has the capacity to image and does so daily (dreaming). Applying this innate ability to the athlete's advantage is an option open to the creative coach. Mental imagery is actually a form of stimulation, but the stimulation takes place entirely in the athlete's head (Orlick, 1980). Most athletes use mental imagery or mental practice at one time or another, practicing a particular game-ending play, for instance. This type of imagery is not usually done in any systematic way; but for athletes who use it regularly, imagery can be a great asset.

Imagery is more than just picturing something; it also involves capturing the feelings of a situation. Imagery is an inner state of mind. To image effectively, athletes must place themselves in a state in which they can be aware of their inner processes. "The desire to break through the labels and abstractions that enclose literate man has prompted him to rediscover the importance of imagery. For imagery enables him to be at one with his world once again" (Samuels & Samuels, 1984). Many rich benefits await the athlete who uses imagery:

1. A differentiated sense of identity and self-awareness.
2. A gain in self-confidence and security.
3. High levels of self-control.
4. More positive affective experiences.
5. Augmented resources for dealing with stress.
   (Tower & Singer, 1981)

Even though mental imagery can provide many benefits, some athletes have difficulty achieving it. Imagery is a skill and, like all skills, must be learned and perfected. Once this skill is mastered, it is readily apparent how it can be utilized to treat staleness. Coaches can encourage imagery by having the entire team practice it together during regular practice time. This is often helpful because the athletes are in the same environment in which athletic performance will take place. Having the athletes develop a practice routine for imagery every day is a good idea. Examples of imagery exercises follow.

Exercise: Interaction between tension and relaxation Close your eyes. . . . Be aware of the tension of your body . . . and imagine that it is filled with different colored lights, for example, a soft blue light for relaxation and a red light for tension. . . . Allow the lights to change from blue to red, or from red to blue, and be aware of any physical sensations you may experience while this is taking place. Pause. . . . Change all the lights in your body to a soft blue and experience the overall feeling of relaxation. (Davis, McKay, & Eshelman, 1983)

Exercise: The happiness room Imagine you are standing at the bottom of a staircase. Look up toward the top of the stairs and see a large door. Grasp the handrail and slowly climb the stairs. When you reach the top, grab the doorknob and open the door. When the door is open, imagine a totally vacant room. As you are standing in the doorway, decorate this room with everything that pleases you. Carpets (plush), lights, wall hangings, waterbed, girlfriends or boyfriends, refrigerator, etc. Money is no object. Everything in this room is there to please you. This is your happiness room and there is no other room like it in the world.

Position yourself very comfortably in front of one wall. On this wall of your happiness room is a three-foot by three-foot television screen. It is only about one inch thick. Take your remote control and turn on the television. The picture on the television screen is *you* performing your sport. Watch yourself very carefully. You are performing perfectly. Imagine how good it feels to perform so well. You are excellent.

After watching yourself perform for a little while, turn off your television. Look around your happiness room and again see how good it feels. Walk to the door, open it, turn off the lights, and slowly descend the stairs. When you reach the bottom of the stairs you will be fully awake and rejuvenated.

Athletes should practice this simple guided imagery exercise daily for optimum results. The happiness room allows athletes to watch and feel themselves performing perfectly without any negative reinforcement.

Exercise: Music listening   Get into a comfortable position and close your eyes. . . . Allow yourself to flow with the music. . . . Permit the music to let various thoughts float through your mind. Do not dwell on any of the thoughts. Passively allow them to float in and out of your mind. As one thought seems to disappear, another takes its place. Ignore all negative ideas and concentrate only on the positive thoughts. Allow the music to relax you deeply. . . . As you are listening to the music, think of a special friend. Experience yourself talking to your friend.

You and your friend are going to examine the tension and stress in your life. . . . Ask your friend what is causing your tension and stress. . . . Ask your friend, "How can I become less tense and deal with stress better?" You and your friend will meet and discuss this problem daily. After a few days, your friend will suggest a number of solutions to your problem.

Again, allow yourself to flow with the music and become relaxed.

This imagery exercise is best accomplished if the athletes are allowed to select the music they will listen to. The music should be instrumental (without words) and the most relaxing to the individual athletes.

The three preceding exercises are examples of modes for stimulating imagination: visualization, guided imagery, and listening to music. Some athletes will respond better to one mode than the others. Most important is the fact that almost all athletes can use imagery, and this is an ideal method for the treatment of staleness.

SUMMARY

Staleness and burnout are very real psychological and physiological phenomena. Burnout has been defined as a state of mental, emotional, and physical exhaustion brought on by persistent devotion to a goal, the achievement of which is dramatically opposed to reality. Burnout afflicts overly dedicated athletes who are motivated toward high achievement and who work in rather unrewarding situations. It results in negative attitudes and negative self-concepts. Individuals who are perfectionistic, other-oriented, and lacking in assertive interpersonal skills are more susceptible to burnout.

Staleness can be described as a symptom of ensuing burnout, an early warning sign of the state to come. Staleness is characterized by a variety of psychological and physiological variables. The Fatigue Rating Scale and the Profile of Mood States are recommended psychological tools for assessing staleness.

The risk of athletic staleness and burnout can be lessened or prevented by keeping the athletic season reasonably short, keeping training from becoming monotonous, and providing more positive reinforcement and less punitive reinforcement and abusiveness from those in authority. Other steps can be taken to prevent staleness: Schedule time outs, allow athletes to make choices and control outcomes, have mental practice periods, and help athletes to reduce post-competition tension. Generally, thoughts concerning the prevention of staleness center around the concept of enjoyment. Far too many coaches make athletics pure drudgery.

These are the key points in the treatment of staleness and burnout: (1) Each case is unique and should be treated as such. (2) One effective means for treatment of athletic staleness is psychological reprogramming (a variety of techniques were presented here). (3) Reestablishing goals for both practice and competition may help reduce staleness.

REFERENCES

Davis, M., McKay, M., & Eshelman, H. (1983). *The relaxation and stress reduction workbook.* Oakland, Calif.: New Harbinger Publications.

Feigley, D. A. (1984). Psychological burnout in high-level athletes. *Physician and Sportsmedicine, 12*(10), 109–119.

Freudenberger, H. J., & Richelson, G. (1981). *Burnout: How to beat the high cost of success.* New York: Bantam Books.

Harris, D. V., & Harris, B. L. (1984). *The athletes' guide to sports psychology: Mental skills for physical people.* New York: Leisure Press.

Henschen, K. P. (1973, December). Coaches beware: Post-competition tension. *Scholastic Coach*, pp. 52–53.

Kashiwagi, S. (1971). Psychological rating of human fatigue. *Ergonomics, 14,* 17–21.

Kereszty, A. (1971). Overtraining. In L. Larson (Ed.), *Encyclopedia of sport sciences and medicine* (pp. 218–222). New York: Macmillan.

Maslach, C. (1982). Understanding burnout: Definitional issues in analyzing a complex phenomenon. In W. S. Paine (Ed.), *Job stress and burnout: Research, theory, and intervention perspectives* (pp. 29–40). Beverly Hills: Sage Publications.

Maslach, C., & Pines, A. (1977). The burnout syndrome. *Child Care Quarterly, 6,* 100–114.

McNair, D. M., Lorr, M., & Droppleman, L. F. (1971). EDITS manual for the profile of mood states. San Diego, Calif.: Editorial and Industrial Testing Service.

Morgan, W. P. (1984, July). *Selected psychological factors limiting performance: A mental health model.* Paper presented in the Limits on Human Performance Symposium at the 1984 Olympic Scientific Congress, Eugene, Oregon.

Morgan, W. P., & Brown, D. R. (1983, September). *Diagnosis, prevention, and treatment of athletic staleness.* Paper presented at the USOC Sports Medicine Council's Workshop, Long Beach, California.

Morgan, W. P., & Johnson, R. W. (1977). Psychologic characterization of the elite wrestler: A mental health model. *Medicine and Science in Sports, 9,* 55–56.

Morgan, W. P., & Johnson, R. W. (1978). Personality characteristics of successful and unsuccessful oarsmen. *International Journal of Sport Psychology, 9,* 119–133.

O'Block, F., & Evans, F. (1984). Goal setting as a motivational technique. In J. Silya and R. Weinberg (Eds.), *Psychological foundations of sport.* Champaign, Ill.: Human Kinetics.

Orlick, T. (1980). *In pursuit of excellence.* Champaign, Ill.: Human Kinetics.

Pines, A., Aronson, E., & Kafry, D. (1981). *Burnout: From tedium to personal growth.* New York: The Free Press.

Roethlisberger, F. J., & Dickson, W. J. (1947). *Management and the worker.* Cambridge, Mass.: Harvard University Press.

Rotter, J. B., Chance, J. B., & Phares, E. J. (Eds.). (1972). *Applications of a social learning theory of personality.* New York: Holt, Rinehart & Winston.

Samuels, M., & Samuels, N. (1984). *Seeing in the mind's eye.* New York: Random House.

Shank, P. A. (1983, March). Anatomy of burnout. *Parks Recreation, 17,* 52–58.

Tower, R. B., & Singer, J. L. (1981). The measurement of imagery: How can it be clinically useful? In P. C. Kendall & S. Hollon (Eds.), *Assessment strategies for cognitive-behavioral interventions* (pp. 221–222). New York: Academic Press.

21

Stress, Injury, and the Psychological Rehabilitation of Athletes

ROBERT J. ROTELLA

University of Virginia

STEVEN R. HEYMAN

University of Wyoming

Historically, sports medicine specialists have concerned themselves primarily with the physical aspects of injury rehabilitation. As a result, athletes who attained a prescribed level of physical rehabilitation were assumed to be fully prepared for a safe and successful return to competition. Gradually it has become clear that this assumption is not valid for all athletes. Certainly, some athletes psychologically adapt to injury quite readily. If these athletes are provided with physical rehabilitation combined with support, encouragement, and the assurance that it is safe to return to competition, they are ready for a confident return.

However, other athletes, despite physical readiness, are not psychologically ready to return to competition. To them, even the suggestion of returning is a questioned challenge. Doubts, fears, and anxieties surface. Despite assurances from trainers, physicians, and coaches, these athletes do not feel ready. Fears begin to mount concerning the possible risk of returning too quickly. The mind and body get overloaded with thoughts and images of further injury. Sleep is interrupted by recurring dreams of a disastrous return to the playing field or by vivid recall of the feelings of the original injury.

It appears that the frequency with which these apprehensive responses occur has increased as (1) surgical techniques have reduced the time period required for physical rehabilitation, thereby reducing the time frame available for psychological adjustment, and (2) athletes have become more aware of the importance of taking care of their bodies. As a result, the future will demand that injury rehabilitation include both physical and psychological components. It will no longer suffice to argue that athletes who appear to be physically ready to return but who do not feel prepared psychologically to return are malingerers, mentally weak, or lacking in toughness. The old-school approaches of challenging desire and commitment to the team, inducing guilt for letting the team down, or using scare tactics to foster fear, shame, and embarrassment will have to change. These strategies cause more problems than they cure. For example, upon an athlete's initial return to competition, anxiety and tension can lead to one or more of the following:

1. reinjury
2. injury to another body part
3. lowered confidence resulting in a *temporary* performance decrement
4. lowered confidence resulting in a *permanent* performance decrement
5. general depression and fear of further injury, which can sap motivation and the desire to return to competition

Today's athletes are well educated. They usually see through coercive strategies and will distrust individuals who use such approaches. The athletes may respond by simply refusing to return to competition by confidently claiming that they are not ready or by finding other indirect ways to undermine their performance and/or physical rehabilitation. As a result, everyone suffers — the athletes, the team, the coach, and the sport psychologist.

Old approaches to rehabilitation will have to be replaced by sound educational approaches. Coaches and sport psychologists will have to teach athletes how to respond psychologically to injury in a positive and growth-oriented manner rather than in a negative and self-defeating one. We must realize that it is unnatural to be psychologically ready to return to competition after physical rehabilitation is complete unless that rehabilitation takes place in a natural manner. In a world that uses special equipment to shorten the time needed for physical recovery, we need to find special techniques to facilitate an equally rapid psychological adjustment.

Athletes are stronger, quicker, and presumably sturdier than the rest of us. They seem blessed. We forget that what they do is hard. We so rarely see them at their most vulnerable — in pain and out of commission. And we almost never hear, from their perspective, about those injuries that disrupt their existences and play havoc with their futures.

Harry Stein
"Brought to His Knees"
Sport, September 1984, p. 64

FACTORS THAT PREDISPOSE ATHLETES TO INJURY

Common sense, which is important in most situations, can at times cause us to overlook important but subtle relationships when injury occurs. Common sense would seem to tell us that accidents occurring outside of practice and athletic injuries occurring during practice or a game are the result of unfortunate but physically tangible events. Can there be more than just a sequence of physical events relating to an accident or injury?

Research within the general population (e.g., Levenson, Hirschfeld, Hirschfeld, & Dzubay, 1983) and within the athletic population (Bramwell, Masuda, Wagner, & Holmes, 1975; Coddington & Troxell, 1980; Cryan & Alles, 1983; Guttman et al., 1984; Passer & Seese, 1983) suggests that certain specific psychological factors may predispose some individuals to injury and reinjury. In addition, more applied research (Suinn, 1967; Yaffe, 1983) suggests other factors that can influence injuries, illness, and missed practices.

It is important to recognize the use of the word *predispose*. By this we mean that although we cannot predict with complete accuracy who will or will not suffer from a particular problem, we can reasonably predict the group from which those likely to have a problem will come. Even though we still need to develop and more precisely refine our predictive abilities, identifying populations predisposed to injury does allow us to target specific interventions to the group most likely to need them. Identifying predisposed populations also enables us to watch for the earliest signs of the particular problem concerning us.

Life Stress Events

Life stress events—specifically, the amount of change and upset experienced in the year prior to a competitive season—are the most specific factors cited in predisposing some athletes to injury. Most of the studies in this area have involved only football players (Bramwell et al., 1975; Coddington & Troxell, 1980; Cryan & Alles, 1983; Passer & Seese, 1983). The research instruments used in these studies, lists of potentially stressful life events, were modified for athletes by also including stressors specific to athletic participation. Events related to general life stress included death of family members and changes in residence, whereas events related to sports included trouble with coaches and being dropped to a lesser playing status (Bramwell et al., 1975).

A coach or trainer working with athletes individually or with a small team may be aware of these events for his or her athletes; the coach or trainer of a larger team may be less aware of such events unless he or she specifically asks about them. The use of a screening instrument can help to identify individuals who may well be *at risk* for injury. (We will discuss this in more detail later in the chapter.) Once these athletes are identified, we can provide preventive interventions that vary from more formal programs to allowing athletes to ventilate their feelings instead of holding them in and allowing the pressure to intensify. For example, some "at risk" individuals are good candidates for a stress reduction program. (See Chapter 13 for stress intervention techniques.) Such a program might include techniques such as relaxation training or cognitive restructuring. In some cases, it may be most useful for concerned individuals to form support groups for athletes who can get together and share their concerns (Oglesby, 1984). Finally, where levels of stress appear to be extreme, professional counseling may be necessary.

A coach or other individual working with teams should understand the nature of psychological tests before administering stress inventories. Otherwise, these tests may be misinterpreted and misused. For example, a person high in life stress might be more injury-prone in some sports than in others. Our data thus far come from only one sport, a team contact sport (football). Until the results are replicated with other sports, the findings cannot be generalized beyond football. A coach or teammates aware of the results of an athlete's stress score might also add additional pressure with their concerns, comments, expectations, or actions. They may even help to create a self-fulfilling prophecy if they have not been trained in the use and interpretation of tests.

Although life stress was the factor studied most consistently in the research, other factors have been discussed. Sanderson (1977) lists a number of these, including the athlete for whom injury serves as a potent weapon, "You pushed me too hard; now I'm hurt and you feel guilty"; or as an excuse, "I really did not want to do this; now I cannot." If we can see and understand these responses beforehand, we may be able to help athletes eliminate injury and its unpleasant consequences.

Ogilvie (1983) also mentions the frustration of the guilt-ridden athlete who tries to assuage some inner sense of guilt. Even where there is success, it is often hollow and bitter. In some cases the push toward even greater achievement results in physical injury, but in other cases the injury is more indirect. One of the authors has seen in clinical practice of psychotherapy a number of successful high school and college athletes who abuse alcohol and drugs and seem to do so because of the hollowness and bitterness that their very accomplishments force them to recognize. Along these same lines, athletes who are uncertain and lacking in self-esteem may well be placed in greater conflict as successes increase. These individuals are more and more afraid that they will not be able to continue to perform at the levels others expect.

We have described both life stress research and case study evidence of reasons for injury. Although we seem to have identified different factors, the basic processes are, in fact, similar. If we return to our concept of predisposition, what the different researchers are advising is that internal conflicts can create stresses that make injury more likely. Some (Nideffer, 1983) point to the decreased athletic, cognitive, and emotional flexibility that athletes may confront while under stress. Others (Sanderson, 1977) point to more individual ways in which an injury resolves a conflict situation. All would probably agree, however, that an understanding of these factors is essential for coaches, sport psychologists, athletes, and other people concerned with athletic performance and injury. Knowledge of these factors allows for a more integrated understanding of the rehabilitation process, as well as for a remediation of problem situations before the negative consequence occurs. Perhaps even more important, it allows for the possibility of prevention through early detection and intervention.

We *must* keep in mind when using a life events measure that the same stressful event will be experienced differently by different individuals. Several factors are involved. A person's coping mechanisms are critical—some people simply have more effective coping methods. A recent study found that injured volleyball players had lower coping resources than noninjured volleyball players (Williams, Tonymon, & Wadsworth, in press). Social support from family, friends, and significant others, a group likely to include coaches and teammates, is very important. Experience with similar stressors can also be important.

Athletes sometimes experience both internal and external pressure to cope with stress by denial or repression—in essence trying to make believe the stressors are not there. Some athletes elect to suffer in silence rather than to acknowledge their problems and the failing methods of coping. Looking at these athletes, another person might easily say, "There's no problem; they're dealing well with their situation," whereas in fact the opposite is true. The use of the life events measures, which can be modified for more individualized needs, insights, and experiences of coaches and sport psychologists, may be very helpful.

Social support is a concept involving the numbers and types of relationships people have. Research has suggested that certain types of social support systems are helpful in moderating the effects of life stress. In essence, while a greater number of supportive relationships may be desired, the quality of such relationships is also important. For example, a popular member of a team may be very important to other members, and may seem to have a large number of relationships. It may be, however, that although others come to this individual as a resource, he or she may not see others as being similar resources. It may also be that a role traps an individual in relationships in unfulfilling ways. On one football team, a young man with fairly strong religious values felt he had to go out, drink, and chase women with his teammates in order to receive their support and friendship. Although he achieved an external measure of support, the relationships were unfulfilling for him and added to his level of stress. It was, in fact, through a classroom discussion of stress that the athlete sought out someone with whom to discuss his conflicts. Both his coach and his teammates were unaware of the nature and range of his conflicts. After he successfully resolved the conflicts, his coach commented that he was a "much freer person and player." This probably resulted from increased flexibility due to decreased stress. The athlete may well have been an accident that *did not* happen.

Experience and Personality

Previous experience with stress may be potentially useful, but it can also be a detriment. Having experienced a specific or similar situation before may make a person feel better able to deal with a recurrence. On the other hand, if a person's coping mechanisms have been previously taxed or eroded by a stressful situation, then another stress or crisis may increasingly impair functioning.

One factor that makes athletes valued competitors may also make them more vulnerable to injury: the willingness to take risks. A series of research studies (Dahlhauser & Thomas, 1979; Vaillant, 1981; Cohen & Young, 1981) have suggested that this is the case for competitive athletes, particularly when this willingness, even desire, to take risks is related to externally oriented motivations. Some motivations vary from a desire to please others to a belief that one's fate is controlled by external sources.

As we discuss personality there is the hope that a specific "personality" test will be able to predict the more injury-prone athlete. Unfortunately, from those studies that have used measures of more basic, stable personality patterns (with instruments such as Cattel's 16 Personality Factors Questionnaire or the California Personality Inventory), no consistent results have emerged. It may well be that by the time athletes are in high school or college they are able to integrate basic patterns with sport demands. Life stress, on the other hand, taxes athletes' coping abilities and offsets previously established equilibrium, hence predisposing them to injury. Similarly, counterphobics or excessive risk takers, if not held in check or changed, would propel themselves into situations for which they do not have adequate coping skills. As a result they are more vulnerable, not only because of the excessive physical demands, but because the added stress causes an additional drain on the ability to respond.

SUBSTITUTES MAY BE PARTICULARLY VULNERABLE

Coaches and trainers need to keep an especially close lookout for borderline starters and substitutes who mask pain and play through injury. Often such players feel that a missed day of practice will lead to reduced playing time, a missed game may mean losing their position and lost game time. These players may believe that acting tough and masking injury are their only way to get playing time, and they may be very fearful of losing what they had to work so hard to earn.

Potentially Predisposing Attitudes

In their effort to help athletes develop into successful competitors, many coaches and athletic trainers have unknowingly fostered erroneous attitudes concerning successful injury rehabilitation. A clear understanding of these potentially dangerous attitudes is crucial to a complete appreciation of the psychological aspects of injury and rehabilitation.

Act tough and always give 110% Athletes have been systematically taught that mental toughness and giving 110% all of the time are necessary for success in sports. Although mental toughness and giving one's best are important to success, we must realize that when taken to *extremes*, these actions can foster injury and failure.

Certainly athletes must be capable of "playing through" some kinds of pain. However, seldom, if ever, do we educate athletes about the necessity of learning which kinds of pain to ignore and which kinds of pain to listen to and respond to appropriately. The same holds true for learning the amount of pain one should tolerate.

Many highly motivated athletes learn to endure almost any amount or kind of pain. This ability may make for a "tough" athlete, but it may also make for a dumb, often injured athlete who never plays in a fully healthy state. Such athletes often have short-lived careers and a lifetime of suffering.

Especially in many contact sports, athletes who embrace these attitudes are given bountiful rewards. Unfortunately, the rewards often lead to an *extreme* psychological reaction by athletes wishing to win the admiration and respect of coaches, trainers, teammates, and fans. Because the athletes thoroughly enjoy the rewards, they become increasingly involved in earning more rewards by proving and continually displaying their dedication.

With time, the well-intentioned appearance of dedication and commit-

Montreal Expo's President John McHale attempted to describe Andre Dawson's response to the injury and pain in his knee. "Andre is a very unusual man. . . . I'll tell you what's happening here. What's happening is that even with the year he's had, his pride and his commitment to his job are such that he *won't* take himself out—or even excuse himself."

Andre's view was "I'm just not the sort to throw in the towel. I don't know, maybe that's just the way I was raised."

Harry Stein
"Brought to His Knees"
Sport, September 1984, pp. 64, 66

ment develops into the projection of a false image of invulnerability. As athletes attempt to live up to this impossible image, both psychologically and physically, problems begin to appear. Soon, it is accepted as fact that tough athletes never need a rest, never miss a play, never go to the training room, and never let an injury keep them from playing. Failure to live up to the expectations fostered by this image is judged as a sign of weakness.

Eventually, athletes begin to believe in the image of invulnerability off, as well as on, the playing field. They believe that they only deserve the right to feel proud if they give 110%. No one points out to them that giving 110% is impossible or that trying to do so can cause performance at 50% of optimal ability. This belief system persists in spite of the fact that athletes who adhere to these attitudes are unable to perform at their best because they are chronically overtired, playing in pain, and adjusting their style of play to their injuries.

Finally, the athletes become extremely vulnerable and totally unprepared for the incapacitating injury or lifelong pain that will likely follow. A major change in attitude is required to ensure a healthy adaptation to injury and life. Without this change in attitude, athletes will not be able to accept injuries and respond positively to them. As a result, athletes will fail to develop to their fullest potential, and in so doing their coaches and trainers will also fail. True professionals must realize the hazards of these mistaken attitudes of the past before they can use to the fullest the specific psychological strategies that we present later in this chapter.

Injured athletes are worthless Some coaches have been led to believe that the best way to foster a rapid recovery from injury is to make injured athletes feel unimportant as long as they are injured. This is, to say the least, a counterproductive approach. Coaches who hold this view clearly communicate to their athletes that they only care for them as performers. Some coaches communicate this message by isolating injured athletes from healthy team members. Some refuse any form of verbal communication while using body language to suggest that injured athletes should feel guilty for being injured and not helping the team win. Others talk behind the injured athletes' backs and suggest that the athletes are malingerers, lack mental toughness and desire, or are not fully committed to the success of the team.

Leaders in sport must realize that the time during which athletes are recovering from injury is crucial for either developing or destroying *trust*. It is during this time that leaders have a chance to demonstrate *care* and *concern* and show that they are as committed to their athletes as they ask their athletes to be to them.

Most contemporary athletes are intelligent and sophisticated. They realize that actions speak louder than words. Athletes have learned to respect their precious physical gifts, and they expect their coaches and trainers to do likewise.

Successful leaders of present-day athletes must help the athletes realize that attitudes such as desire, pride, and commitment are beneficial at the right time and place but that these attitudes may also be hazardous to present and future health if taken to the extreme. The key is for leaders to do what is in the *best interest* of injured athletes. When this approach is followed, athletes, coaches, trainers, and teams alike will have the best possible chance of attaining their fullest potential. When this approach is not followed, there is still a chance that the athletes themselves will put sport in a proper perspective. But they will do so out of *distrust* rather than trust. This will often lead athletes to decide that sport is unimportant and a place for personal abuse rather than positive growth and fulfillment.

"I went to the doctor with Andre Dawson a couple of times," Pete Rose was saying now. . . . The conversation rapidly turned to the gruesome but unavoidable subject of permanent injury. "Listen," said Rose, "I know a guy who fought the whole organization because he didn't want to jeopardize his health—Johnny Bench. He told them, 'I will not catch anymore, period. I don't plan to be a cripple when I'm through.'"

Rose paused. . . . "And I'm not gonna sit here and tell you that someone who says that is wrong. I mean, hell, when you finish playing this game, you've still got half your life in front of you."

Harry Stein
"Brought to His Knees"
Sport, September 1984, p. 63

ATHLETES' REACTIONS TO INJURY

Regardless of the best efforts of coaches and trainers, injuries still occur. The second step involved in serving the athletes' best interests involves an *understanding* and appreciation of the psychology of injury rehabilitation.

Predictable Psychological Reactions to Injury

Following injury, athletes commonly experience a sequence of predictable psychological reactions similar to those outlined by Kübler-Ross in her classic *On Death and Dying* (1969). These reactions include (1) disbelief, denial, and isolation; (2) anger; (3) bargaining; (4) depression; and (5) acceptance and resignation while continuing to remain hopeful of the eventual return to competition. Athletes initially respond by believing that there is no damage, that the injury is less serious than originally thought, or that the injury will be healed in a day or two. However, when they realize that the injury will prevent practice and competition for an extended time period, athletes often respond by feeling isolated and lonely. As they attend to their injuries, they typically become irritated with themselves and others. Anger is followed by a true sense of loss. Normal comfort and freedom are gone, as are the abilities to enjoy and display physical prowess on center stage. Although each step does not always progress as exactly and routinely as presented here, depression is usually followed by acceptance and hope of a successful return to competition. However, coaches and sport psychologists should be aware of a variety of factors that may intervene, and if not properly managed, delay or prevent this important final adjustment step from occurring.

Perceptual Responses to Injury

Athletes perceive injury in various ways. Some view it as a disaster, others see it as an opportunity to display courage, and still others welcome it as a relief from the drudgery of practice or the embarrassment and frustration of poor performance, lack of playing time, or a losing season.

It is not uncommon for injured athletes to feel concerned about whether they will ever completely recover and return to their previous form. They must be prepared for a quick return to action, a delayed recovery, or the end of their career. Only a positive and enthusiastic response will assure the best possible chance of a complete rehabilitation, both physically and mentally.

Because of the importance of athletic performance to many athletes, injury often leads to an attack on the self-image. Emotional and irrational thinking often become dominant. Athletes responding in this manner may increasingly become lost in the "work of worry" and eventually become overwhelmed by anxiety. Such interfering thought patterns can further delay or sabotage effective rehabilitation.

When athletes think irrationally, they may *exaggerate* the meaning of the injury, *disregard* particularly important aspects of the injury, *oversimplify* the injury as good or bad, right or wrong, *overgeneralize* from this single event, or draw *unwarranted conclusions* when evidence is lacking or contradictory (Beck, 1970). Athletes may, for example, feel sorry for themselves and perceive that training room personnel give preferential treatment to "major sport" athletes or to "mens' team" athletes. They may exaggerate and catastrophize that their career is ended. They may become discouraged after 10 days of therapy even though they have been told that recovery will take at least two to three weeks. Injured athletes may decrease their motivation for rehabilitation and increase their anxiety by focusing on other athletes with similar injuries who failed to recover rather than thinking of numerous other athletes who fully recovered. Some injured athletes may, out of fear, decide they are injury-prone. This thought can lead athletes to grow increasingly anxious and thus actually cause them to become more frequently injured.

REACTING TO INJURED ATHLETES

Danish (1984) makes an excellent point when he reminds us to respond to athletes as people, not just injuries. He also describes a helping skills model that can be of use to those working with athletes.

If we consider the nature of injury to athletes, particularly injuries that are painful, sudden, and moderate to severe in their effects, another model comes to mind: *the crisis intervention model.* Crisis intervention is a short-term intervention method most often used when individuals' coping abilities are overwhelmed or when others recognize that those who are injured are not aware of the extent to which their normal patterns have been impaired and overwhelmed. Crisis intervention consists of getting people through crises until their normal coping abilities return or until more long-term help can be implemented.

Crisis intervention models follow a similar pattern and can be learned fairly easily; they form the basis of most volunteer hotlines. In the case of working with injured athletes, such models can help coaches and sport psychologists to become more aware of the meaning of injuries to athletes, to be appropriately reassuring, to help athletes attend to immediate and practical concerns rather than to more distant worries, and to see injury and the problems it poses in manageable units as opposed to an overwhelming, engulfing catastrophe.

Crisis intervention courses vary in length from 15 to 50 hours. As Gluck (1983) notes: "The person who helps to carry a player off the field is as important as the individuals who administer first aid and cardiopulmonary resuscitation. In most instances, a stretcher may be unnerving to the injured player and to his family" (p. 333). Not only can such a person who is trained deal with athletes but with family members as well. The injury is truly a crisis, and without appropriate responses the bottomless fears, the searing emotions may well set a very poor direction that will need to be countered in subsequent rehabilitation attempts. Such training also helps coaches to recognize more clearly the intellectual and emotional limitations the injury — the crisis — may create for injured athletes: the extreme pessimism or optimism that must be accepted and worked with until a more stable balance can be achieved. If crisis intervention is successful, it can prepare the groundwork for later psychological rehabilitation strategies.

Social support, as mentioned previously, is critical in the rehabilitation process, particularly with moderate to severe injuries. If the athletic identification has been strong, family and friends may have come to respond to athletes primarily through their role as athletes. In many cases, friendships are based exclusively along these lines, particularly with other teammates or with other athletes. Suddenly these important ties may be ruptured. Injured athletes may no longer be seen and may no longer see themselves as athletes. Activities around which their lives centered now move along without them. No one quite knows how to relate to these athletes except perhaps in terms of their past glory or possible future — but not to the injured people in the present.

Coaches and sport psychologists must help ensure that normal contacts are maintained. They should be as reassuringly optimistic about recovery of past abilities as possible, and they should also encourage injured athletes to discover other bases of support for themselves. These actions serve more than some obscure long-term need, as Eldridge (1983) notes. They also help to reestablish and maintain a sense of equilibrium. This will not be the same equilibrium as prior to the injury; it can be an even better one. It does require a sincere interest in knowing and understanding athletes.

As we know, the mind and body function together. When we consider the involvement of injured athletes in the physical rehabilitation program (Danish, 1984; Sanderson, 1978), we must also understand what, if any, attempts are made in the psychological arena. How motivated will athletes be in the journey to recovery? How well will they deal with the often minute steps forward or the reverses that are a part of rehabilitation? How will they manage their fears of lost abilities when they return to competition or their fears of reinjury? Unfortunately, these questions are often met with silence or not asked out loud by athletes. Consequently, they echo internally, and in the echo fears may grow.

What we have been describing is the backdrop to a more holistic view of the psychological rehabilitation process. It is not an attempt to fix an injured part but to address the whole. It seems likely that in most cases athletes' participation and commitment to the physical rehabilitation program will be contingent on psychological factors, and the interaction will form a continuing, holistic pattern.

TEACHING SPECIFIC PSYCHOLOGICAL REHABILITATION STRATEGIES

Coaches and sport psychologists must encourage athletes to view injury from a self-enhancing perspective rather than a self-defeating one. They need to teach athletes that when an injury occurs, it is reasonable and appropriate to think the injury is unfortunate, untimely, and inconvenient, and to feel irritated, frustrated, and disappointed. It is unreasonable for athletes to convince themselves that the situation is hopeless, that injuries are a sign of weakness and should be hidden, or that their season or career is over.

Nancy Mayer, a star guard for the University of Virginia basketball team, describes the role her coaches and trainers played in helping her through a year and a half of rehabilitation following a serious knee injury.

> The trainers Joe Gieck and Sue Halstead Shapiro helped me step by step. They taught me patience. They did more than they think. Our assistant coach Gino Auriemma really helped me get my head up when I was frustrated. It was easy to get down and his reinforcement meant a lot. . . . It was scary. I felt very awkward. I was scared to find out if I was as good as I was before, if I could still play well. (Ratcliffe, 1983)

Athletes with emotional self-control will be able to cope with injury more effectively by responding rationally to it. They can best exert self-control if they have knowledge of the injury and the rehabilitation process. It is difficult, if not impossible, for intelligent athletes to be positive and relaxed if they lack knowledge, are anxious, and wonder why they are doing what they are doing in the training room. Much anxiety results from uncertainty, misconceptions, or inaccurate information. If uncertainty persists, athletes may have trouble getting through the denial and isolation phases of rehabilitation. Honest and accurate information coupled with hope helps athletes move into the acceptance phase (Kavanaugh, 1972). In addition, athletes who realize the purpose of rehabilitation are more likely to work hard and to provide useful information about their progress.

Thought Stoppage

What athletes say to themselves following an injury helps determine their subsequent behavior. Athletes can be taught coping skills to control their inner thoughts. Then when faulty or self-defeating internal dialogues occur, the athletes can use an intervention strategy such as thought stoppage. See Chapter 15 for more information on thought stoppage and other techniques for controlling thoughts.

As an example of the importance of inner dialogue, consider an injury-related situation in which an athlete is in the training room receiving treatment and going through rehabilitation exercises while experiencing a great amount of pain and little apparent improvement in the injured area. If her inner dialogue becomes self-defeating, the athlete worries and questions the benefit of treatment and exercise. "This is awful. This hurts too much to be beneficial. These exercises will probably cause me more harm. Besides, I've been doing this for three days now, and I can't see any progress. It would be a lot easier to just let the injury heal on its own. I don't think I'll come tomorrow. If it's really important, the coach will call me. If she doesn't, it will mean I was right. It really doesn't matter if I get treatment." The athlete does not get much out of today's treatment and begins to develop excuses for not continuing therapy.

On the other hand, if the athlete's inner dialogue is self-enhancing, she worries and questions the benefits of treatment and exercise but then thinks, "*stop;* these exercises hurt, but it's OK—they'll pay off. I'm lucky to have knowledgeable people helping me. I'll be competing soon because I'm doing these exercises. I must not let the pain bother me. If the pain gets too severe, I'll speak up and tell the coach. She'll want to know. Otherwise, I'll live with it and think about how happy I'll be to be competing again." The athlete has a good treatment session and prepares herself to continue for as long as necessary. She develops rapport with the coach, who feels good about the athlete.

By learning a mental self-control strategy such as thought stoppage, athletes can often shorten the time period needed to advance from disbelief to acceptance to a safe and successful return to competition.

Imagery

The athletes' imagination can greatly influence their response to injury. Many imagine the worst that could happen. Athletes may be taught to control their visual images and to direct them productively to reduce anxiety and to aid in rehabilitation. Imagery strategies include visual rehearsal, emotive imagery rehearsal, and body rehearsal (Lazarus, 1974; Moss, 1979). See Chapter 14 for more detailed information on what imagery is and techniques that can be used to teach and enhance imagery skills.

Visual rehearsal   Visual rehearsal may include both mastery and coping rehearsal. Mastery rehearsal fosters motivation for rehabilitation and confidence upon the return to competition. While disabled, athletes may vi-

When Philadelphia Phillies pinch-hitter Len Matuszek unloaded against the Chicago Cubs Tuesday night, he released six weeks of frustration.

In his second at bat since coming off the disabled list, Matuszek cracked a leadoff, pinch-hit home run in the seventh inning to give the Phillies a 3–2 victory over the Cubs. He hit the first pitch into the right-field bull pen. "That was all I had on my mind during my time on the disabled list. I kept envisioning some ways to help this team win a game. Even with the injury my attitude has been good."

"Phillie Unloads Frustration on Cubs"
The Daily Progress, July 24, 1984, p. D3

sually rehearse returning to competition and performing effectively. For athletes who experience difficulty viewing themselves vividly in their mind, relaxation exercises should precede the imagery session. Some athletes visualize better with the aid of recordings or video replays of their most effective game performances.

In coping rehearsal, injured athletes visually rehearse anticipated problematic situations or obstacles that may stand in the way of their successful return to competition and then rehearse effectively overcoming these obstacles. Coping rehearsal is the more realistic of the two visual rehearsal methods and prepares athletes for difficulties that might realistically occur.

Emotive rehearsal   Emotive rehearsal enables athletes to feel secure and confident that rehabilitation will be successful. The athletes rehearse various scenes that produce positive, self-enhancing feelings such as enthusiasm, self-pride, and confidence. Athletes may, for instance, rehearse feeling excited about their first game following injury or rehearse thoughts of the admiration coaches, teammates, and friends will have for them on their return from injury. Athletes can also be instructed to think of other athletes like themselves who have overcome similar injuries and then generate other scenes that produce positive feelings.

COPING REHEARSAL: PREPARATION FOR OBSTACLES

There will be excuses for not going to the training room for treatments: "I don't have time," "I'm too busy," "I have a test tomorrow," "The training room hours are ridiculous." I will make sure that I'm ready for these excuses and realize they will work against me. I will always find a way to get my treatments.

Body rehearsal In body rehearsal, the athletes vividly envision what is happening to the injury internally during the rehabilitation process. To do this, the athletes must receive a detailed explanation of their injury. Whenever possible, color pictures should be used to help the athletes develop a mental picture of the injury. The healing process and purpose of the rehabilitation techniques are then explained. After visualizing the healing process, athletes are asked to imagine in vivid color the healing occurring during treatment sessions and at intervals during the day. Although there is a need for further research to determine the effectiveness of body rehearsal, it appears to be a beneficial strategy for aiding the healing process.

ATHLETES ARE HUMAN

Injuries vary from major to minor. It is important to remember that the seriousness of an injury does not necessarily determine the ease or difficulty of psychological rehabilitation. And psychological rehabilitation is necessary to ensure a healthy *future* for athletes, a future that must include more than *just* their playing careers.

Rehabilitation is both a mental and physical process. Because athletes are human, this process includes an emotional component that will change from day to day. It is crucial to strive to make this process a positive experience in which athletes are actively involved.

An example describes the importance of appreciating this emotional component. A university-age athlete was drafted out of high school by a professional baseball team but chose to go to college before turning professional. In the fall of his freshman year in college he tore ligaments in his throwing arm, which required surgery. The following advice and program were outlined for him as he psychologically prepared for his return to practice the following spring. The program was designed to facilitate a safe return and a successful future.

The athlete, a pitcher, was reminded of how excited he would be on the first day of spring practice to find out if he still "had it," if he could still throw hard. He was reminded of the need to be smart, emotionally controlled, disciplined, and patient in order to control himself when his personal excitement over being back on the field with his teammates was combined with the high of a beautiful spring day following a long winter. He was also told that he would feel great and have an almost overpowering urge to overthrow on the first day his arm felt good. In addition, he would want to try all of his different pitches. The desire to help his teammates be successful and the thrill of getting back on stage and becoming a star again would be highly motivating. He was told of the importance of realizing the temptation of these feelings and cautioned not to fall victim to them.

Together, this athlete, his coaches, and his trainers outlined a specific plan. They decided on a set number of throws each day, the distance of the throws, the approximate speed of the throws, and the kinds of throws. For the first three weeks, the athlete's catcher and a coach would help to make sure that the plan was adhered to on a daily basis. Short-term and long-term goals were detailed so that by the fifth game of the year, the athlete would be ready to return to the pitching mound for three innings of relief pitching.

A similar plan was detailed for physical treatments. Both plans were reinforced by coaches, trainers, and teammates, as well as by daily visualization of the good feelings and results that would occur from sticking to the plan. Despite many days of questioning, doubt, and uncertainty, the athlete generally remained positive, stayed with the plan, and made a highly successful return to competition one week later than planned.

As with many other athletes, the process from injury to return to competition was a challenge to this athlete's mind and body. Because the process was managed properly, it allowed for a positive and bright future.

THE INJURED ATHLETE: LESSONS TO BE LEARNED FROM COMBAT REACTIONS

Modern sports, particularly many competitive and contact sports, have their roots in war and combat. As we conclude our consideration of the psychological rehabilitation of injured athletes, we can learn valuable lessons from the principles used with those injured in combat. Kardiner (1959) notes:

> The soldier lives in an atmosphere of continuous fatigue, anxiety, and boredom, deprived of sex and opportunity for complete relaxation. Moreover, his weaknesses are exposed to public gaze, and his failure to be an effective member of a team may inflict a blow to his self-esteem from which he may never recover. (p. 248)

Certainly these sound like some of the factors others have linked to predisposing athletes to injury. More extensive symptoms of a problem process include poor appetite, carelessness, unusual jumpiness, irritability, inability to relax, and nightmares, which in their appearance or frequency may indicate the extent of stress for athletes.

In response to the trauma of war or of injury in sport, some people will seek to avoid situations that they assume produced stress. Others will try to adapt themselves to their new, narrowed world. Still others will show signs of psychological disorganization. They may be unable to derive pleasure from sport and nonsport activities. Their thoughts and dreams will often force them to return to the traumatic event.

Within the war situation, the most important consideration is keeping soldiers close to their unit, with a return to regular duty as quickly as possible. What has occurred and the soldiers' reactions to it are to be kept tied together so they do not become separated psychologically and thus more difficult to resolve. This also prevents soldiers from building up the feared situation to overwhelming proportions in the absence of the real stimuli.

As noted earlier, the same factors that predispose soldiers to a psychological breakdown may predispose athletes to injury. This is not where the similarities end. The more significant the injury and its meaning to athletes, the more similar the recovery process will be to that experienced by soldiers. Soldiers feel bound to duty by external motivations: patriotism, peer evaluation, etc. Athletes often tie their identity to sport, and so when sport is taken away, life's meaning is shaken in direct relation to the importance of sport to them.

In war, separating soldiers from their unit exacerbates feelings of letting others down and also ruptures important social ties. Not only do athletes experience these feelings, they often also fear being replaced. The longer athletes are kept away by injury, the longer these feelings and fear fester.

Perhaps an example will further clarify these relationships. Frank, a high school second-string quarterback, injured his knee and was to be out of practice and games for a month. Frank was an average student, and most of his special recognition as a person came during the games in which he played. His coach knew he was highly motivated and always gave his best. Frank felt he had to do this; others were waiting to take his place, and he desperately wanted to be the starting quarterback in his senior year. Given the importance of athletics to Frank, the depression he experienced after being injured was not surprising. It was also not surprising that his dreams involved reliving the accident or seeing himself walk away uninjured. The pressures under which he played may have predisposed him to the injury, although there is no sure way to ascertain this. His rehabilitation, however, was modeled very much along the lines of soldiers' rehabilitation. As soon as he was able to join his team at practice, he did — even if it meant just helping out. Frank changed clothes with the rest of the team, was there through practice, and showered with the team. He was on the sidelines for games. As he was able, he gradually resumed all of his usual activities. When he had to run slower or lift less weight, he did, but his routine approximated his normal routine. The dreams ceased and the depression lifted relatively quickly. Although at times he wanted to move more quickly than was advisable, the coach underscored the importance of Frank's appropriate recovery to the team. As Frank gradually returned to activity, he had virtually no fear of reinjury when he faced full practice and his first game because he had been close to this in previous practice.

Too often, when athletes are kept away because of injury, they feel that their teammates and time have marched on. There are new jokes, new alignments, in essence a new situation that excludes injured athletes and into which they must try to reintegrate themselves. By being there, other athletes have grown and developed with the situation.

We would go so far as to say as soon as athletes can rejoin a team—even if on crutches or bandaged—they should do so. It is sometimes too much to ask someone to get back on a horse after being thrown, but a modified approach allows a gradual remount while preventing the consolidation of fears of overwhelming obstacles.

For many individual sport athletes the case is somewhat different. There is usually not the same group support system or as much fear of replacement. There is still involvement with others, however. The basic

---

Duke Snider, the Hall of Famer who broadcasts games for the Montreal Expos, comments on Andre Dawson's desire to keep playing despite suggestions that he should stop and have surgery. Snider himself had his career subverted by a severe injury at the age of 31.

"After the injury I was a shell of my old self. . . . I sit up there every day and I see one of the best young players in such pain he simply can't do the job he's trying to do. I see his knee buckle when he swings. I see him overswing to try and compensate . . . hobbling down the first base line, and being unable to slow down to make a slide—so many little things."

"It's easy for me to say, but I think he shouldn't play the rest of the year."

But it was pointed out Dawson doesn't want to sit out the year.

Snider nodded. "Andre has an awful lot of pride, and I respect him for it. But common sense and judgment have to enter into it, too." He stopped. "The thing is you still *think* you can do what you've always done. It takes a while for it to sink in that you can't." He stops again. "The truth is, when Arthur—that is, arthritis—comes to live in your knee, he never leaves."

Harry Stein
"Brought to His Knees"
Sport, September 1984, p. 67

process of separation from an activity that means a great deal remains. So does the opportunity for the separation of event and feelings, and the consolidation of fears. Thus, as soon as possible after injury, athletes should develop routines similar to prior training and competition. If this is not possible, coaches should consider involving recuperating athletes in the training of others.

As this section ends, it is important to return to our original example of soldiers and athletes. To underscore the important similarities, let us remember that while we may say soldiers fight for something and "against others," competitive athletes certainly do no less. The psychological wounds of battle are not inflicted by others on soldiers but by the soldiers themselves, and such wounds affect rehabilitation. Helping soldiers gain control over this situation is a critical part of the rehabilitation process. The reaction of athletes to injury is also something personally created. The rehabilitation process for athletes, as for soldiers, must prevent the development and exacerbation of damage and must provide athletes with the tools to move forward and live healthy and successful lives.

SUMMARY

Sports medicine has made great advances in the physical rehabilitation of injured athletes, but little attention has been given to the psychological rehabilitation of these athletes. Although some athletes have effective psychological responses, others do not. This chapter focuses on factors that may predispose athletes to injuries, patterns of negative reactions to injuries, and ways in which coaches and sport psychologists can help athletes respond psychologically to injuries in positive, growth-oriented ways.

Although no clear injury-prone personality has been identified, some factors such as life stress are predictive of injury. This and other factors related to injury are described, and possible preventive interventions are presented. More and less adaptive responses to injury are illustrated, including comparisons to Kübler-Ross's model of loss. Crisis intervention responses, systems of social support, and cognitive–behavioral interventions are ways to help injured athletes respond to injury in a more positive psychological way.

REFERENCES

Beck, A. (1970). Cognitive therapy: Nature and relation to behavior therapy. *Behavior Therapy. 2,* 194–200.

Bramwell, S. T., Masuda, M., Wagner, N. N., & Holmes, T. H. (1975). Psychosocial factors in athletic injuries. *Journal of Human Stress, 2,* 6–20.

Coddington, R. D., & Troxell, J. R. (1980). The effects of emotional factors on football injury rates—a pilot study. *Journal of Human Stress, 7,* 3–5.

Cohen, D. A., & Young, M. L. (1981). Self-concept and injuries among female high school basketball players. *Journal of Sports Medicine and Physical Fitness, 21,* 55–61.

Cryan, P. D., & Alles, W. F. (1983). The relationship between stress and college football injuries. *Journal of Sports Medicine, 23,* 52–58.

Dahlhauser, M., & Thomas, M. D. (1979). Visual disembedding and locus of control as variables associated with high school football injuries. *Perceptual and Motor Skills, 49,* 254.

Danish, S. J. (1984). Psychological aspects in the care and treatment of athletic injuries. In P. E. Vinger & E. F. Hoerner (Eds.), *Sports injuries: The unthwarted epidemic* (2nd ed.). Boston, Mass.: John Wright PSG.

Eldridge, W. D. (1983). The importance of psychotherapy for athletic-related orthopedic injuries among athletes. *International Journal of Sport Psychology, 14,* 203–211.

Gluck, J. M. (1983). The doctor's bag. *Orthopedic Clinics of North America, 14,* 323–336.

Guttman, M. C., Knapp, D. M., Foster, C., Pollack, M. L., & Ropowski, B. L. (1984). *Age, experience, and gender as predictors of psychological response to training in Olympic speedskaters.* Paper presented at the 1984 Olympic Scientific Congress, Eugene, Oregon.

Kardiner, A. (1959). Traumatic neuroses of war. In S. Arieti (Ed.), *American handbook of psychiatry* (Vol. 1) (pp. 246–257). New York: Basic Books.

Kavanaugh, R. E. (1972). *Facing death.* Los Angeles: Nash Publishing.

Kübler-Ross, E. (1969). *On death and dying.* New York: Macmillan.

Lazarus, A. (1974). Psychological stress and coping in adaptation and illness. *International Journal of Psychiatric Medicine, 5,* 321–333.

Levenson, H., Hirschfeld, L., Hirschfeld, A., & Dzubay, B. (1983). Recent life events and accidents: The role of sex differences. *Journal of Human Stress, 10,* 4–11.

Moss, R. H. (1979). *The crisis of illness: An overview in coping with physical illness.* New York: Plenum Medical Book Co.

Nideffer, R. M. (1983). The injured athlete: Psychological factors in treatment. *Orthopedic Clinics of North America, 14,* 374–385.

Ogilvie, B. C. (1983). The orthopedist's role in children's sports. *Orthopedic Clinics of North America, 14,* 361–372.

Oglesby, C. (1984, June). Personal communication with author.

Passer, M. W., & Seese, M. D. (1983). Life stress and athletic injury: Examination of positive versus negative events and three moderator variables. *Journal of Human Stress, 10,* 11–16.

Ratcliffe, J. (1983, June 19). Saga of UVA Blue Chipper. *The Daily Progress,* p. D3.

Rotella, R. (1984). Psychological care of the injured athlete. In L. Bunker, R. J. Rotella, & A. S. Reilly (Eds.), *Sport psychology: Psychological considerations in maximizing sport performance*. Ithaca, N.Y.: Mouvement Publications.

Sanderson, F. H. (1977). The psychology of the injury-prone athlete. *British Journal of Sports Medicine, 11*, 56–57.

Sanderson, F. H. (1978). The psychological implications of injury. *British Journal of Sports Medicine, 12*, 41–43.

Suinn, R. M. (1967). Psychological reactions to disability. *Journal of the Association for Physical and Mental Rehabilitation, 13–15.*

Vaillant, P. M. (1981). Personality and injury in competitive runners. *Perceptual and motor skills, 53*, 251–253.

Williams, J. M., Tonymon, P., & Wadsworth, W. A. (in press). Relationship of life stress to injury in intercollegiate volleyball. *Journal of Human Stress.*

Yaffe, M. (1983). Sports injuries: Psychological aspects. *British Journal of Hospital Medicine, 27*, 224–232.

22 The Trauma of Termination from Athletics

BRUCE C. OGILVIE

San Jose State University

MAYNARD HOWE

U.S. International University

The termination of an athletic career often creates a major life crisis for which the athlete is not prepared. An extensive review of related literature (which is surprisingly limited) indicates that the social, psychological, and financial problems associated with termination have received very little attention. In both Europe and North America, only the exceptional coach or team manager includes career termination as a part of his or her professional responsibility to the athletes. Considering the potentially traumatic effects of termination, it is most unfortunate that this reality, which occurs in the life of every competitive athlete, has not been addressed in a more sensitive and responsible manner.

In this chapter we will discuss the fundamental elements of sport termination trauma and also examine the role of the coach and sport psychologist in dealing with this phenomenon. We also include several fascinating case studies to support the thesis of this chapter.

THE TERMINATION

Although the cause of termination of an athletic career can spring from a variety of reasons, it usually relates to one of three major factors: the selection process, chronological age, and injury.

The Selection Process

The process of selection, which occurs at every competitive level, accounts for the largest attrition rate. Consider, for example, the following statistics (Mueller & Blyth, 1984):

	Basketball	*Football*
High School	700,000	1,300,000 +
College (NCAA Vars.)	15,000	75,000
Draft	200 (NBA)	320 (NFL)
Final Selection	50	150

Less than 1% of those competing in basketball or football at the collegiate level are successful in making the transition into the NBA or NFL.

No matter what the sport, a rigid selection criterion is imposed upon every athlete. Those who are successful in surviving the cut, at whatever level, will once again experience the philosophy of survival of the fittest at some later time in their competitive life. Each and every athlete must be prepared for the consequences of functioning in a Darwinian sports world.

Chronological Age

The aging process, of course, affects everyone, but it can be deadly to the athletic career. As physiological changes begin to occur, many athletes start to fight the long uphill battle to maintain their career. The presence of younger, faster, and stronger athletes significantly increases the pressures on the aging competitor.

Although the longevity of athletic careers varies among different sports (Arnold Palmer may still be able to make an occasional tournament cut at the age of 51; however, gymnast Olga Korbut, after winning the gold medal in 1972 at the age of 17, appeared "too old" for competition only four years later), the endurance and agility of youth diminish as every athlete is faced with the inevitable reality that models the mortality in all of us.

One of the most comprehensive studies of termination trauma was conducted in 1981 by Svoboda and Vanek. The 163 successful athletes who participated in the survey had made uncharacteristic (for the West) preparation for a life after sports, yet 83% reported that no amount of foresight could protect them from the anxiety that developed out of an awareness of the temporal dimension: Time was ceaselessly "working against them." (With respect to this study, although Svoboda and Vanek did not report the number of athletes who refused to provide data, they recognized the selective nature of the 163 athletes who agreed to be subjects. Indeed, Svoboda and Vanek believed that those who experienced the more severe stress reactions to career termination were poorly represented in their data.)

Injury

Athletic injury may also bring on a termination crisis. Bernie Parent, all-star goaltender for the Philadelphia Flyers, sustained a severe eye injury that brought his athletic career to an abrupt and unexpected end. Now in public relations with the Flyers, Parent openly shares the bouts of severe depression and alcoholism he faced following his sudden termination from professional hockey. Parent's case is only one of the many thousands of examples on all levels of how a major injury can end an athlete's career.

A professional athlete who sustains an injury that results in termination generally receives wide publicity. However, the long-range consequences of major injuries attract comparatively little attention and must be taken into more serious consideration. Permanent damage to bones, cartilage, ligaments, and nerves, as well as varying degrees of brain damage and arthritis, may significantly hamper the athlete's ability to lead a productive and fulfilling life. In many instances the variety of possible career options is limited. For example, brain damage incurred from contact sports such as hockey, football, and boxing may limit an athlete's capacity to realize a career goal that he may have previously considered. An additional consequence might also be the prevention of the athlete's involvement in recreational sports.

THE TRANSITION

Whatever the cause of termination, each individual faces a period of adjustment during the transition from athlete to ex-athlete. Some people handle this transition more successfully than others, but for most, it is a time of existential dilemmas and identity crises. Before the termination of their athletic career, athletes' primary focus of attention on sports can cause them to neglect many other aspects of life.

The Childhood Conditioning Factor

The strong identification that most athletes make with sports begins in childhood and continues to intensify through the developmental and adult years. According to Erik Erickson, a child begins to develop a sense of identity between the ages of 7 and 12. During this same period, the child is also involved in the process of ego integration.

Research supports what any sensitive observer of youth sports would conclude: There are primary motives for a child's participation in sports. Children are interested in the development of skills and competence, and they wish to form friendships and socialize with others. Some seek recognition through success in sports, whereas others seek to expend energy and to know the excitement of challenges or taking risks.

Children are naturally curious about a variety of activities. They will generally choose to develop activities that are internally pleasurable and/or externally rewarded. If a child is internally and externally rewarded for developing a multiplicity of skills and interests, the child's self-worth will not be solely dependent on success in only one role. However, if the child's identity as an athlete is reinforced to the exclusion of other facets of his or her personality, then the child's feeling of self-worth will be almost totally contingent upon success or failure as an athlete.

As the child continues to develop athletic competencies, the social and cultural expectations to excel also increase. This creates a marriage between the athlete's sense of self-worth and the expectations of others. Unfortunately, too many adults who are responsible for youth programs adhere to the concept of survival of the fittest and continue to parrot the overworked view that children must learn that selection will occur at every significant point in their lives. Too many adults also feel that the earlier children confront this reality, the better able they will be to cope with it in the future.

The "Sports Only" Identification

The degree to which athletes derive an identity through the athletic role determines the intensity of the identity crisis they will face at termination. When ex-athletes attempt to adjust to the new world into which they must now assimilate themselves, they experience a feeling of social and cultural limbo and no clear personal identity.

The emotional and psychological responses to this career crisis are nearly universal, and they are much like those experienced with any major loss. Such responses often closely parallel the psychological process that begins when a person is told that he or she is terminally ill.

Advisors to the U.S. Olympic Sports Medicine Committee invariably discuss termination issues with elite performers. Special concern has been generated for athletes who have either sacrificed their education, delayed important career decisions, or uprooted themselves from home environments that provided them with security during the transition from sportsperson to average citizen. Among the elite performers studied by Svoboda and Vanek, 41% admitted that they had paid no attention to profession or career associated with retiring from sports; 31% began to consider a future profession only immediately before termination.

Tragically, the philosophy behind athletic management often directs the athlete away from activities that detract from the sports-only identification. Consider, for example, the attempted initiation of a program in career counseling for the San Francisco 49ers in 1968.

Case Study: Attempted Pro Athlete Counseling Program

In an effort to generate increased team morale and to help athletes acknowledge the temporary nature of their football playing careers, San Francisco 49ers management was introduced to a concept that would provide career counseling for the athletes. With the help and cooperation of the team president, Lou Spadia, the S.F. 49er Career Planning Committee was formed. This was a service offered to any contracted player who wished to prepare for a career beyond his playing days or to develop skills that he could use to supplement his football salary.

A committee of seven of the most prominent business leaders in San Francisco agreed to provide counseling for selected team members. The executives and athletes were to discuss education, special aptitudes, and particular goals for both off-season and long-range employment. A psychologist was to assess the athletes' personal attributes, to collect data on education and work experience, and to determine special aptitudes that could become the basis for a nonathletic career.

The committee was to assess the career potentialities of the athletes and to give both counseling and direction. A special function that the members of the committee particularly enjoyed was to open doors so that the athletes could personally explore career options and opportunities with men and women who were successful in areas in which the athletes had career interest. At the career planning sessions, the psychologist shared all of the psychological insights and personal information that was essential to help with the career information provided by the referrals. All information shared at the committee meetings was subject to each athlete's approval and collaboration.

Unfortunately, what appeared on the surface to be a fine opportunity to achieve major goals of both the players and the organization did not survive even to the middle of the season. The executives proved to be diligent and reliable. In every case they followed through in offering their valuable counsel and in providing introductions that could lead to further training or employment. The personal contact with the professional athletes caused the executives to develop a stronger, more positive relationship with the team. The athletes were quick to share the positive nature of the counseling sessions with their fellow players. Every player who used the planning committee made a commitment to an off-season training program or job. Some were encouraged to return to their university and finish their degree work. So what happened?

In spite of the team's total commitment to the program, the head coach rejected the concept. Because of the fact that by mid-season the team was out of contention (in spite of their great preseason promise), the coach took the position that he did not want anything distracting his players from their sport. He forbade any player from making an appointment to meet with the committee. It was his opinion that any distraction from practice or game preparation would result in a reduced commitment to winning. Even though the program had extremely positive motivational value, including the building of morale and team commitment, the coach thought it would have negative effects. Often, the best laid plans of team psychologists, even when based upon sound, empirical findings, may be sacrificed when a team begins to lose.

Such a fine instrument has unusual potential for providing athletes with a more objective view of their career options. Established professional athletes welcome this opportunity. The business community enjoys the opportunity for involvement. However, the coaching staff, as in the case above, may become threatened. They see these "outside activities" as a possible means of distracting or splitting the athlete's intentions and interests.

Special sensitivity must be employed in educating the coaching staff as to their misconceptions relative to this concern. As athletes begin to examine the possibility of termination, anxiety surrounding what they will do with the rest of their life also begins to mount. If this anxiety is not alleviated, the athletes will continue to be preoccupied with such concerns to the detriment of their performance. However, if they do not have to worry about the future, then their ability to maintain the single focus that the coaching staff desires will not only be restored but enhanced.

The Reaction Pattern

The transition process begins with the recognition of the impending termination and follows a predictable course consisting of several stages. The upcoming role change will require a wide variety of coping skills: dealing with the loss of an identity; having to move to a new location; settling for anonymity after years of recognition; lowering of economic status; and moving on to more routine living circumstances or to a more traditional family role. The possible requirements for coping are endless. Whatever the new role, the new choices and options will require athletes to relinquish former means of self-fulfillment and seek new ways to establish self-worth.

When athletes first start to consider termination as an imminent reality, their reaction may be one of shock and numbness. As this initial feeling begins to subside, the athletes often engage in denial, a defensive coping mechanism, by refusing to believe what is actually happening. Behavioral manifestations of this denial can include continuing to report for practices, arguing with the coach or the general manager, insisting that a mistake has been made, or making persistent attempts at training and reentering the sport at the previous or even lower levels of competition.

Most of the athletes in Svoboda and Vanek's study were highly motivated to continue in competition even after becoming aware of impending termination. Ninety percent reported that they increased their training effort, further regimented their lives, and altered their daily living patterns in order to regain former levels of performance.

The ability of athletes to relinquish this denial and accept the reality of the situation depends primarily on how well they are prepared for the inevitable outcome. If they have engaged in the denial of athletic mortality throughout their career, then they are likely to engage in further denial at this stage.

When denial can no longer be successfully maintained as a coping mechanism, it often gives way to anger. Many athletes respond to their loss and frustration by getting angry with other family members, coaches, their general manager, and peers. Some athletes generalize their anger and direct it toward God, fate, and life. Still others direct their rage against themselves. When asked the question of who provided the most help during the transitional phase, 43% of Svoboda and Vanek's sample answered that they had depended on only their inner resources and rejected the help of others.

Some manifestations of this internalized aggression include self-destructive behaviors such as overindulgence in drugs and alcohol. In the Svoboda and Vanek study, neurotic defenses and an increase in the incidence of psychosomatic disorder (even the extreme reaction of suicidal thoughts or preoccupations) were evident in those athletes who fell at the extreme maladaptive end of the continuum.

Although the reactions of denial and anger are intense and painful, they are usually temporary, and otherwise healthy athletes progress through them. Maintaining massive denial and extreme rage over an extended period of time is only characteristic of individuals with serious psychopathology.

The third stage of the reaction pattern encompasses the major symptoms of a reactive depression. Typically, in this stage the athletes withdraw from others, including significant individuals who could provide much needed support. The athletes may then experience a sense of loneliness and helplessness in the isolation created by their withdrawal. At one time consumed by a life-style that provided purpose and meaning, life is now void of significance and direction. Depending on the external circumstances and the character of the particular athlete, this reaction may be of short duration or turn into a major depressive episode.

No matter how successful the athletes are at working through this stage, they will always have some unresolved feelings. No activity can ever be experienced as intensively satisfying, fulfilling, and rewarding as their involvement in sports. In his book *Life on the Run,* Bill Bradley, a retired 10-year professional with the New York Knicks, wrote of the Faustian bargain that the athlete makes: In return for fame and glory, the athlete must live with the reality of never being able to experience anything else with the same intensity or degree of involvement as was provided by athletics. This same sentiment was echoed by the victorious 1980 U.S. Olympic ice hockey team after winning the gold medal.

Related Difficulties

The terminated athlete is often confronted with social difficulties that further compound the transition process. The experienced loss of social recognition is one of the more immediate changes the athlete must face; the athlete is quickly forgotten by once ardent fans and the media. This loss of recognition is most poignantly exemplified by the athlete's "friends" who seem to disappear when they find they no longer can share in the glory.

In addition, the athlete's immediate family is deeply affected as they now face a transition process of their own. Family members have enjoyed a participation in and identification with the fame and prestige associated with the athlete. When considering the adolescent athlete's termination, parents are confronted with their own bitter disappointment and may find it impossible to resolve their own feelings without amplifying the emotional trauma experienced by their child. Upon termination of the adult athlete's career, both spouse and children lose a shared sense of importance. Children can no longer boast of their "star football father" or their "mother in professional tennis." The spouse must deal with his or her own experience of loss as well as provide the understanding and support the ex-athlete needs to progress through the painful transition process. Unfortunately, many marriages do not survive this crisis. The NFL Players Association estimates that during the first year following termination, 50% of the marriages of professional ex-football players end in divorce.

Terminated professional athletes and their families must also deal with new economic realities. There are many misconceptions concerning the salaries of professional athletes. Most professional athletes do not make the inflated salaries that a few superstars enjoy. While the average salaries of professional athletes may seem high, it is important to keep in mind that the standard professional sports career is extremely short. For example, the average NFL player is retired by the age of 28; however, he does not receive his pension until he is 55. The following figures will further illustrate this point.

	NBA	NFL
Average 1985 salary:	$231,000	$160,000
Average career:	3.4 seasons	4.2 years

Nevertheless, following termination, it is the rare athlete who is able to maintain the same life-style that he or she enjoyed as a professional. Therefore, most athletes become overwhelmed as the financial pressures compound the interpersonal problems precipitated by their termination.

Fortunately, even in the face of these hardships, most athletes eventually accept their termination without making irreversible decisions such as suicide. Once resigned to the facts, the athletes will experience an interesting shift in values. When a group of retired (and/or terminated) athletes were asked to rank a number of relevant psychosocial issues first as they would have as participating athletes, then as retirees, their responses were as follows:

As athletes	As retirees
1. to be first	family
2. travel	friends
3. friends	to be first
4. family	quiet job
5. money	money
6. contacts	travel
7. quiet job	fortune
8. fortune	contacts

Though their need for achievement remained high, their needs for family and warm social contacts had taken precedence in their lives.

Nevertheless, because of a general lack of concern and planning for life-after-termination, the transition is never easy and is occasionally fatal. In the face of this evidence, the coach and sport psychologist must address the issue of termination trauma and develop strategies to help athletes deal with it.

THE COACH AND SPORT PSYCHOLOGIST'S ROLE

Even in light of the aging factor, the issue of termination is universal for athletes of all age groups and levels of competition. Athletes may be terminated because of injury or the selection process at any stage of their career. As we have seen, personal identification with a sport and the role of an athlete begins at a very early age and even relatively young competitors may face a serious identity crisis if they can no longer fulfill the role of an athlete. Although economic issues are different for the professional athlete and the amateur, the social difficulties and the necessary adaptation exist for both. The sport psychologist and coach must be aware of the universality of the issues of termination.

Psychology and Termination Trauma

Svoboda and Vanek took the opportunity to collect data that would enable them to determine whether termination stress reactions were related to basic personality structure. They were interested in "conditionability" as a factor in determining different responses to the termination experience. In relation to the psychometric evidence, they addressed the effect of declining motor activity as a form of sensory deprivation (many of their athletes were unfulfilled by recreational sports). This withdrawal phenomenon is an almost universal complaint among athletes who were terminated before they were psychologically ready. Injury, deselection, changing skill requirements within their sport, or any of the other possible causes of termination often evokes statements regarding the loss of recognition and attention that comes with being an elite performer. Frequently heard is "It's more than we can bear."

Evidently, an elite athlete's age, sex, and marital status play significant roles in how well he or she is able to cope with the various stresses associated with termination. Svoboda and Vanek found that the developmental level of an athlete's personality greatly determines the adaptive process. Athletes over 30, who had greater life experience, and athletes with stable marital relationships found the transition easier. Those who were forced out of sports because of family quarrels perceived the decision as unpleasant. Socioeconomic status and level of self-esteem also played significant roles in adaptation to termination. Athletes who rated high on adaptation skills in general seemed more able to translate sport success into termination success.

Although an endless list of psychological factors can affect individual responses to the termination experience, it is neither possible nor worthwhile for the sport psychologist and coach to analyze all of them. The more productive approach is to concentrate on the clinical evidence and the various practical applications.

Youth Sports

Care for assuring athletes a less traumatic transition from athlete to ex-athlete extends into three primary levels of responsibility. The first level is that of the pubescent and adolescent youth who is competing in age-group programs of regional, district, or even national scope. Working with youth sport programs often requires a sensitive concern for the needs that the child, as an aspiring athlete, brings to the activity. We should take care to protect the freedom of expression, joy, and emotional release that the child would naturally experience in a recreational setting as the child enters competition. During this extremely important developmental time, the child's self-concept is forming, and it is important for significantly involved adults to help the child understand the nature of a role in sports and the nature of competition. Parents, coaches, and sport psychologists must be sensitive to the degree of the child's ego involvement in the sport. They must ensure that the child's feelings of self-worth are not solely dependent upon winning or losing. Children tend to experience judgments of their athletic ability as direct reflections of their total worth as people. Therefore, if children are exposed to social rejection or humiliation as a response to athletic performance, feelings of self-doubt and low self-esteem may become ingrained in their character. It is essential that coaches and sport psychologists who work at this level teach young athletes to put athletics and athletic prowess in the proper perspective.

The unique factors associated with the termination experience for young athletes have particular significance when we are dealing with the elite or subelite performer. The role of coaches and sport psychologists also requires a high degree of social sensitivity when working with young adults or adolescents who are students or performers in sports that are more characteristic of the upper middle class or the wealthy. These sports include tennis, golf, figure skating, and gymnastics, all of which require a significant financial investment from the parent. In gymnastics and figure skating the rules of the game are such that actual performance criteria become significantly less objective as the young athlete moves higher up the performance scale. This blurring of objective criteria is particularly distressing for the young athletes where the final judgment and ranking is often made on a less objective basis than in other sports. The test for both the coach and psychologist comes when they seek to provide counseling for the young men and women in sports in which judges, committees, and other authorities have the power to determine or set the criteria for acceptable performance. It will not take the novice coach or sport psychologist long to become totally aware that athletic justice in such sports is capricious at best.

How does the psychologist function as an ethical professional and the coach as a responsible leader, when confronted with the politics in the world of the elite child performer? What are their responsibilities to the child's parents, who are expending emotional energy and making considerable financial sacrifices? (Skating in the United States can cost between $18,000 and $20,000 a year.) What should be the role of the sport psychologist in relation to the coach, who has both an emotional and a financial investment in his or her students? We could endlessly review the special nature of responsibility when seeking to honor the needs of children.

Case Study: Elite Figure Skating Female, Age 17

A young figure skater was referred to the senior author by her coach, who is one of the renowned woman teachers in U.S. figure skating. The problem, as described initially, was that the skater's style of expression no longer met the contemporary criteria: She had meticulously developed the ballet style of skating, which had been replaced by the newer acrobatic style. As a result, her student practices and actual performances had reached a plateau. She seemed unable to relate to her new routines, became enraged about her musical arrangements, and even rejected the recommendations of her choreographer. She had become sullen and increasingly rebellious. Though she had been quite independent since adolescence, she had never before been particularly difficult to coach. Her relationship with her coach had extended over a period of two and one-half years, and they had enjoyed a fine student–teacher relationship.

When the young woman arrived for therapy, the first area of exploration was to determine the degree to which she was personally committed to continued skating. Again, the primary issue was the degree to which this activity was fulfilling her intrinsic needs. This commitment to interpersonal needs would be distinct from seeking to serve the social needs of others. Within a very short time it became clear that her identity was deeply and wholesomely tied to achievement in skating. There was no question that the dream she possessed was her own and not one imposed by others.

The psychological evaluation of this young lady provided strong evidence that she was not only a remarkable athlete but also that she possessed most of the personal attributes of a world-class athlete: She had unusual ambition and set extremely high goals for herself and others; she was independent and had a great need to dominate; she had very high psychological endurance and could stay with projects for long periods if necessary; she was free to use her aggression in a positive way; she was a thoughtful, plan-ahead, organized type of person; she had great self-confidence; she was tough-minded and had a great capacity to bounce back after adversity or emotional shock; she functioned at a very low level of body tension; she had very high self-control; she was emotionally more mature than the elite performers that she was compared with; she possessed very high mental flexibility.

A summary of the psychometric data would place her in the upper 20% of the elite female population. After her six years of eight hours a day, six days a week of physical, emotional, and social sacrifice, the sport psychologist asked her to examine the options open to her so that she could enjoy a future of reasonable mental health. In this case, the approach of the sport psychologist was a difficult one since it tried to provide the athlete with a reasonably comfortable escape from an activity to which she had devoted a good part of her life.

College/Olympic Level Sports

At a second level of responsibility, the level of the college and the Olympic athlete, the coach and sport psychologist must learn to function in a variety

of complex situations, often dealing with a bureaucracy of medical committees, consultants, and administrators and a variety of politically oriented
factors. The needs of the individual performer within this kind of structure
are easily ignored. Yet the greatest possibility for exploitation and manipulation of the athlete for the benefit of others exists at this level. This is most
evident in colleges and universities where the entire careers of administrators and coaches, as well as the multimillion-dollar "business" of college
athletics, are at stake. In an effort to acquire talented athletes, recruiters
often promise a college education and paint unrealistic pictures of professional possibilities. Once recruited, the athlete is pressured into making a
total commitment to his or her sport, often neglecting the social and academic areas important to a college education. For example, consider a
typical day in the life of a collegiate football player and figure skater:

	Football player	Figure skater
5:00 – 7:00 A.M.		Practice
7:30 – 8:00	Breakfast	Breakfast
8:00 – 11:30	Classes	Classes
11:30 – 12:00	Lunch	
12:00 – 12:30 P.M.		Lunch
1:00 – 2:00		Dance class
2:00 – 3:00	Weight room	Practice
3:00 – 3:30	Taping and pep talk	"
3:30 – 6:00	Practice	Lessons
6:30 – 7:30	Dinner	Dinner
7:30 – 9:00	Game films and meetings	Study
9:00 – 9:30	Tutoring and study	"
9:30 – 11:30	" "	Retire (9:30)
11:30	Retire	

Many athletes spend their five years of eligibility competing in their
sport and never receive even the slightest preparation for a career that can
provide them with a decent living. They are often guided into courses
designed only to keep them eligible, with little or no regard for the actual
completion of a degree.

Many colleges show no concern about recruiting and using academically unqualified athletes in their programs and are reluctant to let these
same athletes graduate once their eligibility expires. According to Dr. Harry
Edwards, noted sport sociologist at the University of California at Berkeley,
75% to 80% of black athletes who go to college on scholarship never graduate. In his studies, Dr. Edwards estimates that 20% to 25% of black athletes
at four-year colleges are functionally illiterate. Although the NBA and the

NFL draft almost exclusively from colleges and universities, only 20% of the players in the NBA and 32% of the players in the NFL have a college degree. These figures point to the unfulfilled promises made during recruiting and leave the athlete feeling betrayed, a sacrificial victim of the sport.

Although the manipulation and exploitation of athletes at both the college and the Olympic levels appears to be increasing in some programs, action is being taken in other programs that shows an increased sense of responsibility for the education of athletes. Again, keeping athletics in the proper perspective will usually lessen the potential trauma resulting from termination from athletics.

Professional Sports

At the professional level, athletes develop a life-style that gives every appearance of being a secure and stable reality. This life-style is comfortable and relatively affluent, and for most, it provides a ready-made entry into certain exclusive segments of society. There is little concern for career termination, and the majority of athletes are not prepared for the vast array of psychological, social, and economic problems they must face when this inevitable reality touches them. It is difficult to ascertain where the responsibility lies in assisting athletes in preparing for and adjusting to termination. Exceptional salaries, in and of themselves, may not be sufficient to alleviate management's responsibility in preparing the athletes. Although large sums of money can pay for an education (as well as career, financial, and personal counseling), athletes are generally not oriented toward the importance of these services. The coach and sport psychologist must assist management and athletes in addressing and fulfilling obligations to prepare the individual athlete for retirement from sport. This role involves a continual learning, adjusting, and coping process in order to function effectively and still honor the primary professional commitment. The following example illustrates some of the problems that can occur when athletes are not prepared for retirement. The trauma of career termination can become so severe and complex as to require the skills of a professional psychologist.

Case Study: Professional Hockey Player, Age 26

This case of termination demanded the highest level of professional attention, not only because of its complexity but also because of the pathological nature of the individual involved. This young professional fits the description of extreme career-termination trauma as reported by Svoboda and Vanek. The athlete was referred for therapy by his coach and general manager who became distressed by the athlete's violent mood shifts and extreme forms of behavior.

As a result of clinical examinations and interviews, a number of salient features about the athlete's personality and the nature of his struggle became evident. During the previous season, he had had a serious knee injury that required surgery. Although the operation had been a success, the medical advice was that he should consider terminating active play. Contrary to medical judgment, he had chosen to participate in the preseason training. The general manager, the coach, and the scouts in attendance were of the same opinion: The athlete's days as a professional hockey player were over. In the absence of any contractual commitment, he was given an outright release.

His determination to stay in the game resulted in his trying out with two other teams in the lower leagues; in each case, he was released for physical reasons. He appeared next at the parent club, angrily demanding that they give him a genuine chance to make the team. It was at this point that management became aware of the extent of his irrational conduct and offered him a chance to spend some time with the team psychologist.

Clinical impressions during a two-day period were consistent with the diagnosis of a manic-depressive reaction. The athlete's mood alterations ranged from grandiose claims about his past playing behavior and accomplishments to periods of intense depression and sadness. As the story of his life unfolded, it became increasingly evident that the only identity he had ever known since the age of 9 was that of "Harry, the future hockey great." He came from a hockey family, both his father and his brother having had short professional careers.

He stated that he had been conditioned from the age of 9 for a career in professional hockey. By the time he was 16, scouts and coaches were predicting that he would be drafted into the National Hockey League. It became evident that he, like so many other gifted athletes, had learned to value himself only in terms of a single dimension: the athlete. His total worth and self-esteem were supported only by this single attribute. His identity as a person was so restricted that there were no options open to him, certainly none that would permit him to feel that he was a valuable or worthwhile human being.

During this period he would share his despair and frustration about the fact that his career was over (and also that he was powerless to do anything about it); he also exposed a suicidal preoccupation. His attempt to escape in liquor and narcotics only provided him with temporary relief from emotional pain. In his hurtful rage, he was attempting to drive everyone away from him: his family, his friends, and—most importantly—a fine and supporting woman. In a real sense, he was committing social suicide before doing so physically.

His strengths were that in every team situation, he had ended up as the team captain, and he had been sufficiently ambitious to continue his education in the off-season and earn a B.A. degree in business. He also had unusually fine work habits and was noted for his reliability in both his professional and personal life. As an athlete, he had been the enforcer when playing hockey, but he remained unusually civilized when off the ice. His relationship with his parents was reasonably secure, but in some ways he still remained dependent upon them for approval.

In comparison with the norms for professional hockey players, his overall psychological evaluation was as follows: He was more ambitious than his fellow athletes and set very high goals for himself and other people; he had a strong need to be in control and dominate others; he had above-average freedom to express and use aggression; he described himself as a person who never turned away from a responsibility once he had made an ego commitment; and he had the capacity to place faith in other people.

However, he fell below the norms in several areas: He had considerable difficulty controlling his emotions when in a stressful or critical situation; he was much more sensitive to criticism or disapproval and found it very difficult to bounce back after performing poorly or receiving criticism; he was seriously lacking in self-confidence, and he had a strong tendency toward self-punishment when things were not going well; he was slow to take responsibility for his need to change; he had a hypomanic personality style (his highs were often too high and his lows too low); he tended to be more critical than rewarding in his treatment of others; and he only formed close relationships with females who exhibited highly maternal attitudes toward him.

The sport psychologist had to compare the 48 hours of psychological and social data with the foregoing clinical insights and explore his role as a responsible counselor in order to deal with the reality of this athlete's career termination.

CONCLUSIONS AND CONSIDERATIONS

It would be ideal if we could provide some form of desensitization service for those whose commitment to sports results in a one-dimensional personality structure. The committed athlete usually lacks the opportunity to develop a rounded, full personality and to capitalize on other options and aptitudes. There has been a tendency for too many of our young athletes to determine their self-worth on the basis of a single attribute. The athletes who make the extreme sacrifice in terms of emotion, time, and energy, to the point that their sport has taken precedence in their lives, are the ones who will suffer the most from career termination.

There is little chance that we can make any impact upon the traditional social values that provide athletes with the motivation to become elite performers. Instead, the goal of the coach and sport psychologist should be that of acting as a preventive mental hygienist. In this capacity, we can make a continual effort to educate parents and others with respect to the role that sports should play in the lives of children. This education process should include an indoctrination of all concerned adults with a psychologically wholesome system of values that will carry over to provide protection well into adulthood. Included in this system of values are helping children gain insights into primary needs; enabling them to comprehend the danger of succumbing to external motivational factors to the exclusion of more personal motives; guiding children away from making the sport experience a measure of their worth as people; helping them avoid making the sport experience a proving ground; enabling them to comprehend that the pursuit of physical excellence can only be measured in uniquely personal terms and that their limits have been set by constitutional factors; reminding them that coming to know and like themselves is the most worthy goal of all; and finally, helping them to see that no matter how remarkable the physical athletic gift, it can never be used to prove one's worth as a human being.

The coach and sport psychologist can also function as mental hygienists in the lives of those who are caught up in the system by helping them with some healthy forms of transition into a less competitive life. To protect athletes against the possibility of extreme traumas, we can remind them of the temporary nature of the rewards that can accrue from a life as an athlete performing at any level of competition.

University faculty and administrators must share the responsibility for protecting athletes from becoming so restricted in their development that they fail to see the realities of the termination of athletic life. The day must come when academically capable athletes earn an academic degree in coordination with their athletic eligibility. Responsibility for developing this attitude and goal lies not only with college coaches but also with youth sport and high school coaches.

There are also a number of unique considerations at the professional level. The short professional life of the athlete requires provisions for termination so that the experience will be less traumatic. It remains an unfortunate truth that it is the rare athlete who has been prepared with career options. The professional athlete and the organization with which he or she is affiliated must be directed in ways that can help to promote opportunities for a smooth transition into another career.

The sport experience promotes not only strong positive feelings about one's body and a sense of mastery over the physical world but also the ability to work with others as part of a team and a vehicle for enhancing self-esteem. These positive attributes should not be lost when an individual's athletic career is terminated. It becomes the challenge of the sport psychologist as mental hygienist to assist the athlete in safeguarding those attributes.

REFERENCES

Botterill, C. (1982). What "endings" tell us about "beginnings." *Mental training for coaches and athletes* (pp. 164–166). Ottawa: Coaching Association of Canada, Sports in Perspective.

Bradley, B. (1976). *Life on the run.* N.Y. Quadrangle/Times Book Co.

Broom, F. (1982). De-training and retirement from high level competition: A reaction to retirement from high level competition and career crises in sports. *Mental training for coaches and athletes* (pp. 183–187). Ottawa: Coaching Association of Canada, Sports in Perspective.

Coakley, J. J. (1983). Leaving competitive sport, retirement or rebirth? *Quest, 35,* 1–11.

Dubois, P. E. (1980). The occupational attainment of former college athletes: A comparative study. *Journal of Sports Behavior, 2*(4), 211–219.

Edwards, H. Personal communication, April 1981.

Magill, R. A., Ash, M. F., & Smoll, F. L. (Eds.). (1982). *Children in sport.* Champaign, Ill.: Human Kinetics.

Martens, R. M. (Ed.). (1978). *Joy and sadness in children's sports.* Champaign, Ill.: Human Kinetics.

Mueller, F. O., & Blyth, C. S. (1984). Can we continue to improve injury statistics? *Physician and Sportsmedicine, 12*(9), 79–84.

Orlick, T., & Botterill, C. (1975). *Every kid can win.* Chicago: Nelson-Hall.

Passer, M. W. (1982). Children in sport: participation motives and psychological stress. *Quest, 33,* 231–244.

Sack, A. L., & Thiel, R. (1979). College football and social mobility. A case study of Notre Dame football players. *Sociology of Education, 52*(1), 60–66.

Sands, R. A. (1978). A socio-psychological investigation of the effects of role discontinuity on outstanding high school athletes. *Journal of Sports Behavior, 1*(4), 174–185.

Singer, R. N., & Gerson, R. F. (1980). Athletic competition for children: motivational considerations. *International Journal of Sports Psychology, 11,* 249–262.

Snyder, E. E., & Baber, L. (1979). A profile of former collegiate athletes and non-athletes: Leisure activities, attitudes toward work, and aspects of satisfaction with life. *Journal of Sport Behavior, 2*(4), 211–219.

Stevenson, C. (1982). Identity transformation and competitive sports. *Mental training for coaches and athletes* (pp. 192–193). Ottawa: Coaching Association of Canada, Sports in Perspective.

Svoboda, B., & Vanek, M. (1981, August). Retirement from high level competition. *Proceedings, Fifth World Congress of Sports Psychology* (pp. 26–31). Ottawa, Canada.

Werthner, P., & Orlick, T. (1982). Transitions from sports: Coping with the end. *Mental training for coaches and athletes* (pp. 187–188). Ottawa: Coaching Association of Canada, Sports in Perspective.

Author Index

Subject Index